THE ROMAN FESTIVALS

OF THE

PERIOD OF THE REPUBLIC

THE

ROMAN FESTIVALS

OF THE

PERIOD OF THE REPUBLIC

*AN INTRODUCTION TO THE STUDY OF THE
RELIGION OF THE ROMANS*

BY

W. WARDE FOWLER, M.A.

FELLOW AND SUB-RECTOR OF LINCOLN COLLEGE, OXFORD

KENNIKAT PRESS
Port Washington, N. Y./London

FRATRIS FILIIS

I . C . H . F

H . G . C . F

BONAE SPEI ADOLESCENTIBUS

THE ROMAN FESTIVALS

First published in 1899
Reissued in 1969 by Kennikat Press
Library of Congress Catalog Card No: 75-101038
SBN 8046-0704-4

Manufactured by Taylor Publishing Company   Dallas, Texas

KENNIKAT CLASSICS SERIES

PREFACE

A WORD of explanation seems needed about the form this book has taken. Many years ago I became specially interested in the old Roman religion, chiefly, I think, through studying Plutarch's *Quaestiones Romanae*, at a time when bad eyesight was compelling me to abandon a project for an elaborate study of all Plutarch's works. The 'scrappy' character not only of the *Quaestiones*, but of all the material for the study of Roman ritual, suited weak eyes better than the continual reading of Greek text; but I soon found it necessary to discover a thread on which to hang these fragments in some regular order. This I naturally found in the *Fasti* as edited by Mommsen in the first volume of the *Corpus Inscriptionum Latinarum*; and it gradually dawned on me that the only scientific way of treating the subject was to follow the calendar throughout the year, and to deal with each festival separately. I had advanced some way in this work, when Roscher's *Lexicon of Greek and Roman Mythology* began to appear in parts, and at once convinced me that I should have to do my work all over again in the increased light afforded by the indefatigable industry of the writers of the Roman articles. I therefore dropped my work for several years while the Lexicon was in progress, and should have waited still longer for its completion, had not Messrs. Macmillan invited me to contribute a volume on the Roman religion to their series of *Handbooks of Archaeology and Antiquities*.

Having once set out on the plan of following the *Fasti*, I could not well abandon it, and I still hold it to be the only sound one: especially if, as in this volume, the object is to exhibit the religious side of the native Roman character, without getting entangled to any serious extent in the *colluvies religionum* of the last age of the Republic and the earlier Empire. The book has thus taken the form of a commentary on the *Fasti*, covering in a compressed form almost all the public worship of the Roman state, and including incidentally here and there certain ceremonies which strictly speaking lay outside that public worship. Compression has been unavoidable; yet it has been impossible to avoid stating and often discussing the conflicting views of eminent scholars; and the result probably is that the book as a whole will not be found very interesting reading. But I hope that British and American students of Roman history and literature, and possibly also anthropologists and historians of religion, may find it useful as a book of reference, or may learn from it where to go for more elaborate investigations.

The task has often been an ungrateful one—one indeed of

> Dipping buckets into empty wells
> And growing old with drawing nothing up.

The more carefully I study any particular festival, the more (at least in many cases) I have been driven into doubt and difficulty both as to reported facts and their interpretation. Had the nature of the series permitted it, I should have wished to print the chief passages quoted from ancient authors in full, as was done by

Mr. Farnell in his *Cults of the Greek States*, and so to present to the reader the actual material on which conclusions are rightly or wrongly based. I have only been able to do this where it was indispensable: but I have done my best to verify the correctness of the other references, and have printed in full the entries of the ancient calendars at the head of each section. Professor Gardner, the editor of the series, has helped me by contributing two valuable notes on coins, which will be found at the end of the volume: and I hope he may some day find time to turn his attention more closely to the bearing of numismatic evidence on Roman religious history.

It happens, by a curious coincidence, that I am writing this on the last day of the old Roman year; and the lines which Ovid has attached to that day may fitly express my relief on arriving at the end of a very laborious task:

> Venimus in portum, libro cum mense peracto,
> Naviget hinc alia iam mihi linter aqua.

W. W. F.

Oxford: *Feb.* 28, 1899.

CONTENTS

ABBREVIATIONS.

The following are the most important abbreviations which occur in the notes:

C. I. L. stands for *Corpus Inscriptionum Latinarum.* Where the volume is not indicated the reference is invariably to the *second* edition of that part of vol. i which contains the *Fasti* (Berlin, 1893).

Marquardt or Marq. stands for the third volume of Marquardt's *Römische Staatsverwaltung,* second edition, edited by Wissowa (Berlin, 1885). It is the sixth volume of the complete *Handbuch der Römischen Alterthümer* of Mommsen and Marquardt.

Preller, or Preller-Jordan, stands for the third edition of Preller's *Römische Mythologie* by H. Jordan (Berlin, 1881).

Myth. Lex. or *Lex.* stands for the *Ausführliches Lexicon der Griechischen und Römischen Mythologie,* edited by W. H. Roscher, which as yet has only been completed to the letter N.

Festus, or Paulus, stands for K. O. Müller's edition of the fragments of Festus, *De Significatione Verborum,* and the *Excerpta ex Festo* of Paulus Diaconus; quoted by the page.

INTRODUCTION

—✦—

I. The Roman Method of Reckoning the Year[1].

There are three ways in which the course of the year may be calculated. It can be reckoned—

1. By the revolution of the moon round the earth, twelve of which = 354 days, or a ring (*annus*), sufficiently near to the solar year to be a practicable system with modifications.

2. By the revolution of the earth round the sun, i.e. $365\frac{1}{4}$ days; a system which needs periodical adjustments, as the odd quarter (or, more strictly, 5 hours 48 minutes 48 seconds) cannot of course be counted in each year. In this purely solar year the months are only artificial divisions of time, and not reckoned according to the revolutions of the moon. This is our modern system.

3. By combining in a single system the solar and lunar years as described above. This has been done in various ways by different peoples, by adopting a cycle of years of varying length, in which the resultants of the two bases of calculation should be brought into harmony as nearly as possible. In

[1] The difficult questions connected with this subject cannot be discussed here. Since Mommsen wrote his *Römische Chronologie* it has at least been possible to give an intelligible account of it, such as that in the *Dict. of Antiquities* (second edition), in Marquardt's *Staatsverwaltung*, iii. 281 foll., and in Bouché-Leclercq, *Pontifes*, p. 230 foll. There is a useful summary in H. Peter's edition of Ovid's *Fasti* (p. 19). Mommsen's views have been criticized by Huschke, *Das Römische Jahr*, and Hartmann, *Der Röm. Kalender*; the former a very unsafe guide, and the latter, unfortunately, an unfinished and posthumous work. The chief ancient authority is Censorinus, *De die natali*, a work written at the beginning of the third century A D., on the basis of a treatise of Suetonius.

other words, though the difference between a single solar year and a single lunar year is more than 11 days, it is possible, by taking a number of years together and reckoning them as lunar years, one or more of them being lengthened by an additional month, to make the whole period very nearly coincide with the same number of solar years. Thus the Athenians adopted for this purpose at different times groups or cycles of 8 and 19 years. In the Octaeteris or 8-year cycle there were 99 lunar months, 3 months of 30 days being added in 3 of the 8 years—a plan which falls short of accuracy by about 36 hours. Later on a cycle of 19 years was substituted for this, in which the discrepancy was greatly reduced. The Roman year in historical times was calculated on a system of this kind, though with such inaccuracy and carelessness as to lose all real relation to the revolutions both of earth and moon.

But there was a tradition that before this historical calendar came into use there had been another system, which the Romans connected with the name of Romulus. This year was supposed to have consisted of 10 months, of which 4— March, May, July, October—had 31 days, and the rest 30 ; in all 304. But this was neither a solar nor a lunar year ; for a lunar year of 10 months = 295 days 7 hours 20 minutes, while a solar year = $365\frac{1}{4}$. Nor can it possibly be explained as an attempt to combine the two systems. Mommsen has therefore conjectured that it was an artificial year of 10 months, used in business transactions, and in periods of mourning, truces[1], &c., to remedy the uncertainty of the primitive calculation of time ; and that it never really was the basis of a state calendar. This view has of course been the subject of much criticism[2]. But no better solution has been found ; the hypothesis that the year of 10 months was a real lunar year, to which an undivided period of time was added at each year's end, to make it correspond with the solar year and the seasons, has not much to recommend it or any analogy among other peoples. It was not, then, the so-called year of Romulus which was the basis of the earliest state-calendar, but another system which the Romans them-

---

[1] *Chron.* 48 foll. ; Marq. 284 and notes.
[2] Huschke, *op. cit.* 8 foll. ; Hartmann, p. 13.

selves usually ascribed to Numa. This was originally perhaps a lunar year; at any rate the number of days in it is very nearly that of a true lunar year (354 days 8 hours 48 minutes) [1]. It consisted of 12 months, of which March, May, July, October had 31 days, and the rest 29, except February, which had 28. All the months therefore had an odd number of days, except the one which was specially devoted to purification and the cult of the dead; according to an old superstition, probably adopted from the Greeks of Southern Italy [2], that odd numbers were of good omen, even numbers of ill omen. This principle, as we shall see, holds good throughout the Roman calendar.

But this reckoning of the year, if it ever existed at all, could not have lasted long as it stood. As we know it in historical times, it has become modified by applying to it the principle of the solar year. The reason for this should be noted carefully. A lunar year, being about 11 days short of the solar year, would in a very short time become out of harmony with the seasons. Now if there is one thing certain about the Roman religious calendar, it is that many at least of its oldest festivals mark those operations of husbandry on which the population depended for its subsistence, and for the prosperous result of which divine agencies must be propitiated. These festivals, when fixed in the calendar, must of course occur at the right seasons, which could not be the case if the calendar were that of a purely lunar year. It was therefore necessary to work in the solar principle; and this was done [3] by a somewhat rude expedient, not unlike that of the Athenian Octaeteris, and probably derived from it [4]. A cycle of 4 years was devised, of which the first had the 355 days of the lunar year, the second 355 + 22, the third 355 again,

---

[1] Censorinus, *De die natali*, 20. 4.

[2] Mommsen (*Chron.* 13) believes it to have been a Pythagorean doctrine which spread in Southern Italy. Hartmann, on the contrary, calls it an old Italian one adopted by Pythagoras. See a valuable note in Schwegler, *Röm. Gesch.* i. 561, inclining to the latter view.

[3] Probably by the Decemvirs, B.C. 450, who are said to have made some alteration in the calendar (Macrob. 1. 13. 21).

[4] See *Dict. Ant.* i. 337 and 342. It is highly probable that there was a still older plan, which gave way to this at the time of the Decemvirate: the evidence for this, which is conjectural only, is stated by Mommsen in the first chapter of his *Chronologie*. The number of days in this cycle (also of 4 years) is computed at 1475, and the average in each year at 368¾.

and the fourth $355 + 23$. The extra periods of 22 and 23 days were inserted in February, not at the end, but after the 23rd (*Terminalia*)[1]. The total number of days in the cycle was 1465, or about 1 day too much in each year; and in course of time even this system got out of harmony with the seasons and had to be rectified from time to time by the Pontifices, who had charge of the calendar. Owing to ignorance on their part, misuse or neglect of intercalation had put the whole system out of gear before the last century of the Republic. All relation to sun and moon was lost; the calendar, as Mommsen says, 'went on its own way tolerably unconcerned about moon and sun.' When Caesar took the reform of the calendar in hand the discrepancy between it and the seasons was very serious; the former being in advance of the latter probably by some weeks. Caesar, aided by the mathematician Sosigenes, put an end to this confusion by extending the year 46 B.C. to 445 days, and starting afresh on Jan. 1, 45 B.C.[2] — a day henceforward to be that of the new year—with a cycle of 4 years of 365 days[3]; in the last of which a single day was added, after the *Terminalia*. This cycle produced a true solar year with a slight adjustment at short intervals; and after a few preliminary blunders on the part of the Pontifices, lasted without change until A.D. 1582, when Pope Gregory XIII set right a slight discrepancy by a fresh regulation. This regulation was only adopted in England in 1752, and is still rejected in Russia and by the Greek Church generally.

[1] Or, according to Mommsen, in alternate years after the 23rd and 24th, i.e. in the year of 378 days 23 days were inserted after the *Terminalia*; in the year of 377 days 22 days were inserted after the 24th (*Regifugium*). Thus February would in the one case have 23, and in the other 24 days; the remaining 5 and 4 being added to the intercalated period. The object of the Decemvirs (if it was they who made this change) in this curious arrangement was, in part at least, to keep the festival of the god Terminus on its original day (Mommsen, *Chron.* 38). Terminus would budge neither from his seat on the Capitol (Liv. 1. 55) nor from his place in the calendar.

[2] Probably in order that the beginning of the year might coincide with a new moon; which actually happened on Jan. 1, 45, and was doubtless regarded as a good omen.

[3] He added 10 days to the normal year of 355: January, Sextilis, December, receiving two; April, June, September, November, one only. These new days were placed at the end of the months, so that the days on which religious festivals fell might remain as before.

II. Order of Months in the Year.

That the Roman year originally began with March is certain [1], not only from the evidence of the names of the months, which after June are reckoned as 5th (Quinctilis), 6th (Sextilis), and so on, but from the nature of the March festivals, as will be shown in treating of that month. In the character of the religious festivals there is a distinct break between February and March, and the operations both of nature and of man take a fresh turn at that point. Between the festivals of December and those of January there is no such break. No doubt January 1, just after the winter solstice, was even at an early time considered in some sense as a beginning; but it is going too far to assume, as some have done, that an ancient religious or priestly year began at that point [2]. It was not on January 1, but on March 1, that the sacred fire in the Aedes Vestae was renewed and fresh laurels fixed up on the Regia, the two buildings which were the central points of the oldest Roman religion [3]. March 1, which in later times at least was considered the birthday of the special protecting deity of the Romans, continued to be the Roman New Year's Day long after the official beginning of the year had been changed to January 1 [4]. It was probably not till 153 B. C., when the consuls began to enter on office on January 1, that this official change took place; and the date was then adopted, not so much for religious reasons as because it was convenient, when the business of administration was increasing, to have the consuls in Rome for some time before they left for their provinces at the opening of the war season in March.

No rational account can in my opinion be given of the Roman religious calendar of the Republic unless it be taken as beginning with March; and in this work I have therefore restored the old order of months. With the Julian calendar I am not concerned; though it is unfortunate that all the

[1] Mommsen, *Chron.* 220. In no other Italian calendar of which we have any knowledge is March the first month (ib. 218 foll.) : but there cannot be much doubt that these too had undergone changes. Festus (150), representing Verrius Flaccus, says, ' Martius mensis initium fuit anni et in Latio et post Romam conditam,' &c.

[2] Huschke, *Röm. Jahr,* 11 foll.

[3] See below, under March 1.

[4] Mommsen, *Chron.* 103 foll.

Roman calendars we possess, including the *Fasti* of Ovid. date from after the Julian era, and therefore present us with a distorted view of the true course of the old Roman worship.

Next after March came Aprilis, the month of opening or unfolding vegetation; then Maius, the month of growing, and Junius, that of ripening and perfecting. After this the names cease to be descriptive of the operations of nature; the six months that follow were called, as four of them still are, only by their positions relative to March, on which the whole system of the year thus turned as on a pivot.

The last two months of the twelve were January and February. They stand alone among the later months in bearing names instead of mere numbers, and this is sufficient to suggest their religious importance. That they were not mere appendages to a year of ten months is almost certain from the antique character of the rites and festivals which occur in them—Agonia, Carmentalia, Lupercalia, &c.; and it is safer to consider them as marking an ancient period of religious importance preparatory to the beginning of the year, and itself coinciding with the opening of the natural year after the winter solstice. This latter point seems to be indicated in the name Januarius, which, whether derived from janua, 'a gate,' or Janus, 'the god of entrances,' is appropriate to the first lengthening of the days, or the entrance of the sun on a new course; while February, the month of purifying or regenerative agencies (februa), was, like the Lent of the Christian calendar, the period in which the living were made ready for the civil and religious work of the coming year, and in which also the yearly duties to the dead were paid.

It is as well here to refer to a passage of Ovid (*Fasti*, ii. 47 foll.), itself probably based on a statement of Varro, which has led to a controversy about the relative position of these two months:

> Sed tamen antiqui ne nescius ordinis erres,
>   Primus, ut est, Iani mensis et ante fuit.
> Qui sequitur Ianum, veteris fuit ultimus anni,
>   Tu quoque sacrorum, Termine, finis eras.
> Primus enim Iani mensis, quia ianua prima est;
>   Qui sacer est imis manibus, imus erat.
> Postmodo creduntur spatio distantia longo
>   Tempora bis quini continuasse viri.

This plainly means that from the time when March ceased to be the first month, the year always began with January and ended with February ; in other words the order was January, March, April, and so on, ending with February ; until the time of the Decemvirate, when February became the second month, and December the last, as at present, January still retaining its place. A little consideration of Ovid's lines will, however, suggest the conclusion that he, and his authority, whoever that may have been, were arguing aetiologically rather than on definite knowledge. January, they thought, must always have been the first month, because janua, 'a door,' is the first thing, the entrance, through which you pass into a new year as into a house or a temple. How, they would argue, could a month thus named have ever been the eleventh month ? This once supposed impossible, it was necessary to infer that the place of January was the first, from the time of its introduction, and that it was followed by March, April, &c., February coming last of all, immediately after December ; and finally that at the time of the Decemvirs, who are known to have made some alterations in the calendar, the positions of January and February were reversed, January remaining the first month, but February becoming the second.

III. The Divisions of the Month.

The Romans, with their usual conservatism, preserved the shell of the lunar system of reckoning long after the reality had disappeared. The month was at all times divided by the real or imaginary phases of the moon, though a week of eight days was introduced at an early period, and though the month was no longer a lunar one.

The two certain points in a lunar month are the first appearance of the crescent [1] and the full moon ; between these is the point when the moon reaches the first quarter, which is a less certain one. Owing to this uncertainty of the reckoning of the first days of the month there were no festivals in the calendars on the days before the first quarter (Nones), with a single exception of the obscure *Poplifugia* on July 5. The day of

---

[1] Not the real new moon, which is invisible. The period between the new moon and the first quarter varies.

the new moon was called Kalendae, as Varro tells us, 'quod
his diebus calantur eius mensis nonae a pontificibus, quintanae
an septimanae sint futurae, in Capitolio in curia Calabra sic :
Dies te quinque calo, Iuno Covella. Septem dies te calo Iuno
Covella'[1]. All the Kalends were sacred to Juno, whose connexion with the moon is certain though not easy to explain.

With the Nones, which were sacred to no deity, all uncertainty ceased. The Ides, or day of the full moon, was always
the eighth after the first quarter. This day was sacred to
Jupiter ; a fact which is now generally explained as a recog-
nition of the continuous light of the two great heavenly bodies
during the whole twenty-four hours[2]. On the Nones the *Rex
sacrorum* (and therefore before him the king himself) announced
the dates of the festivals for the month.

There was another internal division of the month, with
which we are not here specially concerned, that of the Roman
week or nundinal period of eight days, which is indicated in all
the calendars by the letters A to H. The *nundinae* were
market days, on which the rustic population came into Rome ;
whether they were also feast days (*feriae*) was a disputed
question even in antiquity.

IV. The Days.

Every day in the Roman calendar has a certain mark
attached to it, viz. the letters F, C, N, NP, EN, Q.R.C.F.,
Q.St.D.F., or FP. All of these have a religious significance,
positive or negative.

F, i. e. *fas* or *fastus*, means that on the day so marked civil
and especially judicial business might be transacted without
fear of divine displeasure[3]. Correctness in the time as well as
place of all human actions was in the mind of the early Roman
of the most vital importance ; and the floating traditional ideas
which governed his life before the formation of the State were

---

[1] Varro, *L. L.* 6. 27. This was the method before the publication of the
calendar by Flavius : Macr. 1. 15. 9. The meaning of Covella is doubtful ;
it has generally been connected with *cavus* and κοῖλις, and explained of
the 'hollow' crescent of the new moon. See Roscher, *Lex.* s.v. Iuno 586.

[2] Aust, s.v. Iuppiter, in Roscher's *Lexicon*, p. 655.

[3] Varro, *L. L.* 6. 29 'Dies fasti, per quos praetoribus omnia verba
(i.e. do, dico, addico) sine piaculo licet fari.'

systematized and kept secret by kings and priests, as a part, so to speak, of the science of government. Not till B.C. 304 was the calendar published, with its permissive and prohibitive regulations[1].

C (*comitialis*) means that the day so marked was one on which the *comitia* might meet[2], and on which also legal business might be transacted, as on the days marked F, if there were no other hindrance. The total number of days thus available for secular business, i. e. days marked F and C, was in the Julian calendar 239 out of 365.

N, i. e. *nefastus*, meant that the day so marked was *religiosus, vitiosus*, or *ater*; as Gellius has it[3], 'tristi omine et infames impeditique, in quibus et res divinas facere et rem quampiam novam exordiri temperandum est.' Some of these days received the mark in historical times for a special reason, e. g. a disaster to the State ; among these were the *postriduani* or days following the Kalends, Nones and Ides, because two terrible defeats had occurred on such days[4]. But most of them (in all they are 57) were probably so marked as being devoted to lustrations, or worship of the dead or of the powers of the earth, and therefore unsuitable for worldly business. One long series of such *dies nefasti* occurs Feb. 1–14, the time of purification ; another, April 5–22, in the month occupied by the rites of deities of growing vegetation ; a third, June 5–14, when the rites of the Vestals preparatory to harvest were taking place ; and a fourth, July 1–9, for reasons which are unfortunately by no means clear to us.

NP was not a mark in the pre-Julian calendars, for it was apparently unknown to Varro and Ovid. Verrius Flaccus seems to have distinguished it from N, but his explanation is mutilated, even as it survives in Festus[5]. No one has yet determined for certain the origin of the sign, and discussion of the various conjectures would be here superfluous[6]. It appears

[1] Liv. 9. 46.
[2] Macr. 1. 16. 14.　Cp. the mutilated note of Verrius in *Fasti Praenestini* (Jan. 3).
[3] Gell. 4. 9. 5.　Varro, *L. L.* 6 29. 30.
[4] Livy, 6. 1. 11.　Macrob. i. 16. 22.
[5] Festus 165.　See Mommsen's restoration of the passage in *C. I. L.* 290 B. ; another, less satisfactory, in Huschke, *Röm. Jahr*, 240.
[6] Mommsen (*C. I. L.* 290, A) still holds to his view that NP is only an old form of N, brought into use for purposes of differentiation. His

to distinguish, in the Julian calendars, those days on which
fell the festivals of deities who were not of an earthly and
therefore doubtful character from those marked N. Thus in
the series of *dies nefasti* in February and April the Ides in
each case have the mark NP as being sacred to Jupiter.

EN. We have a mutilated note in the calendar of Praeneste
which indicates what this abbreviation meant, viz. *endotercisus*
= *intercisus*, i.e. 'cut into parts'[1]. In morning and evening,
as Varro tells us, the day was *nefastus*, but in the middle,
between the slaying of the victim and the placing of the entrails
upon the altar, it was *fastus*. But why eight days in the
calendar were thus marked we do not know, and have no data
for conjecturing. All the eight were days coming before some
festival, or before the Ides. Of the eight two occur in January
and two in February, the others in March, August, October and
December. But on such facts no conjectures can be built.

Q.R.C.F. (*Quando Rex Comitiavit Fas*) will be explained
under March 24; the only other day on which it occurs is
May 24. Q.St.D.F. (*Quando stercus delatum fas*) only occurs
on June 15, and will there be fully dealt with.

FP occurs thrice, but only in three calendars. Feb. 21
(*Feralia*) is thus marked in Caer.[2], but is F in Maff. April 23
(*Vinalia*) is FP in Caer. but NP in Maff. and F in Praen.
Aug. 19 (*Vinalia rustica*) is FP in Maff. and Amit, F in Antiat.
and Allif., NP in Vall. Mommsen explains FP as *fastus principio*, i.e. the early part of the day was *fastus*, and suggests that
in the case of the *Feralia*, as the rites of the dead were performed at night, there was no reason why the earlier part
of the day should be *nefastus*. But in the case of the two
Vinalia we can hardly even guess at the meaning of the mark,
and it does not seem to have been known to the Romans
themselves.

criticism of other views makes it difficult to put faith in them; but
I cannot help thinking that the object of the mark was not only to
distinguish the religious character of the days from those marked N, but
to show that civil business might be transacted on them after the
sacrificial rites were over, owing to the rapid increase of legal business.
Ovid may be alluding to this, though confusing NP with EN, in *Fasti*
i. 51, where the words, 'Nam simul exta deo data sunt, licet omnia
fari,' do not suit with Verrius' note on EN, but may really explain NP.

[1] *Fasti Praen.*, Jan. 10. Varro, *L. L.* 6. 31. Macr. 1. 16. 3.
[2] For the names of the fragments of *Fasti*, see next section.

V. The Calendars still surviving.

The basis of our knowledge of the old Roman religious year is to be found in the fragments of calendars which still survive. None of these indeed is older than the Julian era ; and all but one are mere fragments. But from the fragments and the one almost perfect calendar we can infer the character of the earlier calendar with tolerable certainty.

The calendar, as the Romans generally believed, was first published by Cnaeus Flavius, curule aedile, in 304 B. C., who placed the *fasti* conspicuously in the Forum, in order that every one might know on what days legal business might be transacted[1] ; in other words, a calendar was published with the marks of the days and the indications of the festivals. After this we hear nothing until 189 B. C., when a consul, M. Fulvius Nobilior, adorned his temple of Hercules and the Muses with a calendar which contained explanations or notes as well as dates[2]. These are the only indications we have of the way in which the pre-Julian calendar was made known to the people.

But the rectification of the calendar by Julius, and the changes then introduced, brought about a multiplication of copies of the original one issued under the dictator's edict[3]. Not only in Rome, but in the municipalities round about her, where the ancient religious usage of each city had since the enfranchisement of Italy been superseded, officially at least, by that of Rome, both public and private copies were made and set up either on stone, or painted on the walls or ceiling of a building.

Of such calendars we have in all fragments of some thirty, and one which is all but complete. Fourteen of these fragments were found in or near Rome, eleven in munici-

---

[1] 'Fastos circa forum in albo proposuit, ut quando lege agi posset sciretur,' Liv. 9. 46. 5 ; Cic. *Att*. 6. 1. 8. On the latter passage Mommsen has based a reasonable conjecture that the Fasti had been already published in one of the last two of the Twelve Tables, and subsequently again withdrawn. (*Chron*. 31 and note.)

[2] Macrob. 1. 12. 16.

[3] *C. I. L*. 207 B. Petronius (*Cena* 30) suggests the way in which copies might be set up in private houses. In municipia copies might be made and given to the town by private persons (so probably were Maff. and Praen.) or put up by order of the decuriones.

palities such as Praeneste, Caere, Amiternum, and others as
far away as Allifae and Venusia ; four are of uncertain origin [1] ;
and one is a curious fragment from Cisalpine Gaul [2]. Most
of them are still extant on stone, but for a few we have
to depend on written copies of an original now lost [3]. No day
in the Roman year is without its annotation in one or more
of these ; the year is almost complete, as I have said, in the
Fasti Maffeiani ; and several others contain three or four months
nearly perfect [4]. Two, though in a fragmentary condition,
are of special interest. One of these, that of the ancient
brotherhood of the Fratres Arvales, discovered in 1867 and
following years in the grove of the brethren near Rome,
contains some valuable additional notes in the fragments which
survive of the months from August to November. The other,
that of Praeneste, containing January, March, April and parts
of February and December, is still more valuable from the
comments it contains, most of which we can believe with
confidence to have come from the hand of the great Augustan
scholar Verrius Flaccus. We are told by Suetonius that
Verrius put up a calendar in the forum at Praeneste [5], drawn
up by his own hand ; and the date [6] and matter of these
fragments found at Praeneste agree with what we know of the
life and writings of Verrius. It is unlucky that recent
attempts to find additional fragments should have been entirely
without result ; for the whole annotated calendar, if we
possessed it, would probably throw light on many dark corners
of our subject.

To these fragments of Julian calendars, all drawn up
between B.C. 31 and A.D. 46, there remain to be added
two in MSS.: (1) that of Philocalus, A.D. 354, (ii) that of
Polemius Silvius, A.D. 448 ; neither of which are of much
value for our present purpose, though they will be occasionally
referred to. Lastly, we have two farmer's almanacs on cubes

---

[1] Including the Fasti Maffeiani, which is almost complete.

[2] No. 20 in C. I. L. (Guidizzolenses), found at Guidizzolo between
Mantua and Verona.

[3] Maffeiani, Tusculani, Pinciani, Venusini.

[4] Those of Caere, Praeneste, Amiternum, and Antium.

[5] Suet. de Grammaticis, 19.

[6] Circ. A D. 10: cf. C. I. L. 206. There are a few additional notes
apparently by a later hand.

of bronze, which omit the individual days, but are of use
as showing the course of agricultural operations under the later
Empire[1].

All these calendars, some of which had been printed wholly
or in part long ago, while a few have only been discovered
of late, have been brought together for the first time in the
first volume of the *Corpus Inscriptionum Latinarum*, edited
by Mommsen with all his incomparable skill and learning,
and furnished with ample elucidations and commentaries. And
we now have the benefit of a second edition of this by the
same editor, to whose labours in this as in every other
department of Roman history it is almost impossible to
express our debt in adequate words. All references to the
calendars in the following pages will be made to this second
edition.

A word remains to be said about the *Fasti* of Ovid[2], which
is a poetical and often fanciful commentary on the calendar
of the first half of the Julian year, i.e. January to June
inclusive; each month being contained in one book. Ovid
tells us himself[3] that he completed the year in twelve books;
but the last six were probably never published, for they are
never quoted by later writers. The first six were written but
not published before the poet's exile, and taken in hand again
after the death of Augustus, but only the first book had been
revised when the work was cut short by Ovid's death.

Ovid's work merits all praise as a literary performance, for
the neatness and felicity of its versification and diction; but
as a source of knowledge it is too much of a medley to be used
without careful criticism. There is, however, a great deal in
it that helps us to understand the views about the gods and
their worship, not only of the scholars who pleased themselves
and Augustus by investigating these subjects, but also of the
common people both in Rome and in the country. But the
value varies greatly throughout the work. Where the poet
describes some bit of ritual which he has himself seen, or tells

---

[1] Menologium rusticum Colotianum, and Men. rusticum Vallense in
C. I. L. 280, 281.

[2] Merkel's edition (1841), with its valuable Prolegomena, is indispensable; very useful too is that by H. Peter, Leipzig, 1889.

[3] *Tristia,* ii. 549.

some Italian story he has himself heard, he is invaluable ; but as a substitute for the work of Varro on which he drew, he only increases our thirst for the original.   No great scholar himself, he aimed at producing a popular account of the results of the work of scholars, picking and choosing here and there as suited his purpose, and not troubling himself to write with scientific accuracy.   Moreover, he probably made free use of Alexandrine poets, and especially of Callimachus, whose *Actia* is in some degree his model for the whole poem ; and thus it is that the work contains a large proportion of Greek myth, which is often hard to distinguish from the fragments of genuine Italian legend which are here and there imbedded in it.   Still, when all is said, a student of the Roman religion should be grateful to Ovid ; and when after the month of June we lose him as a companion, we may well feel that the subject not only loses with him what little literary interest it can boast of, but becomes for the most part a mere investigation of fossil rites, from which all life and meaning have departed for ever.

VI. The Calendar of the Republic and its Religious Festivals.

All the calendars still surviving belong, as we saw, to the early Empire, and represent the Fasti as revised by Julius. But what we have to do with is the calendar of the Republic. Can it be recovered from those we still possess ?   Fortunately this is quite an easy task, as Mommsen himself has pointed out [1] ; we can reconstruct for certain the so-called calendar of Numa as it existed throughout the Republican era.   The following considerations must be borne in mind :

1. It is certain that Caesar and his advisers would alter the familiar calendar as little as possible, acting in the spirit of persistent conservatism from which no true Roman was ever free.   They added 10 days to the old normal year of 355 days, i. e. two at the end of January, August, and December, and one at the end of April, June, September, and November ; but they retained the names of the months, and their division by Kalends, Nones, and Ides, and also the signs of the days,

[1] *C. I. L.* 297 foll. (de feriis).

and the names of all festivals throughout the year. Later on further additions were made, chiefly in the way of glorification of the Emperors and their families; but the skeleton remained as it had been under the Republic.

.2. It is almost certain that the Republican calendar itself had never been changed from its first publication down to the time of Caesar. There is no historical record of any alteration, either by the introduction of new festivals or in any other way. The origin of no festival is recorded in the history of the Republic, except the second Carmentalia, the Saturnalia, and the Cerealia[1]; and in these three cases we can be morally certain that the record, if such it can be called, is erroneous.

3. If Julius and his successors altered only by slight additions, and if the calendar which they had to work on was of great antiquity and unchanged during the Republic, how, in the next place, are we to distinguish the skeleton of that ancient calendar from the Julian and post-Julian additions? Nothing is easier; in Mommsen's words, it is not a matter of calculation; a glance at the Fasti is sufficient. In all these it will be seen that the numbers, names, and signs of the days were cut or painted in *large* capital letters; while ludi, sacrifices, and all additional notes and comments appear in *small* capital letters. It cannot be *demonstrated* that the large capital letters represent the Republican calendar; but the circumstantial evidence, so to speak, is convincing. For inscribed in these large capitals is all the information which the Roman of the Republic would need; the *dies fasti, comitiales, nefasti,* &c.; the number of the days in the month; the position of the Nones and the Ides and the names of those days on which fixed festivals took place; all this in an abbreviated but no doubt familiar form. The minor sacrificial rites, which concerned the priests and magistrates rather than the people, he did not find there; they would only have confused him. The moveable festivals, too, he did not find there, as they changed their date from year to year and were fixed by the priesthood as the time for each came round. The *ludi,* or public games, were also absent from the old calendar, for they were, originally at least, only adjuncts to certain

---

[1] To these we may perhaps add the *Poplifugia* and *Lucaria* in July, the legends about which we can neither accept nor refute.

festivals out of which they had grown in course of time. Lastly, all rites which did not technically concern the State as a whole, but only its parts and divisions [1], i. e. of gentes and curiae, of pagi (*paganalia*), montes (*Septimontium*) and sacella (*Sacra Argeorum*), could not be included in the public calendar of the Roman people.

But the Roman of the Republic, even if his calendar were confined to the indications given by the large capital letters in the Julian calendar, could find in these the essential outline of the yearly round of his religious life. This outline we too can reconstruct, though the detail is often wholly beyond our reach. For this detail we have to fall back upon other sources of information, which are often most unsatisfactory and difficult to interpret. What are these other sources, of what value are they, and how can that value be tested?

Apart from the surviving Fasti, we have to depend, both for the completion of the religious calendar, and for the study and interpretation of all its details, chiefly on the fragmentary remains of the works of the two great scholars of the age of Julius and Augustus, viz. Varro and Verrius Flaccus, and on the later grammarians, commentators, and other writers who drew upon their voluminous writings. Varro's book *de Lingua Latina*, though not complete, is in great part preserved, and contains much information taken from the books of the pontifices, which, did we but possess them, would doubtless constitute our one other most valuable record besides the *Fasti* themselves [2]. Such, too, is the value of the dictionary of Verrius Flaccus, which, though itself lost, survives in the form of two series of condensed excerpts, made by Festus probably in the second century, A. D., and by Paulus Diaconus as late as the beginning of the ninth [3]. Much of the work of Varro and Verrius is also imbedded in the grammatical writings of Servius the commentator on Virgil, in Macrobius, Nonius, Gellius, and

---

[1] See Festus, 245 ; and *Dict. Ant.* s. v. Sacra.

[2] Varro's works, *de Antiquitatibus humanis* and *divinis*, and many others, only survive in the fragments quoted by later authors.

[3] Paul the deacon was one of the scholars who found encouragement at the court of Charles the Great. His work is an abridgement of that of Festus, not of Verrius himself. On Verrius and his epitomators, as well as on the other writers who used his glosses, see H. Nettleship's valuable papers in *Essays in Latin Literature*, p. 201 foll.

many others, and also in Pliny's *Natural History*, and in some of the Christian Fathers, especially St. Augustine and Tertullian ; but all these need to be used with care and caution, except where they quote directly from one or other of their two great predecessors. The same may be said of Laurentius Lydus [1], who wrote in Greek a work *de Mensibus* in the sixth century, which still survives. To these materials must be added the great historical writers of the Augustine age ; Livy, who, uncritical as he was, and incapable of distinguishing the genuine Italian elements in religious tradition from the accretions of Greek and Graeco-Etruscan myth, yet supplies us with much material for criticism ; and Dionysius of Halicarnassus, who as a foreigner resident for some time in Rome, occasionally describes ritual of which he was himself a witness. The Roman lives of Plutarch, and his curious collection entitled *Roman Questions*, also contain much interesting matter, taken from several sources, e. g. Juba. the learned king of Mauritania, but as a rule ultimately referable to Varro. Beyond these there is no one author of real importance ; but the 'plant' of the investigator will include of course the whole of Roman literature, and Greek literature so far as it touches Roman life and history. Of epigraphical evidence there is not much for the period of the Republic, beyond the fragments of the Fasti ; by far the most valuable Italian religious inscription is not Roman but Umbrian ; and the *Acta Fratrum Arvalium* only begin with the Empire. Yet from these [2], and from a few works of art, however hard of interpretation, some light has occasionally been thrown upon the difficulties of our subject ; and the study of early Italian culture is fast progressing under the admirable system of excavation now being supervised by the Italian government.

All this material has been collected, sifted, and built upon by modern scholars, and chiefly by Germans. The work of collecting was done to a great extent in the sixteenth and seventeenth centuries ; the rest of the process mainly in the

[1] For more information about Lydus see Bury, *Later Roman Empire*, ii. 183, and below under March 14.

[2] They will be found in Bücheler's *Umbrica* (containing the processional inscription of Iguvium with commentary and translation), and Henzen's *Acta Fratrum Arvalium*.

nineteenth. The chief writers will be quoted as occasion demands; here can only be mentioned, *honoris causa*, the writings of Ambrosch, Preller, Schwegler, Marquardt [1], and of some of the writers in the *Mythological Lexicon*, edited by Roscher, especially Professor Wissowa of Berlin, whose short but pithy articles, as well as his treatises *de Feriis* and *de Dis Indigetibus* are models of scholarly investigation [2]. Of late, too, anthropologists and folk-lorists have had something to say about Roman religious antiquities; of these, the most conspicuous is the late lamented Dr. Mannhardt, who applied a new method to certain problems both of the Greek and the Roman religion, and evolved a new theory for their interpretation. Among other works of this kind, which incidentally throw light on our difficulties, the most useful to me have been those of Professor Tylor, Mr. Frazer, Mr. Andrew Lang, and the late Professor Robertson Smith. In the *Religion of the Semites*, by the last named scholar, I seem to see a deeper insight into the modes of religious thought of ancient peoples than in any other work with which I am acquainted.

Yet in spite of all this accumulation of learning and acumen, it must be confessed that the study of the oldest Roman religion is still one of insuperable difficulty, and apt to try the patience of the student all the more as he slowly becomes aware of the conditions of the problem before him. There are festivals in the calendar about which we really know nothing at all, and must frankly confess our ignorance; there are others about which we know just enough to be doubtful; others again, in interpreting which the Romans themselves plainly went astray, leaving us perhaps nothing but a baseless legend to aid us in guessing their original nature. It must be borne in mind that the Roman religion was in ruins when the Julian calendar was drawn up, and that the archaeological research which was brought to bear upon it by Varro and Verrius was not of a strictly scientific character. And during

---

[1] Preller's *Römische Mythologie* (ed. 3, by H. Jordan) and Marquardt's third volume of his *Staatsverwaltung* (ed. Wissowa) are both masterpieces, not only in matter but in manner.

[2] Among the others may especially be mentioned Aust, a pupil of Wissowa, to whom we owe the excellent and exhaustive article on Jupiter; and R. Peter, the author of the article Fortuna and others, who largely reflects the views of the late Prof. Reifferscheid of Breslau.

the last two centuries of the Republic, as the once stately building crumbled away, it became overlaid with growths of foreign and especially of Greek origin, under which it now lies hopelessly buried. The ground-plan alone remains, in the form of the calendar as it has been explained above; to this we must hold fast if we would obtain any true conception of the religion of the earliest Roman State[1]. Here and there some portion of the building of which it was the basis can however still be conjecturally restored by the aid of Varro and Verrius and a few other ancient writers, tested by the criticism of modern scholars, and sometimes by the results of the science of comparative religion. Such particular restoration is what has been attempted in this work, not without much misgiving and constant doubt.

The fall of the Republic is in any case a convenient point from which to survey the religious ideas and practice of the conquerors of the civilized world. It is not indeed a more significant epoch in the history of the Roman religion than the era of the Punic wars, when Rome ceased to be a peninsular, and began to be a cosmopolitan state; but it is a turning-point in the history of the calendar and of religious worship as well as of the constitution. Henceforward, in spite of the strenuous efforts of Augustus to revive the old forms of worship, all religious rites have a tendency to become transformed or over-shadowed, first by the cult of the Caesars[2]; secondly, by the steadily increasing influence of foreign and especially of Oriental cults; and lastly, by Christianity itself[3].

Taking our stand, then, in the year 46 B.C., the last year of the pre-Julian calendar, we are able in a small volume, by carefully working through that calendar, to lay a firm foundation of material for the study of the religious life and thought of the Roman people while it was still in some sense really Roman. The plan has indeed its disadvantages; it excludes the introduction of a systematic account of certain departments of the subject, such as the development of the priesthoods, the sacrificial ritual, the auspicia, and the domestic

[1] 'Hoc paene unum superest sincerum documentum,' Wissowa, de Feriis, p. 1.

[2] This is well illustrated in the *Acta Fratrum Arvalium* referred to above.

[3] A succinct account of these tendencies will be found in Marquardt, p. 72 foll. There is a French translation of this invaluable volume.

practice of religious rites[1]. But if it is true, as it undoubtedly is, that in dealing with the Roman religion we must begin with the cult[2], and that for the cult the one 'sincerum documentum' is to be found in the surviving Fasti, these drawbacks may fairly be deemed to be counterbalanced by distinct advantages. And in order to neutralize any bewilderment that may be caused by the constant variety of the rites we shall meet with, both in regard to their origin, history, and meaning, some attempt will be made, when we have completed the round of the year, to sum up our results, to sketch in outline the history of Roman religious ideas, and to estimate the influence of all this elaborate ceremonial on the life and character of the Roman people.

In order to fit the calendar of each month into a single page of this work it has been necessary to print the names of the festivals, and the indications of Kalends, Nones, &c. in *small* capital letters instead of the large capitals in which they appear in the originals (see above, p. 15). In the headings to the days as they occur throughout the book the method of the originals will be reproduced exactly, i. e. large capitals represent in every case the most ancient calendar of the Republic, and small capitals the *additamenta ex fastis*.

---

[1] A short account of these will be found in the author's articles in the new edition of Smith's *Dictionary of Antiquities*, on 'Sacra,' 'Sacerdos,' and 'Sacrificium.' On the domestic rites, there is an excellent book in Italian, which might well be translated : *Il Culto privato di Roma antica*, by Prof. De-Marchi of Milan, of which only Part I, *La Religione nella vita domestica*, has as yet appeared.

[2] Marquardt, *Staatsverwaltung*, iii. p. 2.

MENSIS MARTIUS

Fasti antiquissimi.			Additamenta ex fastis.	Additamenta ex scriptoribus.
1	KAL.	N͞P	1. Feriae Marti. Iunoni Lucinae.	1. Matronalia (?).
2		F		
3		C		
4		C		
5		C		
6		N͞P		
7	NON.	F	7. Vediovi.	
8		F		
9		C		9. Arma ancilia movent.
10		C		
11		C		
12		C		
13		EN		
14		N͞P	EQUIRRIA	14 (or 15 ?). Feriae Marti.	14. Mamuralia (?).
15	EID.	N͞P		15. Feriae Annae Perennae.	
16		F			16 (and 17 ?). Sacra Argeorum.
17		N͞P	LIBERALIA AGONIA		
18		C			
19		N	QUINQUATRUS	19. Feriae Marti.	
20		C			
21		C			
22		N			
23		N͞P	TUBILUSTRIUM		
24	Q.R.C.	F			
25		C			
26		C			
27		N͞P			
28		C			
29		C			
30		C			
31		C		31. Lunae in Aventino.	

MENSIS APRILIS

Fasti antiquissimi.			Additamenta ex fastis.	Additamenta ex scriptoribus.
1	KAL.	F		1. Veneralia (?).
2		F		Fortunae virili
3		C		in balneis
4		C	4. Matri Magnae.	(Verr. Flacc.).
5	NON.	N	4-10. Ludi Mega-lesiaci.	
6		NP	5. Fortunae publicae citeriori in colle.	
7		N		
8		N		
9		N	9-10 or 10-11. Ora-culum Fortunae patet (at Prae-neste).	
10		N		
11		N		
12		N	12-19. Ludi Cereales	
13	EID.	NP		
14		N		
15		NP FORDICIDIA		
16		N		
17		N		
18		N		
19		N CEREALIA	19. Cereri Libero Liberae.	
20		N		
21		NP PARILIA		21. Natalis urbis (Philoc.).
22		N		
23		NP VINALIA	23. Veneri Erycinae. Iovi.	
24		C		24. Feriae Latinae (conceptivae) usually about this time.
25		NP ROBIGALIA	25. Sacrificium et ludi.	
26		F		
27		C		
28		NP	28. Ludi Florae, to V. Non. Mai. (May 3).	28. Floralia(Plin.).
29		C		

22

MENSIS MAIUS

	Fasti antiquissimi.		Additamenta ex fastis.	Additamenta ex scriptoribus.
1	KAL.	F	1. Laribus (praestiti-	1. Dies natalis of
2		F	bus).	temple of Bona
3		C		Dea (Ovid).
4		C		
5		C		
6		C		
7	NON.	¹F		
8		F		
9		N	LEMURIA	
10		C		
11		N	LEMURIA	
12		NP		
13		N	LEMURIA	
14		C		
15	EID.	NP	15. Feriae Iovi Mer-	15. Sacra Argeo-
16		F	curio Maiae.	rum (Ovid, &c.).
17		C		
18		C		
19		C		
20		C		
21		NP	AGONIA	21. Vediovi.
22		N		
23		NP	TUBILUSTRIUM	23. Volcano.
24	Q.R.C.	F		
25		C		25. Fortunae publi-
26		C		cae Populi Ro-
27		C		mani.
28		C		
29		C		29. Ambarvalla
30		C		(feriae concep-
31		C		tivae).

¹ N. Maff. Cf. Mommsen, *C. I. L.* 294 b.

Fasti antiquissimi.			Additamenta ex fastis.	Additamenta ex scriptoribus.
1	KAL.	N	1. Iunoni Monetae.	1. Kalendae fabariae (Plin.) Ludi.
2		F		
3		C	3. Bellonae in circo.	
4		C		
5	NON.	N	5. Dio Fidio in colle.	
6		N		
7		N		
8		N	8. Menti in Capitolio.	
9		N VESTALIA		
10		N		
11		N MATRALIA		
12		N		
13	EID.	NP	13. Feriae Iovi.	13. Quinquatrus minusculae.
14		[1]N		
15	Q.ST.D.	F		
16		C		
17		C		
18		C	18. Annae sacrum.	
19		C		
20		C	20. Summano ad circum maximum.	
21		C		
22		C		
23		C		
24		C	24. Forti Fortunae.	
25		C		
26		C		
27		C		
28		C		
29		F		

[1] F. Tusc. Cf. Mommsen, *C. I. L.* 294 b.

MENSIS QUINTILIS

Fasti antiquissimi.			Additamenta ex fastis.	Additamenta ex scriptoribus.
1	KAL.	N		
2		N		
3		N		
4		NP		
5		NP	POPLIFUGIA	
6		N	6-13. Ludi Apolli	
7	NON.	N	nares.	7. Nonae Capro-
8		N		tinae (Varro).
9		N		9. Vitulatio
10		C		(Varro).
11		C		
12		C		
13		C		
14		C	14-19. Mercatus.	
15	EID.	NP		
16		F		
17		C		
18		C	18. Dies Alliensis.	
19		NP	LUCARIA	
20		C		
21		NP	LUCARIA	
22		C		
23		NP	NEPTUNALIA	
24		N		
25		NP	FURRINALIA	
26		C		
27		C		
28		C		
29		C		
30		C	30. Fortunae huius-	
31		C	que diei in campo.	

Fasti antiquissimi.			Additamenta ex fastis.	Additamenta ex scriptoribus.
1	KAL.	F	1. Spei ad forum holitorium.	1. Laribus compitalibus? (Ovid, 5. 147).
2		NP		
3		C		
4		C		
5	NON.	F	5. Saluti in colle Quir.	
6[1]		F		
7		C		
8		C	8 (or 9?) Soli Indigiti in colle Quir.	
9		F		
10		C		
11		C		
12		C	12. Herculi invicto ad circ. max.	
13	EID.	NP	13. Feriae Iovi.	
14		F	Dianae in Aventino.	
15		C	Vortumno in Aventino, &c.	
16		C	(see p. 198).	
17		NP	PORTUNALIA	17. Iano ad theatrum Marcelli.	
18		C		
19[2]		FP	VINALIA		
20		C		
21		NP	CONSUALIA	21. Conso in Aventino.	
22		EN		
23		NP	VOLCANALIA	23. Volcano in circo Flaminio, &c.	
24		C		24. Mundus patet (Festus).
25		NP	OPICONSIVIA		
26		C		
27		NP	VOLTURNALIA		
28		C		
29		F		

---

[1] NP. Antiat. N. minores 6. [2] F. Antiat. Allif. NP Vall.

MENSIS SEPTEMBER

Fasti antiquissimi.		Additamenta ex fastis.	Additamenta ex scriptoribus.
1 KAL. F			
2 F			
3 F			
4 C		4-12. Ludi Romani.	
5 NON. F			
6 F			
7 C			
8 C			
9 C			
10 C			
11 C			
12[1] N			
13 EID. NP		13. Iovi epulum. Feriae Iovi.	
14 F		14. Equorum probatio.	
15[2] N		15-19. Ludi Romani in circo.	
16 C			
17 C			
18 C			
19 C			
20 C		20-23. Mercatus.	
21 C			
22 C			
23 F			
24 C			
25 C			
26 C			
27 C			
28 C			
29 F			

[1] NP Vall. C. Antiat.   *C. I. L.* 294.   [2] C. Vall. Antiat.

27

Fasti antiquissimi.			Additamenta ex fastis.	Additamenta ex scriptoribus.
1	KAL.	N	1. Tigillo sororio ad compitum Acili. Fidei in Capitolio.	
2		F		
3		C		
4		C		
5		C		5. Mundus patet.
6[1]		C		
7	NON.	F	7. Iovi fulguri. Iunoni Curriti in campo.	
8		F		
9		C		
10		C		
11		NP	MEDITRINALIA	
12		C		
13		NP	FONTINALIA	13. Feriae Fonti.
14		EN		
15	EID.	NP		15. Feriae Iovi.	15. Sacrifice of October horse (Festus).
16		F		
17		C		
18		C		
19		NP	ARMILUSTRIUM	
20		C		
21		C		
22		C		
23		C		
24		C		
25		C		
26		C		
27		C		
28		C		
29		C		
30		C		
31		C		

[1] N. Antiat. Cf. *C. I. L.* 294.

MENSIS NOVEMBER

Fasti antiquissimi.		Additamenta ex fastis.	Additamenta ex scriptoribus.
1	KAL. F		
2	F		
3	C		
4	C	4–17. Ludi plebeii.	
5	F		
6	NON. F		
7	C		
8	C		
9	C		
10	C		
11	C	13. Feriae Iovi.	
12	C	Iovi epulum.	
13	EID. NP	13 (or 14?). Feroniae	
14	F	in campo.	
15	C	Fortunae Primigeniae in colle.	
16	C	14. Equorum probatio.	
17	C		
18	C	18-20. Mercatus.	
19	C		
20	C		
21	C		
22	C		
23	C		
24	C		
25	C		
26	C		
27	C		
28	C		
29	F		

MENSIS DECEMBER

Fasti antiquissimi.			Additamenta ex fastis.	Additamenta ex scriptoribus.
1	KAL.	N	1. Neptuno ⎫ ad circ. Pietati ⎭ max.	1. Fortunae mu- liebri (Dionys.).
2		N		
3		N		3. Sacra Bonae
4		C		Deae (Plutarch, &c.).
5	NON.	F		5. Faunalia rus-
6		F		tica (Horace).
7		C		
8		C	8. Tiberino in in- sula.	
9		C		
10		C		
11		NP	AG[ONIA] IN.	11. Septimontium
12		EN	12. Conso in Aven- tino.	(Festus;Varro).
13	EID.	NP	13. Telluri et Cereri in Carinis.	
14		F		
15		NP	CONSUALIA	
16		C		
17		NP	SATURNALIA	
18		C		
19		NP	OPALIA	
20		C		
21		NP	DIVALIA	
22		C	22. Laribus perma- rinis in porticu	
23		NP	LARENTALIA	Minucia.
24		C		
25		C		
26		C		
27		C		
28		C		
29		F		

30

MENSIS IANUARIUS

Fasti antiquissimi.			Additamenta ex fastis.	Additamenta ex scriptoribus.
1	KAL.	F	1. Aesculapio ⎱ in insula. Vediovi ⎰	
2		F		
3		C		3-5 (circa). Compitalia or ludi compitales.
4		C		
5	NON.	F		
6		F̄		
7		C		
8		C		
9		[NP] AGONIA		
10		EN		
11		NP CARMENTALIA		11. 'Iuturnalia' Servius.
12		C		
13	EID.	NP		
14		EN		
15		NP CARMENTALIA		
16		C		
17		C		
18		C		
19		C		
20		C		
21		C		
22		C		
23		C		
24		C		24-26. Sementivae or Paganalia (Ovid) (feriae conceptivae).
25		C		
26		C		
27		C		27. Castori et Polluci (dedication of temple).
28		C		
29		F		

Fasti antiquissimi.			Additamenta ex fastis.	Additamenta ex scriptoribus.
1	KAL.	N		1. Iunoni Sospitae (Ovid).
2		N		
3		N		
4		N		
5	NON.	NP	5. Concordiae in arce (Praen.).	
6		N		
7		N		
8		N		
9		N		
10		N		
11		N		
12		N		
13	EID.	NP	13. Fauno in insula (Esq.).	13 21. Parentalia.
14		N		
15		NP	LUPERCALIA	
16		EN		
17		NP	QUIRINALIA	17. Last day of Fornacalia (feriae conceptivae). 'Stultorum feriae' (Paulus, &c.).
18		C		
19		C		
20		C		
21[1]		FP	FERALIA	
22		C		
23		NP	TERMINALIA	
24		N	REGIFUGIUM	
25		C		
26		EN		
27		NP	EQUIRRIA	
28		C		

[1] F. Maff.

MENSIS MARTIUS.

THE mensis Martius stands alone among the Roman months. Not only was it the first in matters both civil and religious down to the time of Julius Caesar, but it is more closely associated with a single deity than any other, and that deity the protector and ancestor of the legendary founder of the city. It bears too the name of the god, which is not the case with any other month except January; and it is less certain that January was named after Janus than that March was named after Mars. The cult of Janus is not specially obvious in January except on a single day; but the cult of Mars is paramount all through March, and gives a peculiar character to the month's worship.

It follows on a period which we may call one of purification, or the performance of piacular duties towards dead ancestors and towards the gods; and this has itself succeeded a time of general festivity in the homestead, the group of homesteads, the market, and the cross-roads. The rites of December and January are for the most part festive and social, those of February mystic and melancholy—characteristics which have their counterpart in the Christian Christmas, New Year, and Lent. The rites of March are distinct from those of either period, as we shall see. They again are followed by those of April, the opening month, which are gay and apt to be licentious; then comes the mensis Maius or month of growth, which is a time of peril for the crops, and has a certain character of doubt and darkness in its rites; lastly comes June, the month of maturity, when harvest is close at hand, and life

D

begins to brighten up once more. After this the Roman months cease to denote by their names those workings of nature on which the husbandman's fortune for the year depends.

By a process of elimination we can make a guess at the kind of ideas which must have been associated with the month which the Romans called Martius, even before examining its rites in detail. It is the time when the spring, whose first breath has been felt in February, begins to show its power upon the land[1]. Some great *numen* is at work, quickening vegetation, and calling into life the powers of reproduction in man and the animals. The way in which this quickening Power or Spirit was regarded by primitive man has been very carefully investigated of recent years, and though the variation is endless both in myth and in ritual, we may now safely say that he was looked on as coming to new life after a period of death, or as returning after an absence in the winter, or as conquering the hostile powers that would hinder his activity. Among civilized peoples these ideas only survive in legend or poetry, or in some quaint bit of rural custom, often semi-dramatic, which may or may not have found its way into the organized cults of a city-state of Greece or Italy, or even into the calendar of a Christian Church. But when these survivals have been collected in vast numbers both from modern Europe and from classical antiquity, and compared with the existing ideas and practices of savage peoples, they can leave no doubt in our minds as to the general character of the primitive

---

[1] See Nissen, *Italienische Landeskunde*, i. 404 ; Ovid, *Fasti*, 3. 235 —

> Quid, quod hiems adoperta gelu tunc denique cedit,
>   Et pereunt victae sole tepente nives,
> Arboribus redeunt detonsae frigore frondes,
>   Uvidaque in tenero palmite gemma tumet :
> Quaeque diu latuit, nunc se qua tollat in auras,
>   Fertilis occultas invenit herba vias.
> Nunc fecundus ager : pecoris nunc hora creandi,
>   Nunc avis in ramo tecta laremque parat.
> Tempora iure colunt Latiae fecunda parentes
>   Quarum militiam votaque partus habet.

Here we have the fertility of man, beast, and crop, all brought together : the poet is writing of March 1. The Romans reckoned spring from Favonius (Feb. 7) to about May 10 (Varro, *R. R.* 1. 38) ; March 1 would therefore usually be a day on which its first effects would be obvious to every one.

husbandman's conception of the mysterious power at work in spring-time.

It was this Power, we can hardly doubt, that the Latins knew by the name of Mars, the god whose cult is so prominent throughout the critical period of the quickening processes. We know him in Roman literature as a full-grown deity, with characteristics partly taken from the Greeks, partly extended and developed by a state priesthood and the usage of a growing and cosmopolitan city. We cannot trace him back, step by step, to his earliest vague form as an undefined Spirit, Power, or *numen* ; it is very doubtful whether we can identify him, as mythologists have often done, with anything so obvious and definite as the sun, which by itself does not seem to have been held responsible by primitive peoples for the workings of nature at this time of year. We do not even know for certain the meaning of his name, and can get no sure help from comparative philology. Nevertheless there is a good deal of cumulative evidence which suggests a comparatively humble origin for this great god, some points of which we shall meet with in studying his cult during the month. The whole subject has been worked up by Roscher in the article on Mars in his *Mythological Lexicon*, which has the great advantage of being based on an entire re-examination of the Mars-cult, which he had handled in an earlier essay on Apollo and Mars.

KAL. MART. (MARCH 1). NP.

FERIAE MARTI. (PRAEN.)

N̄ MARTIS. (PHILOC.)

IUN[O]NI LUCINAE E S QUILIIS QUOD EO DIE AEDES EI DEDICA TA EST PER MATRONAS QUAM VOVERAT ALBI[NIA] . . . VEL UXOR . . . SI PUERUM . . . [AT]QUE IPSA M . . . . (PRAEN.)

This was the New Year's day of the Roman religious calendar. From Macrobius[1] we learn that in his day the sacred fire of Vesta was now renewed, and fresh laurels fixed on the Regia, the Curiae, and the houses of the flamens ; the custom therefore was kept up long after the first of March had ceased to be the

---

[1] Sat. 1. 12. 6; Ovid, *Fasti*, 3. 135 foll.

civil New Year.   Ovid alludes to the same rites, and adds the
Aedes Vestae as also freshly decorated [1]:

> Neu dubites, primae fuerint quin ante Kalendae
>   Martis, ad haec animum signa referre potes.
> Laurea flaminibus quae toto perstitit anno
>   Tollitur, et frondes sunt in honore novae.
> Ianua tunc regis posita viret arbore Phoebi ;
>   Ante tuas fit idem, curia prisca, fores.
> Vesta quoque ut folio niteat velata recenti,
>   Cedit ab Iliacis laurea cana focis.

The mention of these buildings carries us back to the very
earliest Rome, when the rex and his sons and daughters [2]
(Flamines and Vestales, in their later form) performed between
them the whole religious duty of the community; to these we
may perhaps add the warrior-priests of Mars (Salii).   The connexion of the decoration with the Mars-cult is probable, if not
certain ; the laurel was sacred to Mars, for in front of his
sacrarium in the regia there grew two laurels [3], and it has been
conjectured that they supplied the boughs used on this day [4].

March 1 is also marked in the calendar of Philocalus as the
birthday of Mars ($\bar{N}$ = natalis Martis).   This appears in no other
calendar as yet discovered, and is conspicuously absent in the
Fasti Praenestini ; it is therefore very doubtful whether any
weight should be given to a fourth-century writer whose
calendar had certainly an urban and not a rustic basis [5].   There
is no trace of allusion to a birth of Mars *on this day* in Latin
literature, though the day is often mentioned.   There was
indeed a pretty legend of such a birth, told by Ovid under

----

[1] Ovid only mentions one 'curia': in Macrobius the word is in the
plural.   Ovid must, I think, refer to the curia Saliorum on the Palatine
(Marq. 431), as this was the day on which the Salii began their rites.
Macrobius may be including the curia of the Quirinal Salii (Preller,
i. 357).

[2] See below, on the Vestalia in June, p. 147.

[3] Julius Obsequens, 19.

[4] Roscher, *Myth. Lex.* s.v. Mars, 2427.   Roscher regards the use of laurel
in the Mars-cult as parallel with that in the Apollo-cult and not derived
from it.   The point is not however certain.   The laurel was used as an
ἀποτρόπαιον at the Robigalia, which seems closely connected with the
Mars-cult (Plin. *N. H.* 18. 161) ; here it could hardly have been taken over
from the worship of Apollo.

[5] Mommsen, *C. I. L.* 254.

May 2 [1], which has its parallels in other mythologies; Juno became pregnant of Mars by touching a certain flower of which the secret was told her by Flora:

> Protinus haerentem decerpsi pollice florem;
> Tangitur et tacto concipit illa sinu.
> Iamque gravis Thracen et laeva Propontidis intrat
> Fitque potens voti, Marsque creatus erat.

Of this tale Preller remarked long ago that it has a Greek setting: it is in fact in its Ovidian form a reflex from stories such as those of the birth of Athena and of Kora. Yet it has been stoutly maintained [2] that it sprang from a real Italian germ, and is a fragment of the lost Italian mythology. Now, though it is certainly untrue that the Italians had no native mythology, and though there are faint traces, as we shall see, of tales about Mars himself, yet the Latins at least so rarely took these liberties with their deities [3], that every apparent case of a divine myth needs to be carefully examined and well supported. In this case we must conclude that there is hardly any evidence for a general belief that March 1 was the birthday of Mars; and that Ovid's story of Juno and Mars must be looked on with suspicion so far as these deities are concerned.

The idea that Mars was born on March 1 might arise simply

---

[1] *Fasti*, 5. 253. There is a good parallel in Celtic mythology: the wife of Llew the Sun-hero was born of flowers (Rhys, *Celt. Myth.* 384). The myth is found in many parts of the world (*Lang*, ii. 22, and note).

[2] By Usener, in his remarkable paper in *Rhein. Museum*, xxx. 215 foll., on 'Italische Mythen.' He unluckily made the mistake of supposing that Ovid told this story under June 1 (i. e. *nine months* before the supposed birthday of Mars). There is indeed a kind of conjunction of June and Mars on June 1, as both had temples dedicated on that day; but neither of these can well be earlier than the fourth century B.C., and no one would have thought of them as having any bearing on the birth of Mars but for Usener's blunder (Aust, *de Aedibus sacris Pop. Rom.* pp. 8 and 10, and his valuable note in Roscher's article on Mars, p. 2390). Usener also adduces the derivation of Gradivus in Fest. 97 ' quia gramine sit ortus.'

[3] The practical Roman mind applied the myth chiefly to the history of its *state*, and in such a way that its true mythic character was lost, or nearly so. What became in Greece mythic literature became quasi-history at Rome. Thus it is that Romulus is so closely connected with Mars in legend: the race-hero and the race-god have almost a mythical identity. The story of the she-wolf may be at least as much a myth of the birth of Mars as Ovid's story of Juno, in spite of the fatherhood of Mars in that legend.

from the fact that the day was the first of his month and also the first of the year. It is possible however to account for it in another way. It was the *dies natalis* of the temple of Juno Lucina on the Esquiline, as we learn from the note in the Fasti Praenestini; and this Juno had a special power in childbirth. The temple itself was not of very ancient date[1], but Juno had no doubt always been especially the matrons' deity, and in a sense represented the female principle of life[2]. To her all kalends were sacred, and more especially the first kalends of the year, on which we find that wives received presents from their husbands[3], and entertained their slaves. In fact the day was sometimes called the Matronalia[4], though the name has no technical or religious sense. Surely, if a mother was to be found for Mars, no one could be more suitable that Juno Lucina; and if a day were to be fixed for his birth, no day could be better than the first kalends of the year, which was also the dedication-day of the temple of the goddess. At what date the mother and the birthday were found for him it is impossible to discover. The latter may be as late as the Empire; the former may have been an older invention, since Mars seems to have been apt to lend himself, under Greek or Etruscan influence, somewhat more easily to legendary treatment than some other deities[5]. But we may at any rate feel pretty sure that it was the Matronalia on March 1 that suggested the motherhood of Juno and the birth of Mars; and we cannot, as Roscher does, use the Matronalia to show that these myths were old and native[6].

Yet another legend was attached to this day. It was said that the original *ancile*, or sacred shield of Mars, fell down from heaven[7], or was found in the house of Numa[8], on March 1. This was the type from which were copied the other

---

[1] Aust, as quoted above. The date was probably 379 B.C. (Plin. *N. H.* 16. 235).

[2] Roscher in *Lex.* s. v. Juno, p. 576.

[3] Marq. 571, where is a list of passages referring to these gifts. Some are familiar, e.g Horace, *Od.* 3. 8, and Juvenal, 9. 53 (with the scholiast in each case).

[4] *Schol. Cruq.* on Horace, l. c., and the scholiast on Juvenal, l. c.

[5] See e. g. the mysterious scene on a cista from Praeneste given in Roscher, *Lex.* 2407, to which the clue seems entirely lost.

[6] *Lex.* s. v. Mars, 2399; s. v. Juno, 584.

[7] Ovid, 3. 351 foll. ; Plut. *Numa*, 13.   [8] Dion. Hal. 2. 71.

eleven belonging to the collegium of Salii Palatini; in the legend the smith who did this work was named Mamurius, and was commemorated in the Salian hymn[1]. These are simply fragments of a tangle of myth which grew up out of the mystery attaching to the Salii, or dancing priests of Mars, and to the curious shields which they carried, and the hymns which they sang[2]; in the latter we know that the word *Mamuri* often occurred, which is now generally recognized as being only a variant of the name Mars[3]. We shall meet with the word again later in the month. This also was the first day on which the shields were 'moved,' as it was called; i.e. taken by the Salii from the *sacrarium Martis* in the Regia[4], and carried through the city in procession. Dionysius (ii. 70) has left us a valuable description of these processions, which continued till the 24th of the month; the Salii leaped and danced, reminding the writer of the Greek Curetes, and continually struck the shields with a short spear or staff[5] as they sang their ancient hymns and performed their rhythmical dances.

The original object and meaning of all these strange performances is now fairly well made out, thanks to the researches of Müllenhoff, Mannhardt, Roscher, Frazer and others. Roscher, in his comparison of Apollo and Mars[6], pointed out the likeness in the spring festivals of the two gods. At Delphi, at the Theophania (7th of Bysios = March), there were decorations, sacrifices, dances, and songs; and of these last, some were

---

[1] Ovid, l. c. 381 foll. [2] Marq. 430, and note.

[3] Festus, p. 131; Usener in *Rhein. Mus.* xxx. 209 foll. Wordsworth, *Fragments and Specimens of Early Latin*, p. 564 foll. Jordan (Preller, i. 336) had however doubts about the identification of Mars and Mamurius.

[4] The place is not quite certain. Ambrosch (*Studien*, 7), who believed them to be part of the armour of the god, placed them in his *sacrarium* in the king's house, with Serv. Aen. 7. 603, and this falls in with Dionysius' version of the myth, that the shield was found in Numa's house. With this view Preller agreed. Marquardt, (431) however, believed they were part of the armour of the priests, and as such were kept in the Curia Saliorum, which might also be called *sacrarium Martis*. The question is not of the first importance.

[5] Dionysius (2. 70. 2) says that each was girt with a sword, and carried in his right hand, λόγχην ἢ ῥάβδον ἤ τι τοιοῦθ' ἕτερον. Apparently, assuming that he had seen the procession, he did not see or remember clearly what these objects were. A relief from Anagnia (*Annali del Inst.* 1869, 70 foll.) shows them like a double drumstick, with a knob at each end.

[6] See also *Myth. Lex.* s. v. Mars, p. 2404 and Apollo, p. 425.

ὕμνοι κλητικοί, or invocations to the god to appear, some παιᾶ ες, or shouts of encouragement in his great fight with the dragon, or perhaps intended to scare the dragon away. For Apollo was believed to return in the spring, to be born anew, and to struggle in his infancy with the demon of evil. At other places in Greece similar performances are found; at Delos[1], at Ortygia[2] near Ephesus, at Tegyra, and elsewhere. At Ortygia the Κουρῆτες stood and clashed their arms to frighten away Hera the enemy of Apollo's mother Leto, in the annual dramatic representation of the perilous labour of the mother and the birth of her son. These practices (and similar ones among northern peoples) seem to be the result of the poetical mythology of an imaginative race acting on still more primitive ideas. From all parts of the world Mr. Frazer has collected examples of rites of this kind occurring at some period of real or supposed peril, and often at the opening of a new year, in which dances, howling, the beating of pots and pans, brandishing of arms, and even firing of guns are thought efficacious in driving out evil spirits which bring hurt of some kind to mankind or to the crops which are the fruits of his labour[3]. This notion of evil spirits and the possibility of expelling them is at the root of the whole series of practices, which in the hands of the Greeks became adorned with a beautiful mythical colouring, while the Romans after their fashion embodied them in the cult of their city with a special priesthood to perform them, and connected them with the name of their great priest king.

In an elaborate note[4] Mr. Frazer has attempted to explain the rites of the Salii in the light of the material he has collected. He is inclined to see two objects in their performances: (1) the routing out of demons of all kinds in order to collect them for transference to the human scapegoat, Mamurius Veturius (see

---

[1] Virg. *Aen.* 4. 143.

[2] Strabo, 639 foll. The same also appear in the cult of Zeus; Preller-Robert, *Greek Myth.* i. 134.

[3] *G. B.* ii. 157–182; Tylor, *Prim. Cu't.* i. 298 foll. We have survivals at Rome, not only in the periodic Salian rites, but on particular occasions; Martial 12. 57. 15 (of an eclipse); Ovid, *Fasti*, 5. 441; Tibull. 1. 8. 21; Tac. *Ann.* 1. 28 (this was in Germany). I have known the church bells rung at Zermatt in order to stop a continuous downpour of rain in hay-harvest.

[4] *G. B.* ii. 210.

below on March 14), who was driven out a fortnight later; and (2) to make the corn grow, by a charm consisting in leaping and dancing, which is known in many parts of the world. It will perhaps be safer to keep to generalities in matters of which we have but slender knowledge; and to conclude that the old Latins believed that the Spirit which was beginning to make the crops grow must at this time be protected from hostile demons, in order that he might be free to perform his own friendly functions for the community. Though the few words preserved of the Salian hymns are too obscure to be of much use [1], we seem to see in them a trace of a deity of vegetation; and the prayer to Mars, which is given in Cato's agricultural treatise, is most instructive on this point [2].

The Salii in these processions were clothed in a *trabea* and *tunica picta* [3], the 'full dress' of the warrior inspired by some special religious zeal, wearing helmet, breastplate, and sword. They carried the *ancile* on the left arm, and a staff or club of some kind to strike it with [4]. At certain sacred places they stopped and danced, their praesul giving them the step and rhythm; and here we may suppose that they also sang the song of which a few fragments have come down to us, where the recurring word Mamurius seems beyond doubt to be a variant of Mars [5]. Each evening they rested at a different place—*mansiones Saliorum*, as they were called—and here the sacred arms were hung up till the next day, and the Salii feasted. They were twenty-four in number, twelve Palatini and twelve Collini (originally Agonales or Agonenses), the former specially devoted to the worship of Mars Gradivus, the latter to that of Quirinus [6]. The antiquity of the priest-

---

[1] Jordan, *Krit. Beiträge*, p. 203 foll.   [2] Cato, *R. R.* 143.

[3] Liv. 1. 20. Cp. 9. 40, where the chosen Samnite warriors wore *tunicae versicolores*. In each case the dress is a religious one, of the same character as that of the *triumphator*, and would have its ultimate origin in the war-paint of savages, which probably also has a religious signification. The *trabea* was the old short cavalry coat.

[4] See Marq. 432, and *Dict. of Antiq.* s. v. Salii for details.

[5] Fest. 131. The fragments may be seen in Wordsworth's *Fragments and Specimens of Early Latin*, pp. 564 foll. In the chief fragment the name of Janus seems almost certainly to occur (cf. Lydus, 4. 2); and in another Lucetius (= Iupiter?). Juno and Minerva are also mentioned. See *Dict. of Antiq.* s. v. Salii. It is curious that Mars is more prominent in the song of the Arval Brothers.

[6] Liv. 5. 52. 7.

hood is proved by the fact that the Salii must be of patrician birth, and *patrimi* and *matrimi* (i. e. with both parents living) according to the ancient rule which descended from the worship of the household [1].

It has been suggested that the shields (*ancilia*) which the Salii carried, being twelve in number for each of the two guilds, represented the twelve months of the year, either as twelve suns [2] (the sun being renewed each month), or as twelve moons, which is a little more reasonable. This idea implies that the number of the Salii (which was the same as that of the Fratres Arvales) was based on the number of months in the year, which is very far from likely; it would seem also to assume that the shape of the shields was round, like sun or moon, which was almost certainly not the case. According to the legend, the original shield fell on the first new moon of the year; but it is quite unnecessary to jump to the conclusion that the others represent eleven other new moons. It would rather seem probable to a cautious inquirer that though an incrustation of late myth may have grown upon the Salii and their carmen and their curious arms, no amount of ingenious combination has as yet succeeded in proving that such myths had their origin in any really ancient belief of the Romans. What we know for certain is that there were twelve warrior-priests of the old Palatine city, and that they carried twelve shields of an antique type, which Varro compares to the Thracian peltae (*L. L.* 7. 43); shaped not unlike the body of a violin, with a curved indentation on each side [3], which,

---

[1] Dionysius, 2. 71.

[2] Usener in *Rhein. Mus.* xxx. 218; Roscher, *Lex.* s. v. Mars 2419, can only quote two very vague and doubtful passages from late writers in support of the view that the shields were symbols of the months: Lydus 4. 2, who says that the Salii sang in praise of Janus, κατὰ τὸν τῶν Ἰταλικῶν μηνῶν ἀριθμόν; and Liber glossarum, Cod. Vat. Palat. 1773 f. 40 v.: Ancilia: scuta unius anni.

[3] For the evidence on this point, and others connected with the Salii, I must refer the reader to Mr. G. E. Marindin's excellent article 'Salii' in the new edition of Smith's *Dict of Antiquities*, the most complete and at the same time sensible account that has appeared in recent years. (The article 'Ancilia' in the new edition of Pauly's *Real-Encycl.* is disappointing.) Dionysius, Varro, and Plutarch are all at once about the shape of the shields, and Mr. Marindin is quite right in insisting that Ovid does not contradict them. (See the passages quoted in the article.) The coins of Licinius Stolo and of Antoninus Pius (Cohen, *Méd. Cons.*

when the shield was slung on the back, would leave space for the arms to move freely. In this respect, as in the rest of his equipment, the Salius simply represented the old Italian warrior in his 'war-paint.' In the examples of expulsion of evils referred to above as collected by Mr. Frazer, it is interesting to notice how often the expellers use military arms, or are dressed in military fashion. This may perhaps help us to understand how attributes apparently so distinct as the military and the agricultural should be found united in Mars and his cult.

Non. Mart. (March 7). F.

. . . [VEDI]OVI. ARTIS VEDIOVIS INTER DUOS LUCOS. (PRAEN.)

Various conjectures have been made for correcting this note. We may take it that the first word is rightly completed : some letters seem to have preceded it, and *feriae* has been suggested[1], but not generally accepted. The next word, *Artis*, must be a slip of the stone-cutter. That it was not Martis we are sure, as Ovid says that there was no note in the Fasti for this day except on the cult of Vediovis[2]. Even Mommsen is in despair, but suggests *Aedis* as a possibility, and that *dedicata* was accidentally omitted after it.

We do not know when the temple was dedicated[3]. The cult of Vediovis seems to have no special connexion with other March rites : and it seems as well to postpone consideration of it till May 21, the dedication-day of the temple *in arce*. See also on Jan. 1.

VII Id. Mart. (March 9). C.

ARMA ANCILIA MOVENT. (PHILOC.)

As we have seen, the first 'moving' of the ancilia was on the 1st. This is the second mentioned in the calendars ;

plate xxiv. 9, 10, and *Méd. Imp.* ii, no. 467) give the same peculiar shape. The bronze of Domitian, A.D. 88 (Cohen, *Méd. Imp.* i. plate xvii), and the coins of Sanquinius, B.C. 16 (both issued in connexion with ludi saeculares), on which are figures supposed to be Salii with round shields, have certainly been misinterpreted (e. g. in Marq. 431). See note at end of this work.

[1] Jordan, in *Commentationes in hon. Momms.* p. 365. There could not be *feriae* on this day, as it was a *dies fastus*.

[2] *Fast.* 3. 429 'Una nota est Marti Nonis ; sacrata quod illis Templa putant lucos Vediovis ante duos.'   [3] Aust, *de Aedibus sacris*, p. 33.

the third, according to Lydus (4. 42), was on the 23rd (Tubilustrium, q. v.). As the Salii seem to have danced with the shields all through the month up to the 24th [1], it has been supposed that these were the three principal days of 'moving'; and Mr. Marindin suggests that they correspond to the three most important *mansiones Saliorum*, of which two were probably the Curia Saliorum on the Palatine and the Sacrarium Martis in the Regia [2].

Prid. Id. Mart. (March 14). NP.

EQUIRR[IA]. (MAFF. VAT. ESQ.)
FERIAE MARTI. (VAT.)
SACRUM MAMURIO. (RUSTIC CALENDARS [3].)
MAMURALIA. (PHILOC.)

These notes involve several difficulties. To begin with, this day is an even number, and there is no other instance in the calendar of a festival occurring on such a day. Wissowa [4], usually a very cautious inquirer, here boldly cuts the knot by conjecturing that the Mars festival of this day had originally been on the next, i. e. the Ides, but was put back one day to enable the people to frequent both the horse-races (Equirria) and the festival of Anna Perenna [5]. The latter, he might have added, was obviously extremely popular with the lower classes, as we shall see from Ovid's description ; and though the scene of it was close to that of the Equirria, or certainly not far away, it is not impossible that it may have diverted attention from the nobler and more manly amusement. Wissowa strengthens

---

[1] Polyb. 21. 10 (13) ; Liv. 37. 33.

[2] See his article in *Dict. Ant.* He further suggests that in Philocalus' note *ancilia* is an adjective, and that *arma ancilia* means the shields only, as the spears of Mars do not seem to have been used by the Salii.

[3] The day is of course not given in these almanacs ; but the position is between Isidis navigium (March 5) and Liberalia (March 17).

[4] *de Feriis*, ix. foll. Cp. *C. I. L.* 311.

[5] The usual sacrifice to Jupiter on the Ides is also mentioned by Wissowa in this connexion ; but I should hardly imagine that it would have had a sufficiently popular character to cause any such alteration as he is arguing for. But the first full moon of the year may have become over-crowded with rites ; and it was the day on which at one time the consuls entered on office, B.C. 222 to 154 (Mommsen, *Chron.* 102 and notes).

his argument by pointing out an apparent parallel between the festival dates of March and October. Here, as elsewhere, in the calendar, we find an interval of three days between two festivals, viz. between March 19 (Quinquatrus) and March 23 (Tubilustrium), and between Oct. 15 ('October horse') and Oct. 19 (Armilustrium). Now, as we shall see, the rites of March 19 and Oct. 19 seem to correspond to each other [1]; and if there were a chariot-race on March 15, it would also answer to the race on the day of the 'October horse,' Oct. 15, with a three days' interval as in October. The argument is not a very strong one, but there is a good deal to be said for it.

A much more serious difficulty lies in the discrepancy between the three older calendars in which we have notes for this day and the almanacs of the later Empire, viz. that of Philocalus (A.D. 354) and the rustic calendars. The former tell us of a Mars-festival, with a horse-race ; the latter know nothing of these, but note a festival of Mamurius, a name which, as we saw, occurred in the Saliare Carmen apparently as a variant of Mars, and came to be affixed to the legendary smith who made the eleven copies of the ancile. How are we to account for the change of Mars into Mamurius, and of feriae Marti into Mamuralia? And are we to suppose that the later calendars here indicate a late growth of legend, based on the name Mamurius as occurring in the Carmen Saliare, or that they have preserved the shadow of an earlier and popular side of the March rites, which the State-calendars left out of account?

Apparently Mommsen holds the former opinion [2]. In his note on this day he says that it is easy to understand how the second Equirria came to be known to the *vulgus* as Mamuralia (i. e. so distinguished from the first Equirria on Feb. 27), seeing that Mamurius who made the ancilia belongs wholly to the cult of Mars, and that this day was one of those on which the Salii and the ancilia were familiar sights in the streets of Rome. In other words, the Salian songs gave rise to the legend of Mamurius, and this in its turn gave a new name to the second Equirria or feriae Marti. And this I believe to be the most rational

---

[1] Wissowa takes both as lustrations of cavalry. Mommsen, *C. I. L.* 332, disapproves of Wissowa's reasoning about this day.

[2] *C. I. L.* 311.

explanation of our difficulty, seeing that we have no mention of a feast of Mamurius earlier than the calendar of Philocalus in the fourth century A. D., which cannot be regarded as in any sense representing learning or research [1].

But of recent years much has been written in favour of the other view, that the late calendars have here preserved for us a trace of very ancient Roman belief and ritual [2]. This view rests almost entirely on a statement of a still later writer, Laurentius Lydus of Apamea, who wrote a work, de Mensibus, in the first half of the sixth century A. D., preserved in part in the form of two summaries or collections of extracts. Lydus was no doubt a man of learning, as is shown by his other work, de Magistratibus; but he does not give us his authority for particular statements, and his second- or third-hand knowledge must always be cautiously used.

Lydus tells us that on the Ides of March (a mistake, it is supposed [3], for the 14th—which, however, he should not have made), a man clothed in skins was led out and driven with long peeled wands (out of the city, as we may guess from what follows) and shouted at as 'Mamurius.' Hence the saying, when any one is beaten, that they are 'playing Mamurius with him.' For the legend runs that Mamurius the smith was beaten out of the city because misfortune fell on the Romans when they substituted the new shields (made by Mamurius) for those that had fallen from heaven [4].

This is clearly a late form of the Mamurius-myth : in all the earlier accounts [5] only one ancile is said to have fallen from heaven. Lydus seems rather to be thinking of twelve original ones [6], and twelve copies—perhaps of the Palatine and Colline ancilia respectively. If the form of the myth, then, is of late

---

[1] C. I. L. 254.

[2] Cf. Usener's article on Italian Myths in Rhein. Mus vol. xxx—a most interesting and suggestive piece of work, which, however, needs to be read with a critical mind, and has been too uncritically used by later writers, e.g. Roscher in his article on Mars. Frazer (G. B. ii. 208) adopts his conclusions about Mamurius, but, with his usual care, points out some of the difficulties in a footnote.   [3] Usener, p. 211.

[4] Lydus, 3. 29 and 4. 36. The words are rather obscure, but the meaning is fairly obvious. See Usener's paraphrase, p. 210.

[5] See above, p. 38.

[6] Cp. what he says of the Salii singing of Janus κατὰ τὸν τῶν Ἰταλικῶν μηνῶν ἀριθμόν (4. 2).

growth, suspicion may well be aroused as to the antiquity of
the rite it was meant to explain, for with the older type of
myth the rite does not seem to suit. And this suspicion is
strengthened by the fact that in the whole of Latin literature
there is no certain allusion to a rite so striking and peculiar,
and only one that can possibly, even by forcible treatment, be
taken as such. In Propertius v (iv.) 2. 61, we have the
following lines, put into the mouth of the god Vertumnus:

> At tibi, Mamuri, formae caelator aenae,
>   Tellus artifices ne premat Osca manus,
> Qui me tam docilis potuisti fundere in usus.
>   Unum opus est : operi non datur unus honos.

Usener took this to mean, or to imply, that Mamurius was
driven out of the city to its enemies the Oscans; but how we
are to get this out of the words, which will bear very different
interpretations, obscure as they are, it is not easy to see. And
can we easily believe that, with this exception, no allusion
should be found to the rite in either Latin or Greek writers —
not in Ovid, Dionysius, Servius, Plutarch [1], or in the fragments
of Varro, Varrius, and others—if that curious rite had really
been enacted year by year before the eyes of the Roman people?
It certainly is not impossible that it may have slipped their
notice, or have been mentioned in works that are lost to us ;
but it is so improbable as to justify us in hesitating to base
conclusions as to the antiquity of the rite on the statement of
Lydus alone.

There are indeed one or two passages which seem to prove
that *skins* were used by the Salii, and that these skins were
beaten. Servius [2] says of Mamurius that they consecrated a day
to him, on which 'pellem virgis caedunt ad artis similitudinem,'
i. e. on which they imitate the smith's art by beating a skin.
So also Minucius Felix [3]: 'alii (we should probably read *Salii*)
incedunt pileati, scuta vetera [4] circumferunt, pelles caedunt.'
If we may judge by these passages of writers of the second
century, there was something done by the Salii which involved
the beating of skins ; but if it was a skin-clad Mamurius who

---

[1] e. g. in Numa 13.
[2] *Aen.* 7. 188. Thilo and Hagen seem to think that Servius wrote
peltas (shields) on the evidence of one MS , wrongly, I think.
[3] *Octavius*, 24. 3.   [4] What is the meaning of *vetera* here ?

was beaten, why is he not mentioned, and why did they, as Servius says (and the context shows that he is speaking of him with all respect), set apart a day in his honour?

Yet Lydus' account is so interesting from the point of view of folk-lore, that Usener was led by it into very far-reaching conclusions. These have been so well condensed in English by Mr. Frazer that my labour will be lightened if I may borrow his account [1]:

'Every year on March 14 a man clad in skins was led in procession through the streets of Rome, beaten with long white rods, and driven out of the city. He was called Mamurius Veturius [2], that is, "the old Mars," and as the ceremony took place on the day preceding the first full moon of the old Roman year [3] (which began on March 1), the skin-clad man must have represented the Mars of the past year, who was driven out at the beginning of a new one. Now Mars was originally not a god of war, but of vegetation. For it was to Mars that the Roman husbandman prayed for the prosperity of his corn and vines, his fruit-trees and his copses; it was to Mars that the Arval Brothers, whose business it was to sacrifice for the growth of the crops, addressed their petitions almost exclusively. . . . Once more, the fact that the vernal month of March was dedicated to Mars seems to point him out as the deity of the sprouting vegetation. Thus the Roman custom of expelling the old Mars at the beginning of the New Year in spring is identical with the Slavonic custom of "carrying out Death [4]," if the view here taken of the latter custom is correct.

---

[1] *Golden Bough*, ii. 208.

[2] Mr. Frazer is careful to point out in a note that Lydus only mentions the name Mamurius. But as we know that Mamurius was called Veturius in the Salian hymn, and as Veturius may perhaps mean *old*, it is inferred that the skin-clad man was 'the old Mars.' The argument is shaky; its only strength lies in the Slavonic and other parallels.

[3] Lydus is thought to have made a mistake in attributing it to the 15th (Ides); if so, he may have confused other matters in this curious note. But he is certainly explicit enough here (4. 36), and refers to the usual sacrifice to Jupiter on the Ides, and to ' public prayers for the salubrity of the coming year,' which we may be sure would be on the Ides, and not on a day of even number. I do not feel at all sure that Lydus was wrong as to the date, the more so as the Ides of May (which month has a certain parallelism with March) is the date of another curious ceremony of th's primitive type, that of the *Argei*.

[4] This was first noticed by Grimm (*Teutonic Mythology*, Eng. Trans., vol. ii. 764 foll.). Since then Mannhardt (*Baumkultus*, 410 foll.) and

The similarity of the Roman and Slavonic customs has been already remarked by scholars, who appear, however, to have taken Mamurius Veturius and the corresponding figures in the Slavonic ceremonies to be representatives of the old year rather than of the old god of vegetation. It is possible that ceremonies of this kind may have come to be thus interpreted in later times even by the people who practised them. But the personification of a period of time is too abstract an idea to be primitive. However, in the Roman, as in the Slavonic ceremony, the representative of the god appears to have been treated, not only as a deity of vegetation, but also as a scape-goat [1]. His expulsion implies this; for there is no reason why the god of vegetation, as such, should be expelled the city. But it is otherwise if he is also a scape-goat; it then becomes necessary to drive him beyond the boundaries, that he may carry his sorrowful burden away to other lands. And, in fact, Mamurius Veturius appears to have been driven away to the lands of the Oscans, the enemies of Rome [2].'

My examination of the evidence will, I hope, have made it clear why I hesitate to endorse these conclusions in their entirety (as I did for many years), interesting as they are. I rather incline to believe that the whole Mamurius-legend grew out of the Carmen Saliare, and that we may either have here one of those comparatively rare examples of later ritual growing itself out of myth, or a point of ancient ritual, such as the use of skins—perhaps those of victims—misinterpreted and possibly altered under the influence of the

Mr. Frazer (G. B. i. 257 foll. and 264 foll.) have worked it out and explained it (see especially i. 275). It is generally believed that Death, or whatever be the name applied to the human being or figure expelled in these rites, signifies the extinct spirit of vegetation of the past year. I agree with Mr. Frazer, as against Usener and Roscher (Lex. s. v. Mars), that it is not any abstract conception of the year, or at least was not such originally.

[1] This fusion of two apparently different ideas in a single ceremony has previously been explained by Mr. Frazer, pp. 205 foll. On p. 210 he notices the curious and well-authenticated rite of driving out hunger at Chaeronea (Plutarch, Quaest. Conviv. 6. 8), which would offer an interesting parallel to the Roman, if we could but be sure of the details of the latter. Another from Delphi (Plut. Quaest. Graec. 12, mentioned by Usener, does not seem to me conclusive; but that of the 'man in cowhide' from the Highlands (G. B. ii. 145) is singularly like the Roman rite as Lydus describes it, and took place on New Year's eve.

[2] See above, p. 47.

E

myth. As to Lydus' statement, it is better to suspend our judgement; he may, for all we know, have confused some foreign custom, or that of some other Italian town where there were Salii, with the ritual of a Roman priesthood[1]. In any case, his account is too much open to question to bear the weight of conjecture that has been piled upon it.

ID. MART. (MARCH 15). NP.

FERIAE[2] ANNAE PERENNAE VIA FLAM[INIA] AD LAPIDEM PRIM[UM]. (VAT.)

ANNAE PER. (FARN.)

This is a survival of an old popular festival, as is clearly seen from Ovid's account of it; but the absence of any mention of it in the rustic calendars or in those of Philocalus and Silvius leads us to suppose that it had died out in the early Empire. This may be accounted for by the fact that the people came to be more and more attracted by spectacles and games; and also by the ever-increasing cosmopolitanism of the city populace, which would be continually losing interest in old Roman customs which it could not understand.

On this day, Ovid tells us[3], the 'plebs' streamed out to the 'festum geniale' of Anna Perenna, and taking up a position in the Campus Martius, not far from the Tiber[4], and lying

---

[1] I am the more disposed to suspect Lydus' account, as in the same sentence he mentions a sacrifice which is conducted by priests of the Magna Mater Idaea : ἱεράτευον δὲ καὶ ταῦρον ἐξέτη ὑπὲρ τῶν ἐν τοῖς ὄρεσιν ἀγρῶν, ἡγουμένου τοῦ ἀρχιερέως καὶ τῶν κανηφόρων τῆς μητρόχου· ἤγετο δὲ καὶ ἄνθρωπος κ.τ.λ. For the difficulties of this passage, and suggested emendations, see Mommsen, C. I. L. 312, note on Id. Mart ; Marq. 394, note 5. What confusion of cults may not have taken place, either in Lydus' mind or in actual fact ?

[2] Both these notes are *additamenta* : Anna does not appear in the large letters of the Numan calendar. We cannot, however, infer from this that her festival was not an ancient one ; for, as Wissowa points out, the same is the case with the very primitive rite of the 'October horse' (*de Feriis*, xii). The day is only marked EID in *Maff. Vat.*, the two calendars in which this part of the month is preserved ; i. e. the usual sacrifice to Jupiter on the Ides was indicated (cp. Lydus, 4. 36), and the Ides fixed for the 15th. The additional notes, according to Wissowa, were for the use of the priests ; but, considering the popular character of the festival, I am inclined to doubt this rule holding good in the present instance.

[3] Ovid, *Fasti*, 3. 523 foll.

[4] 'Via Flaminia ad lapidem primum' (Vat.) : this would be near the present Porta del Popolo, and close to the river.

about on the grass in pairs of men and women, passed the day in revelry and drinking [1]. Some lay in the open; some pitched tents, and some constructed rude huts of stakes and branches, stretching their togas over them for shelter. As they drank they prayed for as many years of life as they can swallow cups of wine; meanwhile singing snatches of song with much gesticulation and dancing. The result of these performances was naturally that they returned to the city in a state of intoxication. Ovid tells us that he had seen this spectacle himself [2].

Whether there was any sacrificial rite in immediate connexion with these revels we do not know. Macrobius indeed tells us [3] that sacrifice was offered in the month of March to Anna Perenna 'ut annare perannareque commode liceat' [4]; and Lydus, that on the Ides there were εὐχαὶ δημόσιαι ὑπὲρ τοῦ ὑγιεινὸν γενέσθαι τὸν ἐνιαυτόν; but we do not know what was the relation between these and the scene described by Ovid.

Who was the Anna Perenna in whose honour these revels, sacrifices, and prayers took place, whatever their relation to each other? Ovid and Silius Italicus [5] tell legends about her which are hardly genuine Italian, and in which Anna Perenna is confused with the other Anna whom they knew, the sister of Dido. Hidden under such stories may sometimes be found traces of a belief or a cult of which we have no other knowledge; but in this poetical medley there seems to be only one feature that calls on us to pause. After her wanderings Anna disappears in the waters of the river Numicius:

> Corniger hanc cupidis rapuisse Numicius undis
> Creditur, et stagnis occuluisse suis.

---

[1] See Robertson Smith, *Religion of the Semites*, p. 240, for the jovial character of some primitive forms of religion, and the absence of a sense of sin.

[2] Ov. l. c. 541 'Occurri nuper: visa est mihi digna relatu Pompa. Senem potum pota trahebat anus.

[3] *Sat.* 1. 12. 6. Cp. Lydus, *de Mens.* 4. 36.

[4] *Annare perennare* is to complete the circle of the year: cp. Suet. *Vespas.* 5 'puella nata non *perennavit.*' Anna Perenna herself is probably a deity manufactured out of these words, and the idea they conveyed (cf. Janus Patulcius and Clusius, Carmenta Prorsa Postverta); not exactly a *deity of the year*, but one whom it would be desirable to propitiate at the beginning of the year.

[5] Ov. l.c. 545 foll. Sil. Ital. 8. 50 foll. Ovid also says that some thought she was the moon, 'quia mensibus impleat annum' (3. 657): but this notion has no value, except as indicating the belief that she represented the circle of the year.

Her companions traced her footsteps to the bank: she seemed to tell them

> Placidi sum nympha Numici,
> Amne perenne latens Anna Perenna vocor.

This tale led Klausen[1] into some very strange fancies about the goddess, whom he regarded as a water-nymph, thinking that all her other characteristics (e. g. the year) might be explained symbolically; the running water representing the flow of time, &c. But it is probable that she only came into connexion with the river Numicius because Aeneas was there already. If Aeneas, as Jupiter Indiges, was buried on its banks[2], what could be more natural than that another figure of the Dido legend should be brought there too? There does not indeed seem to be any reason for connecting the real Anna Perenna with water[3]. All genuine Roman tradition seems to represent her, as we shall see directly, as an old woman; and when she appears in another shape, she must have become mixed up with other ideas and stories. It may perhaps be just possible that on this day some kind of an image of her may have been thrown into the Tiber, as was the case with the straw puppets (Argei) on May 15, and that the ceremony dropped out of practice, but just survived in the Numicius legend[4]. But this is simply hypothesis.

The fact is that, whatever else Anna Perenna may have been, all that we can confidently say of her is that she represented in some way the circle or ring of the year. This is indicated not only by the name, which can hardly be anything but a feminine form of *annus*, but by the time at which her

---

[1] *Aeneas und die Penaten*, ii. 717 foll. The cautious Merkel long ago repudiated such fancies; preface to Ovid's *Fasti*, p. 177.

[2] Liv. 1. 2. The Punic legend is now thought to be a deity = Dido = Elissa : see Rossbach in the new edition of Pauly's *Encycl.* i. 2223.

[3] Her grove was not even on the Tiber-bank, but somewhere between the Via Flaminia and the Via Salaria, i. e. in the neighbourhood of the Villa Borghese : as we see from the obscure lines of Martial, 4. 64. 17 (he is looking from the Janiculum):

> Et quod virgineo cruore gaudet
> Annae pomiferum nemus Perennae.
> Illinc Flaminiae Salariaeque
> Gestator patet essedo tacente, &c.

There is no explanation of *virgineo cruore* : but I would rather retain it than adopt even H. A. J. Munro's *virgine nequiore*. See Friedländer, ad loc.

[4] This seems to be Usener's suggestion, p. 207.

festival took place, the first full moon of the new year. The one legend preserved about her which is of undoubted Italian origin is thought to point in the same direction. Ovid, wishing to explain 'cur cantent obscena puellae' in that revel of the 'plebs' on the Tiber-bank, tells us [1] how Mars, once in love with Minerva [2], came to Anna and asked her aid. It was at length granted, and Mars had the nuptial couch prepared: thither a bride was led, but not the desired one; it was old Anna with her face veiled like a bride who was playing the passionate god such a trick as we may suppose not uncommon in the rude country life of old Latium.

There is no need to be startled at the rude handling of the gods in this story, which seems so unlike the stately and orderly ideas of Roman theology. It must be borne in mind that folk-tales like this need not originally have been applied to the gods at all. They are probably only ancient country stories of human beings, based on some rude marriage custom —stories such as delighted the lower farm folk and slaves on holiday evenings; and they have survived simply because they became in course of time attached to the persons of the gods, as the conception of divinities grew to be more anthropomorphic. Granted that Anna or Perenna [3] was the old woman of the *past* year, that Mars was the god of the first month, and that the story as applied to human beings was a favourite one, we can easily understand how it came to attach itself to the persons of the gods [4].

Yet another story is told by Ovid of an Anna [5], in writing of whom he does not add the name Perenna. The Plebs had seceded to the Mons Sacer, and were beginning to suffer from starvation, when an old woman from Bovillae, named Anna, came to the rescue with a daily supply of *rustica liba*. This myth seems to me to have grown out of the custom, to be described directly, of old women [6] selling *liba* on the 17th

---

[1] *Fasti*, 3. 675.

[2] No doubt this should be Nerio: see below on March 17.

[3] There is some ground for believing that the two words implied two deities on occasion or originally: Varro, *Sat. Menipp.* fr. 506 'Te Anna ac Peranna' (Riese, p. 219).

[4] Wissowa (*de Feriis* x) thinks Ovid's tale mere *nugae*: but this learned scholar never seems to be able to comprehend the significance of folk-lore.

[5] *Fasti*, 3 661 foll.

[6] Varro (*L. L.* 6. 14) calls them 'sacerdotes Liberi,' by courtesy, we may

(Liberalia), the custom having been transferred to that day through an etymological confusion between *liba* and *Liberalia*. Usener, however, saw here a connexion between Anna and Annona[1]; and recently it has been suggested that a certain Egyptian Anna, who is said by Plutarch to have invented a mould for bread-baking, may have found her way to Rome through Greek channels[2].

XVI KAL. APR. (MARCH 17). N̅P̅.

LIB[ERALIA]. (MAFF. FARN. RUST.)
LIB. AG[ONIA]. LIBERO LIB. (CAER.)
AG[ONIA]. (VAT.)
LIBERO IN CA[PITOLIO]. (FARN.)

This is one of the four days marked AG. or AGON. in the Fasti (Jan. 9, May 21, Dec. 11)[3]. It is curious that on this day two of the old calendars should mark the Liberalia only, and one the Agonia only, and one both. The day was generally known as Liberalia[4]; the other name seems to have been known to the priests only, and more especially to the Salii Collini or Agonenses[5], who must have had charge of the sacrifice. Wissowa seems to be right in thinking (*de Feriis* xii) that the conjunction of Liberalia and Agonia is purely accidental, and that the day took its common name from the former simply because, as the latter occurred four times in the year, confusion would be likely to arise.

Liber is beyond doubt an old Italian deity, whose true nature, like that of so many others, came to be overgrown with Greek ideas and rites. There is no sign of any connexion between this festival and the cult of Dionysus; hence we

presume : and it is noticeable that Ovid describes this old Anna as wearing a *mitra*, which, in Propert. v. (iv.) 2. 31, is characteristic of Bacchus : 'Cinge caput mitra : speciem furabor Iacchi.'

[1] Op. cit. 208.
[2] See Pauly, *Encycl.* vol. i. 2223. This is Wissowa's opinion.
[3] See on Jan. 9.
[4] Cic. *ad Fam.* 12. 25. 1 ; *Att.* 9. 9. 4 ; *Auct. Bell. Hisp.* 31.
[5] Varro, *L. L.* 6. 14 'In libris Saliorum, quorum cognomen Agonensium, forsitan hic dies ideo appellatur potius Agonia.' So Masurius Sabinus (in Macrob. *Sat.* 1. 4. 15), 'Liberalium dies a pontificibus agonium Martiale appellatur.'

infer that there was an old Latin Liber before the arrival of
the Greek god in Italy. What this god was, however, can
hardly be inferred from his cult, of which we only know
a single feature, recorded by Ovid[1]. He tells us that old
women, *sacerdotes Liberi*, sat crowned with ivy all about
the streets on this day with cakes of oil and honey (*liba*), and
a small portable altar (*foculus*), on which to sacrifice for the
benefit of the buyer of these cakes. This tells us nothing
substantial, and we have to fall back on the name—always
an uncertain method. The best authorities seem now agreed
in regarding the word Liber (whatever be its etymology) as
having something of the same meaning as *genius*, forming
an adjective *liberalis* as *genius* forms *genialis*, and meaning
a creative, productive spirit, full of blessing, and so generous,
free, &c.[2] If this were so it would not be unnatural that the
characteristics and rites of Dionysus should find here a stem
on which to engraft themselves, or that Liber should become
the object of obscene ceremonies which need not be detailed
here, and also the god of the Italian vine-growers.

It is possible that Liber may have been an ancient cult-title
of Jupiter; we do in fact find a Jupiter Liber in inscriptions,
though the combination is uncommon[3]. In that case Liber
may have been an emanation or off-shoot from Jupiter, as
Silvanus probably was from Mars[4]. But I am disposed to think
that the characteristics of Liber, so far as we know them, are
not in keeping with those of Jupiter; and that the process was
rather of the opposite kind, that is, the cult of Liber in its
later form became attached to that of Jupiter, who was always
the presiding deity of vineyards and wine-making[5].

---

[1] See above, p. 53, where I have expressed a doubt whether this
custom originally belonged to the Liberalia. It is alluded to in Ovid,
Fasti, 3. 725 foll., and Varro, *L. L.* 6. 14.

[2] This is the view of Wissowa in *Myth. Lex.* s. v. Liber, 2022. Cp. Aust,
Lex. s. v. Iuppiter, 662.

[3] It is only once attested of Roman worship, viz. in the calendar of the
Fratres Arvales (Sept. 1 'Iovi Libero, Iunoni Reginae in Aventino,'
C. I. L. i. 214); but is met with several times among the Osco-Sabellian
peoples.

[4] So Hehn, *Kulturpflanzen*, &c., p. 70 foll. But Hehn is only thinking
of the later Liber, whom he considers an 'emanation' from Jupiter Liber
= Dionysus, introduced with the vine from Greece. See Aust, *Lex.* s. v.
Iuppiter, 662.

[5] See on April 23.

This was also the usual day on which boys assumed the toga virilis (toga recta, pura, *libera*):

> Restat ut inveniam quare toga libera detur
> Lucifero pueris, candide Bacche, tuo.
>
> . . . .
>
> Sive quod es Liber, vestis quoque libera per te
> Sumitur et vitae liberioris iter [1].

We know indeed that in the late Republic and Empire other days were used for this ceremony: Virgil took his toga on Oct. 15, Octavian on Oct. 18, Tiberius on April 24, Nero on July 7 [2]; but it is likely that this day was in earlier times the regular one, in spite of the inconvenience of a disparity of age thence resulting amongst the tirones. For whether or no the *toga libera* has any real connexion with the Liberalia, this was the time when the army was called out for the year, and when the tirones would be required to present themselves [3]. Ovid tells us that on this day the rustic population flocked into the city for the Liberalia, and the opportunity was doubtless taken to make known the list of tirones, as the boys were called when the toga was assumed and they were ready for military service.

They sacrificed, it appears, before leaving home and again on the Capitol, either to Pubertas or Liber, or both [4].

On this day also, according to Ovid, and also on the previous one, some kind of a procession 'went to the Argei' [5]; by which word is meant, we may be almost sure, the Argeorum sacella. There were in various parts of the four regions of the Servian city a number of sacella or sacraria, which were called Argei, Argea, or Argeorum sacella [5]. What these were we never

---

[1] Ovid, *Fasti*, 3. 771 foll.   [2] Marq. *Privatleben*, i. 122 note 2.

[3] Ovid, l. c., 783 foll.; Marq. l. c. and 123, 124. Military service began anciently at seventeen (Tubero, ap. Gell. 10. 28): though even praetextati sometimes served voluntarily (Marq. op. cit. 131). Even if not called out at once, the boys would begin the practice of arms from the assumption of the toga virilis.

[4] Marq. op. cit. 124. Libero in Ca[pitolio], Farn. For Iuventas, Dion. Hal. 3. 69, 4. 15.

[5] This result is obtained by comparing Ovid, *Fasti*, 3. 791

> Itur ad Argeos—qui sint, sua pagina dicet—
> Hac, si commemini, praeteritaque die.

(where he refers to his description of the rite of May 15, and appears to identify the *simulacra* and *sacella*\, with Gell. *N. A.* 10. 15, who says that the Flaminica Dialis, ' cum it ad Argeos ' was in mourning dress: also

shall know for certain ; but we may be fairly sure that their
number was twenty-four, six for each region; the same number
as that of the rush puppets or simulacra also called Argei,
which were thrown into the Tiber by the Vestal Virgins on
May 15. The identity of the name and number leads to the
belief that there was a connexion between these sacella and the
simulacra ; but the very difficult questions which arose about
both must be postponed till we have before us the whole of the
ceremonial, i. e. that of May 15 as well as that of March 17.
About this last we know nothing and can at best attempt to
infer its character from the ceremony in May, of which we
fortunately have some particulars on which we can fully rely.

KAL. XIV APR. (MARCH 19). ℞ CAER. VAT. N. MAFF.
QUINQ[VATRUS]. (CAER. MAFF. PRAEN. VAT. FARN.)
QUINQUATRIA. (RUST. PHIL. SILV.)

A note is appended in Praen., which is thus completed by
Mommsen with the help of a Verrian gloss (Fest. 254).

[RECTIUS TAMEN ALII PUTARUNT DICTUM AB EO QUOD HIC DIES
EST POST DIEM V IDUS . QUO]D IN LATIO POST [IDUS DIES
SIMILI FERE RATIONE DECLI]NARENTUR.

FERIAE MARTI (VAT.)

[SALI] FACIUNT IN COMITIO SALTUS [ADSTANTIBUS PO]NTIFICIBUS
ET TRIB[UNIS] CELER[UM]. Praen., in which we find yet
another note: ARTIFICUM DIES [QUOD MINERVAE] AEDIS IN
AVENTINO EO DIE EST [DEDICATA].

The original significance of this day is indicated by the note
Feriae Marti in Vat., and also by that in Praen., which has been
amplified with tolerable certainty. The Salii were active this
day in the worship of Mars, and the scene of their activity
was the *Comitium*. With this agrees, as Mommsen has pointed
out, the statement of Varro [1] that the *Comitium* was the scene

with the fragments of the 'Sacra Argeorum' in Varro, *L. L.* 5. 46-54.
These have been shown by Jordan (*Topogr.* ii. 271 foll.) to be fragments of
an itinerary, meant for the guidance of a procession, an idea first suggested
by O. Müller. The further questions of the route taken, and the distribution of the sacella in the four Servian regiones, are very difficult, and
need not be discussed here. See Mommsen, *Staatsrecht*, iii. 123 foll.

[1] *L. L.* 5. 85 'Salii a salitando, quod facere in comitio in sacris quotannis et solent et debent.'

of some of their performances, though he does not mention which. More light is thrown on the matter by the grammarian Charisius [1], who, in suggesting an explanation of the name Quinquatrus by which this day was generally known, remarks that it was derived from a verb *quinquare*, to purify, 'quod eo die arma ancilia lustrari sint solita.' His etymology is undoubtedly wrong, but the reason given for it is valuable [2]. The ancilia were purified on this day (perhaps by the Salii dancing around them), and thus it exactly answers to the Armilustrium on Oct. 19, just as the horse-races on the Ides of March, if that indeed were the original day, correspond to the ceremony of the 'October horse' [3].

The object and meaning of the lustratio in each case is not, however, quite clear. Since in March the season of war began, and ended, no doubt, originally in October [4], and as the Salii seem to be a kind of link between the religious and military sides of the state's life, we are tempted to guess that the lustration of the ancilia represented in some way the lustration of the arms of the entire host, or perhaps that the latter were all lustrated so as to be ready for use, on this day, and once again on Oct. 19 before they were put away for the winter. In this latter case the Salii would be the leaders of, as well as sharers in, a general purifying process. And that this is the right view seems to be indicated by Verrius' note in the Prae-nestine calendar, from which it is clear that the *tribuni celerum* were present, and took some part in the ceremony. These tribuni were almost certainly the three leaders of the original cavalry force of the three ancient tribes, and they seem to have united both priestly and military characteristics [5]; and from their presence in the Comitium may perhaps also be inferred that of the leaders of the infantry *tribuni militum*. In the earliest times, therefore, the arms of the whole host may have been lustrated in the presence of its leaders, the Salii, so to

---

[1] i. p. 81 (Keil). Why the *Comitium* was the scene does not appear. Preller has suggested a reason (i. 364), which is by no means convincing.

[2] It was adopted by Usener (p. 222, note 6), but has obtained no further support. For another curious etymology of the latter part of the word -*atrus*, which, however, does not assist us here, see Deecke, *Falisker*, p 90 (*Dies ater = dies alter = postridie*).

[3] Wissowa, *de Feriis*, ix. [4] Mommsen, in *C. I. L.* 312.

[5] Mommsen, *R. H.* i. 78, note 1.

speak, performing the service; but in later times the Salii alone were left, and their arms alone lustrated, though possibly individuals representing the ancient *tribuni celerum* may have appeared as congregation.

But this day was generally known as Quinquatrus, simply because it was the fifth day after the Ides [1]; i.e. there was a space of three days between the Ides and the festival. Such intervals of three days, either between the Ides and the festival or between one festival and another, occur several times in the Roman calendar [2], though in this instance alone the day following the interval appears in the calendars as Quinquatrus. The term was no doubt a pontifical one, and the meaning was unknown to the common people; in any case it came to be misunderstood, and was in later times popularly applied to the four days following the festival as well as the festival itself; its first syllable being taken to indicate a five-day period instead of the fifth day after the Ides. This popular mistake led to still further confusion owing to a curious change in the religious character of these days, about the nature of which there can be no serious doubt.

The 19th came to be considered as sacred to Minerva [3], because a temple to that goddess was consecrated on this day, on the Caelian or the Aventine, or possibly both [4]. There is no obvious connexion between Mars and Minerva; and it is now thought probable that Minerva has here simply taken

---

[1] Festus, 254 'Quinquatrus appellari quidam putant a numero dierum qui fere his (? feriis iis) celebrantur: qui scilicet errant tam hercule quam qui triduo Saturnalia, et totidem diebus Compitalia; nam omnibus his singulis diebus fiunt sacra. Forma autem vocabuli eius exemplo multorum populorum Italicorum enuntiata est, quod post diem quintum Iduum est is dies festus, ut apud Tusculanos Triatrus,' &c.

[2] Wissowa, *op. cit.* viij. We find one in April, between the Fordicidia (April 15) and Cerialia (April 19).

[3] Ovid, *Fasti*, 3. 809 'Una dies media est, et fiunt sacra Minervae,' &c.

[4] Ovid, *Fasti*, 3. 835 foll.

> Caelius ex alto qua mons descendit in aequum,
> Hic ubi non plana est sed prope plana via,
> Parva licet videas Captae delubra Minervae
> Quae dea natali coepit habere suo.

As from the note in Praen. we learn that March 19 was also the dedication-day of Minerva on the Aventine, there must either be a confusion between the two, or both had the same foundation-day. About the day of Minerva Capta there is no doubt; for that of Minerva on the Aventine see Aust, *de Aedibus*, p. 42.

the place of another goddess, Nerio — one almost lost to sight in historical times, but of whose early connexion with Mars some faint traces are to be found. Thus where we find Minerva brought into close relation with Mars, as in the myth of Anna Perenna, it is thought that we should read Nerio instead of Minerva [1]. This conclusion is strengthened by a note of Porphyrion on Horace *Epist.* ii. 2. 209 'Maio mense religio est nubere, et etiam Martio, in quo de nuptiis habito certamine a Minerva Mars victus est: obtenta virginitate Neriene est appellata.' As Neriene must = Nerio [2], this looks much like an attempt to explain the occurrence of two female names, Minerva and Nerio, in the same story ; the original heroine, Nerio, having been supplanted by the later Minerva [3].

Of this Nerio much, perhaps too much, has been made in recent years by ingenious scholars. A complete love-story has been discovered, in which Mars, at first defeated in his wooing, as Porphyrion tells us in the passage just quoted, eventually becomes victorious ; for Nerio is called wife of Mars in a fragment of an old comedy by Licinius Imbrex, in a passage of Plautus, and in a prayer put into the mouth of Hersilia by Gellius the annalist, when she asked for peace at the hand of T. Tatius [4]. And this story has been fitted on, without sufficient warrant, to the Mars-festivals of this month. Mars is supposed to have been born on the Kalends, to have grown wondrously between Kalends and Ides, to have fallen then in love with Nerio, to have been fooled as we saw by Anna Perenna, to have been rejected and defeated by his sweetheart, and finally to have won her as his wife on the 19th [5]. Are we to find here a fragment of real Italian mythology, or an elaborate example of the Graecizing anthropomorphic tendencies of the third and second centuries B. C. ?

The question is a difficult one, and lies rather outside the scope of this work. Those who have read Usener's brilliant

---

[1] Preller, i. 342 ; Usener, *Rh. Mus.*, xxx. 221 ; Roscher, *Myth. Lex.* s. v. Mars, 2410 ; *Lyd. de Mens.* 4. 42 ; Gell. 13. 23 (from *Gellii Annales*) is the *locus classicus* for Nerio.

[2] Nerio gen. Nerienis (Gell. l. c., who compares Anio Anienis).

[3] Ovid, *Fasti*, 3. 850 : '*forti* sacrificare deae,' though clearly meant to refer to Minerva, is thought to be a reminiscence of a characteristic of Nerio (' the strong one '), attached to her supplanter.

[4] Aul. Gell. l. c.   [5] Usener, l. c., *passim*.

paper will find it hard to shake themselves free of the conviction that he has unearthed a real myth, unless they carefully study the chapter of Aulus Gellius which is its chief foundation. Such a study has brought me back to the conviction that Plautus and the others were writing in terms of the fashionable modes of thought of their day, and were not appealing to popular ideas of the relations of Italian deities to each other[1]. Aulus Gellius begins by quoting a *comprecatio* from the book of the *Libri sacerdotum populi Romani*. 'In his scriptum est: Luam Saturni, Salaciam Neptuni, Horam Quirini, Virites Quirini, Maiam Volcani, Heriem Iunonis, Moles Martis Nerienemque Martis.' A glance at the names thus coupled together is enough to show that Mars is not here thought of as the husband of Neriene; the names Lua, Salacia, &c., seem rather to express some characteristic of the deity with whose name they are joined or some mode of his operation[2]; and Gellius himself, working on an etymology of Nerio which has generally been accepted as correct, explains the name thus: 'Nerio igitur Martis vis et potentia et maiestas quaedam esse Martis demonstratur.' In the latter part of his chapter, after quoting Plautus, he says that he has heard the poet blamed by an eminent critic for the strange and false notion that Nerio was the wife of Mars; but he is inclined to think that there was a real tradition to that effect, and cites his namesake the annalist and Licinius Imbrex in support of his view.

But neither annalist nor play-writer can stand against that passage from the sacred books with which he began his chapter; and if we give the latter its due weight, the value of the others is relatively diminished. It appears to me that

[1] H. Jordan expressed a somewhat different view in his *Symbolae ad hist. Ital. religionum alterae*, p. 9. He thinks that 'volgari opinione hominum feminini numinis cum masculo coniunctionem non potuisse non pro coniugali aestimari.' But this would seem to imply that the *opinio volgaris* was a mistaken one: and if so, how should it have arisen but under Greek influence?

[2] Mommsen, in a note on the *Feriale Cumanum* (*Hermes*, 17. 637), calls them *weibliche Hilfsgöttinnen*; and this is not far removed from the view I have expressed in the text. The other alternative, viz that we have in these names traces of an old Italian anthropomorphic age, with a mythology, is in my view inadmissible. I see in them survivals of a mode of thought about the supernatural which might easily lend itself to a foreign anthropomorphizing influence.

the one represents the true primitive Italian idea of divine
powers, which with its abundance of names offered excellent
opportunities to anthropomorphic tendencies of the Graecizing
school, while the others show those tendencies actually
producing their results. Any conclusion on the point must
be of the nature of a guess; but I am strongly disposed
to think (1) that Nerio was not originally an independent
deity, but a name attached to Mars expressive of some aspect
of his power, (2) that the name gradually became endowed
with personality, and (3) that out of the combination of Mars
and Nerio the Graecizing school developed a myth of which the
fragments have been taken by Usener and his followers as
pure Roman.

Having once been displaced by Minerva, Nerio vanished
from the calendar, and with her that special aspect of Mars—
whatever it may have been—which the name was intended
to express. The five days, 18th to 23rd, became permanently
associated with Minerva. The 19th was the dedication-day
of at least one of her temples, and counted as her birthday[1]:
the 23rd was the Tubilustrium, with a sacrifice to 'dea fortis,'
who seems to have been taken for Minerva, owing to an
incorrect idea that the latter was specially the deity of
trumpet-players[2]. She was no doubt an old Italian deity
of artificers and trade-guilds; but the Tubilustrium was really
a Mars-festival, and Minerva had no immediate connexion
with it.

x Kal. Apr. (March 23).   NP.

TUBILUST[RIUM].   (caer. maff. vat. farn. min. iii.)
tubilustrium.   (philoc.)

Note in Praen. : [feriae] marti[3]. hic dies appellatur ita,
quod in atrio sutorio tubi lustrantur, quibus in sacris
utuntur. lutatius quidem clavam eam ait esse in
ruinis pala[ti i]ncensi a gallis repertam, qua romulus
urbem inauguraverit.

[1] Ovid, *Fasti*, 3. 835 foll.
[2] Wissowa in *Lex.* s. v. Minerva 2986 : a model article, to which the
reader must be referred for further information about Minerva.
[3] Lydus, 4. 42, adds 'Nerine,' and further tells us that this was the last
day on which the *ancilia* were 'moved' (κίνησις τῶν ὅπλων). The Salii
were also active on the 24th (Fest. 278).

IX KAL. APR. (MARCH 24). NP.

Q.R.C.F. (VAT. CAER.)
Q.REX.C.F. (MAFF. PRAEN.)

Note in Praen.: HUNC DIEM PLERIQUE PERPERAM INTERPRE-
TANTES PUTANT APPELLAR[I] QUOD EO DIE EX COMITIO FUGERIT
[REX : N]AM NEQUE TARQUINIUS ABIIT EX COMITIO [URBIS], ET
ALIO QUOQUE MENSE EADEM SUNT [IDEMQUE S]IGNIFICANT.
QU[ARE COMITIIS PERACTIS IUDICI]A FIERI INDICA[RI IIS MAGIS
PUTAMUS][1].

These two days must be taken in connexion with the
23rd and 24th of May, which are marked in the calendars
in exactly the same way. The explanation suggested by
Mommsen is simple and satisfactory[2]; the 24th of March and
of May were the two fixed days on which the *comitia curiata*
met for the sanctioning of wills[3] under the presidency of the
Rex. The 23rd in each month, called Tubilustrium, would
be the day of the lustration of the *tubae* or *tubi* used in
summoning the assembly. The letters Q. R. C. F. (quando rex
comitiavit fas) mean that on the days so marked proceedings
in the courts might only begin when the king had dissolved
the Comitia.

The *tuba*, as distinguished from the *tibia*, which was the
typical Italian instrument, was a long straight tube of brass
with a bell mouth[4]. It was used chiefly in military[5] and

---

[1] The note is thus completed by Mommsen from Varro, *L. L.* 6. 31
'Dies qui vocatur sic, Quando Rex Comitiavit Fas, is dictus ab eo quod
eo die rex sacrificulus itat [we should probably read *litat*] ad comitium, ad
quod tempus est nefas, ab eo fas' (see Marq. 323, note 8). The MS. has
'*dicat* ad comitium.' If we adopt *litat* with Hirschfeld and Jordan, we
are not on that account committed to the belief corrected in Praen.,
that it was on this day and May 24 that the Rex fled after sacrificing in
comitio (see Hartmann, *Röm. Kal.* 162 foll.). The question will be discussed under Feb. 24.

[2] *Röm. Chronol.* p. 241 ; *Staatsrecht*, iii. 375.

[3] Gaius, 2. 101 'Comitia calata quae bis in anno testamentis faciendis
destinata erant.' Cp. Maine, *Ancient Law*, 199.

[4] It may have been of Etruscan origin : Müller-Deecke, *Etrusker*, ii. 206.
A special kind of *tuba* seems to have been used at funerals : Gell. *N. A.*
20. 2 ; Marq. *Privatleben*, i. 341.

[5] For the military use, Liv. ii. 64. They were also used in *sacris
Saliaribus* Paul. 19, s. v. Armilustrium. Wissowa (*de Feriis* xv) mentions
a relief in which the Salii are preceded by *tubicines laureati* (published in
St. Petersburgh by E. Schulze, 1873).

religious ceremonies; and as the *comitia curiata* was an assembly both for military and religious objects, this would suit well with Mommsen's idea of the object of the lustration. The Tubilustrium was the day on which these instruments, which were to be used at the meeting of the comitia on the following day, were purified by the sacrifice of a lamb. Of the Atrium Sutorium, where the rite took place, we know nothing.

There are some words at the end of Verrius' note in the Praenestine Calendar, which, as Mommsen has pointed out[1], come in abruptly and look as if something had dropped out: 'Lutatius quidem clavam eam ait esse in ruinis Pala[ti i]ncensi a Gallis repertam, qua Romulus urbem inauguraverit.' This *clava* must be the *lituus* of Romulus, mentioned by Cicero[2], which was found on the Palatine and kept in the Curia Saliorum. We cannot, however, see clearly what Verrius or his excerptor meant to tell us about it; there would seem to have been a confusion between *lituus* in the sense of *baculum* and *lituus* in the sense of a *tuba incurva*. The latter was in use as well as the ordinary straight *tuba*[3]; in shape it closely resembled the *clava* of the augur, and perhaps the resemblance led to the notion that it was the *clava* of Romulus and not a *tuba* which was this day purified with the other *tubae*.

We can learn little or nothing from the calendar of this month about the origin of Mars, and we have no other sufficient evidence on which to base a satisfactory conjecture. But from the cults of the month, and partly also from those of October, we can see pretty clearly what ideas were prominent in his worship even in the early days of the Roman state. They were chiefly two, and the two were closely connected. He was the Power who must be specially invoked to procure the safety of crops and cattle; and secondly, in his keeping were the safety and success of the freshly-enrolled host with its armour and its trumpets. In short, he was that deity to whom the most ancient Romans looked for aid at the season when all living things, man included, broke into fresh activity. He repre-

---

[1] *C. I. L.* 313. He is of opinion that the note was among those 'non tam a Verrio scriptas quam male ex scriptis eius excerptas.'

[2] *de Div.* i. 17. 30.   [3] Varro, *L. L.* 5. 91.

sents the characteristics of the early Roman more exactly than any other god ; for there are two things which we may believe with certainty about the Roman people in the earliest times—(1) that their life and habits of thought were those of an agricultural race ; and (2) that they continually increased their cultivable land by taking forcible possession in war of that of their neighbours.

MENSIS APRILIS.

THERE can hardly be a doubt that this month takes its name, not from a deity, but from the verb *aperio*; the etymology is as old as Varro and Verrius, and seems perfectly natural[1]. The year was opening and the young corn and the young cattle were growing. It was therefore a critical time for crops and herds; but there was not much to be done by man to secure their safety. The crops might be hoed and cleaned[2], but must for the most part be left to the protection of the gods. The oldest festivals of the month, the Robigalia and Fordicidia, clearly had this object. So also with the cattle; *oves lustrantur*, say the rustic calendars[3]; and such a *lustratio* of the cattle of the ancient Romans survived in the ceremonies of the Parilia.

Thus, if we keep clear of fanciful notions, such as those of Huschke[4], about these early months of the year, which he seems to imagine was thought of as growing like an organic creature, we need find no great difficulty in April. We need not conclude too hastily that this was a month of purification preliminary to May, as February was to March. Like February, indeed, it has a large number of *dies nefasti*[5], and its festivals

---

[1] Varro, *L. L.* 6. 33 ; Censorinus, 2. 20. Verrius Flaccus in the heading to April in Fasti Praen.: . . . 'quia fruges flores animaliaque et maria et terrae aperiuntur.' Mommsen, *Chron.* 222. Ovid quaintly forsakes the scholars to claim the month for Venus (Aphrodite), *Fasti*, 4. 61 foll. I do not know why Mr. Granger should call it the boar-month (from *aper*), in his *Worship of the Romans*, p. 294.

[2] *Segetes runcari*, Varro, *R. R.* I. 30. Columella's instructions are of the same kind (II. 2).

[3] *C. I. L.* 280.   [4] *Röm. Jahr*, 216.

[5] February has thirteen, all but two between Kal. and Ides. The Nones and Ides are NP. April has thirteen between Nones and 22nd ; or fourteen if we include the 19th, which is NP in Caer. The Ides are NP, Nones N.

are of a cathartic character, while March and May have some
points in common; but beyond this we cannot safely venture.
The later Romans would hardly have connected April with
Venus [1], had it been a sinister month; it was not in April, but
in March and May, that weddings were ill-omened.

We may note the prevalence in this month of female deities,
or of those which fluctuate between male and female—a sure
sign of antiquity. These are deities of the earth, or vegetation,
or generation, such as Tellus, Pales, Ceres, Flora, and perhaps
also Fortuna. Hence the month became easily associated in
later times with Venus, who was originally, perhaps, a garden
deity [2], but was overlaid in course of time with ideas brought
from Sicily and Greece, and possibly even from Cyprus and the
East. Lastly, we may note that the Magna Mater Idaea found
a suitable position for her worship in this month towards the
end of the third century B. C.

KAL. APR. (APRIL 1). F.

VENERALIA : LUDI. (PHILOC.)

Note in Praen. : 'FREQUENTER MULIERES SUPPLICANT FOR-
TUNAE VIRILI, HUMILIORES ETIAM IN BALINEIS, QUOD IN IIS
EA PARTE CORPOR[IS] UTIQUE VIRI NUDANTUR, QUA FEMINARUM
GRATIA DESIDERATUR.'

Lydus [3] seems to have been acquainted with this note of Verrius
in the Fasti of Praeneste ; if so, we may guess that some words
have been omitted by the man who cut the inscription, and

---

[1] See the fragmentary heading to the month in Fasti Praen. ; Ovid, l.c. ;
Lydus, 4. 45 ; Tutela Veneris, in rustic calendars ; Veneralia (April 1),
Philocalus.

[2] Varro, R. R. I. 1. 6: 'Item adveneror Minervam et Venerem, quarum
unius procuratio oliveti, alterius *hortorum*.' Cp. L. L. 6. 20 'Quod tum
(Aug. 19) dedicata aedes et horti ei deae dicantur ; c tum fiant feriati
holitores.' Cf. Preller, *Myth.* i. 434 foll. The oldest Venus-temple was in
the low ground of the Circus Maximus (B.C. 295). Venus, like Ceres, may
have been an old Roman deity of the plebs, but she never entered into
the State-worship in early times. Macrob. I. 12. 12 quotes Cincius
(*de Fastis*) and Varro to prove that she had originally nothing to do with
April, and that there was no *dies festus* or *insigne sacrificium* in her honour
during the month.

[3] 4. 45 Ταῖς τοίνυν καλάνδαις ἀπριλλίαις αἱ σεμναὶ γυναικῶν ὑπὲρ ὁμονοίας καὶ
βίου σώφρονος ἐτίμων τὴν Ἀφροδίτην· αἱ δὲ τοῦ πλήθους γυναῖκες ἐν τοῖς τῶν
ἀνδρῶν βαλανείοις ἐλούοντο, πρὸς θεραπείαν αὐτῆς μυρσίνῃ ἐστεμμέναι, κ.τ.λ.
Cp. Macrob. I. 12. 15.

we should insert with Mommsen [1], after 'supplicant,' the words
'honestiores Veneri Verticordiae.' If we compare the passage of
Lydus with the name Veneralia given to this day in the
calendar of Philocalus, we may guess that the cult of Venus on
April 1 came into fashion in late times among ladies of rank,
while an old and gross custom was kept up by the humiliores
in honour of Fortuna Virilis [2]. This seems to be the most
obvious explanation of the concurrence of the two goddesses
on the same day ; they were probably identified or amalgamated
under the Empire, for example by Lydus, who does not mention
Fortuna by name, and seems to confuse her worship on this
day with that of Venus. But the two are still distinct in
Ovid, though he seems to show some tendency to amal-
gamation [3].

Fortuna Virilis, thus worshipped by the women when
bathing, would seem from Ovid to have been that Fortuna
who gave women good luck in their relations with men [4].
The custom of bathing in the men's baths may probably be
taken as some kind of lustration, more especially as the women
were adorned with myrtle, which had purifying virtues [5]. How
old this curious custom was we cannot guess. Plutarch [6]
mentions a temple of this Fortuna dedicated by Servius
Tullius ; but there was a strong tendency, as we shall see later
on, to attribute all Fortuna-cults to this king.

The Venus who eventually supplanted Fortuna is clearly
Venus Verticordia [7], whose earliest temple was founded in
114 B. C., in obedience to an injunction of the Sibylline books,
after the discovery of incest on the part of three vestal virgins,
'quo facilius virginum mulierumque mens a libidine ad pudici-

---

[1] C. I. L. 315.
[2] We shall find some reason for believing that in the early Republican
period new cults came in rather through plebeian than patrician agency
(see below, on Cerealia). But in the period of the new nobilitas the
lower classes seem rather to have held to their own cults, while the upper
social stratum was more ready to accept new ones. See below, on
April 4, for the conditions of such acceptance. The tendency is to be
explained by the wide and increasing sphere of the foreign relations of
the Senatorial government.
[3] Fasti, 4. 133-164.
[4] Ovid, l. c. 149 foll.
[5] Robertson Smith, Religion of the Semites, p. 456.
[6] Quaest. Rom. 74.
[7] Ovid, l. c., 4. 160 'Inde Venus verso nomina corde tenet.'

tiam converteretur[1].' Macrobius insists that Venus had originally
no share in the worship of this day or month[2]; she must
therefore have been introduced into it as a foreigner. Robertson Smith[3] has shown some ground for the conjecture that
she was the Cyprian Aphrodite (herself identical with the
Semitic Astarte), who came to Rome by way of Sicily and
Latium. For if Lydus can be trusted, the Roman ceremony
of April 1 was found also in Cyprus, on the same day, with
variations in detail. If that be so, the addition of the name
Verticordia is a curious example of the accretion of a Roman
cult-title expressive of domestic morality on a foreign deity of
questionable reputation[4].

PRID. NON. APR. (APRIL 4). C.

MATR[I] MAG[NAE]. (MAFF.)
LUDI MEGALESIACI. (PHILOC.)

Note in Praen.: LUDI M[ATRI] D[EUM] M[AGNAE] I[DAEAE].
MEGALESIA VOCANTUR QUOD EA DEA MEGALE APPELLATUR.
NOBILIUM MUTITATIONES CENARUM SOLITAE SUNT FRE-
QUENTER FIERI, QUOD MATER MAGNA EX LIBRIS SIBULLINIS
ARCESSITA LOCUM MUTAVIT EX PHRYGIA ROMAM.

The introduction of the Magna Mater Idaea into Rome can
only be briefly mentioned here, as being more important for
the history of religion at Rome than for that of the Roman
religion. In B. C. 204, in accordance with a Sibylline oracle
which had previously prophesied that the presence of this deity
alone could drive the enemy out of Italy, the sacred stone
representing the goddess arrived at Rome from Pessinus in
Phrygia[5]. Attalus, King of Pergamus, had acquired this
territory, and now, as a faithful friend to Rome, consented to
the transportation of the stone, which was received at Rome
with enthusiasm by an excited and now hopeful people[6].

---

[1] Aust, *de Aedibus sacris*, p. 28. About a century earlier a statue of this
Venus was said to have been erected (Val. Max. 8. 15. 12; Plin. *H. N.* 7.
120), as Wissowa pointed out in his Essay, 'de Veneris Simulacris,' p. 12.
[2] See above, p. 67, note 2.
[3] *Religion of the Semites*, p. 450 foll.   [4] Preller, i. 446.
[5] Livy, 29. 10 and 14; Ovid (*Fasti*, 4. 259 foll.) has a fanciful edition
of the story which well illustrates the character of his work, and that of
the legend-mongers; cp. Preller, ii. 57.
[6] Preller, ii. 55.

Scipio was about to leave with his army for Africa; a fine harvest followed; Hannibal was forced to evacuate Italy the next year; and the goddess did everything that was expected of her [1].

The stone was deposited in the temple of Victory on the Palatine on April 4 [2]. The day was made a festival; though no Roman festival occurs between the Kalends and Nones of any month, the rule apparently did not hold good in the case of a foreign worship [3]. Great care was taken to keep up the foreign character of the cult. The name of the festival was a Greek one (Megalesia), as Cicero remarked [4]; all Romans were forbidden by a senatus consultum to take any part in the service of the goddess [5]. The temple dedicated thirteen years later on April 10 [6] seems to have been frequented by the nobilitas only, and the custom of giving dinner-parties on April 4, which is well attested, was confined to the upper classes [7], while the plebs waited for its festivities till the ensuing Cerealia. The later and more extravagant developments of the cult did not come in until the Empire [8].

The story told by Livy of the introduction of the goddess is an interesting episode in Roman history. It illustrates the far-reaching policy of the Senate in enlisting Eastern kings, religions, and oracles in the service of the state at a critical time, and also the curious readiness of the Roman people to believe in the efficacy of cults utterly foreign to their own religious practices. At the same time it shows how careful the government was then, as always, to keep such cults under strict supervision. But the long stress of the Hannibalic War had its natural effect on the Italian peoples; and less than

---

[1] Plin. *H. N.* 18. 16; Arnobius, 7. 49.　　　　[2] Livy, 29. 10, 14.

[3] See above, Introduction, p. 7.

[4] *de Harusp. Resp.* 12. 24 'Qui uni ludi ne verbo quidem appellantur Latino, ut vocabulo ipso et appetita religio externa et Matris Magnae nomine suscepta declaretur.'

[5] Dion. Hal. 2. 19. A very interesting passage, in which, among other comments, the historian points out that in receiving the goddess the Romans eliminated ἅπασαν τερθρείαν μυθικήν.

[6] Aust, *de Aedibus sacris*, pp. 22 and 49.

[7] Gell. 18. 2. 11 (patricii); cp. 2. 24. 2 (principes civitatis). Cp. Lydus, 4. 45; Verrius' note in Praen., '*Nobilium mutitationes cenarum* solitae sunt frequenter fieri,' &c.

[8] See Marq. 370 foll. The Ludi eventually extended from the 4th to the 10th inclusive (*C. I. L.* 314).

twenty years later the introduction of the Bacchic orgies forced the senate to strain every nerve to counteract a serious danger to the national religion and morality.

XVII KAL. MAI. (APRIL 15). ΓP.

FORD[ICIDIA]¹. (CAER. MAFF. VAT. PRAEN.)

This is beyond doubt one of the oldest sacrificial rites in the Roman religion. It consisted in the slaughter of pregnant cows (*hordae* or *fordae*), one in the Capitol and one in each of the thirty *curiae*²; i.e. one for the state and the rest for each of its ancient divisions. This was the first festival of the *curiae*; the other, the *Fornacalia*, will be treated of under February 17. The cows were offered, as all authorities agree, to Tellus³, who, as we shall see, may be an indigitation of the same earth power represented by Ceres, Bona Dea, Dea Dia, and other female deities. The unborn calves were torn by attendants of the virgo vestalis maxima from the womb of the mother and burnt⁴, and their ashes were kept by the Vestals for use at the Parilia a few days later⁵. This was the first ceremony in the year in which the Vestals took an active part, and it was the first of a series of acts all of which are connected with the fruits of the earth, their growth, ripening and harvesting. The object of burning the unborn calves seems to have been to procure the fertility of the corn now growing in the womb of mother earth, to whom the sacrifice was offered⁶.

¹ Or Hordicidia, Fest. 102; Hordicalia, Varro, *R. R.* 2. 5. 6; Fordicalia, Lydus, 4. 49. 'Forda ferens bos est fecundaque, dicta ferendo,' Ovid, *Fasti*, 4. 631.

² Ovid, l. c. 635 'Pars cadit arce Iovis. Ter denas curia vaccas Accipit, et largo sparsa cruore madet.' Cp. Varro, *L. L.* 6. 15. Preller, ii. 6, understands Ovid's 'pars' as meaning more than one cow.

³ Ovid, l. c. 633 'Nunc gravidum pecus est, gravidae nunc semine terrae; Telluri plenae victima plena datur.'

⁴ Ovid, l. c. 637

Ast ubi visceribus vitulos rapuere ministri,
Sectaque fumosis exta dedere focis,
Igne cremat vitulos quae natu maxima Virgo,
Luce Palis populos purget ut ille cinis.

⁵ See below, p. 83.

⁶ This appears plainly in Ovid's account (*Fasti*, 4. 633 foll.), and also in that of Lydus (4. 49): περὶ τὰ σπόριμα ὑπὲρ εὐετηρίας ἱεράτευον. Both doubtless drew on Varro. Lydus adds one or two particulars, that the ἀρχιερεῖς (?)

Many charms of this sacrificial kind have been noticed by various writers; one may be mentioned here which was described by Sir John Barrow, when British Ambassador in China in 1804. In a spring festival in the temple of Earth, a huge porcelain image of a cow was carried about and then broken in pieces, and a number of small cows taken from inside it and distributed among the people as earnests of a good season[1]. This must be regarded as a survival of a rite which was no doubt originally one of the same kind as the Roman.

III Id. Apr. (April 11). N.

On this day[2] the oracle of the great temple of Fortuna Primigenia at Praeneste was open to suppliants, as we learn from a fragment of the Praenestine Fasti. Though not a Roman festival, the day deserves to be noticed here, as this oracle was by far the most renowned in Italy. The cult of Fortuna will be discussed under June 25 and Sept. 13. It does not seem to be known whether the oracle was open on these days only; see R. Peter in *Myth. Lex.* s. v. Fortuna, 1545.

XIII Kal. Mai. (April 19). NP.

CER[IALIA]. (caer. maff. praen. esq.)
cereri libero (liberae) esq.

Note: All the days from 12th to 19th are marked ludi, ludi Cer., or ludi Ceriales, in Tusc. Maff. Praen. Vat., taken together: loid. Cereri in Esq., where the 18th only is preserved: loedi C in Caer. Philocalus has Cerealici c. m. (circenses missus) xxiv on 12th and 19th.

The origin of the ludi Cereales, properly so called, cannot be proved to be earlier than the Second Punic War. The games

scattered flowers among the people in the theatre, and went in procession outside the city, sacrificing to Demeter at particular stations; but he may be confusing this festival with the Ambarvalia.

[1] See Mannhardt, *Myth. Forsch.* 190; cp. Frazer, *G. B.* ii. 43.

[2] Fasti Praen.; *C. I. L.* 235, and Mommsen's note (where Apr. is misprinted Aug.). '[Hoc biduo sacrific]ium maximum Fortunae Prim[i]g. utro eorum die oraclum patet, IIviri vitulum I.'

first appear as fully established in B.C. 202 [1]. But from the fact that April 19 is marked CER in large letters in the calendars we may infer, with Mommsen [2], that there was a festival in honour of Ceres as far back as the period of the monarchy. The question therefore arises whether this ancient Ceres was a native Italian deity, or the Greek Demeter afterwards known to the Romans as Ceres.

That there was such an Italian deity is placed almost beyond doubt by the name itself, which all authorities agree in connecting with cerus = genius, and with the *cerfus* and *cerfia* of the great inscription of Iguvium [3]. The verbal form seems clearly to be *creare* [4]; and thus, strange to say, we actually get some definite aid from etymology, and can safely see in the earliest Ceres, if we recollect her identification with the Greek goddess of the earth and its fruits, a deity presiding over or representing the generative powers of nature. We cannot, however, feel sure whether this deity was originally feminine only, or masculine also, as Arnobius seems to suggest [5]. Judging from the occurrence of forms such as those quoted above, it is quite likely, as in the case of Pales, Liber, and others, that this numen was of both sexes, or of undetermined sex. So anxious were the primitive Italians to catch the ear of their deities by making no mistake in the ritual of addressing them, that there was a distinct tendency to avoid marking their sex too distinctly ; and phrases such as 'sive mas sive femina,' 'si deus si dea,' are familiar to all students of the Roman religion [6].

We may be satisfied, then, that the oldest Ceres was not simply an importation from Greece. It is curious, however,

[1] Liv. 30. 39; Friedländer in Marq. 500 ; Mommsen, *Münzwesen*, p. 642, note ; *Staatsrecht*, i. 586.

[2] *C. I. L.* 298.

[3] In the Salian hymn *duonus cerus = creator bonus* (of Janus): cf. Varro, *L L.* 7. 26 ; Mommsen, *Unteritalische Dialekten*, 133. See articles *cerus* (Wissowa) and *Ceres* (Birt) in *Myth. Lex.* ; Bücheler, *Umbrica*, 80 and 99.

[4] ' Ceres a creando dicta,' Serv. Georg. 1. 7. It is worth noting that in Nonius Marcellus, 44, *cerriti = larvati*, where *cerus* seems to mean a ghost. If so, we have a good example of a common origin of ghosts and gods in the animistic ideas of early Italy.

[5] Arnob. 3. 40, quoting one Caesius, who followed Etruscan teaching, and held that Ceres = Genius Iovialis et Pales. See Preller-Jordan, i. 81.

[6] Preller-Jordan, i. 62. They were not even certain whether the Genius Urbis was masculine or feminine ; Serv. *Aen.* 2. 351.

that Ceres is not found exactly where we should expect to find her, viz. in the ritual of the Fratres Arvales [1]. Yet this very fact may throw further light on the primitive nature of Ceres. The central figure of the Arval ritual was the nameless Dea Dia ; and in a ritual entirely relating to the fruits of the earth we can fairly account for the absence of Ceres by supposing that she is there represented by the Dea Dia—in fact, that the two are identical [2]. No one at all acquainted with Italian ideas of the gods will be surprised at this. It is surely a more reasonable hypothesis than that of Birt, who thinks that an old name for seed and bread (i. e. Ceres) was transferred to the Greek deity who dispensed seed and bread when she was introduced in Rome [3]. It is, in fact, only the name Ceres that is wanting in the Arval ritual, not the numen itself ; and this is less surprising if we assume that the names given by the earliest Romans to supernatural powers were not fixed but variable, representing no distinctly conceived personalities ; in other words, that their religion was pandaemonic rather than polytheistic, though with a tendency to lend itself easily to the influence of polytheism. We may agree, then, with Preller [4], that Ceres, with Tellus, and perhaps Ops and Acca Larentia, are different names for, and aspects of, the numen whom the Arval brothers called Dea Dia. At the same time we cannot entirely explain why the name Ceres was picked out from among these to represent the Greek Demeter. Some light may, however, be thrown on this point by studying the early history of the Ceres-cult.

The first temple of Ceres was founded, according to tradition, in consequence of a famine in the year 496 B. C., in obedience to a Sibylline oracle [5]. It was at the foot of the Aventine, by the Circus Maximus [6], and was dedicated on April 19, 493, to Ceres, Liber and Libera, representing Demeter, Dionysus,

---

[1] Henzen, *Acta Fr. Arv.* p. 48. In later times Ceres took the place of Mars at the Ambarvalia, under Greek influence.

[2] So Henzen, l. c. and his Introduction, p. ix.

[3] *Myth. Lex.* s. v. Ceies, 861. He does not, however, dogmatize, and has little to adduce in favour of his opinion, save the statement of Servius (Georg. I. 7) that 'Sabini Cererem Panem appellant.'

[4] Preller-Jordan, ii. 26.

[5] Aust, *de Aedibus*, pp. 5 and 40. Preller-Jordan, ii. 38.

[6] Birt (*Myth. Lex.* 862) gives the authorities.

and Persephone[1]. Thus from the outset the systematized cult of Ceres in the city was not Roman but Greek. The temple itself was adorned in Greek style instead of the Etruscan usual at this period[2]. How is all this to be accounted for?

Let us notice in the first place that from the very foundation of the temple it is in the closest way connected with the plebs. The year of its dedication is that of the first secession of the plebs and of the establishment of the tribuni and aediles plebis[3]. The two events are connected by the fact, repeatedly stated, that any one violating the *sacrosanctitas* of the tribune was to be held *sacer Cereri*[4]; we are also told that the fines imposed by tribunes were spent on this temple[5]. It was under the care of the plebeian aediles, and was to them what the temple of Saturnus was to the quaestors[6]. Its position was in the plebeian quarter, and at the foot of the Aventine, which in B. C. 456 is said to have become the property of the plebs[7].

Now it can hardly be doubted that the choice of Ceres (with her fellow deities of the *trias*), as the goddess whose temple should serve as a centre for the plebeian community, had some definite meaning. That meaning must be found in the traditions of famine and distress which we read of as immediately following the expulsion of Tarquinius. These traditions have often been put aside as untrustworthy[8], and may indeed be so in regard to details; but there is some reason for thinking them to have had a foundation of fact, if we can but accept the other tradition of the foundation of the temple and its connexion

---

[1] The *trias* of itself would prove the Greek origin : cf. Kuhfeldt, *de Capitoliis*, p. 77 foll.

[2] Plin. *H. N.* 35. 154. The names of two Greek artists were inscribed on the temple.

[3] Mommsen, *Staatsrecht*, ii.[2] 468, note.

[4] Dion. Hal. 6. 89 ; 10. 42 ; Liv. 3. 55 says *sacer Iovi*, but the property was to be sold at the temple of Ceres, Liber, and Libera. The cornstealer also was *sacer Cereri*.

[5] Liv. 10. 23 ; 27. 6; 33. 25.

[6] Mommsen, *Hist.* i. 284, note. Cp. Schwegler, *Röm. Gesch.* ii. 275, note 3, who thinks of an *aerarium plebis* there. See also i. 606 and ii. 278, note 3. According to Liv. 3. 55 senatus consulta had to be deposited in this temple.

[7] Burn, *Rome and the Campagna*, p. 204 ; Liv. 3. 31 and 32 fin. ; cp. 10. 31.

[8] e. g. by Ihne, vol. i. p. 160.

with the plebs. It is likely enough that under Tarquinius the population was increased by 'outsiders' employed on his great buildings. Under pressure from the attack of enemies, and from a sudden aristocratic reaction, this population, we may guess, was thrown out of work, deprived of a *raison d'être*, and starved [1]; finally rescuing itself by a secession, which resulted in the institution of its officers, tribunes and aediles, the latter of whom seem to have been charged with the duty of looking after the corn-supply [2].

How the corn-supply was cared for we cannot tell for certain; but here again is a tradition which fits in curiously with what we know of the temple and its worship, though it has been rejected by the superfluous ingenuity of modern German criticism. Livy tells us that in B. C. 492, the year after the dedication of the temple, corn was brought from Etruria, Cumae, and Sicily to relieve a famine [3]. We are not obliged to believe in the purchase of corn at Syracuse at so early a date, though it is not impossible; but if we remember that the decorations and ritual of the temple were Greek beyond doubt, we get a singular confirmation of the tradition *in outline* which has not been sufficiently noticed. If it was founded in 493, placed under plebeian officers, and closely connected with the plebs; if its rites and decorations were Greek from the beginning; we cannot afford to discard a tradition telling us of a commercial connexion with Greek cities, the object of which was to relieve a starving plebeian population.

And surely there is nothing strange in the supposition that

---

[1] Schwegler, *R. G.* i. 783 foll.

[2] Mommsen, *Staatsrecht*, ii.[2] 468, note 2, is doubtful as to the date of the *cura annonae* of the plebeian aediles. But Plin. *H. N.* 18. 3. 15 attributes it to an aedile of earlier date than Spurius Maelius (B.C. 439); and though the Consuls may have had the general supervision, the immediate *cura*, as far as the plebs was concerned, would surely lie with their officers. Two points should be borne in mind here—(1) that the plebeian population to be relieved would be a surplus population *within the city*, not the farmer-population of the country; (2) that it would probably be easier to transport corn by sea than by land, as roads were few, and enemies all around.

[3] Dion. Hal. 7. 1, exposes the absurdity of Roman annalists in attributing the corn-supply to Dionysius; but he himself talks of Gelo. Cp. Ihne, i. 160. Ihne disbelieves the whole story, believing it to be copied from events which happened long afterwards.

Greek influence gained ground, not so much with the patricians who had their own outfit of religious armour, but with the plebs who had no share in the sacra of their betters, and with the Etruscan dynasty which favoured the plebs [1]. We may hesitate to assent to Mommsen's curious assertion that the merchants of that day were none other than the great patrician landholders [2]; we may rather be disposed to conjecture that it was the more powerful plebeians, incapable of holding large areas of public land, who turned their attention to commerce, and came in contact with the Greeks of Italy and Sicily. The position of the plebeian quarter along the Tiber bank, and near the spot where the quays of Rome have always been, may possibly point in the same direction [3].

To return to the Cerealia of April 19. We have still to notice a relic of apparently genuine Italian antiquity which survived in it down to Ovid's time, and may be taken as evidence that there was a real Roman substratum on which the later Greek ritual was superimposed.

Every one who reads Ovid's account of the Cerealia will be struck by his statement that on the 19th it was the practice to fasten burning brands to the tails of foxes and set them loose to run in the Circus Maximus [4]:

> Cur igitur missae vinctis ardentia taedis
> Terga ferant volpes, causa docenda mihi est.

He tells a charming story to explain the custom, learnt from an old man of Carseoli, an Aequian town, where he was seeking information while writing the *Fasti*. A boy of twelve years' old caught a vixen fox which had done damage to the farm, and tied it up in straw and hay. This he set on fire, but the fox escaped and burnt the crops. Hence a law at Carseoli forbidding — something about foxes, which the

---

[1] Ambrosch, *Studien*, p. 208. Tradition told that the Tarquinii had stored up great quantities of corn in Rome, i.e. had fed their workmen. Cp. Liv. 1. 56 and 2. 9.

[2] Mommsen, *R. H*, bk. i. ch. 13 fin.

[3] See under August 13 (below, p. 198) for the parallel foundation of the temple of Diana on the Aventine, which also had a Greek and plebeian character.

[4] *Fasti*, 4. 681 foll. Ovid does not distinctly say that the foxes were let loose in the Circus, but seems to imply it.

corruption of the MSS. has obscured for us[1]. Then he concludes:

> Utque luat poenas gens haec, Cerialibus ardet ;
> Quoque modo segetes perdidit, ipsa perit.

We are, of course, reminded of Samson burning the corn of the Philistines[2]; and it is probable that the story in each case is a myth explanatory of some old practice like the one Ovid describes at Rome. But what the practice meant it is not very easy to see. Preller has his explanation ready[3]; it was a 'sinnbildliche Erinnerung' of the *robigo* (i. e. 'red fox'), which was to be feared and guarded against at this time of year. Mannhardt thinks rather of the corn-foxes or corn-spirits of France and Germany, of which he gives many instances[4]. If the foxes were corn spirits, one does not quite see why they should have brands fastened to their tails[5]. No exactly parallel practice seems to be forthcoming, and the fox does not appear elsewhere in ancient Italian or Greek folk-tales, as far as I can discover. All that can be said is that the fox's tail seems to have been an object of interest, and possibly to have had some fertilizing power[6], and some curious relation to ears of corn. Prof. Gubernatis believes this tail to have been a phallic symbol[7]. We need not accept his explanation, but we may be grateful to him for a modern Italian folk-tale, from the region of Leghorn and the Maremma, in which a fox is frightened away by chickens which carry each in its beak an

---

[1]   'Factum abiit, monimenta manent ; †nam vivere captam†
          Nunc quoque lex volpem Carseolana vetat.'

The best MSS. have 'nam dicere certam.' Bergk conjectured 'namque icere captam.' The reading given above is adopted from some inferior MSS. by H. Peter (Leipzig, 1889), following Heinsius and Riese. Mr. S G. Owen of Ch. Ch., our best authority on the text of Ovid, has kindly sent me the suggestion *namque ire repertam*, comparing, for the use of *ire*, Ovid, *Am.* 3. 6. 20 'sic aeternus eas.' This conjecture, which occurred independently to myself, suits the sense and is close to the reading of the best MSS.

[2] J. Grimm, *Reinhardt der Fuchs*, cclxix (quoted by Peter). Ovid's explanation is of course wrong; the story is beyond doubt meant to explain the ritual, or a law to which the ritual gave rise.

[3] Preller-Jordan, ii. 43. See under Robigalia.

[4] *Myth. Forsch.* 107 foll.

[5] Ovid's word is *terga*, but he must, I think, mean 'tails.'

[6] Mannhardt, op. cit. 185. Cp. Frazer, *Golden Bough*, i. 408 ; ii. 3 and 28 (for fertilizing power of tail).

[7] *Zoological Mythology*, ii. 138.

ear of millet; the fox is told that these ears are all foxes' tails, and runs for it.

Here we must leave this puzzle[1]; but whoever cares to read Ovid's lines about his journey towards his native Pelignian country, his turning into the familiar lodging—

> Hospitis antiqui solitas intravimus aedes,

and the tales he heard there—among them that of the fox—will find them better worth reading than the greater part of the *Fasti*.

XI KAL. MAI. (APR. 21). N.[2]

PAR[ILIA]. (CAER. MAFF. PRAEN.)
ROMA COND[ITA] FERIAE CORONATIS OM[NIBUS]. (CAER.)
N[ATALIS] URBIS. CIRCENSES MISSUS XXIV. (PHILOC.)

[A note in Praen. is hopelessly mutilated, with the exception of the words IGNES and PRINCIPIO AN[NI PAS-TORICII[3] ?]

The Parilia[4], at once one of the oldest and best attested festivals of the whole year, is at the same time the one whose features have been most clearly explained by the investigations of parallels among other races.

The first point to notice is that the festival was both public and private, urban and rustic[5]. Ovid clearly distinguishes

---

[1] It may be as well to note that the custom of tying some object in straw—wheel, pole with cross-piece, man who slips out in time, &c.—and then burning it and carrying it about the fields, is common in Europe and elsewhere (Frazer, *G. B.* ii. 246 foll.). At the same time animals are sometimes burnt in a bonfire : e.g. squirrels, cats. foxes, &c. (*G. B.* ii. 283). The explanation of Mannhardt, adopted by Mr. Frazer, is that they were corn-spirits burnt as a charm to secure sunshine and vegetation. If the foxes were ever really let loose among the fields, damage might occasionally be done, and stories might arise like that of Carseoli, or even laws forbidding a dangerous practice.

[2] In *C. I. L.* 315 this mark is confused with those of the 23rd.

[3] The letters *an* also appear in a fragment of a lost note in Esq. Mommsen quotes Ovid, *Fasti*, 4. 775, and Tibull. 2. 5. 81 for the idea of an *annus pastorum* beginning on this day. I can find no explanation of it, astronomical or other. Dion. Hal. 1. 88 calls the day the beginning of spring, which it certainly was not.

[4] For the form of the word see Mommsen, *C. I. L.* 315. (In Varro, *L. L.* 6. 15, it is Palilia.) Preller-Jordan, i. 416.

[5] 'Palilia tam privata quam publica sunt.' Varro, ap Schol. in Persium, 1. 75. See on Compitalia, below, p. 279.

the two; lines 721–734 deal with the urban festival, 735–782 with the rustic. The explanations which follow deal with both. Pales, the deity (apparently both masculine and feminine [1]) whose name the festival bears, was, like Faunus, a common deity of Italian pasture land. A Palatium was said by Varro to have been named after Pales at Reate, in the heart of the Sabine hill-country [2]; and though this may not go for much, the character of the Parilia, and the fact that Pales is called *rusticola*, *pastoricia*, *silvicola*, &c., are sufficient to show the original non-urban character of the deity. He (or she) was a shepherd's deity of the simplest kind, and survived in Rome as little more than a name [3] from the oldest times, when the earliest invaders drove their cattle through the Sabine mountains. Here, then, we seem to have a clear example of a rite which was originally a rustic one, and survived as such, while at the same time one local form of it was kept up in the great city, and had become entangled with legend and probably altered in some points of ritual. We will take the rustic form first.

Here we may distinguish in Ovid's account [4] the following ritualistic acts.

1. The sheep-fold [5] was decked with green boughs and a great wreath was hung on the gate:

> Frondibus et fixis decorentur ovilia ramis,
> Et tegat ornatas longa corona fores.

With this Mannhardt [6] aptly compares the like concomitants of the midsummer fires in North Germany, Scotland, and England. In Scotland, for example, before the bonfires were kindled on midsummer eve, the houses were decorated with

---

[1] Serv. *Georg*. 3. 1: 'Pales . . . dea est pabuli. Hanc . . . alii, inter quos Varro, masculino genere vocant, ut hic Pales.' There can be no better proof of the antiquity of the deity in Italy.

[2] *L. L.* 5. 53.

[3] There was a *flamen Palatualis* (Varro, *L. L.* 7. 45, and Fest. 245) and an offering *Palatuar* (Fest. 348), connected with a *Diva Palatua* of the Palatine, who may have been the urban and pontifical form of Pales.

[4] Ovid is borne out or supplemented by Tibull. 2. 5. 87 foll.; Propert. 4. 4. 75 foll.; Probus on Virg. *Georg*. 3. 1; Dionys. 1. 88, &c.

[5] It is noticeable that sheep alone are mentioned in the ritual as Ovid describes it.

[6] *A. W. F.* p. 310. Cp. Frazer, *G. B.* ii. 246 foll.

foliage brought from the woods [1]. The custom of decoration at special seasons, May-day, mid-summer, harvest, and Christmas, is even now, with the exception of midsummer, universal, and is probably descended from these primitive rites, by which our ancestors sought in some mysterious way to influence the working of the powers of vegetation.

2. At the earliest glimmer of daybreak the shepherd purified the sheep. This was done by sprinkling and sweeping the fold ; then a fire was made of heaps of straw, olive-branches, and laurel, to give good omen by the crackling, and through this apparently the shepherds leapt, and the flocks were driven [2]. For this we have, of course, numerous parallels from all parts of the world. Burning sulphur was also used :

> Caerulei fiant vivo de sulfure fumi
> Tactaque fumanti sulfure balet ovis [3].

3. After this the shepherd brought offerings to Pales, of whom there may perhaps have been in the farmyard a rude image made of wood [4] ; among these were baskets of millet and cakes of the same, pails of milk, and other food of appropriate kinds. The meal which followed the shepherd himself appears to have shared with Pales [5]. Then he prays to the deity to avert all evil from himself and his flocks ; whether he or they have unwittingly trespassed on sacred ground and caused the nymphs or fauni to fly from human eyes ; or have disturbed the sacred fountains, and used branches of a sacred tree for secular ends. In these petitions the genuine spirit of Italian

---

[1] *Chambers' Journal*, July, 1842. For the custom in London, Brand, *Pop. Antiquities*, p. 307.

[2] So I understand Ovid : but in line 742 *in mediis focis* might rather indicate a fire in the *atrium* of the house, and so Mannhardt takes it. In that case the fire over which they leaped (line 805) was made later on in the ceremony.

[3] Cp. Hom. *Od.* 22. 481 Οἶσε θέειον, γρηΰ, κακῶν ἄκος, οἶσε δέ μοι πῦρ, Ὄφρα θεειώσω μέγαρον.

[4] Tibull. 2. 5. 28 ' Et facta agresti lignea falce Pales.' Tib. seems here to be transferring a rustic practice of his own day to the earliest Romans of the Palatine. But he may be simply indulging his imagination ; and we cannot safely conclude that we have here a rude Italian origin of anthropomorphic ideas of the gods.

[5] Ovid, *Fasti*, 4. 743–746, esp. ' dapibus resectis.' We can hardly escape the conclusion that the idea of the common meal shared with the gods was a genuine Italian one ; it is found here, in the Terminalia (Ovid, *Fasti*, 2. 655), and in the worship of Jupiter. See on Sept. 13 and Feb. 23.

religion—the awe of the unknown, the fear of committing
unwittingly some act that may bring down wrath upon you—
is most vividly brought out in spite of the Greek touches and
names which are introduced. He then goes on to his main
object[1] :

> Pelle procul morbos : valeant' hominesque gregesque,
>   Et valeant vigiles, provida turba, canes.
>
> .   .   .   .   .   .
>
> Absit iniqua fames. Herbae frondesque supersint,
>   Quaeque lavent artus, quaeque bibantur, aquae.
> Ubera plena premam : referat mihi caseus aera,
>   Dentque viam liquido vimina rara sero.
> Sitque salax aries, conceptaque semina coniunx
>   Reddat, et in stabulo multa sit agna meo.
> Lanaque proveniat nullas laesura puellas,
>   Mollis et ad teneras quamlibet apta manus.
> Quae precor eveniant : et nos faciamus ad annum
>   Pastorum dominae grandia liba Pali.

This prayer must be said four times over[2], the shepherd
looking to the east and wetting his hands with the morning
dew[3]. The position, the holy water, and the prayer in its
substance, though now addressed to the Virgin, have all
descended to the Catholic shepherd of the Campagna.

4. Then a bowl is to be brought, a wooden antique bowl
apparently[4], from which milk and purple *sapa*, i. e. heated
wine, may be drunk, until the drinker feels the influence of the
fumes, and when he is well set he may leap over the burning
heaps :

> Moxque per ardentes stipulae crepitantis acervos
>   Traiicias celeri strenua membra pede[5].

The Parilia of the urbs was celebrated in much the same
way in its main features ; but the day was reckoned as the

---

[1] *Fasti*, 4. 763 foll.

[2] Four is unusual ; three is the common number in religious rites.

[3] 'Conversus ad ortus Dic quater, et vivo perlue rore manus.' Ovid may
perhaps be using *ros* for fresh water of any kind ; see H. Peter's note
(Pt. II, p. 70). But the virtues of dew are great at this time of year (e. g.
May-day). See Brand, *Pop. Ant.* 218, and Mannhardt, *A. W. F.* 312. Pepys
records that his wife went out to gather May-dew ; *Diary*, May 10. 1669.

[4] The word is *camella* in Ovid, *Fasti*, 4. 779 ; cp. Petron. *Sat*, 135, and
Gell. *N. A.* 16. 7.

[5] Or as Propertius has it (4. 4. 77) :

> 'Cumque super raros foeni flammantis acervos
>   Traiicit immundos ebria turba pedes.'

birthday of Rome, and doubtless on this account it came under
the influence of priestly organization [1]. It is connected with
two other very ancient festivals : that of the Fordicidia and
that of the 'October horse.' The blood which streamed from
the head of the horse sacrificed on the Ides of October was
kept by the Vestals in the Penus Vestae, and mixed with
the ashes of the unborn calves burnt at the Fordicidia ; and
the mixture seems to have been thrown upon heaps of burning
bean-straw to make it smoke, while over the smoke and flames
men and women leaped on the Palatine Hill [2]. The object
was of course purification ; Ovid calls the blood, ashes, and
straw *februa casta,* i. e. holy agents of purification, and adds
in allusion to their having been kept by the Vestals :

> Vesta dabit : Vestae munere *purus* eris.

Ovid had himself taken part in the rite ; had fetched the
suffimen, and leaped three times through the flames, his
hands sprinkled with dew from a laurel branch. Whether
the *februa* were considered to have individually any special
significance or power, it is hard to say. Mannhardt, who
believed the 'October horse' to be a corn-demon, thought that
the burning of its blood symbolized the renewal of its life
in the spring, while the ashes thrown into the fire signified
the safe passage of the growing crops through the heat of the
summer [3]; but about this so judicious a writer is naturally
not disposed to dogmatize. We can, however, be pretty sure
that the purification was supposed to carry with it protection
from evil influences both for man and beast, and also to aid
the growth of vegetation. The theory of Mannhardt, adopted
by Mr. Frazer, that the whole class of ceremonies to which the

---

[1] Ovid, *Fasti,* 4. 801 foll. ; Prop. 4. 4. 73 ; Varro, *R. R.* 2. 1. 9. Many
other references are collected in Schwegler, *R. G.* i. 444, note 1. The
tradition was certainly an ancient one, and the pastoral character of the
rite is in keeping with that of the legend. It is to be noted that the
sacrificing priest was originally the Rex Sacrorum (Dionys. 1. 88), a fact
which may well carry us back to the earliest Roman age.

[2] Ovid, *Fasti,* 4. 733 foll. 'Sanguis equi suffimen erit vitulique favilla,
Tertia res durae culmen inane fabae.' Whether the bonfire was burnt
on the Palatine itself does not seem certain, but it is a reasonable
conjecture.

[3] He points out (p. 316) that the throwing of bones or burnt pieces of
an animal into the flames is common in northern Europe : hence bonfire
= bonefire.

Parilia clearly belongs, i. e. the Easter and Midsummer fires and Need-fires of central and northern Europe, may best be explained as charms to procure sunshine[1], has much to be said for it, but does not seem to find any special support in the Roman rite.

It may be noted in conclusion that a custom of the same kind, and one perhaps connected with a cult of the sun[2], took place not far from Rome, at Mount Soracte; at what time of year we do not know. On this hill there was a worship of Apollo Soranus[3], a local deity, to which was attached a kind of guild of worshippers called Hirpi Sorani, or wolves of Soranus[4]; and of these we may guess, from the legend told of their origin, that in order to avert pestilence, &c., they dressed or behaved themselves like wolves[5]. Also on a particular day, perhaps the summer solstice, these Hirpi ran through the flames, 'super ambustam ligni struem ambulantes non aduruntur[6],' and on this account were excused by a senatus consultum from all military or other service. A striking parallel with this last feature is quoted by Mannhardt, from Mysore, where the Harawara are degraded Brahmins who act as priests in harvest-time, and make a living by running through the flames unhurt with naked soles: but in this case there seems to be no animal representation. Mannhardt tries to explain the Hirpi as dramatic representations of the Corn-wolf or vegetation spirit[7]. On the other hand, it is possible to consider them as survivals of an original clan who worshipped

---

[1] A. W. F. 316; Frazer, G. B. ii. 274 foll.

[2] Preller-Jordan, i. 268. Soranus is thought to be connected etymologically with Sol. With this, however, Deecke disagrees (Falisker, 96).

[3] So called by Virg. Aen. 11. 785 and Serv. ad loc. Who the deity really was, we do not know. Apollo here had no doubt a Graeco-Etruscan origin. Deecke (Falisker, 93) thinks of Dis Pater or Vediovis; quoting Servius' account and explanation of the cult. That the god was Sabine, not Etruscan, is shown by the word hirpi.

[4] Or of Soracte, if Soranus = Soractnus (Deecke).

[5] Serv. l. c. tells the aetiological legend. Cp. Plin. N. H. 7. 11. It has been dealt with fully by Mannhardt, A. W. F. 318 foll.

[6] Plin. l. c.; Varro (ap. Serv. l. c.) asserted that they used a salve for their feet which protected them. The same thing is said, I believe, of the Harawara in India.

[7] According to Strabo, p. 226, this fire-ceremony took place in the grove of Feronia, at the foot of the hill. Feronia may have been a corn- or harvest-deity, and of this Mannhardt makes all he can. We may at least guess that the rite took place at Midsummer.

the wolf as a totem[1]; a view adopted by Mr. Lang[2], who compares the *bear*-maidens of Artemis at Brauron in Attica. But the last word has yet to be said about these obscure animalistic rites.

IX KAL. MAI. (APR. 23). FP (CAER.) ℕP (MAFF.)
F (PRAEN.)[3]

VEIN[ALIA] (CAER.) VIN[ALIA] (MAFF. PRAEN. ESQ.)

Praen. has a mutilated note beginning 10[VI], and ending with [CUM LATINI BELLO PREME]RENTUR A RUTULIS, QUIA MEZENTIUS REX ETRUS[CO]RUM PACISCEBATUR, SI SUBSIDIO VENISSET, OMNIUM ANNORUM VINI FRUCTUM. (Cp. Festus, 65 and 374, where it appears that libations of all new wine were made to Jupiter.)

VENERI (CAER.)

[V]ENERI ERUC. [EXTR]A PORTAM COLLIN[AM]. (ARV.)

This day was generally known as Vinalia Priora, as distinguished from the Vinalia Rustica of August 19. Both days were believed to be sacred to Venus[4]; the earlier one, according to Ovid, was the foundation-day of the temple of Venus Erycina, with which he connected the legend of Aeneas and Mezentius. But as both Varro and Verrius are agreed that the days were sacred, not to Venus but to Jupiter[5], we may leave the legend alone and content ourselves with asking how Venus came into the connexion.

The most probable supposition is that this day being, as

---

[1] Cp. the cult of Zeus Lykaios in Arcadia; Farnell, *Cults of the Greek States*, i. 41.

[2] *Myth., Ritual, and Religion*, ii. 212.

[3] This peculiar notation is common to this day and Aug. 19 (the Vinalia Rustica), and to the Feralia (Feb. 21). See Introduction, p. 10.

[4] Ovid, *Fasti*, 4. 877, asks: 'Cur igitur Veneris festum Vinalia dicant, Quaeritis?'

[5] Varro, *L. L.* 6. 16; Fest. 65 and 374. The latter gloss is: 'Vinalia diem festum habebant, quo die vinum novum Iovi libabant.' Ovid, *Fasti*, 4. 899, after telling the Mezentius story (alluded to in the note in Praen.), adds

Dicta dies hinc est Vinalia: Iuppiter illam
Vindicat, et festis gaudet inesse suis.

Ovid implies, the dies natalis of one of the temples of Venus [1], the Vinalia also came to be considered as sacred to the goddess. The date of the foundation was 181 B. C., exactly at a time when many new worships, and especially Greek ones, were being introduced into Rome [2]. That of the Sicilian Aphrodite, under the name of Venus, seems to have become at once popular with its *Graecus ritus* and *lascivia maior* [3]; and the older connexion of the festival with Jupiter tended henceforward to disappear. It must be noted, however, that the day of the Vinalia Rustica in August was also the dies natalis of one if not two other temples of Venus [4], and one of these was as old as the year B. C. 293. Thus we can hardly avoid the conclusion that there was, even at an early date, some connexion in the popular mind between the goddess and wine. The explanation is perhaps to be found in the fact that Venus was specially a deity of gardens, and therefore no doubt of vineyards [5]. An interesting inscription from Pompeii confirms this, and attests the connexion of Venus with wine and gardens, as it is written on a wine-jar [6]:

PRESTA MI SINCERU[M] ITA TE AMET QUE
CUSTODIT ORTU[M] VENUS.

The Vinalia, then, both in April and August, was really and originally sacred to Jupiter. The legendary explanation is given by Ovid in ll. 877–900. Whatever the true explanation may have been, the fact can be illustrated from the ritual employed; for it was the Flamen Dialis [7] who 'vindemiam auspicatus est,' i. e. after sacrificing plucked the first grapes. Whether this auspicatio took place on either of the Vinalia has indeed been doubted, for even August 19 would hardly seem

[1] Ovid, *Fasti*, 4. 871

Templa frequentari Collinae proxima portae
Nunc decet; a Siculo nomina colle tenent.

He seems to have confused this temple with that on the Capitol (Aust, *de Aedibus*, 23).

[2] Liv. 40. 34. 4.

[3] Aust, ib. p. 24. Varro wrote a satire 'Vinalia περὶ ἀφροδισίων.' Plutarch (*Q. R.* 45) confuses Vinalia and Veneralia.

[4] Festus, 264 and 265; in the Vallis Murcia (or Circus maximus), and the lucus Libitinae. (In 265, xiii Kal. Sept. should be xiv.) For the date of the former temple, 293 B. C., Liv. 10. 31. 9.

[5] Varro, *R. R.* 1. 1; Fest. 265; Preller-Jordan, i. 441.

[6] *C. I. L.* iv. 2776.

[7] Varro, *L. L.* 6. 16. See *Myth. Lex.* s. v. Iuppiter, 704 foll.

to suit the ceremony Varro describes[1] ; but the fact that it was performed by the priest of Jupiter is sufficient for our purpose.

Of this day, April 23, we may guess that it was the one on which the wine-skins were first opened, and libations from them made to Jupiter. These are probably the libations about which Plutarch[2] asks 'Why do they pour much wine from the temple of Venus on the Veneralia' (i. e. Vinalia)? The same libations are attested by Verrius : ' Vinalia diem festum habebant quo die vinum novum Iovi libabant'[3]. After the libation the wine was tasted, as we learn from Pliny[4]; and it seems probable that it was brought from the country into Rome for this purpose only a few days before. Varro has preserved an interesting notice which he saw posted in vineyards at Tusculum : 'In Tusculanis hortis (MSS. sortis) est scriptum : 'Vinum novum ne vehatur in urbem ante quam vinalia kalentur'[5]; i. e. wine-growers were warned that the new wine was not to be brought into the city until the Vinalia had been proclaimed on the Nones. It must, however, be added that this notice may have had reference to the Vinalia in August; for Verrius, if he is rightly reported by Paulus[6], gives August 19 as the day on which the wine might be brought into Rome. Paulus may be wrong, and have confused the two Vinalia[7]; but in that case we remain in the dark as to what was done at the Vinalia Rustica, unless indeed we explain it as a rite intended to secure the vintage that was to follow against malignant influences. This would seem to be indicated by Pliny (*H. N.* 18. 284), where he classes this August festival with the Robigalia and Floralia[8], and further on quotes Varro to prove

---

[1] Mommsen, *C. I. L.* 326. Vindemia is the *grape*-harvest. Hartmann, *Röm. Kal.* 138, differs from Mommsen on this point.

[2] *Q. R.* 45.   [3] Fest. 65.   [4] *H. N.* 18. 287.

[5] *L. L.* 6. 16. *Hortis* is Mommsen's very probable emendation for *sortis* of the MSS. O. Müller has *sacris*, which is preferred by Jordan (Preller, i. 196).   [6] 264.

[7] Mommsen (*C. I. L.* 326) thinks that there is no mistake in the gloss ; but that the Vinalia Rustica represent a later and luxurious fashion of allowing a whole year to elapse before tasting the wine, instead of six months. From the vintage, however (end of September or beginning of October), to August 19 is not a whole year. See under August 19.

[8] 'Tria namque tempora fructibus metuebant, propter quod instituerunt ferias diesque festos, Robigalia, Floralia, Vinalia.' That the Vinalia here referred to is the August one is clear, not only from the order of the words, but from what follows, down to the end of sec. 289. Secs. 287

that its object was to appease the storms (i. e. to be expected in September).

As regards the connexion of the vine-culture with Jupiter, it should be observed that the god is not spoken of as Jupiter Liber, but simply Jupiter; and though the vine was certainly introduced into Italy from Greece, we need not assume that Dionysus, coming with it, was from the beginning attached to or identified with Jupiter. The gift of wine might naturally be attributed to the great god of the air, light, and heat; the Flamen Dialis who 'vindemiam auspicatus est' was not the priest of Jupiter Liber; nor does the aetiological legend, in which the Latins avoid the necessity of yielding their first-fruits to the Etruscan tyrant Mezentius by dedicating them to Jupiter, point to any other than the protecting deity of Latium [1].

VII KAL. MAI. (APRIL 25). ℞.

[ROB]IGALIA.   (CAER. ESQ. MAFF. PRAEN.)

Note in Praen : FERIAE ROBIGO VIA CLAUDIA AD MILLIARIUM V NE ROBIGO FRUMENTIS NOCEAT. SACRIFICIUM ET LUDI CUR-SORIBUS MAIORIBUS MINORIBUSQUE FIUNT. FESTUS EST PUERORUM LENONIORUM, QUIA PROXIMUS SUPERIOR MERE-TRICUM EST.

Robigo means red rust or mildew which attacks cereals when the ear is beginning to be formed [2], and which is better known and more dreaded on the continent than with us. This destructive disease is not caused by the sun's heat, as Pliny [3]

to end of 288 deal with the Vinalia priora *parenthetically*; in 289 Pliny returns to the Vinalia altera (or rustica), after thus clearing the ground by making it clear that the April Vinalia ' nihil ad fructus attinent.' He then quotes Varro to show that in August the object is to avert storms which might damage the vineyards. Mommsen, *C. I. L.* 326, seems to me to have misread this passage.

[1] Ovid, *Fasti*, 877 foll. : the legend was an old one. for it is quoted by Macrob. (*Sat.* 3. 5. 10) from Cato's *Origines*. See also Hehn, *Kulturpflanzen*, 65 foll., who is, however, in error as to the identification of Jupiter (Liber) with Ζεὺς Ἐλευθέριος.

[2] See Columella, 2. 12; Plin. *N.H.* 18. 91; and article, 'Mildew,' in *Encycl. Brit.* For the botanical character of this parasite see Worthington Smith's *Diseases of Field and Garden Crops*, chs. 21 and 23 ; and Hugh Macmillan's *Bible Teachings from Nature*, p. 120 foll.

[3] *N H.* 18. 273 : cp. 154. Pliny thought it chiefly the result of *dew* (cf. mil*dew*, German mehl*thau*), and was not wholly wrong.

tells us was the notion of some Italians, but by damp acting in
conjunction with a certain height of temperature, as Pliny
himself in fact explains it.

Robigus [1] is the spirit who works in the mildew; and it has
been conjectured that he was a form or indigitation of Mars [2],
since Tertullian tells us that 'Marti et Robigini Numa ludos
instituit' [3]. This is quite consistent with all we know of the
Mars of the farm-worship, who is invoked to avert evil simply
because he can be the creator of it [4]. The same feature is found
in the worship of Apollo, who had at Rhodes the cult-title
$ἐρυθίβιος$ [5], or Apollo of the blight, as elsewhere he is Apollo
Smintheus, i.e. the power that can bring and also avert the
pest of field-mice.

Robigus had a grove of his own at the fifth milestone on the
Via Claudia; and Ovid relates in pretty verses how, as he was
returning from Nomentum (doubtless by way of his own
gardens, which were at the junction of the Via Claudia with
the Via Flaminia near the Milvian bridge [6]), he met the
Flamen Quirinalis with the *exta* of a dog and a sheep to offer
to the god [7]. He joined the procession, which was apparently
something quite new to him, and witnessed the ceremony,
noting the *meri patera*, the *turis acerra*, and the rough linen
napkin [8], at the priest's right hand. He versified the prayer
which he heard, and which is not unlike that which Cato
directs the husbandman to address to Mars in the lustration of
the farm [9]:

> Aspera Robigo, parcas Cerialibus herbis,
> Et tremat in summa leve cacumen humo.

[1] The masc. is no doubt correct. Ovid, *Fasti*, 4. 907, uses the feminine
Robigo, but is alone among the older writers in doing so: see Preller-
Jordan, ii. 44, note 2.

[2] Indigitation is the fixing of the *local action* of a god to be invoked, by
means of his name, if I understand rightly Reifferscheid's view as given
by R. Peter in *Myth. Lex.* s. v. Indigitamenta, p. 137. The priest of the
Robigalia was the flamen Quirinalis: Quirinus is one form of Mars.

[3] *de Spectaculis*, 5.

[4] Cato, *R. R.* 141; Preller-Jordan, i. 340.

[5] Strabo, 613: see Roscher, *Apollo and Mars*, p. 62. $Ἐρυσίβη$ = mildew,
of which $ἐρυθίβη$ is the Rhodian form.

[6] See Mommsen's ingenious explanation in *C. I. L.* 316.

[7] *Fasti*, 4. 901 foll. The victims had been slain at Rome and in the
morning; and were offered at the grove later in the day (see Marq. 184).

[8] Villis mantele solutis (cp. Serv. *Aen.* 12. 169).

[9] *R. R.* 141.

> Tu sata sideribus caeli nutrita secundi
> Crescere, dum fiant falcibus apta, sinas.
>
> . . . .
>
> Parce, precor, scabrasque manus a messibus aufer,
> Neve noce cultis : posse nocere sat est, &c.

Ovid then asked the flamen why a dog—*nova victima*—was
sacrificed, and was told that the dangerous Dog-star was in the
ascendant[1] :

> Est Canis, Icarium dicunt, quo sidere moto
> Tosta sitit tellus, praecipiturque seges.
> Pro cane sidereo canis hic imponitur arae,
> Et quare pereat, nil nisi nomen habet.

In this, however, both he and the priest were certainly
mistaken. Sirius does not rise, but disappears on April 25, at
sunset ; and it is almost certain that the sacrifice of the dog
had nothing to do with the star. The real meaning of the
choice of victim was unknown both to priest and poet : but
modern research has made a reasonable attempt to recover it[2].

We are told[3] of a sacrifice of reddish sucking whelps, and of
augury made from their *exta*, which must have been closely
connected with the Robigalia, if not (in later times at least)
identified with it. Originally it was not on a fixed day, as
is proved by an extract from the *commentarii pontificum* quoted
by Pliny[4] ; but it is quite possible that for convenience, as the
religio of the urbs got more and more dissociated from the
agriculture in which it had its origin, the date was fixed for
April 25—the rites of the Robigalia being of the same kind,
and the date suitable. The whelps were red or reddish ; and
from the language of Festus, quoting Ateius Capito, we gather

---

[1] So we may perhaps translate *quo sidere moto* : . but Ovid certainly
thought the star rose (cf. 904). Hartmann explains Ovid's blunder by
reference to Serv. *Georg.* 1. 218 (*Röm. Kal.* 193). See also H. Peter, ad loc.

[2] Mannhardt, *My'h. Forsch.* 107 foll.

[3] Festus, 285 ; Paul. 45. It was outside the Porta Catularia, of which,
unluckily, nothing is known.

[4] *N. H.* 18. 14 'Ita est in commentariis pontificum : Augurio canario
agendo dies constituantur priusquam frumenta vaginis exeant et antequam in vaginas perveniant.' For '*et* antequam' we should perhaps read
'*nec* antequam.' The *vagina* is the sheath which protects the ear and from
which it eventually protrudes ; and it seems that in this stage, which in
Italy would occur at the end of April or beginning of May, the corn is
peculiarly liable to 'rust.' (So Virg. *Georg.* 1. 151 'Ut mala *culmos* Esset
robigo' : i. e. the stalks including the *vagina*.) See Hugh Macmillan,
op. cit. p. 121.

that this colour was supposed to resemble that of the corn when
ripe: 'Rufae canes immolabantur, ut fruges *flavescentes* ad matu-
ritatem perducerentur' (p. 285). We should indeed naturally
have expected that the rufous colour was thought to resemble
the red mildew, as Mannhardt explains it [1]; but we do not know
for certain that these puppies were offered to Robigus. In any
case, however, we may perhaps see in them an animal representation of the corn, and in the rite a piece of 'sympathetic
magic' [2], the object of which was to bring the corn to its
golden perfection, or to keep off the robigo, or both. If we
knew more about the dog-offering at the grove of Robigus,
we might find that it too, if not indeed identical with the
augurium, had a similar intention.

The red mildew was at times so terrible a scourge that the
Robigalia must in early Rome, when the population lived
on the corn grown near the city, have been a festival of very
real meaning. But later on it became obscured, and gave way
to the races mentioned in the note in the Praenestine calendar [3],
and under the later empire to the Christian *litania maior*, the
original object of which was also the safety of the crops [4]. The
25th is at present St. Mark's day.

iv Kal. Mai. (Apr. 28). ℞.

loedi flor[ae] (caer.) ludi flor[ae]. (maff. praen.)

v Non. Mai. (May 3). C.

florae (ven.).
On the intervening days were also ludi (*C. I. L.* 317).

Note in Praen. (Apr. 28): eodem die aedis florae, quae
rebus florescendis praeest, dedicata est propter ste-
rilitatem frugum.

---

[1] *Myth. Forsch.* 106. Mr. Frazer (*G. B.* ii. 59 : cp. i. 306) takes the other
view of this and similar sacrifices, but with some hesitation.

[2] It must be confessed that the occurrence of red colour in victims
cannot well be always explained in this way ; e. g. the red heifer of the
Israelites (Numbers xix), and the red oxen of the Egyptians (Plut. *Isis and
Osiris*, 31). But in this rite, occurring so close to the Cerialia, where, as
we have seen, *foxes* were turned out in the *circus maximus*, the colour of
the puppies must have had some meaning in relation to the growing crops.

[3] 'Ludi cursoribus maioribus minoribusque.' What these were is not
known : Mommsen, *C. I. L.* 317.

[4] Usener, *Religionsgeschichte*, i. 298 foll.

This was not a very ancient festival and is not marked in the Calendars in those large letters which are believed to indicate extreme antiquity [1]. Its history seems to be as follows: in 238 B. C. in consequence of a dearth, the Sibylline Books were consulted, and games in honour of Flora were held for the first time by plebeian aediles [2]; also a temple was dedicated to her *ad circum maximum* on April 28 of that year [3]. There seems to be a certain connexion between the accounts of the institution of the Floralia and the Cerialia. Dearth was the alleged cause in each case; and the position of the temple of Flora near that of Ceres: the foundation by plebeian magistrates, in this case the two Publicii [4], who as aediles were able to spend part of the fines exacted from defaulting holders of *ager publicus* on this object [5]: and the coarse character of the games as Ovid describes them, all seem to show that the foundation was a plebeian one, like that of the Cerialia [6].

There may, however, have been something in the nature of ludi before this date and at the same time of year, but not of a regular or public character. Flora was beyond doubt an old Italian deity [7], probably closely related to Ceres and Venus. There was a Flamen Floralis of very old standing [8]; and Flora is one of the deities to whom piacula were offered by the Fratres

---

[1] See Introduction, p. 15.

[2] Plin. *N. H.* 18. 286; two years earlier, according to Velleius, 1. 14. This is, I think, the only case in which a deity taken in hand by the *decemviri sacris faciundis* cannot be traced to a Greek origin; but the characteristics of Flora are so like those of Venus that in the former, as in the latter, Aphrodite may be concealed. The games as eventually organized had points in common with the cult of Aphrodite at Hierapolis (Lucian, *Dea Syr.* 49; Farnell, *Cults*, ii. 643); and it is worth noting that their date (173 B. C.) is subsequent to the Syrian war. Up to that time the games were not regular or annual (Ovid, *Fasti*, 5. 295).

[3] Tac. *Ann.* 2. 49; Aust, p. 17.

[4] Plebis ad aediles: Ovid, ib. v. 287; Festus, 238, probably in error, calls the Publicii *curule* aediles.

[5] Ovid, ib. 5. 277 foll., in which he draws a picture of the misdoings of the landholders. Cp. Liv. 33. 42, for the temple of Faunus *in insula*, founded by the same means.

[6] Ovid, ib. 5. 352.

[7] Steuding in *Myth. Lex.* s. v. Flora. There was a Sabine month Flusalis (Momms. *Chron.* 219) = Floralis, and answering to July. Varro considered Flora a Sabine deity (*L. L.* 5. 74).

[8] Varro, *L. L.* 7. 45. Flora had an ancient temple *in colle*, near the so-called Capitolium vetus (Steuding, l. c.), i.e. in the 'Sabine quarter.'

Arvales[1]—a list beginning with Janus and ending with Vesta. There is no doubt, then, that there was a Flora-cult in Rome long before the foundation of the temple and the games in 238; and though its character may have changed under the influence of the Sibylline books, we may be able to glean some particulars as to its original tendency.

In the account of Ovid and from other hints we gather—

1. That indecency was let loose[2] at any rate on the original day of the ludi (April 28), which were in later times extended to May 3. The numen of Flora, says Ovid, was not strict. Drunkenness was the order of the day, and the usual results followed:

> Ebrius ad durum formosae limen amicae
> Cantat: habent unctae mollia serta comae.

The prostitutes of Rome hailed this as their feast-day, as well as the Vinalia on the 23rd; and if we may trust a story told by Valerius Maximus[3], Cato the younger withdrew from the theatre rather than behold the mimae unclothe themselves, though he would not interfere with the custom. Flora herself, like Acca Larentia, was said by late writers to have been a harlot whose gains enabled her to leave money for the ludi[4]. These characteristics of the festival were no doubt developed under the influence of luxury in a large city, and grew still more objectionable under the Empire[5]. But it is difficult to believe that such practices would have grown up as they did at this particular time of year, had there not been some previous customs of the kind existing before the ludi were regularly instituted.

2. We find another curious custom belonging to the last days of the ludi, which became common enough under the Empire[6], but may yet have had an origin in the cult of Flora.

---

[1] Henzen, *Acta Fratr. Arv.* 146.
[2] Ov. 5. 331 foll 'Volt sua plebeio sacra patere choro.
[3] Val. Max. 2. 10. 8. Steuding in *Myth. Lex.* has oddly misunderstood this passage, making Val. Max. write of this custom as an ancient one, whereas he clearly implies the opposite. It was no doubt the relic of some rude country practice, degenerated under the influence of city life.
[4] Lactantius, *De falsa religione*, i. 20.
[5] Aug. *Civ. Dei*, ii. 27.
[6] Friedländer on Martial, 8. 67. 4.

Harés and goats were let loose in the Circus Maximus on these days. Ovid asks Flora:

> Cur tibi pro Libycis clauduntur rete [1] leaenis
> Imbelles capreae sollicitusque lepus?

and gets the answer:

> Non sibi, respondit, silvas cessisse, sed hortos
> Arvaque pugnaci non adeunda ferae.

If we take this answer as at least appropriate, we may add to it the reflection that hares and goats are prolific animals and also that they are graminivorous. Flora as a goddess of fertility and bloom could have nothing in common with fierce carnivora. But we are also reminded of the foxes that were let loose in the Circus at the Cerialia [2], and may see in these beasts as in the foxes animal representations of the spirit of fertility.

3. Another custom is possibly significant in something the same way. From a passage in Persius we learn that vetches, beans, and lupines were scattered among the people in the circus [3]. The commentators explain this as meaning that they were thrown simply to be scrambled for as food; and we know that other objects besides eatables were thrown on similar occasions, at any rate at a later time [4]. But it is noticeable that among these objects were medals with obscene representations on them; and putting two and two together it is not unreasonable to guess that the original custom had a meaning connected with fructification. Dr. Mannhardt [5] has collected a very large number of examples of the practice of sprinkling and throwing all kinds of grain, including rice, peas, beans, &c., from all parts of the world, in the marriage rite and at the birth of children; amply sufficient to prove that the custom is symbolic of fertility. Bearing in mind the time of year, the nature of Flora, the character of the April rites generally, and

---

[1] H. Peter takes this to mean that they were let loose from a net and hunted into it again. See note ad loc. 5. 371.

[2] See above, p. 77.

[3] *Sat.* 5. 177: Vigila et cicer ingere large
    Rixanti populo, nostra ut Floralia possint
    Aprici meminisse senes.—Cp. Hor. *Sat.* 2. 3. 182.

[4] Friedländer, *Sittengeschichte*, ii. 286; and his note on Martial, 8. 78.

[5] *Kind. u. Korn.* 351 foll.

the occurrence of the women's cult of the Bona Dea on May 1, viz. one of the days of the ludi, we may perhaps conjecture that the custom in question was a very old one—far older than the organized games—and had reference to the fertility both of the earth and of man himself[1].

FERIAE LATINAE.

A brief account may be here given of the great Latin festival which usually in historical times took place in April. Though it was not held at Rome, but on the Alban Mount, it was under the direct supervision of the Roman state, and was in reality a Roman festival. The consuls on their entrance upon office on the Ides of March had to fix and announce the date of it[2]; and when in 153 B.C. the day of entrance was changed to January 1, the date of the festival does not seem to have been changed to suit it. The consuls must be present themselves, leaving a *praefectus urbi* at Rome[3]; or in case of the compulsory absence of both consuls a dictator might be appointed *Feriarum Latinarum causa*. Only when the festival was over could they leave Rome for their provinces.

It was therefore a festival of the highest importance to the Roman state. But the ritual will show that it must in fact have been much older than that state as we know it in historical times; it was a common festival of the most ancient Latin communities[4], celebrated on the lofty hill which arose in their midst, where dwelt the great protecting deity of their race. At what date Rome became the presiding city at the festival we do not know. The foundation of the temple on the hill was

---

[1] Another point that may strike the reader of Ovid is the wearing of parti-coloured dress on these days (5. 355: cp. Martial, 5. 23)—

Cur tamen ut dantur vestes Cerialibus albae,

Sic haec est cultu versicolore decens?

Flora answers him doubtfully. Was this a practice of comparatively late date? See Friedländer, *Sittengeschichte* ii. 275.

[2] Mommsen in *C. I. L.* vi. p. 455 (Tabula fer. Lat.). The day was March 15 from B.C. 222 to 153; in earlier times it had been frequently changed. See Mommsen. *Chron.* p. 80 foll.

[3] On this office and its connexion with the *feriae* see Vigneaux, *Essai sur l'histoire de la praefectura urbis*, p. 37 foll.

[4] Plin. *H. N.* 3. 69; Dionys. 4. 49. The difficult questions arising out of the numbers given by these authorities are d scussed by Beloch, *Italischer Bund*, 178 foll., and Mommsen in *Hermes*, vol. xvii. 42 foll.

ascribed to the Tarquinii, and this tradition seems to be borne out by the character of the foundations discovered there, which resemble those of the Capitoline temple[1]. No doubt the Tarquinii may have renovated the cult or even given it an extended significance; but the Roman presidency must conjecturally be placed still further back. Perhaps no festival, Greek or Roman, carries us over such a vast period of time as this; its features betray its origin in the pastoral age, and it continued in almost uninterrupted grandeur till the end of the third century A. D., or even later[2].

The ritual as known to us was as follows[3]. When the magistrates or (their deputies) of all the Latin cities taking part had assembled at the temple, the Roman consul offered a libation of milk, while the deputies from the other cities brought sheep, cheeses, or other such offerings. But the characteristic rite was the slaughter of a pure white heifer that had never felt the yoke. This sacrifice was the duty of the consul, who acted on behalf of the whole number of cities. When it was concluded, the flesh of the victim was divided amongst all the deputies and consumed by them. To be left out of this common meal, or sacrament, would be equivalent to being excluded from communion with the god and the Latin league, and the desire to obtain the allotted flesh is more than once alluded to[4]. A general festivity followed the sacrifice, while *oscilla*, or little puppets, were hung from the branches of trees as at the Paganalia[5]. As usual in Italy, the least oversight in the ceremony or evil omen made it necessary to begin it all over again; and this occasionally happened[6]. Lastly, during the festival there was a truce between all the cities, and it

---

[1] Aust, in *Myth. Lex.* s. v. Iuppiter, p. 689.

[2] *C. I. L.* vi. 2021.

[3] Condensed from the account given by Aust, l. c. See also Preller-Jordan, i. 210 foll. The chief authority is Dionys. 4. 49.

[4] e. g. Liv. 32. 1, 37. 3, in which cases some one city had not received its portion. The result was an *instauratio feriarum*.

[5] See below, p. 294 (Feriae Sementivae). The meaning of the *oscilla* was not really known to the later Romans, who freely indulged in conjectures about them. Macrob. 1. 7. 34; Serv. *Georg.* 2. 389; Paul. 121. My own belief is that, like the *bullae* of children, they were only one of the many means of averting evil influences.

[6] See the passages of Livy quoted above, and add 40. 45 (on account of a storm); 41. 16 (a failure on the part of Lanuvium).

would seem that the alliance between Rome and the Latins was yearly renewed on the day of the Feriae [1].

Some of the leading characteristics of the Italian Jupiter will be considered further on [2]. But this festival may teach us that we are here in the presence of the oldest and finest religious conception of the Latin race, which yearly acknowledges its common kinship of blood and seals it by partaking in the common meal of a sacred victim, thus entering into communion with the god, the victim, and each other [3]. The offerings are characteristic rather of a pastoral than an agricultural age, and suggest an antiquity that is fully confirmed by the ancient utensils dug up on the Alban Mount [4]. As Helbig has pointed out, the absence of any mention of wine proves that the origin of the festival must be dated earlier than the introduction of the grape into Italy. The white victim may be a reminiscence of some primitive white breed of cattle. The common meal of the victim's flesh is a survival from the age when cattle were sacred animals, and were never slain except on the solemn annual occasions when the clan renewed its kinship and its mutual obligations by a solemn sacrament [5].

As Rome absorbed Latium, so Jupiter Latiaris gave way before the great god of the Capitol, who is the symbol of the later victorious and imperial Rome ; but the god of the Alban hill and his yearly festival continued to recall the early share of the Latins in the rise of their leading city, long after the population of their towns had been so terribly thinned that some of them could hardly find a surviving member to represent them at the festival and take their portion of the victim [6].

---

[1] Macrob. 1. 16. 16 'Cum Latiar, hoc est Latinarum solemne concipitur, nefas est proelium sumere : quia nec Latinarum tempore. quo publice quondam indutiae inter populum Romanum Latinosque firmatae sunt, inchoari bellum decebat.'

[2] See under Sept. 13.

[3] For the characteristics and meaning of the common sacrificial meal see especially Robertson Smith, *Religion of the Semites*, Lect. viii.

[4] Helbig, *Die Italiker in der Poebene*, 71.

[5] Robertson Smith, op. cit., 278 foll.

[6] Cic. *pro Plancio*, 9. 23.

MENSIS MAIUS.

WAS the name of this month taken from a deity Maia, or had it originally only a signification of *growing* or *increasing*, such as we might expect in a word derived from the same root as *maior, maiestas*, &c.? The following passage of Macrobius will show how entirely the Roman scholars were at sea in their answer to this question [1]:

'Maium Romulus tertium posuit. De cuius nomine inter auctores lata dissensio est. Nam Fulvius Nobilior in Fastis quos in aede Herculis Musarum posuit [2] Romulum dicit postquam populum in maiores iunioresque diuisit, ut altera pars consilio altera armis rem publicam tueretur, in honorem utriusque partis hunc Maium, sequentem Iunium mensem uocasse [3]. Sunt qui hunc mensem ad nostros fastos a Tusculanis transisse commemorent, apud quos nunc quoque uocatur deus Maius, qui est Iuppiter, a magnitudine scilicet ac maiestate dictus [4]. Cingius [5] mensem nominatum putat a Maia quam Vulcani dicit uxorem, argumentoque utitur quod flamen Vulcanalis Kalendis Maiis huic deae rem diuinam facit. Sed Piso uxorem Vulcani Maiestam non Maiam dicit uocari. Contendunt alii Maiam Mercurii matrem mensi nomen dedisse, hinc maxime probantes quod hoc mense mercatores omnes

---

[1] Sat. 1. 12. 16.   [2] See above, Introduction, p. 11.

[3] So Varro also (*L. L.* 6. 33). But Censorinus (*De die natali,* 20. 2) expressly ascribes to Varro the derivation from Maia ; the great scholar apparently changed his view.

[4] For Iup. Maius see Aust, in *Myth. Lex.* s. v. Iuppiter, p. 650.

[5] This was probably not the early historian Cincius Alimentus, but a contemporary of Augustus, Teuffel, *Hist. of Roman Literature,* sec. 106. For the flamen Volcanalis see on Aug 23.

Maiae pariter Mercurioque sacrificant[1]. Adfirmant quidam, quibus Cornelius Labeo consentit, hanc Maiam cui mense Maio res diuina celebratur terram esse hoc adeptam nomen a magnitudine, sicut et Mater Magna in sacris uocatur adsertionemque aestimationis suae etiam hinc colligunt quod sus praegnans ei mactatur, quae hostia propria est terrae. Et Mercurium ideo illi in sacris adiungi dicunt quia uox nascenti homini terrae contactu datur, scimus autem Mercurium uocis et sermonis potentem. Auctor est Cornelius Labeo huic Maiae id est terrae aedem Kalendis Maiis dedicatam sub nomine Bonae Deae et eandem esse Bonam Deam et terram ex ipso ritu occultiore sacrorum doceri posse confirmat. Hanc eandem Bonam deam Faunamque et Opem et Fatuam pontificum libris indigitari, &c.'

It is clear from this passage that the Romans themselves were not agreed, either in the case of May or June, that the name of the month was derived from a deity. No Roman scholar doubted that Martius was derived from Mars, the characteristic god of the Roman race; but Maia was a deity known apparently only to the priests and the learned. Had she been a popular one, what need could there have been to question so obvious an etymology? And if she were an obscure one, how could she have given her name to a month? As a matter of fact March is the only month of which we can be sure that it was named after a god. Even January is doubtful, June still more so. The natural assumption about this latter word would be that it comes from Juno, more especially as we find in Latium the words Junonius and Junonalis as names of months[2]. But if Junius came from Juno, it must have come by the dropping out of a syllable; and this, in the case of a long and accented o, would be at least unlikely to happen[3]. Nor can we discover any sufficient reason why the month of June should be called after Juno; none at any rate such as accounts for the connexion of Mars with the initial month of the year. This is enough to show

---

[1] i.e. on the Ides: see below, p. 120. The connexion between Mercurius and Maia seems to arise simply from the fact that the dedication of the temple of the former was on the Ides of this month.

[2] Ovid, *Fasti*, 6. 59 foll. ; Mommsen, *Chron.* 218.

[3] The etymology was defended by Roscher in Fleckeisen's *Jahrbuch* for 1875, and in his *Iuno und Hera*, p. 105.

that the derivation of June from Juno must be left doubtful ; and if so, certainly that of May from Maia.   In the case of this month, not only does the natural meaning of mensis Maius suit well as following the mensis Aprilis, but there is no cult of a deity Maia which is found throughout the month.

Any one who reads the passage of Macrobius with some knowledge of the Roman theological system will hardly fail to conclude that Maia is only a priestly *indigitation* of another deity, and that the name thus invented was simply taken from the name of the month as explained above.   This deity was more generally known, as Macrobius implies, by the name Bona Dea, and her temple was dedicated on the Kalends of May.

It is difficult to characterize the position of the month of May in the religious calendar.   It was to some extent no doubt a month of purification.   At the *Lemuria* the house was purified of hostile ghosts ; the curious ceremony of the Argei on the Ides is called by Plutarch the greatest of the purifications ; and at the end of the month took place the *lustratio* of the growing crops.   We note too that it was considered ill-omened to marry in May, as it still is in many parts of Europe.   The agricultural operations of the month were not of a marked character.   Much work had indeed to be done in oliveyards and vineyards ; some crops had to be hoed and cleaned, and the hay-harvest probably began in the latter part of the month.   In the main it was a time of somewhat anxious expectation and preparation for the harvest to follow; and this falls in fairly well with the general character of its religious rites.

KAL. MAI. (MAY 1.) F.

LAR[IBUS].   (VEN.)   L——. (ESQ.)

This was the day on which, according to Ovid [1], an altar and ' parva signa ' had been erected to the Lares praestites. They were originally of great antiquity, but had fallen into decay in Ovid's time :

> Bina gemellorum *quaerebam* signa deorum,
> Viribus annosae facta caduca morae [2].

---

[1] *Fasti*, 5. 129 foll.   For the doubtful reading *Curibus* in 131 see Peter, ad loc. ; Preller-Jordan, ii. 114.

[2] *Fasti*, 5. 143 ; Plutarch, *Quaest. Rom.* 51.

Ovid himself had apparently not seen the *signa*, though he looked
for them ; and no doubt he took from Varro the description he
gives. They had the figure of a dog at their feet[1], and, according
to Plutarch, were clothed in dogs' skins. Both Ovid and Plutarch
explained the dog as symbolizing their watch over the city ;
though Plutarch, following, as he says, certain Romans, preferred
to think of them rather as evil demons searching out and
punishing guilt like dogs. The mention of the skins is very
curious, and we can hardly separate it from the numerous
other instances in which the images of deities are known
to have been clothed in the skins of victims sacrificed to them[2].
We may indeed fairly conclude that the Lares were chthonic
deities, and as such were originally appeased, like Hekate in
Greece[3], by the sacrifice of dogs. We have already had one
example of the dog used as a victim[4]. Two others are
mentioned by Plutarch[5] ; in one case the deity was the
obscure Genita Mana, and in the other the unknown god of
the Lupercalia, both of which belong in all probability to the
same stratum of Italian religious antiquity as the Lares.
Whether we should go further, and infer from the use of the
skins that the Lares were originally worshipped in the form of
dogs[6], is a question I must leave undecided ; the evidence
is very scanty. There is no trace of any connexion with the
dog in the cult of the Lares domestici[7], or Compitales.

This is also the traditional day of the dedication of a temple
to the Bona Dea, on the slopes of the Aventine, under a big
sacred rock. It is thus described by Ovid[8] :

> Est moles nativa loco. Res nomina fecit :
> Appellant Saxum. Pars bona montis ea est.
> Huic Remus institerat frustra, quo tempore fratri
> Prima Palatinae signa dedistis aves.

---

[1] This appears on coins of the gens Caesia : Cohen, *Méd. Cons.* pl. viii.
Wissowa, in *Myth. Lex.*, s.v. Lares, gives a cut of the coin, on which the
Lares are represented sitting with a dog between them. See note at the
end of this work (Note B) on the further interpretation of these coins.

[2] See Robertson Smith, *Religion of the Semites*, 414 foll.

[3] Farnell, *Cults*, ii. 515. Hekate was certainly a deity of the earth. Cf.
Plut. *Q. R.* 68.   [4] See on Robigalia, April 25.

[5] *Quaest. Rom.* 52 and 111 ; cf. *Romulus* 21.

[6] So Jevons, *Roman Questions*, Introduction, xli.

[7] De-Marchi, *La Religione nella vita domestica*, 48. Wissowa (*Myth. Lex*, s.v.
Lares, p. 1872) prefers the old interpretation, much as Plutarch gives it.

[8] *Fasti*, 5. 149 foll.

Templa Patres illic oculos exosa viriles
    Leniter acclivi constituere iugo.
Dedicat haec veteris Clausorum nominis heres,
    Virgineo nullum corpore passa virum.
Livia restituit, ne non imitata maritum
    Esset et ex omni parte secuta virum.

The allusion to Remus fixes the site on the Aventine.   The
date is uncertain[1]; so too the alleged foundation by Claudia,
which may be only a reflection from the story of the part
played by a Claudia in the introduction of the *Magna Mater
Idaea* to Rome[2].   The temple, as Ovid says, was restored
by Livia, in accordance with the policy of her husband, also
at an unknown date.

Of the cult belonging to this temple we have certain traces,
which also help us to some vague conception of the nature
of the deity.   It should be observed that though in one
essential particular, viz. the exclusion of men, this cult was
similar to that of December, it must have been quite distinct
from it, as the latter took place, not in a temple, but in the
house of a magistrate *cum imperio*[3].

1. The temple was cared for, and the cult celebrated, by
women only[4].   There was an old story that Hercules, when
driving the cattle of Geryon, asked for water by the cave
of Cacus of the women celebrating the festival of the goddess,
and was refused, because the women's festival was going
on, and men were not allowed to use their drinking-vessels;
and that this led to the corresponding exclusion of women from
the worship of Hercules[5].   The myth obviously arose out
of the practice.   The exclusion of men points to the earth-

___

[1] Aust, *De Aedibus sacris*, p. 27.   It was apparently before 123 B.C., when
a Vestal Virgin, Licinia, added an *aedicula*, *pulvinar*, and *ara* to it (Cic. *de
Domo*, 136).

[2] Wissowa, in Pauly's *Real-Encyclopädie*, s. v. Bona Dea, 690.   See above,
p. 69.

[3] See below, under Dec. 3.   There can be hardly a doubt that this
December rite was the one famous for the *sacrilegium* of Clodius in 62 B. C.,
though Prof. Beesly rashly assumed the contrary in his essay on Clodius
(*Catiline, Clodius, and Tiberius*, p. 45 note).   Plutarch, *Cic.* 19 and 20; Dio
Cass. 37. 35.

[4] Ovid, l. c. 'oculos exosa viriles.'   Cp. *Ars Amat.* 3. 637.   On this and
other points in the cult see R. Peter in *Myth. Lex.*, and Wissowa, l. c.   The
latter seems to refer most of them to the December rite; but Ovid and
Macrobius expressly connect them with the *temple*.   Macr. 1. 12. 25 foll.

[5] Propert. 4. 9; Macr. 1. 12. 28.

nature of the Bona Dea ; the same was the case in the worship of the Athenian Demeter Thesmophoros. The earth seems always to be spiritualized as feminine even among savage peoples [1], and the reason of the exclusion of men is not difficult to conjecture, just as the exclusion of women from the worship of Hercules is explained by the fact that Hercules represents the male principle in the ancient Roman religion [2].

2. Macrobius [3] tells us that wine could not be brought into the temple *suo nomine,* but only under the name of milk, and that the vase in which it was carried was called *mellarium,* i.e. a vase for honey. A legend grew up to account for the custom, to which we shall refer again, that Faunus had beaten his daughter Fauna (i.e. Bona Dea) with a rod of myrtle because she would not yield to his incestuous love or drink the wine he pressed on her [4]. This may indicate a survival from the time when the herdsman used no wine in sacred rites, but milk and honey only ; Pliny tells us of such a time [5], and his evidence is confirmed by the poets. In any case milk would be the appropriate offering to the Earth-mother, and it is hard to see why it should have been changed to wine, unless it were that life in the city and Greek influence altered the character both of the Bona Dea and her worshippers. The really rustic deities had milk offered them, e. g. Silvanus, Pales, and Ceres. The general inference from this survival is that the Bona Dea was originally of the same nature with these deities, but lost her rusticity when she became part of an organized city worship.

3. Myrtle was not allowed in this temple ; hence the myth that Faunus beat his daughter with a myrtle rod [6]. But could

---

[1] Tylor, *Primitive Culture,* ii. 245 foll.

[2] See below, p. 143. *Lex. Myth.* s. v. Hercules, 2258.

[3] Macr. l. c. Plutarch also knew of this (*Quaest. Rom.* 20).

[4] Otherwise in Lactantius, 1. 22. 11, and Arnob. 5. 18, where Fauna is said to have been beaten because she drank wine ; no doubt a later version. Lactantius quotes Sext. Clodius, a contemporary of Cicero.

[5] *H. N.* 14. 88. See above on feriae Latinae, p. 97. Virg. *Ecl.* 5. 66; *Georg.* 1. 344 ; *Aen.* 5. 77. In the last passage milk is offered to the *inferiae* of Anchises : we may note the similarity of the cult of Earth-deities and of the dead.

[6] Plut. *Q. R.* 20 ; Macrob. l. c. ; Lactant. l. c. The myth has been explained as Greek (Wissowa, in Pauly, 688), but its peculiar feature, the whipping, could hardly have become attached to a Roman cult unless there were something in the cult to attach it to, or unless the cult itself were

the exclusion of myrtle by itself have suggested the beating?
Dr. Mannhardt answers in the negative, and conjectures that
there must have been some kind of beating in the cult itself,
which gave rise to the story[1]. Dr. Mannhardt never made
a conjecture without a large collection of facts on which to base
it; and here he depends upon a number of instances from
Greece and Northern Europe, in which man or woman, or
some object such as the image of a deity, is whipped with rods,
nettles, strips of leather, &c., in order, as it would seem,
to produce fertility and drive away hostile influences. We
shall see the same peculiarity occurring at the Lupercalia in
February[2], where its object and meaning are almost beyond
doubt. Many of these practices occur, it is worth noting,
on May-day. If the Bona Dea was a representative in any
sense of the fertility of women, as well as of the fructifying
powers of the earth—and the two ideas seem naturally to
have run together in the primitive mind—we may provisionally
accept Dr. Mannhardt's ingenious suggestion. If it be objected
that as myrtle was excluded from the cult it could not have
been used therein for the purpose of whipping, the answer
is simply that as being invested with some mysterious power
it was tabooed from ordinary use, but, like certain kinds of
victims, was introduced on special and momentous occasions.

4. The temple was a kind of *herbarium* in which herbs were
kept with healing properties[3]. A group of interesting inscriptions shows that the Bona Dea did not confine her healing
powers to cases of women, but cured the ailments of both
sexes[4]. This attribute of the goddess is borne out by the
presence of snakes in her temple, the usual symbol of the
medicinal art, and at the same time appropriate to the Bona
Dea as an Earth-goddess[5]. It is possible that this feature
is a Greek importation; but on the whole I see no reason why

---

borrowed from the Greek. That the latter was the case it is impossible
to prove; and I prefer to believe that both cult and myth were Roman.

[1] *Mythologische Forschungen*, 115 foll. Cp. Frazer, *Golden Bough*, ii. 213 foll.

[2] Below, p. 320. See also on July 7 (Nonae Caprotinae).

[3] Macrob. l. c. ' Quidam Medeam putant, quod in aede eius omne genus
herbarum sit ex quibus antistites dant plerumque medicinas.'

[4] *C. I. L.* vi. 54 foll.

[5] This no doubt gave rise to the myth that Faunus 'coisse cum filia'
in the form of a snake. Here again the myth may possibly be Greek,
but we have no right to deny that it may have had a Roman basis.

the female ministrants of the temple should not have exercised such healing powers, or have sold or given herbs at request, even at a very early period. No doubt Greek medicinal learning became associated with it, but that the knowledge of simples was indigenous in Italy we have abundant proof [1]; and that it should have been connected with no cult of a deity until Aesculapius was introduced from Greece, is most improbable.

5. The sacrifice mentioned is that of a *porca* [2]. The pig is also the victim in the worship of Ceres, of Juno Lucina [3] (as alternative for a lamb), and as a piacular sacrifice in the ritual of the deity of the Fratres Arvales (Dea Dia); it seems in fact, as in Greece, to be appropriate to deities of the earth and of women. There is no reason to suppose that wherever it is found it had a Greek origin; even in the cult of Ceres, which, as we saw, became early overlaid with Greek practice [4], the pig may have been the victim before that change took place. But it is a singular fact that in the worship of the Bona Dea, either at the temple of the Aventine, or in the December rite—more probably perhaps in the latter—the victim was called by a name which looks suspiciously Greek, viz. *Damium* [5]. It seems that there was a deity Damia who was worshipped here and there in Greece, and also in Southern Italy, e. g. at Tarentum, where she had a festival called Dameia [6]. It looks as if this Greek deity had at one time migrated from Tarentum to Rome, and become engrafted upon the indigenous Bona Dea ; for we are expressly told that Damia was identical with the Bona Dea, and that the priestess of the latter was called *Damiatrix* [7]. Much has been written about these very obscure names, without any very definite result; but it seems to be

Snakes were kept in great numbers both in temples and houses in Italy (Preller-Jordan, i. 87, 385).

[1] Plin. *H. N.* 29 *passim*, especially 14, &c., where Cato is quoted as detesting the new Greek art, and urging his son to stick to the old simples ; some of which, with their absurd charms, are given in Cato, *R. R.* 156 foll.　　　　　　　　　　　　　[2] Macrob. l. c. ; Juv. *Sat.* 2. 86.

[3] Marq. 173. Gilbert (*Gesch. und Topogr.* ii. 159, note) has some impossible combinations on this subject, and concludes that the Bona Dea was a moon-goddess.　　　　　　　　　　　[4] See above, p. 72 foll.

[5] Paulus, 68 'Damium sacrificium, quod fiebat in operto in honorem Bonae deae, . . . dea quoque ipsa Damia et sacerdos eius damiatrix appellabatur.'

[6] R. Peter in *Myth. Lex.*, s. v. Damia ; Wissowa, l. c.

[7] Paulus, l. c.

generally agreed that the form of the word *damiatrix* indicates a high antiquity for the Graecized form of the cult, and may indeed possibly suggest an Italian origin for the whole group of names.   In this uncertainty conjectures are almost useless.

We have seen enough of the cult to gain some idea of the nature of this mysterious deity, whose real name was not known, even if she had one[1].   We need not identify her with Vesta, as some have done[2], nor with Juno Lucina, nor with any other female deity of the class to which she seems to have belonged.   She must at one time have been, whatever she afterwards became, a protective deity of the female sex, the Earth-mother[3], a kindly and helpful, but shy and unknowable deity of fertility.   The name Bona Dea is probably to be regarded as one indigitation of the Earth-spirit known by a variety of other names and appearing in a number of different phases.   There is indeed a remarkable indefiniteness about the Italian female deities of this class ; they never gained what we may call complete specific distinctness, but are rather half-formed species developed from a common type.   They form, in fact, an excellent illustration of the nature of that earliest stratum of Roman religious belief which has been called pan-daemonism—a belief in a world of spiritual powers not yet grown into the forms of individual deities, but ready at any moment, under influences either native or foreign, to take a more definite shape.

VII. Id. Mai. (May 9).   N.
LEM[VRIA].   (ven. maff.)

V. Id. Mai. (May 11).   N.
LEM[VRIA].   (tusc. ven. maff.)

III. Id. Mai. (May 13).   N.
LEM[VRIA].   (tusc. ven. maff.)

The word Lemuria indicates clearly enough some kind of worship of the dead ; but we know of no such *public* cult on

[1] Lactantius, 1. 22 ; Serv. *Aen.* 8. 314.
[2] Preuner, *Hestia-Vesta*, 407 foll.   For Lucina, Gilbert, l. c.
[3] The combination of the idea of female fecundity with that of the earth is of course common enough.   Here is a good example from Abyssinia : 'She (Atetie) is the goddess of fecundity, and women are her

these three days except from the calendars. What Ovid describes as taking place at this time is a private and domestic rite performed by the head of the household[1]; and Ovid is our only informant in regard to details. In historical times the public festival of the dead was that of the *dies parentales* in February, ending with the Feralia on the 21st. How, then, is it that the three days of the Lemuria appear in those large letters in the ancient calendars, which, as we have seen[2], indicate the public festivals of the religious system of the Republic? There is no certain answer to this question. We can but guess that the Lemuria was at one time, like the Feralia, a public festival, but descended from a more ancient deposit of superstition which in historical times was buried deep beneath the civilization of a developed city life[3]. Ovid himself implies that the Lemuria was an older festival than the Feralia[4], and we may suppose him to be following Varro as a guide. And if we compare his account of the grotesque domestic rites of the Lemuria with those of February, which were of a systematic, cheerful, and even beautiful character, we may feel fairly sure that the latter represents the organized life of a city state, the former the ideas of an age when life was wilder and less secure, and the fear of the dead and of demons generally was a powerful factor in the minds of the people. If we may argue from Ovid's account, to be described directly, it is not impossible that the Lemuria may have been one of those periodical expulsions of demons of which Mr. Frazer has told us so much in his *Golden Bough*[5], and which are performed on behalf of the community as well as in the domestic circle amongst savage peoples. It is noticeable that the offering of food to the demons is a feature common to these practices, and that it also appears in those described by Ovid.

The difference of character in the two Roman festivals of the dead is perhaps also indicated by the fact that the days of the Lemuria are marked in the calendars with the letter N,

---

principal votaries; but, as she can also make the earth prolific, offerings are made to her for that purpose' (Macdonald, *Religion and Myth*, p. 42).

[1] *Fasti*, 5. 421 foll.   [2] See Introduction, p. 15.

[3] Huschke (*Röm. Jahr*, 17) tried to prove that the Lemuria was the 'Todtenfest' of the Sabine city, the Feralia that of the Latin; but his arguments have convinced no one.   [4] *Fasti*, 5. 423.

[5] *G. B.* ii. 157 foll.; Macdonald, *Religion and Myth*, ch. vi.

while the Feralia is marked F or FP[1]. This may perhaps
point to two different views of the attitude of the dead to the
living, affecting the character of the festival days; they are
friendly or hostile, as they have been buried with due rites
and carefully looked after, or as they have failed of these dues
and are consequently angry and jealous[2]. The latter of these
attitudes is more in keeping with the notions of uncivilized
man, and of a life not as yet wholly brought under the influence of the civilization of the city-state. To be more certain,
however, on this point, we must try and discover the real
meaning of the word *lemur*.

The definition given by Porphyrio is 'Umbras vagantes
hominum ante diem mortuorum atque ideo metuendas[3].'
Nonius has the following: 'Lemures larvae nocturnae et terrifi-
cationes imaginum et bestiarum[4].' From these passages it
would seem that *lemures* and *larvae* mean much the same
thing; on the other hand Appuleius[5] implies that *lemures* is
a general word for spirits after they have left the body, while
those that haunt houses are especially called *larvae*. But on a
question of this kind, the philosophical and uncritical Appuleius
is not to be weighed as an authority against either Nonius or
Porphyrio, who may quite possibly be here representing the
learning of the Augustan age; and a perusal of the whole of
his passage will show that he is simply trying to classify ghosts
by the light of his own imagination. Judging from the hints
of the two other scholars, we may perhaps conclude that *lemures*
and *larvae* are to be distinguished as hostile ghosts from *manes,*
the good people (as the word is generally explained), i. e. those
duly buried in the city of the dead, and whom their living
descendants have no need to fear so long as they pay them
their due rites at the proper seasons as members of the family.
And this conclusion is confirmed by the curious etymology of
Ovid[6], reproduced by Porphyrio, deriving Lemuria from Remus,

[1] Introduction, p. 10.
[2] Tylor, *Prim. Cult.* ii. 24. The friendly attitude is well illustrated in
F. de Coulanges' *La Cité antique*, ch. ii.   [3] On Hor. *Ep.* 2. 2. 209.
[4] Non. p. 135. Cp. Festus, s. v. faba: ' Lemuralibus iacitur larvis,' i. e.
' the bean is thrown to *larvae* at the Lemuralia.' Serv. *Aen.* 3. 63.
[5] *de Genio Socratis*, 15. The passage is interesting, but historically
worthless, as is that of Martianus Capella, 2. 162.
[6] *Fasti,* 5. 451 foll.; Porph. l.c. Remus, as one dead before his time,
would not lie quiet: ' Umbra cruenta Remi visa est adsistere lecto,' &c.

whose violent death was supposed to have been expiated by the institution of the festival. The difficulty is to see why, if the *lemures* were unburied, evil, or hostile spirits, a special festival of three days should have been necessary to appease or quiet them ; and I can only account for this by supposing that such spirits were especially numerous in an age of un-civilized life and constant war and violence, and that they formed a large part of the whole world of evil demons whose expulsion was periodically demanded. It may have been the case that at this particular time in May, when the days were *nefasti* and marriages were ill-omened, these spirits became particularly restless and needed to be laid.

Such an explanation as this of the Lemuria is on the whole preferable to that which would regard it as the original Roman festival of *all* the dead ; for there is now abundant evidence that even in the earliest ages of Italian life the practice of orderly burial in necropoleis was universal [1], and this is a practice that seems inconsistent with a general belief in the dead as hostile and haunting spirits.

The following is Ovid's description of the way in which the ghosts were laid at the Lemuria by the father of a family. At midnight he rises, and with bare feet [2] and washed hands, making a peculiar sign with his fingers and thumbs to keep off the ghosts, he walks through the house. He has black beans in his mouth, and these he spits out as he walks, looking the other way, and saying, 'With these I redeem me and mine.' Nine times he says this without looking round ; then come the ghosts behind him, and gather up the beans unseen. He proceeds to wash again and to make a noise with brass vessels ; and after nine times repeating the form-ula 'manes [3] exite paterni,' he at last looks round, and the ceremony is over.

---

[1] See e. g. Von Duhn's paper on Italian excavations, translated in the *Journal of Hellenic Studies* for 1897.

[2] 'Habent vincula nulla pedes' (*Fasti*, 5. 432). In performing sacred rites a man must be free ; e. g. the Flamen Dialis might not wear a ring, or any-thing binding, and a fettered prisoner had to be loosed in his house (Plut. Q R. 111). Cp. Numa in his interview with Faunus (Ov. *Fasti*, 4. 658), ' Nec digitis annulus ullus inest.' Serv. *Aen.* 4. 518 ; Hor. *Sat.* 1. 8. 24.

[3] *Manes* must be here used, either loosely by the poet, or euphemistically by the house-father.

The only point in this quaint bit of ritual which need detain us is the use of beans. We have had bean-straw used at the Parilia, and we shall find that beans were also used at the festival of the dead in February. Assuredly it is not easy to see what could have made them into such valuable 'medicine.' Beans were not a newly discovered vegetable. Their exclusion from the rites of Demeter must have been of great antiquity, and the notions of the Pythagoreans about them were probably based on very ancient popular superstitions[1]. No one, as far as I know, has as yet successfully solved the problem why beans had so strange a religious character about them[2]; they probably were an ancient symbol of fertility, but it is impossible now to discover how or why the ideas grouped themselves around them, which we so constantly find both in Greece and Italy. If we ask why the ghosts picked them up, or were supposed to do so, there is some reason for believing that by eating them they might possibly hope to get a new lease of life[3]. Whatever was the real basis of the superstition, it was a widely spread one, and ramified in more than one direction; the Roman priest of Jupiter, for example, might not touch beans nor even mention them[4]. In his case the taboo was no doubt very old, but might have grown out of some such practice as that just described, all things ill-omened and mysterious being carefully kept out of his reach.

The days from May 7 to 14 were occupied by the Vestal Virgins in preparing the *mola salsa*, or sacred salt-cake, for use at the Vestalia in June, on the Ides of September, and at the Lupercalia[5]. This was made from the first ears of standing corn in

---

[1] It is curious to find them used for the very same purpose of ghost-ridding as far away as Japan (Frazer, *Golden Bough*, ii. 176). For their antiquity as food, Hehn, *Kulturpflanzen*, 459; Schrader, *Sprachvergleichung*, 362.

[2] A. Lang, *Myth*, &c., ii. 265; Jevons, *Roman Questions*, Introd. p. lxxxvi; O. Crusius. *Rhein. Mus.* xxxix. 164 foll.; and especially Lobeck, *Aglaoph.* 251 foll. For superstitions of a similar kind attached to the mandrake and other plants see Sir T. Browne's *Vulgar Errors*, bk. ii. ch. 6; Rhys, *Celtic Mythology*, p. 356 (the berries of the rowan).

[3] There was a notion that beans sown in a manure-heap produced men. Cp. Plin. *H. N.* 18. 118 'quoniam mortuorum animae sint in ea.'

[4] Gell. 10. 15. 2 (from Fabius Pictor).

[5] Serv. *Ecl.* 8. 82; Marq. 343 note. Mannhardt, *A. W. F.* 269, attempts an explanation of the difficulty arising here from the fact that in historical times the calendar was some weeks in advance of the seasons, but without much success.

a primitive fashion by the three senior Vestals, and is no doubt, like most of their ritual, a relic of the domestic functions of the daughters of the family. But we must postpone further consideration of the Vestals and their duties till we come to the Vestalia in June.

ID. MAI. (MAY 15). NP.

FER[IAE] IOVI. MERCUR[IO] MAIAE. (VENUS [1].)
MAIAE AD CIRC[UM] M[AXIMUM]. (CAER.) MERC[URIO]. (TUSC.)

The very curious rite which took place on this day is not mentioned in the calendars ; it belonged to those which, like the Paganalia, were *publica* indeed and *pro populo*, but represented the people as divided in certain groups rather than the State as a whole [2]. But its obvious antiquity, and the interesting questions which arise out of it, tempt me to treat it in detail, at the risk of becoming tedious.

I have already mentioned [3] that there was a procession in March, as we infer from the *sacra Argeorum* quoted by Varro, which went round the *sacella Argeorum,* or twenty-four chapels situated in the four Servian regions of the city [4]. What was done at these *sacella* we do not know ; the procession and its doings had become so obscure in Ovid's time that he could dispose of it in two lines of his *Fasti*, and express a doubt as to whether it took place on one day or two [5]. Nor do we know what the *sacella* really were. The best conjecture is that of Jordan, who has brought some evidence together to show that they were small chapels or sacred places where holy things

[1] This note is wrongly entered in the Fasti Venusini, under May 16.

[2] Festus, 245, s. v. Publica sacra. Cp. Mommsen, *Staatsrecht*, iii. 123. Festus distinguishes *pagi, montes, sacella*, of which the festivals would seem to be the Paganalia, Septimontium, and sacra Argeorum, respectively.

[3] See under March 17. We arrive at the procession by comparing the Varronian extracts from the sacra Argeorum (*L. L.* 545) with Gellius, 10. 15. 30, and Ovid, *Fasti*, 3. 791. See a restoration of the itinerary of the procession in Jordan, *Topogr.* ii. 603.

[4] Sacella in Varro (*L. L.* 545) ; sacraria, ib. 548 ; Argea in Festus, 334, where the word seems to be an adjective ; Argei in Liv. 1. 24 ' loca sacris faciendis, quae Argeos pontifices vocant.' The number depends on the reading of Varro, 7. 44, xxiv or xxvii ; Jordan decided for xxiv : but see Mommsen, *Staatsrecht*, iii. 123.

[5] *Fasti*, 3. 791.

were deposited until the time came round for them to be used in some religious ceremony[1].

But on May 15 there was another rite in which the word *Argei* plays a prominent part ; and here the details have in part at least survived.   The *Argei* in this case are not chapels, but a number of puppets or bundles of rushes, resembling (as Dionysius has recorded) men bound hand and foot, which were taken down to the *pons sublicius* by the Pontifices and magistrates, and cast into the river by the Vestal Virgins[2]. The Flaminica Dialis, the priestess of Jupiter, was present at the ceremony in mourning.   The number of the puppets was probably the same as that of the *sacella* of the same name[3].

Explanations of these rites were invented by Roman scholars. The *sacella* were the graves of Greeks who had come to Italy with Hercules ; and the puppets represented the followers of Hercules who had died on their journey and were to return home as it were by proxy[4].   Apart from the theories of the learned, it was the fact that the common people at Rome believed the puppets to be substitutes for old men, who at one time used to be thrown into the Tiber as victims.   *Sexagenarios de ponte* was a well-known proverb which in Cicero's time was explained by supposing that the bridges alluded to were those over which the voters passed in the Comitia[5] ; but this view may at once be put aside.   Those bridges were certainly a comparatively late invention, while the proverb was of remote antiquity.

But, given the details of the rite, and the popular belief about the old men as victims, what explanation can we hope to arrive at ?   We may freely admit that no satisfactory etymology of the word *Argei* is forthcoming ; but this is perhaps, in

---

[1] Jordan, *Topogr.* ii. 271 foll.

[2] Dionysius, 1. 38 ; Ovid, *Fasti*, 5. 621 foll. ; Festus, p. 334, s. v. Sexagenarii ; Plutarch, *Q. R.* 32 and 86.

[3] Dionysius says there were thirty ; he had probably seen the ceremony, but may have only made a rough guess at the number or have thought of the thirty Curiae.   Ovid writes of two : 'Falcifero libata seni duo corpora gentis Mittite,' &c.   (Jordan proposed to read 'senilia' for 'seni duo.')

[4] Festus, 334.

[5] Festus, l. c. ; Cicero, *pro Roscio Amerino*, 35. 100.   *Sexagenarios de ponte* was apparently an old saying (cp. 'depontani,' Festus, 75) ; the earliest notice we have of it, which comes from the poet Afranius, seems to connect it with the pons sublicius.

a negative sense, an advantage to our inquiry [1]. The Romans derived it from the Greek 'Αργεῖοι ; and to this etymology Mommsen is now disposed to return. The writer of the article 'Argei' in the *Mythological Lexicon* derived it from *varka-s =* 'wolf'; others have believed it to come from a root *arg =* 'white' or 'shining,' and though the termination *eus* is hardly a Latin one, it may be that this is the true basis of the word [2].

Instead of prejudging the case by fanciful etymologies, or by attempting to decide the question whether the Romans ever practised the rites of human sacrifice, we will take the leading features of the ceremony, and see in what direction they may on the whole direct us. That done, it may be possible to sum up the debate, though a final and decisive verdict is not to be expected.

The features which demand attention are (1) the processional character of the rites ; (2) the presence of the Pontifices and the Vestals ; (3) the mourning of the Flaminica Dialis ; (4) the rush-puppets and their immersion in the Tiber.

1. We can hardly doubt that there was a procession to the *pons sublicius*, though the fact is not expressly stated. We are tempted to believe that it visited each *sacellum*, and there found, or possibly made, the puppet (*simulacrum*), which thus represented the district of which the *sacellum* was the sacred centre ; and that it then proceeded, bearing the puppets, probably by the Forum and Vicus Tuscus to the bridge [3]. Now if this feature can help us at all—if we accept the connexion of the March and May ceremonies and their processional character—it must point in the direction of the purification of land or city, on the analogy of other Italian ceremonies of the same kind.

---

[1] 'The etymology will of course explain a word, but only if it happens to be right ; the history of the word is a surer guide' (Skeat). In this case we have not even the history.

[2] See Schwegler, i 383. note ; Marq. 183. Mommsen (*Staatsrecht*, iii. 123) reverts to the opinion that Argei is simply 'Αργεῖοι, and preserves a reminiscence of Greek captives. Nettleship, in his *Notes in Latin Lexicography*, p. 271, is inclined to connect the word with 'arcere,' in the sense of confining prisoners. More fanciful developments in a paper by O. Keller, in Fleckeisen's *Jahrbuch*, cxxxiii. 845 foll.

[3] The puppets may have been made in March, and then hung in the sacella till May : so Jordan, *Topogr.* l. c. The writer in *Myth. Lex.* thinks that human victims were originally kept in these sacella, for whom the puppets were surrogates.

At the end of this month took place the Ambarvalia, when the priests went round the land with prayer and sacrifice to ensure the good growth of the crops; and we have a remarkable instance of the same kind of practice in the celebrated inscription of Iguvium. Not only each city, but each *pagus*, and even each farmer, duly purified his land in some such way, cleansing it from the powers of evil and sterility, while at the same time the boundaries were renewed in the memories of all concerned. Bearing this in mind, and also the season of the year, we may fairly guess that the Argean processions had some relation to agriculture, and to the welfare of the precarious stock of wealth of an agricultural community.

2. *The presence of the Pontifices and Vestals.*—The former would be present, partly as the representative sacred college of the united city [1], partly as having under their special care the sacred bridge from which the puppets were thrown. Whether or no the word *pontifex* be directly derived from *pons* [2], it is certain that the ancient bridge, with its strong religious associations, was under their care, and that the river was an object of their constant liturgical attention [3]. It has been suggested that the whole ceremony was one of bridge-worship [4]; but this view, as we shall see, will hardly explain all the facts. It leaves the March rites unexplained, and also the presence of the Vestals; nor does it seem to suit the season of the year.

The presence of the Vestals is more significant; and it was they, as it seems, who performed the act of throwing the puppets from the bridge [5]. In all the public duties performed by them (as we shall see more fully in dealing with the Vestalia [6]) a reference can be traced to one leading idea, viz. that the food and nourishment of the State, of which the sacred fire was the symbol, depended for its maintenance on

[1] There is an interesting modern parallel in Mannhardt, *A. W. F.* 178.

[2] Varro, *L. L.* 5. 83, and Jordan, *Topogr.* i. 398. The general opinion seems now to favour the view that there was an original connexion between the *pontifices* and the *pons sublicius.*

[3] Varro, *L. L.* 5. 83; Dionys. 2. 73, 3. 45.

[4] This was the suggestion of Mr. Frazer in a note in the *Journal of Philology,* vol. xiv. p. 156. The late Prof. Nettleship once expressed this view to me.

[5] Paulus, p. 15 'per Virgines Vestales'; Ovid, *Fasti,* 5. 621.

[6] See below, p. 149.

the accurate performance of these duties. We have just seen that they spent the seven days preceding the Ides of May in preparing their sacred cakes from the first ripening ears of corn. We shall see them using these cakes in June, September, and at the Lupercalia. At the Parilia and the Fordicidia they also take a prominent part, both of them festivals relating to the fruitfulness of herds and flocks; so also at the harvest festivals in August of Ops Consiva and Consus. And we can hardly suppose that their presence at the rite under discussion should have a different significance from that of their public service on all other occasions. Even if we had no other evidence to go upon, we might on the facts just adduced base a fair inference that this ceremony too had some relation to the processes and perils awaiting the ripening crops.

3. The Flaminica Dialis had on this day to lay aside her usual bridal dress, and to appear in mourning[1]. The same rule was laid down for her during the 'moving' of the *ancilia* in March, and during the Vestalia up to the completion of the purification of the temple of Vesta. It is not easy to see what the meaning of this rule may have been. On the other two occasions there is nothing to lead us to suppose that it was some such terrible rite as human sacrifice which caused the change of costume; we need not therefore suppose that it was so on May 15. But if all three occasions are times of purification and the averting of evil influences: if they each mark the conclusion of an old season, and the necessity of great care in entering on a new one, we can better understand it. This was the case, as we saw, when in March the Salii were pervading the city, and it was so also at the Vestalia, which was preparatory to the ingathering of the crops. Some such critical moment, I think, the day we are discussing must also have been. Some light may be thrown on this aspect of the question by practices which have been collected by Dr. Mannhardt from Northern Europe[2], some of which still

---

[1] Plut. *Quaest. Rom.* 86; Gell. 10. 15; Marq. 318. Her usual head-dress was the *flammeum*, or bride's veil. No mention is made of the Flamen her husband; the prominence of women in all these rites is noticeable.

[2] *Baumkultus*, 155, 411, 416. The cult of Adonis has some features like that of the Argei: e.g. the puppet, the immersion in water and the mourning (see *Lex.* s.v. Adonis, p. 73; Mannhardt, *A. W. F.* 276).

survive. I will give a single instance from Russia. At Murom on June 29 a figure of straw, dressed in female clothing, is laid on a bier and carried to the edge of a lake or river; it is eventually torn up and thrown into the river, while the spectators hide their faces and behave as though they bewailed the death of Kostroma. In another district on the same day an old man carried out of the town a puppet representing the spring, and was followed by the *women* singing mournful songs and expressing by their gestures grief and despair.

4. *The Puppets and their immersion in the Tiber.*—There are two possible explanations of this curious practice.

(1) The puppets were substitutes for human victims, and probably for old men. The evidence for this view is—first, the Roman tradition expressed in the saying *scxagenarios de ponte*[1], and supported by the fact that the puppets appeared, to Dionysius at least, like men bound hand and foot[2]; secondly, the fact that human sacrifice was not entirely unknown at Rome, though there is no trace of any such custom regularly recurring. We may allow that Italy could not have been entirely free from a practice which existed even in Greece, and also that the habit of substituting some object for the original victim is common and well attested in religious history; but whether either the Argei, or the *oscilla* or *maniae*, which are often compared with the Argei, really had this origin, may well indeed be doubted[3]. Thirdly, there is evidence that not only human sacrifice, but the sacrifice of old men, was by no means unknown in primitive times. Passing over the general evidence as to human sacrifice, we know that the old and weak

[1] i.e. 'old men must go over the bridge.' See Cic. *pro Roscio Amerino*, 35, where the old edition of Osenbrüggen has a useful note. Also Varro, apud Lactant. *Inst.* 1. 21. 6. Ovid alludes to the proverb (5. 623 foll.) 'Corpora post decies senos qui credidit annos Missa neci, sceleris crimine damnat avos.'

[2] Dionys. 1. 38. But he may have been deceived simply by the appearance of the bindings of the sheaves or bundles, especially if he had been told beforehand of the proverb.

[3] The best known instances of human sacrifice at Rome are collected in a note to Merivale's *History* (vol. iii. 35); and by Sachse, *Die Argeer*, p. 17. O. Müller thought that it came to Rome from Etruria (*Etrusker*, ii. 20). For Greece, see Hermann, *Griech. Alt.* ii. sec. 27; Strabo. 10. 8. See also some valuable remarks in Tylor, *Prim. Cult.* ii. 362, on substitution in sacrifice.

were sometimes put to death[1]. Being of no further use in the struggle for existence, they were got rid of in various ways— an act perhaps not so much of cruelty as of kindness, and under certain circumstances not incompatible with filial piety[2]. The chief objections to this explanation are—first, that it obliges us to ascribe to the early Romans a habit which seems quite incompatible with their well-known respect for old age and their horror of parricide ; secondly, that it does not explain why a practice, which can hardly have ever been a regularly recurring one, should have passed into a yearly ceremony[3].

(2) The rite was of a dramatic rather than a sacrificial character[4], and belongs to a class of which we have numerous examples both from Greek, Teutonic, and Slavonic peoples. In Greece, or rather in Egypt, we have the cult of Adonis, in which a puppet is immersed in the water amid wailings and lamentations. In Greece proper semi-dramatic rites are found at Chaeronea and Athens[5], though somewhat different in character to those of the Argei and Adonis. Tacitus describes the immersion in water of the image of the German goddess Nerthus[6]. But most significant are the many examples, of which Mannhardt formed an ample collection, in which puppets are found, made as a rule of straw, carried along in procession and thrown into a river or water of some kind, often from a bridge[7]. Sometimes the place of these puppets is taken by a sheaf, a small tree, or a man or boy dressed up in foliage or

---

[1] Caesar, *B. G.* 6. 16; Tac. *Germ.* 9 and 39. Strabo, 10. 8, is interesting, as giving an example of the dropping out of the actual killing, while the form survived. See below on Lupercalia, p. 315.

[2] A point suggested to me some years ago by Mr. A. J. Evans.

[3] Sir A. Lyall (*Asiatic Studies*, p. 19) writes of human sacrifice as having been common in India as a last resort for appeasing divine wrath when manifested in some strange manner ; i. e. it was never regular. So Procopius, *Bell. Goth.* 3. 13. Tacitus, indeed, writes of ' certis diebus ' (*Germ.* 9), but it is not clear that he meant fixed recurring days. As a rule in human sacrifice and cannibalism the victims are captives, who would not be always at hand.

[4] Dionysius (1. 38) speaks of sacrifice *before* the immersion of the puppets : προθύσαντες ἱερὰ τὰ κατὰ τοὺς νόμους.

[5] The βούλιμος and φαρμακός, Mannhardt, *Myth. Forsch.* 129 foll.

[6] *Germania*, 40; Mannhardt, *Baumkultus*, 567 foll. The evidence is perhaps hardly adequate as to detail.

[7] *Baumkultus*, chapters 3, 4, and 5, which should be used by all who wish to form some idea of the amount of evidence collected on this one head.

fastened in the sheaf[1]: but in almost all cases the object is duckᵉd in water or at least sprinkled with it, though now and then it is burnt or buried. The best known example is that of the Bavarian 'Wasservogel,' which is either a boy or a puppet, as the custom may be in different places; he or it was decorated, carried round the fields at Whitsuntide[2], and thrown from the bridge into the stream. So constant and inconvenient was this kind of custom in the Middle Ages that a law of 1351, still extant, forbade the ducking of people at Erfurt in the water at Easter and Whitsuntide[3]. In many of these cases the *simulacrum* may have been substituted for a human being[4]; but I find none where the notion of sacrifice survived, or where there was any trace of a popular belief that the object was a substitute for an actual victim. What these curious customs, according to Dr. Mannhardt, do really represent, is the departure of winter and the arrival of the fruitful season, or possibly the exhaustion of the vernal Power of vegetation after its work is done[5].

Two features in these old customs may strike us as interesting in connexion with the Argei—(1) The fact that the central object is often either actually *an old man,* or is at least called 'the old one.' A Whitsuntide custom at Halle shows us, for example, a straw puppet called *Der alte*[6]. (2) The constant occurrence of white objects in these customs; the puppet is called 'the white man with the white hair, the snow-white husband,' or is dressed in a white shirt[7]. In these expressions it is perhaps not impossible that we may find a clue to the long-lost meaning of the word Argei. Can it be that the Roman puppets were originally called 'the white ones,' i. e. old ones, from a root

---

[1] Our Jack-in-the-Green is probably a survival of this kind of rite.

[2] Nearly all these customs occur either at Whitsuntide or harvest. Mannhardt conjectured that the Argei-rite was originally a harvest custom (*A. W. F.* 269); quite needlessly, I think.

[3] *Baumkultus,* 331.

[4] Mannhardt allows this, *Baumkultus,* 336 note.

[5] *Baumkultus,* 358 foll. His theory is expressed in judicious and by no means dogmatic language. It may be that he runs his Vegetation-spirit somewhat too hard—and no mythologist is free from the error of seeing his own discovery exemplified wherever he turns. But the spirit of vegetation had been found at Rome long before Mannhardt's time (see e.g. Preller's account of Mars and the deities related to him).

[6] *Baumkultus,* 359, 420; *Korndämonen,* 24.

[7] *Baumkultus,* 349 foll., 365, 414.

arg = 'white'[1]; and that from a natural mistake as to the meaning of the word there arose not only the story about the Greek victims, but also the common belief about sexagenarii being thrown over the bridge?

We have to choose between the two explanations given above. I am, on the whole, disposed to agree with Dr. Mannhardt, and in the absence of convincing evidence as to the regular and periodical occurrence of human sacrifice in ancient Italy, to regard these strange survivals as semi-dramatic performances rather than sacrificial rites. This view, however, need not exclude the possibility of the union of both drama and sacrifice at a very remote period, probably before the Latins settled in the district.

The immersion in water, whether or no it involved the death of a victim, is reasonably explained, on the basis of comparative evidence, to have been a *rain-spell*[2]. In the cases already mentioned of Adonis, Nerthus, &c., this idea seems the prominent one. I am inclined to think, however, that the notion of purification was also present—the two uniting in the idea of regeneration. Plutarch calls the Argean rite 'the greatest of the purifications,' and he is here most probably reproducing the opinion of Varro[3]. This is indicated by the presence of the priests and the Vestals, by the processions, and by the mourning of the Flaminica Dialis, as we have already seen. We may regard the rite as in fact a casting out of old things, and in that sense a purification ; and also at the same time as a spell or earnest of rain and fertility in the ensuing year. The puppets

---

[1] Cp. the root *cas-*, which (according to Corssen, *Aussprache*, i. 652 note, appears both in *canus* and *cascus*, and also in the Oscan *casnar* = 'an old man.' The word *casnar* is used by Varro (ap. Nonium, 86) for *sexagenarius*, or possibly *argeus*: 'Vix ecfatus erat cum more maiorum carnales (= casnales) arripiunt et de ponte deturbant.' Cf. Varro, *L. L.* 7. 73 ; Mommsen, *Unter-italische Dialekten*, p. 268. The root *arg* may perhaps have meant *holy* as well as old or white, like the Welsh *gwen* (Rhys, *Celtic Mythology*, 527 note).

[2] *Baumkultus*, 214–16, 355, &c. On p. 356 is a valuable note giving examples from America, India, &c. For a remarkable case from ancient Egypt, of which the object is not rain, but inundation, see Tylor, *Prim. Cult.* ii. 368. See also Grimm, *Teutonic Mythology* (E. T.), p. 593 foll.

[3] *Quaest. Rom.* 86. This work is undoubtedly drawn chiefly from Varro's writings, but largely through the medium of those of Juba the king of Mauretania, who wrote in Greek (Barth de Jubae Ὁμοιότησιν in Plutarcho expressis: Göttingen, 1876).

were perhaps hung in the sacella in the course of the procession in March, as a symbol of the fertility then beginning, and cast into the river as 'the old ones' when that fertility had reached its height[1].

In the last place, it might be asked in honour of what deity the rite was performed. It is hardly necessary, and certainly is not possible, to answer a question about which the Romans themselves were not agreed. Ovid and Dionysius[2] believed it was Saturnus, probably following an old Greek oracle which was known to Varro[3]. Verrius Flaccus thought it was Dis Pater[4]. Modern writers have concluded on the general evidence of the rite that it was the river-god Tiberinus; Jordan, however, regarded the question as irrelevant[5]. We may agree with him, and at least return a verdict of *non liquet*. If it was a sacrificial act, the ancient river-god is indeed likely enough ; if it was a quasi-dramatic one, it does not follow that any deity was specially concerned in it. But we may go so far as to guess that it was connected with the worship of those vaguely-conceived deities of vegetation whose influence on the calendar we have been tracing since March 1.

This same day is marked in one calendar as Feriae Iovi, Mercurio, Maiae. The conjunction of these deities is to some extent accidental. In the first place the Ides of every month were sacred to Jupiter ; and the addition of Mercurius is probably to be explained simply by the adaptation of a Greek myth which made Hermes the son of Jupiter, suggesting the selection of the Ides as an appropriate day for the cult of the Latin representative of Hermes[6]. Mercurius, again, was associated with Maia, perhaps simply because the dedication-day of his oldest temple in Rome (*ad circum maximum*) was the Ides

---

[1] Parallels in *Baumkultus*, pp. 170, 178, 211, 409. These are examples of May-trees and other objects, sometimes decked out as human beings, which are hung up in the homestead for a certain time—e. g. in Austria from May-day to St. John Baptist's day, a period closely corresponding both in length and season to that at Rome, from March 15 to May 15. In the church of Charlton-on-Otmoor, near Oxford, it is hung on the rood-screen from May 1 onwards.

[2] Ovid, *Fasti*, 5. 627 : Dionys. 1. 38.

[3] See Macrob. 1. 7. 28. In Dionysius' version, however, of the line it is ῎Αιδης to whom the sacrifice is offered.

[4] Festus, 334.

[5] *Topogr*. ii. 285.

[6] *Lex*. s. v. Mercurius, p. 2804.

of the Mensis Maius[1]. The Roman Mercurius was considered especially as the god of trade, and dated, like Ceres, from the time when an extensive corn trade first began in Rome[2]. It is highly probable that the Tarquinian dynasty had encouraged Roman trade, and that the increase of population which was the result, together with the wars which followed their expulsion, had occasioned a series of severe famines. To this we trace the Roman knowledge of the Greek or Graeco-Etruscan Hermes, through a trade in corn with Sicilian Greeks or Etruscans, and the appearance of the god at Rome as Mercurius, the god of trade. His first temple was dedicated in B.C. 495, and as in other cases, the dedication was celebrated each year by those specially interested in the worship, in this case the *mercatores*, who were already, at this early period, formed into an organized guild[3].

XII KAL. IUN. (MAY 21). N̄P.

AGON[IA][4]. (ESQ. CAER. VEN. MAFF.)
VEDIOVI. (VEN.)

The other days sacred to Vediovis were January 1 and the Nones of March, from which latter day we postponed the consideration of this mysterious deity, in hopes of future enlightenment. But Vediovis is wrapped still, and always will be, in at least as profound an obscurity for us as he was for Varro and Ovid.

We have but his name to go upon, and two or three indistinct traces of his cult. The name seems certainly to be Vediovis, i e apparently 'the opposite of,' or 'separated from,' Jupiter (= Diovis); or, as Preller has it[5], comparing, like Ovid, *vegrandia farra* ('corn that has grown badly'), *vescus*, &c., Jupiter in a sinister sense. But this last explanation must, on the whole, be rejected. It is true that each deity has a sinister or threatening

---

[1] Aust, *de Aedibus sacris*, p. 5.

[2] It seems to me probable that there was a Mercurius at Rome before the introduction of Hermes; but this cannot be proved. It seems likely that the temple-cult established in 495 B.C. was really that of Hermes under an Italian name, as in the parallel case of Ceres. This was one year later than the date of the Ceres-temple (above, p. 74).

[3] Mercuriales, or Mercatores (Jordan, *Topogr.* i. 1. 278). They belonged to the collegia of the pagi.

[4] See on March 17 and January 9.

[5] i. 262 foll.; Ovid, *Fasti*, 3. 445; Gell. *N. A.* 5. 12.

aspect as well as a smiling one; but in no other case was this separately personified, and the name, if its origin be rightly given as above (which is not indeed certain), might be explained by the well-known Roman habit of calling deities by their qualities and their business rather than by substantival names. In this case the name would be negatively deduced from that of one of the few gods who really had a name.

What we know of the cult is only this. First, it was peculiar, so far as we know, to Rome and Bovillae [1]; secondly, the temples in Rome were in the space between the arx and Capitolium, 'inter duos lucos' [2], and another in the Tiber island [3]—two places outside the Servian wall, and of importance for the security of the city; thirdly, the god was represented as young, holding arrows, and having a goat standing beside him, on account of which characteristics he was usually, according to Gellius, identified with Apollo [4]; fourthly, the usual victim was a goat which was sacrificed *humano ritu* [5].

On such faint traces it will be obvious that no sound conclusion can be based. The connexion with Bovillae and the gens Julia points to a genuine Latin origin. The sites on the Capitol and the island do not lead to any definite conclusion; in the former the god seems to have been connected with the so-called Asylum, in the latter with Aesculapius; but both these connexions may be accidental or later developments. Preller conjectured cleverly that Vediovis was a god of criminals who might take refuge in Rome and there find purification; but the idea of an Asylum, on which this is based, is Greek, and of much later date than any age which could have given a definite meaning to such a deity. We must here, as occasionally elsewhere, give up the attempt to discover the original nature of this god.

[1] *C. I. L.* i. 807; the dedication of an altar (Vediovei Patrei genteiles Iuliei) found at Bovillae.

[2] Ovid, *Fasti*, 3. 429; Gell. 5. 12. It was this temple which had May 21 as its 'dies natalis.'

[3] Liv. 31. 21. 12 (reading Vediovi for deo Iovi, with Merkel and Jordan).

[4] Gell. l. c.; Preller, i. 264, and Jordan's note.

[5] Gell. 5. 12. The meaning of the expression is not clear. Paulus (165) writes : ' Humanum sacrificium dicebant quod mortui causa fiebat '—which does not greatly help us. Preller reasonably suggested that the goat might be a substitutory victim in place of a 'homo sacer' or criminal (i. 265).

x Kal. Iun. (May 23). N͞P.

TUBIL[USTRIUM]. (esq. caer. ven. maff.)
FER[IAE] VOLCANO. (ven. amit.)

I have already explained[1] the view taken by Mommsen
of the two pairs of days, March 23 and 24 and May 23 and 24,
accepting his theory that the 24th in each month was the day
on which wills could be made and witnessed in the Comitia
calata, and that the 23rd in each month was the day on
which the *tubae* were lustrated by which the assembly was
summoned.

But May 23 is also marked in two calendars as *feriae
Volcano*; and Ovid has noticed this in a single couplet[2]:

> Proxima Volcani lux est: Tubilustria dicunt;
> Lustrantur purae, quas facit ille, tubae.

The difficult question of the original character of Volcanus
must be postponed until we come to his festival in August.
We only need here to ask whether Ovid was right in regarding
Volcanus as the smith who made the trumpets. This has been
strenuously denied by Wissowa[3], who goes so far as to believe
that the deity originally invoked on this day was not Volcanus
but Mars—since the corresponding day in March was a festival
of that deity—and that Volcanus was at an early period thrust
into his place under the influence of Greek notions of
Hephaestus as a smith who made armour and also trumpets.
Wissowa has, however, to throw over the two calendars quoted
above (Ven. Amit.) in order to support his argument—and so
far we are hardly entitled to go.

It is safer to take Volcanus as an ancient Roman deity whose
cult was closely connected with that of Maia, or the Bona Dea,
and was prominent in this month as well as in August. The
Flamen Volcanalis sacrificed to the Bona Dea on May 1; and
Maia was addressed in invocations as Maia Volcani[4]. The
coincidence of this festival of his with the Tubilustrium I take
to have been accidental; but it led naturally, as the Romans

---

[1] Above, p. 63.
[2] *Fasti*, 5 725.
[3] *de Feriis*, xv.
[4] Gell. 13. 23.

became acquainted with Greek mythology, to the erroneous view represented by Ovid that Volcanus was himself a smith [1].

VIII KAL. IUN. (MAY 25). C.

FORTUNAE P[UBLICAE] P[OPULI] R[OMANI] Q[UIRITIUM] IN COLLE QUIRIN[ALI]. (CAER.)
FORTUN[AE] PUBLIC[AE] P[OPULI] R[OMANI] IN COLL[E]. (ESQ.)
FORTUN[AE] PRIM[IGENIAE] IN COL[LE]. (VEN.)

This was the dedication-day of one of three temples of Fortuna on the Quirinal; the place was known as 'tres Fortunae [2].' The goddess in this case was Fortuna Primigenia, imported from Praeneste—of whom something will be said later on [3]. The temple was vowed after the Second Punic War in B. C. 204, and dedicated ten years later [4]. Our consideration of Fortuna may be postponed till the festival of Fors Fortuna, an older Roman form of the cult, on June 24.

IV KAL. IUN. (MAY 29). C.

The Ambarvalia, originally a religious procession round the land of the early Roman community, the object of which was to purify the crops from evil influences, does not appear in the Julian calendars, not being *feriae stativae*; but it is indicated in the later rustic calendars by the words, *Segetes lustrantur*. Its date may be taken as May 29 [5]: and this fixity will not appear incompatible with its character as a *sacrum conceptivum*, if we accept Mommsen's explanation of the way in which some feasts might be fixed to a day according to the usage of the Italian farmer, but of varying date according to the civil calendar [6].

There has been much discussion whether the Ambarvalia

---

[1] The Hephaestus-myth has been treated on the comparative method by F. von Schröder (*Griech. Götter u. Heroen*, i. 79 foll.), and by Rapp in *Myth. Lex*. It is of course possible that it may have been known to the early Italians, but what we know of Volcanus does not favour this.

[2] Vitruvius, 3. 2. 2; it was 'proxime portam Collinam.'

[3] See below, pp. 165, 223.

[4] Liv. 34. 53; Aust, *de Aedibus*, p. 20.

[5] This seems to have been the date among the Anauni of N. Italy as late as 393 A. D.: see the *Acta Martyrum*, p. 536 (Verona, 1731). (For the Anauni, Rushforth, *Latin Historical Inscriptions*, p. 99 foll.)

[6] *Chron.* 70 foll.: a difficult bit of calculation.

was identical with the similar festival of the Fratres Arvales.
On the ground that the *acta fratrum Arvalium* seemed to prove
a general similarity of the two in time and place, and at least
in some points of ritual, Mommsen, Henzen, and Jordan
answer in the affirmative [1]. On the other side there is no
authority of any real weight. The judicious Marquardt [2] found
a difficulty in the absence of any mention in the *acta fratrum
Arvalium* of a lustratio in the form of a procession; but it
should be remembered (1) that we have not the whole of the
acta; (2) that it is almost certain that, as the Roman territory
continued to increase, the brethren must have dropped the duty
of driving victims round it, for obvious reasons. A passage
in Paulus [3] places the matter beyond doubt if we can be sure of
the reading: '*Ambarvales hostiae dicebantur quae pro arvis a duodecim* (MSS. duobus) *fratribus sacrificantur.*' As no *duo fratres* are
known, the old emendation *duodecim* seems certain, but will of
course not convince those who disbelieve in the identity of
the Ambarvalia and the sacra fratrum Arvalium. The question
is, however, for us of no great importance, as the *acta* do not
add to our knowledge of what was done at the Ambarvalia.

The best description we have of such lustrations as the
Ambarvalia is that of Virgil; it is not indeed to be taken as
an exact description of the Roman rite, but rather as referring
to Italian customs generally:

> In primis venerare deos, atque annua magnae
> Sacra refer Cereri laetis operatus in herbis,
> Extremae sub casum hiemis, iam vere sereno.
> Tum pingues agni, et tum mollissima vina;
> Tum somni dulces densaeque in montibus umbrae.
> Cuncta tibi Cererem pubes agrestis adoret,
> Cui tu lacte favos et miti dilue Baccho,
> Terque novas circum felix eat hostia fruges,
> Omnis quam chorus et socii comitentur ovantes,
> Et Cererem clamore vocent in tecta; neque ante
> Falcem maturis quisquam supponat aristis,
> Quam Cereri torta redimitus tempora quercu
> Det motus inconpositos et carmina dicat [4].

[1] Mommsen, l. c. Henzen, *Acta Fr. Arv.* xlvi–xlviii; Jordan on Preller,
i. 420, and *Topogr.* i. 289, ii. 236. The latter would also identify Ambarvalia and Amburbium; but the two seem clearly distinguished by Servius
(*Ecl.* 3. 77). [2] p. 200. Huschke, *Röm. Jahr*, 63.
[3] p. 5. See Jordan on Preller, i. 420, note 2; Marq. 200, note 3.
[4] *Georg.* 1. 338 foll.

It is not clear to what festival or festivals Virgil is alluding in the first few of these lines [1]; probably to certain rustic rites which did not exactly correspond to those in the city of Rome. But from line 343 onwards the reference is certainly to Ambarvalia of some kind, perhaps to the private *lustratio* of the farmer before harvest began, of which the Roman festival was a magnified copy. His description answers closely to the well-known directions of Cato [2]; and if it is Ceres who appears in Virgil's lines, and not Mars, the deity most prominent in Cato's account, this may be explained by the undoubted extension of the worship of Ceres, and the corresponding contraction of that of Mars, as the latter became more and more converted into a god of war [3].

The leading feature in the original rite was the procession of victims— bull, sheep, and pig—all round the fields, driven by a garlanded crowd, carrying olive branches and chanting. These victims represent all the farmer's most valuable stock, thus devoted to the appeasing of the god. The time was that when the crops were ripening, and were in greatest peril from storms and diseases ; before the harvest was begun, and before the Vestalia took place in the early part of June, which was, as we shall see, a festival preliminary to harvest. Three times the procession went round the land ; at the end of the third round the victims were sacrificed, and a solemn prayer was offered in antique language, which ran, in Cato's formula of the farmer's lustration, as follows: 'Father Mars, I pray and beseech thee to be willing and propitious to me, my household, and my slaves ; for the which object I have caused this threefold sacrifice to be driven round my farm and land. I pray thee keep, avert, and turn from us all disease, seen or unseen, all desolation, ruin, damage, and unseasonable influence ; I pray thee give increase to the fruits, the corn, the vines, and the

---

[1] 'Extremae sub casum hiemis' might possibly suit the Italian April, but certainly not the Italian May. May 1 is the earliest date we have for an agri lustratio, i. e. in Campania (*C. I. L.* x. 3792). 'Tunc mollissima vina' may contain a reference to the Vinalia of April 23, when the new wine was first drunk ; and if that were so, the general reference might be to the Cerialia or its rustic equivalent.

[2] *R. R.* 141. Cp. Siculus Flaccus in *Gromatici Veteres*, p. 164. The lustratio should be celebrated before even the earliest crops (e.g. beans) were cut.

[3] Henzen, *Acta Fr. Arv.* xlviii. .

plantations, and bring them to a prosperous issue. Keep also in safety the shepherds and their flocks, and give good health and vigour to me, my house, and household. To this end it is, as I have said—namely, for the purification and making due lustration of my farm, my land cultivated and uncultivated—that I pray thee to bless this threefold sacrifice of sucklings. O Father Mars, to this same end I pray thee bless this threefold sacrifice of sucklings[1].'

Not only in this prayer, but in the ritual that follows, as also in other religious directions given in the preceding chapters, we may no doubt see examples of the oldest agricultural type of the genuine Italian worship. They are simple rustic specimens of the same type as the elaborate urban ritual of Iguvium, fortunately preserved to us[2]; and we may fairly assume that they stood in much the same relation to the Roman ritual of the Ambarvalia.

Of all the Roman festivals this is the only one which can be said with any truth to be still surviving. When the Italian priest leads his flock round the fields with the ritual of the Litania major in Rogation week he is doing very much what the Fratres Arvales did in the infancy of Rome, and with the same object. In other countries, England among them, the same custom was taken up by the Church, which rightly appreciated its utility, both spiritual and material; the bounds of the parish were fixed in the memory of the young, and the wrath of God was averted by an act of duty from man, cattle, and crops. 'It was a general custom formerly, and is still observed in some country parishes, to go round the bounds and limits of the parish on one of the three days before Ascension-day; when the Minister, accompanied by his Churchwardens and Parishioners, was wont to deprecate the vengeance of God, beg a blessing on the fruits of the earth, and preserve the rights and properties of the parish[3].'

At Oxford, and it is to be hoped in some other places, this laudable custom still survives. But the modern clergy, from

---

[1] Cato, *R. R.* 141. I have availed myself of the Italian translation and commentary of Prof. De-Marchi in his work on the domestic religion of the Romans, p. 128 foll.

[2] Bücheler, *Umbrica*; Bréal, *Les Tables Eugubines.*

[3] Brand, *Popular Antiquities*, p. 292.

want of interest in ritual, except such as is carried on within
their churches, or from some strong distrust of any merry-
making not initiated by their own zeal, are apt to drop the
ceremonies; and there is some danger that even in Oxford
the processions and peeled wands may soon be things of the
past. To all such ministers I would recommend the practice
of the judicious Hooker, as described by his biographer, Isaak
Walton:

'He would by no means omit the customary time of procession, persuading all, both rich and poor, if they desired the
preservation of Love, and their Parish rights and liberties, to
accompany him in his Perambulation—and most did so; in
which Perambulation he would usually express more pleasant
Discourse than at other times, and would then always drop
some loving and facetious Observations, to be remembered
against the next year, especially by the Boys and young people;
still inclining them, and all his present Parishioners, to meek-
ness and mutual Kindnesses and Love.'

At Charlton-on-Otmoor, near Oxford, there was a survival of
the 'agri lustratio' until recent years. On the beautiful rood-
screen of the parish church there is a cross, which was carried
in procession through the parish [1], freshly decorated with
flowers, on May-day; it was then restored to its place on the
screen, and remained there until the May-day of the next year.
It may still be seen there, but it is no longer carried round,
and its decoration seems to have been transferred from May-
day to the harvest-festival [2].

---

[1] I am informed that it visited one hamlet, Horton, which is not at
present in the parish of Charlton; of this there should be some topographical explanation.

[2] The cross is very commonly carried about on the continent, and in
Holland the week is called cross-week for this reason. But at Charlton
there seems to have been a confusion between this cross and the May-
queen or May-doll; for on May-day, 1898, the old woman who decked it
called it 'my lady,' and spoke of 'her waist,' &c. I am indebted to the
Rev. C. E. Prior, the present incumbent, for information about this
interesting survival.

MENSIS IUNIUS.

KAL. IUN. (JUNE 1). N.

IUNONI MONETAE (VEN.)
FABARICI C[IRCENSES] M[ISSUS]. (PHILOC.)

On the name of the mensis Junius some remarks have already been made under May 1. There is no sure ground for connecting it with Juno[1]. The first day of June was sacred to her, but so were all Kalends; and if this was also the *dies natalis* of the temple of Juno Moneta *in arce*, we have no reason to suppose the choice of day to be specially significant[2]. We know the date of this dedication; it was in 344 B. C. and in consequence of a vow made by L. Furius Camillus Dictator in a war against the Aurunci[3]. Of a Juno Moneta of earlier date we have no knowledge; and, in spite of much that has been said to the contrary, I imagine that the title was only given to a Juno of the *arx* in consequence of the popular belief that the Capitol was saved from the attack of the Gauls (390 B. C.) by the warning voices of her sacred geese. What truth there was in that story may be a matter of doubt, but it seems easier to believe that it had a basis of fact than to account for it aetiologically[4]. There may

---

[1] What can be said for this view may be read in Roscher's article in *Lex.* s. v. Iuno, p. 575, note.

[2] Roscher's treatment of Juno Moneta (*Lex.* s. v. Iuno, 593) seems to me pure fancy; this writer is apt to twist his facts and his inferences to suit a prepossession—in this case the notion of a ἱερὸς γάμος of Jupiter and Juno.

[3] Liv. 7. 28; Ovid, *Fasti*, 6. 183; Macrob. 1. 12. 30.

[4] On this point see Lewis, *Credibility of Early Roman Hist.* vol. ii. 345.

K

well have been an altar or *sacellum*[1] of Juno on the *arx*, near
which her noisy birds were kept[2]; and when a temple was
eventually built here in 344 B.C., it was appropriately dedicated
to Juno of the warning voice. From the fact that part of this
temple was used as a mint[3], the word *Moneta* gradually passed
into another sense, which has found its way into our modern
languages[4].

One tradition connected the name of the month with
M. Junius Brutus, who is said to have performed a *sacrum*
on this day after the flight of Tarquinius, on the Caelian Hill[5].
This *sacrum* had no connexion with Juno, and the tradition
which thus absurdly brings Brutus into the question shows
plainly that the derivation from Juno was not universally
accepted[6]. The real deity of the Kalends of June was not
Juno, but an antique goddess whose antiquity is attested both
by the meagreness of our knowledge of her, and the strange
confusion about her which Ovid displays. Had Carna been
more successful in the struggle for existence of Roman deities,
we might not have been so sure of her extreme antiquity;
but no foreign cult grafted on her gave her a new lease of life,
and by the end of the Republic she was all but dead.

What little we do know of her savours of the agricultural
life and folk-lore of the old Latins. Her sacrifices were
of bean-meal and lard[7]; and this day went by the name of
of Kalendae fabariae[8], 'quia hoc mense adultae fabae divinis
rebus adhibentur.' The fact was that it was the time of bean-
harvest[9]; and beans, as we have already seen, were much
in request for sacred purposes. 'Maximus honos fabae,' says

---

[1] Dionys., 13. 7, says, Χῆνες ἱεροὶ περὶ τὸν νεὼν τῆς Ἥρας; but this is no
evidence for an early *temple* of Juno Moneta.

[2] Apparently she was fond of such birds: crows also were 'in tutela
Iunonis' at a certain spot north of the Tiber (Paul. 64), and at Lanuvium
(Preller, i. 283).   [3] Liv. 6. 20.

[4] I have assumed that *Moneta* is connected with *moneo*; but there are other
views (Roscher, *Lex.* 593). Livius Andronicus (ap. Priscian, p. 679) helps
us to the meaning by translating Μνημοσύνη (of the *Odyssey*) by *Moneta*.

[5] Macrob. *Sat.* 1. 12. 22 and·31. There was no temple of Carna there,
but Tertullianus (*ad Nat.* 2. 9) mentions a *fanum*.

[6] Cp. also the explanation from *iuniores* (e. g. in Ovid, *Fasti*, 6. 83 foll.).

[7] Macrob. 1. 12. 33 'Cui pulte fabacia et larido sacrificatur.'

[8] Even in the fourth century A.D. this was so: see the calendar of
Philocalus.

[9] Colum. 11. 2. 20; Pallad. 7. 3; Hartmann, *Das Röm. Kal.* 135.

Pliny[1], alluding to the value of the bean as food, to its supposed narcotic power, and its use in religious ritual. We have already found beans used in the cult of the dead and the ejection of ghosts from the house[2]; and Prof. Wissowa has of late ingeniously conjectured that this day (June 1) was concerned with rites of the same kind[3]. He quotes an inscription, a will in which a legacy is left 'ut rosas Carnar[iis] ducant'[4]. Undoubtedly the reference here is to rites of the dead (cf. Rosalia), and Mommsen may be right in suggesting that by Carnar[iis] is meant the Kalends of June. But it is going a little too far to argue on this slender evidence, even if we add to it the fact that the day was *nefastus*, that the festival of Carna was of the same kind as the Parentalia, Rosalia, &c.; a careful reading of Ovid's comments seems to show that there were curious survivals of folk-lore connected with the day and with Carna which cannot all be explained by reference to rites of the dead.

Ovid does indeed at once mislead his readers by identifying Carna and Cardea, and thus making the former the deity of door-hinges, and bringing her into connexion with Janus[5]. But we may guess that he does this simply because he wants to squeeze in a pretty folk-tale of Janus and Cardea, for which his readers may be grateful, and which need not deceive them. When he writes of the ritual of Carna[6]—our only safe guide— he makes it quite plain that he is mixing up the attributes of two distinct deities. He brings the two together by contriving that Janus, as a reward to Cardea for yielding to his

---

[1] *H. N.* 18. 117. [2] See above on Lemuria, p. 110.
[3] *de Feriis*, xiii. [4] *C. I. L.* iii. 3893.
[5] There is really nothing in common between the two: see Wissowa in *Lex.* s. v. Carna, following Merkel, clxv. What the real etymology of Carna may be is undecided; Curtius and others have connected it with *cor*, and on this O. Gilbert has built much foolish conjecture (ii. 19 foll.). I would rather compare it with the words Garanus or Recaranus of the Hercules legend (Bréal, *Herc. et Cacus*, pp. 59, 60), and perhaps with Gradivus, Grabovius. The name of the 'nymph' Cranae in Ovid's account is in some MSS. Grane or Crane. H. Peter (*Fasti*, pt. ii. p 89) adopts the connexion with *caro*: she is 'die das Fleisch kräftigende Göttin' (cp. Ossipago).
[6] *Fasti*, 6. 169–182. Lines 101–130 are concerned with Cardea; 130 to 168, or the middle section of the comment, seem, as Marquardt suggested (p. 13, note), to be referable to Carna (as the averter of *striges*), though the charms fixed on the *postes* show that Ovid is still confounding her with Cardea.

advances, should bestow on her not only the charge of *cardines*, but also that of protecting infants from the *striges*[1], creatures of the nature of vampires, but described by Ovid as owls, who were wont to suck their blood and devour their vitals. But this last duty surely belonged to Carna, of whom Macrobius says 'Hanc deam vitalibus humanis praeesse credunt': and thus Carna's attribute is conjoined with Cardea's. The lines are worth quoting in which Ovid describes the charms which are to keep off the *striges*, for as preserving a remnant of old Italian folk-lore they are more interesting than the doubtful nature of an obscure deity[2]:

> Protinus arbutea[3] postes ter in ordine tangit
>   Fronde, ter arbutea limina fronde notat:
> Spargit aquis aditus—et aquae medicamen habebant—
>   Extaque de porca cruda bimenstre tenet[4].
> Atque ita 'noctis aves, extis puerilibus' inquit
>   'Parcite: pro parvo victima parva cadit.
> Cor pro corde, precor, pro fibris sumite fibras.
>   Hanc animam vobis pro meliore damus.'
> Sic ubi libavit, prosecta sub aethere ponit,
>   Quique adsint sacris, respicere illa vetat[5].
> Virgaque Ianalis de spina ponitur alba[6]
>   Qua lumen thalamis parva fenestra dabat.
> Post illud nec aves cunas violasse feruntur,
>   Et rediit puero qui fuit ante color.

Having told his folk-tale and described his charms, Ovid returns to Carna, and asks why people eat bean-gruel on the Kalends of June, with the rich fat of pigs. The answer

---

[1] The word *strix* is Greek, or at least identical with the Greek word. But the belief in vampires is so widely spread (cf. Tylor, *Prim. Cult.* ii. 175 foll.) that we must not conclude hastily that it came to Italy with the Greeks: it is met with as early as Plautus (*Pseud.* 3. 2. 20). Cf. Pliny, *H. N.* 11. 232.

[2] *Fasti*, 6. 155 foll.

[3] The *arbutus* does not seem to be mentioned in connexion with charms except in this passage; we might have expected the laurel. Bötticher, *Baumkultus*, 324.

[4] The sucking-pig is sacrificed, as we gather from *prosecta* below; i.e. to Carna: cp. the cakes of *lard* eaten this day (169 foll.).

[5] Cp. in the process of ghost-laying (above, p. 109) the prohibition to look at the beans scattered.

[6] For the blackthorn (Germ. *Weissdorn*) see Bötticher, *Baumkultus*, 361. Varro, ap. Charisium, p. 117 'fax ex spinu alba praefertur, quod purgationis causa adhibetur.'

is that the cult of Carna is of ancient date, and that the
healthy food of man in early times is retained in it[1].

> Sus erat in pretio ; caesa sue festa colebant.
> Terra fabas tantum duraque farra dabat.
> Quae duo mixta simul sextis quicunque Kalendis
> Ederit, huic laedi viscera posse negant.

This was undoubtedly the real popular belief—that by eating
this food on Carna's day your digestion was secured for the
year. Macrobius[2] makes the practice into a much more
definite piece of ritual. 'Prayers are offered to this goddess,'
he says, 'for the good preservation of liver, heart, and the
other internal organs of our bodies. Her sacrifices are bean-
meal and lard, because this is the best food for the nourishment
of the body.' Ovid is here the genuine Italian, Macrobius the
scholar and theologian : both may be right.

Whatever, then, may be the meaning or etymology of the
name Carna, we may at least be sure that the cult belongs
to the age of ancient Latin agriculture[3], since it was in
connexion with her name that the popular belief survived
in Ovid's time of the virtue of bean-eating on the Kalends
of June.

We learn from Ovid (line 191) that this same day was the *dies
natalis* of the temple of Mars *extra portam Capenam*, i.e. on the
Via Appia—a favourite spot for the mustering of armies, and
the starting-point for the yearly *transvectio equitum*[4]. I have
already alluded to the baseless fabric of conjecture built

---

[1] This is the passage that must have inspired O. Crusius in his paper on
beans in *Rhein. Mus.* xxxix. 164 foll. 'Beans,' he says, 'were the oldest
Italian food, and like stone knives, &c., survived in ritual.' We want,
indeed, some more definite proof that they were really the oldest food ;
and anyhow their use had not died out like that of stone implements.
(They were a common article of food at Athens : Aristoph. *Knights*, 41 ;
Lysist. 537 and 691.) But it is not unlikely that their use in the cult of
the dead may be a survival, upon which odd superstitions grafted themselves. For a parallel argument see Roscher, *Nektar und Ambrosia*, 36 ;
Rhys, *Celtic Mythology*, 356.
[2] *Sat.* i. 12. 32.
[3] No safe conclusion can be drawn from Tertullian's inclusion (*ad Nat.* 2.
9) of the *fanum* of Carna on the Caelian among those of *di adventicii*.
O. Gilbert has lately tried to make much of this (ii. 42 foll.), and to find
an Etruscan origin for Carna : but see Aust on the position of temples
outside the *pomoerium* (*de Aedibus sacris*, 47).
[4] Liv. 7. 23 ; Dionys. 6. 13.

on the conjunction of Mars and Juno on this day [1]; and need here only repeat that in no well-attested Roman myth is Mars the son of Juno, or Juno the wife of Jupiter.   And it is even doubtful whether June 1 was the *original* dedication-day of this temple of Mars : the Venusian calendar does not mention it, and Ovid may be referring to a re-dedication by Augustus [2].   There is absolutely no ground for the myth-making of Usener and Roscher about Mars and Juno : but it is to the credit of the latter that he has inserted in his article on Mars a valuable note by Aust, in which his own conclusions are cogently controverted.

III. Non. Iun. (June 3).   C.

BELLON[AE] IN CIRC[O] FLAM[INIO].   (VEN.)

This temple was vowed by the Consul Ap. Claudius in an Etruscan war [3] (296 B.C.): the date of dedication is unknown. In front of the temple was an area of which the truly Roman story is told [4], that being unable to declare war with Pyrrhus with the orthodox ritual of the *fetiales*, as he had no land in Italy into which they could throw the challenging spear [5], they caught a Pyrrhan soldier and made him buy this spot to suit their purpose.   Here stood the 'columella' from which henceforward the spear was thrown [6].

The temple became well known as a suitable meeting-place for the Senate outside the *pomoerium*, when it was necessary to do business with generals and ambassadors who could not legally enter the city [7].   But of the goddess very little is known. There is no sufficient reason to identify her with that Nerio

---

[1] See on March 1, above, p. 37.

[2] Aust, *de Aedibus sacris*, p. 8.   The *Fasti Venusini* are 'omnium accuratis-simi'; ib. p. 43.   Aust goes so far as to doubt the true Roman character of this Mars, and believes him to be the Greek god Ares.   See his note in *Lex.* 2391.   The date of foundation is not certain, but was probably not earlier than the Gallic war, 388 B.C., if it is this to which Livy alludes in 6. 5. 8.

[3] Liv. 10. 19.   There was a tradition that Ap. Claudius, *Cos.* 495 B.C., had dedicated statues of his ancestors in a temple of Bellona (Pliny, *N. H.* 35. 12).   [4] Serv. *Aen.* ix. 53.

[5] Liv. 1. 32. 12 ; Marq. 422.   [6] Ovid, *Fasti*, 6. 205 foll.; Paulus, 33.

[7] Willems, *Le Sénat de la République*, ii. 161.

with whom we made acquaintance in March, as is done too confidently by the writer of the article in Roscher's *Lexicon* [1].

Prid. Non. Iun. (June 4). C.

HERC[ULI] MAGN[O] CUSTO[DI]. (VEN.)
SACRUM HERCULI. (RUST.)

This temple also was near the Circus Flaminius [2]. It was a foundation of Sulla's, 82 B.C., and the cult was Greek, answering to that of Ἡρακλῆς ἀλεξίκακος [3].

Non. Iun. (June 5). N. [4]

DIO FIDIO IN COLLE. (VEN.)

The temple on the Quirinal of which this was the *dies natalis* is said by Dionysius [5] to have been vowed by Tarquinius Superbus, and dedicated by Sp. Postumius in B.C. 466. But that there was a *fanum* or *sacellum* of this deity on or near the same site at a much earlier time is almost certain; such a *sacellum* 'ad portam Sanqualem' is mentioned, also by Dionysius [6], as ἱερὸν Διὸς Πιστίου, and we know that in many cases the final *aedes* or *templum* was a development from an uncovered altar or sacred place.

Dius Fidius, as the adjectival character of his name shows, was a genuine old Italian religious conception, but one that in historical times was buried almost out of sight. Among gods and heroes there has been a struggle for existence, as among animals and plants; with some peoples a struggle between indigenous and exotic deities, in which the latter usually win

---

[1] This was originally suggested by Gellius (13. 23), 'perhaps not without some reason,' says Marquardt (75). This suggestion has grown almost into a certainty for the writer in the *Lexicon*, in a manner very characteristic of the present age of research. There would be some reason to think that Bellona (or Duellona) was an ancient goddess of central Italy, if we could be sure that the inscription on an ancient cup, in the museum at Florence, which may be read 'Belolae poculum' (*C. I. L.* i. 44), refers to this deity. See *Lex.* s. v. Belola.

[2] Ovid, *Fasti*, 6. 209. See *Commentarii in honorem Th. Mommseni*, 262 foll. (Klügmann), and R. Peter in *Lex.* s. v. Herc. p. 2979.

[3] Preller-Jordan, ii. 296.   [4] See below, p. 146.

[5] 9. 60, where Ζεὺς Πίστιος = Dius Fidius.

[6] 4. 58 : cp. Liv. 8. 20; Aust, *de Aedibus sacris*, p. 51. Of the porta Sanqualis I shall have a word to say presently.

the day, and displace or modify the native species[1]. What laws, if any, govern this struggle for existence it is not possible to discern clearly ; the result is doubtless the survival of the fittest, if by the fittest we understand those which flourish best under the existing conditions of society and thought; but it would hardly seem to be the survival of those which are most beneficial to the worshipping race. Among the Romans the fashionable exotic deities of the later Republic and Empire had no such ethical influence on the character of the people as those older ones of the type of Dius Fidius, who in historical times was known to the ordinary Roman only through the medium of an old-fashioned oath.

Ovid knows very little about Dius Fidius[2] :

> Quaerebam Nonas Sanco Fidione referrem,
>   An tibi, Semo pater : cum mihi Sancus ait
> ' Cuicunque ex illis dederis, ego munus habebo ;
>   Nomina trina fero, sic voluere Cures.'

He finds three names for the deity, but two would have sufficed ; the only individual Semo known to us is Sancus himself. The Semones, so far as we can guess, were spirits of the 'pandaemonic' age, nameless like the Lares with whom they are associated in the hymn of the Fratres Arvales[3] ; but one only, Semo Sancus, seems to have taken a name and survived into a later age, and this one was identified with Dius Fidius. Aelius Stilo, the Varro of the seventh century A. U. C., seems to have started this identification[4]. Varro does not comment on it ; but Verrius accepted it : he writes of an 'aedes Sancus, qui deus Dius Fidius vocatur '[5]. The evidence of inscriptions is explicit for a later period ; an altar, for example, found near the supposed site of his temple on the Quirinal, bears the inscription 'Sanco Sancto Semon[i] deo fidio sacrum '[6].

---

[1] Mr. Lang (*Myth, Ritual*, &c., ii. 191) has some excellent remarks on this subject. [2] *Fasti*, 6. 213.

[3] See Wordsworth's *Fragments and Specimens of Early Latin*, p. 157 'Semunes alternos advocapit cunctos.' I follow Jordan's explanation of 'Semunes,' in *Krit. Beiträge*, 204 foll.

[4] Aelius Dium Fidium dicebat Diovis filium, ut Graeci Διόσκορον Castorem, et putabat hunc esse Sancum ab Sabina lingua et Herculem a Graeca ' (Varro, *L. L.* 5. 66).

[5] Festus, 241. This is probably the *sacellum* of Livy, 8. 22.

[6] *C. I. L.* vi. 568 : again (ib. 567), 'Semoni Sanco deo fidio.' Sancus is, of course, a name, not an adjective : we find Sangus in some MSS. of

And there is nothing in the words Sancus and Fidius to forbid the identification, for both point to the same class of ideas—that of the bond which religious feeling places on men in their duties to, and contracts with, each other. They are in fact two different names for the same religious conception. It is interesting to find them both occurring in the great processional inscription of Iguvium in Umbria: Fisus or Fisovius Sancius, who is there invoked next after Jupiter, seems to unite the two deities in a single name[1]. This conjunction would seem to save us from the necessity of discussing the question whether Sancus, as has often been insisted on by scholars both ancient and modern[2], was really the Sabine form of Dius Fidius; for if in Umbria the two are found together, as at Rome, there is no reason why the same should not have been the case throughout central Italy. The question would never have been asked had the fluid nature of the earliest Italian deities and the adjectival character of their names been duly taken account of. We are all of us too apt to speak of this primitive spirit-world in terms of a later polytheistic theology, and to suppose that the doubling of a name implies some distinction of origin or race.

Dius Fidius, then, and Semo Sancus are both Latin names for the same religious conception, the impersonality of which caused it to lose vitality as new and anthropomorphic ideas of the divine came into vogue at Rome. But there is at least some probability that it survived in a fashion under the name of an intruder, Hercules; and the connexion with Hercules will show, what we might already have guessed, that the

---

Livy, 32. 1. For the well-known curious confusion with Simon Magus, Euseb. *H. E.* 2. 13.

[1] Bréal, *Tables Eugubines,* 71 ; Bücheler, *Umbrica,* 65 foll. As Preller remarks, Fisus stands to Fidius as Clausus to Claudius (ii. 271). At Iguvium there was a hill, important in the rites, which bore this name—*ocris fisius.*

[2] Aelius Stilo ap. Varro, l. c. ; Ovid, l. c. ; Propert. 4. 9. 74 ; Lactantius, 1. 15. 8 ; Schwegler, *R. G.* i. 364 ; Preller, ii. 272 ; O. Gilbert, i. 275, note ; Ambrosch, *Studien,* 170. Jordan, however, in a note on Preller (273) emphatically says that the Sabine origin of the god is a fable ; and for the illusory distinction between Latins and Sabines in Rome see Mommsen, *R. H.* i. 67, note, and Bréal, *Hercule et Cacus,* p. 56. Sancus was no doubt a Sabine deity and reputed ancestor of the race (Cato ap. Dionys. 2. 49 : cp. 4. 58) ; but it does not follow that he came to Rome as a Sabine importation.

religious conception we are speaking of was very near akin to
that of Jupiter himself.

There is clear evidence that the best Roman scholars identified
not only Dius Fidius with Semo Sancus, but both of these with
Hercules. Varro, in a passage already quoted, tells us that Stilo
believed Dius Fidius to be the Sabine Sancus and the Greek
Hercules; Verrius Flaccus, if his excerptors represent him
rightly, in two separate glosses identified all these three[1].

Again, the Roman oaths *me dius fidius* and *me hercule* are
synonymous; that the former was the older can hardly be
doubted, and the latter must have come into vogue when the
Greek oath by Heracles became familiar. Thus the origin of *me
hercule* must be found in a union of the characteristics of Hercules
with those of the native Dius Fidius. It is worth noting that
in pronouncing both these oaths it was the custom to go out
into the open air[2]. Here is a point at which both Hercules
and Dius Fidius seem to come into line with Jupiter; for the
most solemn oath of all was *per Iovem* (*lapidem*), also taken
under the light of heaven[3], as was the case with the oath at
the altar of Ζεὺς Ἑρκεῖος in Greece[4]. Yet another point of conjunction is the *ara maxima* at the entrance to the Circus Maximus,
which was also a place where oaths were taken and treaties
ratified[5]; this was the altar of Hercules Victor, to whom the
tithes of spoil were offered; and this was also associated with
the legend of Hercules and Cacus. In the deity by whom
oaths were sworn, and in the deity of the tithes and the legend,
it is now acknowledged on all hands that we should recognize
a great Power whom we may call Dius Fidius, or Semo Sancus,
or the Genius Iovius, or even Jupiter himself[6]. Tithes, oaths,

---

[1] Varro, *L. L.* 5. 66; Festus, 229 (Propter viam); and Paulus, 147
(medius fidius).

[2] Cp. Plutarch, *Quaest. Rom.* 28 ('Why are boys made to go out of the
house when they wish to swear by Hercules?') with Varro, ap. Nonium,
s. v. *rituis*, and *L. L.* 5. 66.

[3] See below on Sept. 13, p. 231. The silex was taken out of the temple
of Jupiter Feretrius (Paulus, 92).

[4] Eustath. ad *Od.* 22. 335; Hermann, *Gr. Ant.* ii. 74. Cp. A. Lang,
Myth, &c. ii. 54: 'the sky hears us,' said the Indian when taking an oath.

[5] Dionys. i. 40.

[6] See the opinions of Hartung, Schwegler, and Preller, summed up by
Bréal, *Hercule et Cacus*, 51 foll.; and R. Peter in *Lex.* s.v. Hercules,
2255 foll.

and the myth of the struggle of light with darkness, cannot be associated with such a figure as the Hercules who came to Italy from Greece ; tithes are the due of some great god, or lord of the land [1], oaths are taken in the presence of the god of heaven, and the great nature-myth only descends by degrees to attach itself to semi-human figures.

We are here indeed in the presence of very ancient Italian religious ideas, which we can only very dimly apprehend, and for the explanation of which—so far as explanation is possible— there is not space in this work. But before we leave Dius Fidius, I will briefly indicate the evidence on which we may rest our belief (1) that as Semo Sancus, he is connected with Jupiter as the god of the heaven and thunder ; and (2) that as Hercules he is closely related to the same god as seen in a different aspect.

1. In the Iguvian inscription referred to above Sancius in one place appears in conjunction with Iovius [2] ; and, as we have seen, it is also found in the same ritual with Fisu or Fisovius. In this same passage of the inscription (which is a manual of ritual for the Fratres Attidii, an ancient religious brotherhood of Iguvium), the priest is directed to have in his hand an *urfita* (*orbita*), i. e. either disk or globe ; and this *urfita* has been compared [3], not without reason, with the *orbes* mentioned by Livy [4] as having been made of brass after the capture of Privernum and placed in the temple of Semo Sancus. If we may safely believe that such symbols occur chiefly in the worship of deities of sun and heaven, as seems probable, we have here some evidence, however imperfect, for the common origin of Sancus and Jupiter.

Again, there was in Roman augural lore a bird called *sanqualis avis,* which can hardly be dissociated from the cult of

[1] Robertson Smith, *Religion of the Semites,* p. 233.

[2] Bücheler, *Umbrica,* 7 ; Bréal, *Tables Eugubines,* 270.

[3] Preller, ii. 273, and Jordan's note. In M. Gaidoz's *Études de Mythologie Gauloise,* i. 64, will be found figures of a hand holding a wheel, from Bar-le-Duc (the wrist thrust through one of the holes), which may possibly explain the *urfita,* and which he connects with the Celtic sun-god. In this connexion we may notice the large series of Umbrian and Etruscan coins with the six-rayed wheel-symbol (Mommsen, *Münzwesen,* 222 foll.), which, as Professor Gardner tells me, is more probably a sun-symbol than merely the chariot-wheel convenient for unskilful coiners.

[4] 8. 20.

Sancus; for there was also an ancient city gate, the porta Sanqualis, near the sacellum Sancus on the Quirinal [1]. Pliny's language about this bird shows that this bit of ancient lore was almost lost in his time; but at the same time he makes it clear that it was believed to belong to the eagle family, which played such an important part in the science of augury. The only concrete fact that seems to be told us about this bird is that in B. C. 177 one struck with its beak a sacred stone at Crustumerium—a stone, it would seem, that had fallen from heaven, i. e. a thunder-stone or a meteorite [2].

Bearing this in mind, we are not surprised to find further traces of a connexion between Sancus and thunderbolts. There was at Rome a *decuria* of *sacerdotes bidentales*, in close association with the cult of Sancus. Three votive altars are extant, dedicated to the god by this *decuria* [3]; two of them were found on the Quirinal, close to the site of the sacellum Sancus. Now the meaning of the word *bidental* shows that the *decuria* had as its duty the care of the sacred spots which had been struck by thunderbolts; such a spot, which was also called *puteal* from its resemblance to a well fenced with a circular wall, bore the name *bidental*, presumably because two-year-old sheep (*bidentes*) were sacrificed there [4]. Consequently we again have Sancus brought into connexion with the augural lore of lightning, which made it a religious duty to bury the bolt, and fence off the spot from profane intrusion. Yet another step forward in this dim light. A *bidental* was one kind of *templum*, as we are expressly told [5]; and the temple of Sancus itself seems to have had this peculiarity. Varro says that its roof was *per-*

---

[1] For the bird, Plin. *N. H.* 10. 20; Festus, 197 s. v. *oscines*, and 317 (*sanqualis avis*). Bouché-Leclercq, *Hist. de la Divination*, iv. 200. For the gate cp. Paulus, 345, with Liv. 8. 20; Jordan, *Topogr.* ii. 264.

[2] Liv. 41. 13, with Weissenborn's note. The stone was perhaps the same as one which had shortly before fallen into the grove of Mars at Crustumerium (41. 9).

[3] *C. I. L.* vi. 567. 568; and *Bull. dell' Inst.*, 1881, p. 38 foll. (This last with a statue, which, however, may not belong to it: Jordan's note on Preller, ii. 273.) Wilmanns, *Exempla Inscr. Lat.* 1300.

[4] Marq. 263; B.-Leclercq, iv. 51 foll. The Scholiast on Persius, 2. 27, is explicit on the point. But Deecke, in a note to Müller's *Etrusker* (ii. 275) doubts the connexion of the *decuria* with *bidental* = *puteal*.

[5] Festus, s. v. Scribonianum (p. 333: the restoration can hardly be wrong) '[quia ne͜fas est integi, semper ibi forami[ne aper]to caelum patet.'

foratum, so that the sky might be seen through it [1]. In a fragment of augural lore, apparently genuine though preserved by a writer of late date, the *caeli templum* seems to have been ·conceived as a dome, or a ball (*orbis*) cut in half, *with a hole in the top* [2]. We may allow that we are here getting out of our depth ; but the general result of what has been put forward is that Sancus = Dius Fidius was originally a spirit or *numen* of the heaven, and a wielder of the lightning, closely allied to the great Jupiter, whose cult, combined with that of Hercules, had almost obliterated him in historical times.

Finally, it would seem that those moral attributes of Jupiter which give him a unique position in the Roman theology as the god of truth, order, and concord, belonged at one period also to Sancus as Dius Fidius ; for in his temple was kept the most ancient treaty of which the Romans knew, that said to have been made by Tarquinius Superbus with Gabii, which Dionysius must himself have seen [3], and which he describes as consisting of a wooden *clypeus*, bound with the hide of a sacrificed ox, and bearing ancient letters. Here also was the reputed statue of Gaia Caecilia or Tanaquil, the ideal Roman matron ; of which it has been conjectured, rashly perhaps, but by an authority of weight, that it really represented a humanized female form of Dius Fidius, standing to him as the Junones of women stood to the Genii of men, or as Juno in the abstract to Genius in the abstract [4].

---

[1] *L. L.* 5. 66 'ut ea videatur divum, id est caelum.' He connects the word *divum* with *Dius* Fidius. See Jordan in the collection of essays 'in honorem Th. Mommseni,' p. 369.

[2] Martianus Capella, 1. 45 (p. 47 in Eyssenhardt's edition). See Nissen's explanation in *Das Templum*, p. 184, and plate iv. In this account Jupiter occupies the chief place : Sancus is there, alone in the 12th *regio*. But doubt has been cast on Nissen's view by the discovery of an actual representation of the *caeli templum* (see Aust, in *Lex.* s. v. Iupiter, 668).

[3] Dionys. 4. 58. In 9. 60 he says that this temple was only vowed by Tarquinius, and not dedicated till 466 B. C. (Aust, *de Aedibus sacris*, p. 6) ; but there must have been a still earlier sanctuary of some kind (Livy writes of a *sacellum*, 8. 20. 8). Dionysius is interesting and explicit ; he calls Dius Fidius Ζεὺς Πίστιος, and adds the name Σάγκος. The treaties next in date, those with Carthage, were kept in the aedilium thesaurus, close to the temple of Jupiter Capitolinus (Polyb. 3. 22 ; Mommsen, *Staatsrecht*, ii. 1 (ed. 2) 481 note). Here we seem to see the authority of the ancient Dius Fidius already losing ground.

[4] Plut. *Quaest. Rom.* 30 ; Varro, ap. Plin. *N. H.* 8. 194 ; Festus, 238. It was Reifferscheid's conjecture that she was a female Dius Fidius (see

2. The last sentence of the preceding paragraph may aptly bring us to our second point, viz. the relation to Jupiter of Dius Fidius as = Hercules. Those who read the article 'Dius Fidius' in Roscher's *Lexicon* will be struck by the fact that so cautious a writer as Professor Wissowa should boldly identify this deity, at the very outset of his account, with the 'Genius Iovis'; and this conjecture, which is not his own, but rather that of the late Professor Reifferscheid of Breslau [1], calls for a word of explanation.

More than thirty years ago Reifferscheid published a paper in which he compared certain points in the cults of Juno and Hercules, of which we have a meagre knowledge from Roman literature, with some works of art of Etruscan or ancient Italian origin (i. e. not Greek), and found that they seemed to throw new and unexpected light on each other.

The Roman women, we are told [2], did not swear by Hercules, but by 'their Juno'; the men swore by Hercules, Dius Fidius, or by their Genius [3]. Women were excluded from the cult of Hercules at the ara maxima [4]; men were excluded, not indeed from the cult of Juno, but (as Reifferscheid puts it) 'from that of Bona Dea, who was not far removed from Juno [5].' At the birth of a child, a couch (*lectus*) was spread in the *atrium* for Juno, a *mensa* for Hercules [6]. The bride's girdle (*cingulum*) seems to have given rise to a cult-title of Juno, viz. Cinxia, while the knot in it which was loosed by the bridegroom at the *lectus genialis* was called the *nodus herculaneus* [7].

Wissowa, *Lex.* 1190). Fest. 241 adds ' cuius ex zona periclitantes ramenta sumunt.'

[1] *Bull. dell' Inst.*, 1867, 352 foll. Reifferscheid was prevented by death from working his view out more fully; but R. Peter (see *Lex.* s. v. Hercules, 2267) preserved notes of his lectures.

[2] Gellius, 11. 6. 1. For Juno as female equivalent of Genius see article 'Iunones' in *Lex.* But it does not seem proved that this was the old name, and not an idea of comparatively late times.

[3] Seneca, *Ep.* 12. 2.   [4] See below, on Aug. 12, p. 194.

[5] This seems a weak point. Bona Dea was not more closely related to Juno than some others. I do not feel sure that the name Juno is not as much an intrusion here as Hercules, and that the real female counterpart of Genius, &c., was not a nameless *numen* like the Bona Dea. The rise of the cult of Juno Lucina may have produced this intrusion. It is worth noting that in Etruria Minerva takes the place of Juno (*Lex.* 2266, and the illustration on 2267).

[6] Serv. *Ecl.* 4. 62.   [7] Paulus, 63.

Now Reifferscheid believed that he found the same conjunction of Juno and Hercules in several works of art, which
may be supposed to be reflections from the same set of ideas
which produced the usages just indicated. In the most important of these there is indeed no doubt about it; this is
a mirror of Etruscan workmanship[1], in which three figures
are marked with the Latin names IOVEI (Jupiter), IUNO and
HERCELE. Jupiter sits on an altar in the middle, and with his
right hand is touching Juno, who has her left hand on his
shoulder; Hercules stands with his club, apparently expectant,
on the left. From certain indications in the mirror (for which
I must refer the reader to the illustration on p. 2259 of
Roscher's *Lexicon*) Reifferscheid concluded that Jupiter was
here giving Juno in marriage to Hercules; and, in spite of
some criticism, this interpretation has been generally accepted[2].
In other works of art he found the same conjunction, though
no names mark the figures; in these Hercules and Juno, if
such they be, appear to be contending for the mastery, rather
than uniting peacefully in wedlock[3]. This conjunction, or
opposition, of Juno and Hercules, is thus explained by Reifferscheid. The name Juno represents the female principle in
human nature[4]; the 'genius' of a woman was called by this
name, and the cult of Juno as a developed goddess shows many
features that bear out the proposition[5]. If these facts be so,
then the inference to be drawn from the conjunction or opposition
of Juno and Hercules is that the name Hercules indicates the
male principle in human nature. But the male principle is
also expressed in the word Genius, as we see e. g. in the term
lectus genialis; Hercules therefore and Genius mean the same
thing—the former name having encroached upon the domain
of the latter, as a Latinized form of Heracles, of all Greek
heroes or divinities the most *virile*. And if Hercules, Semo

[1] Gerhard, *Etruskische Spiegel*, 147. It is also figured in *Lex.* s. v.
Hercules, 2259.
[2] e. g. by every writer in Roscher's *Lexicon* who has touched on the
subject. Jordan seems to have dissented (Preller, ii. 284).
[3] The opposition or conflict of the two is paralleled by the supposed
myth of the contention of Mars and Minerva (Nerio) (see above, p. 60;
Lex. 2265).
[4] See article 'Iunones' in *Lex.*; and De-Marchi, *La Religione nella vita
domestica*, p. 70.
[5] Roscher's article 'Juno' in *Lex.* passim.

Sancus and Dius Fidius are all different names for the same idea, then the word Genius may be taken as equivalent to the two last of these as well as to Hercules[1].

But why does Reifferscheid go on to tell us that this Genius, i. e. Hercules = Sancus = Dius Fidius, is the *Genius Iovis*? How does he connect this many-titled conception with the great father of the sky? As a matter of fact, he has but slender evidence for this; he relies on the mirror in which he found Jupiter giving Juno to Hercules, and on the conjecture that the Greek Hercules, the son of Zeus, would easily come to occupy in Italy the position of Genius, if the latter were, in an abstract form and apart from individual human life, regarded as the Genius of Jupiter[2]. And in this he is followed by Wissowa and other writers in Roscher's *Lexicon*.

It would perhaps have been wiser not to go so far as this. He has already carried us back to a world of ideas older than these varying names which so often bewilder us in the Roman worship—to a world of spirits, Semones, Lares, Cerri, ghosts of deceased ancestors, vegetation demons, and men's 'other souls.' When he talks of a *Genius Iovis*[3], he is surely using the language of later polytheism to express an idea which belonged, not to a polytheistic age, but to that older world of religious thought. He is doing, in fact, the very thing which the Romans themselves were doing all through the period of the Republic—the one thing which above all others has made

---

[1] I cannot agree with Mr. Jevons (*Introduction to History of Religion*, p. 186 foll.) when he makes the Roman genius a relic of totemism, simply because *genii* were often represented by serpents. The snake was too universally worshipped and domesticated to be easily explained as a totem. Mr. Frazer has an interesting example from Zululand, which is singularly suggestive in connexion with the doctrine of Genius (see *Golden Bough*, ii. 332), which can hardly be explained on a totemistic basis. The doctrine of Genius may certainly have had its roots in a totemistic age; but by the time it reaches us in Roman literature it has passed through so many stages that its origin is not to be dogmatized about.

[2] I cannot attach much weight to the argument (see *Lex.* 2268) that because Aelius Stilo explained Dius Fidius as Diovis Filius he therefore had in his head some such relation of Genius to Jupiter.

[3] If he had written Genius *Iovius*, after the manner of the Iguvian inscription, with its adjectival forms which preserve a reminiscence of the older spirit-world, he might have been nearer the mark. It may be that we get back to Jupiter himself as the Genius *par excellence*, but there is no direct proof of this. The genius of a god is a late idea, as Mr. Jevons points out in a note to *Roman Questions*, p. liii.

the study of their religious ideas such a treacherous quagmire for the modern student.

vi Id. Iun. (June 8). N.

MENTI IN CAPITOLIO. (VEN. MAFF. VI MINORES.)

The temple of Mens was vowed by T. Otacilius (praetor) in 217 B. C., after the battle of Trasimenus 'propter neglegentiam caerimoniarum auspiciorumque [1],' and dedicated in 215 B.C., by the same man as *duumvir aedibus dedicandis* [2]. The vow was the result of an inspection of the Sibylline books, from which we might infer that the goddess was a stranger [3]. If so, who was she, and whence? Reasoning from the fact that in the same year, in the same place, and by the same man, a temple was dedicated to Venus Erycina [4], Preller guessed that this Mens was not a mere abstraction, but another form of the same Venus; for a Venus Mimnermia or Meminia is mentioned by Servius [5], 'quod meminerit omnium.'

However this may be, the foundation of a cult of Mens at so critical a moment of their fortunes is very characteristic of the Roman spirit of that age; it was an appeal to 'something not themselves which made for righteousness' to help them to remember their caerimoniae, and not to neglect their auspicia. It is remarkable that this temple of Mens was restored by M. Aemilius Scaurus probably amid the disasters of the Cimbrian war a century later [6].

vii Id. Iun. (June 7). N.

VESTA APERIT. (PHILOC.)

v Id. Iun. (June 9). N.

VESTALIA. (TUSC. VEN. MAFF.)

xvii Kal. Quinct. (June 15). N.

VESTA CLUDITUR. (PHILOC.)

xvii Kal. Quinct. (June 15). Q. St. D. F.

It would seem from these notes in the calendars, and from

---

[1] Livy, 22. 9; Ovid, *Fasti*, 6. 241 foll.; Aust, *de Aedibus sacris*, p. 19.

[2] Livy, 23. 31 and 32; Marq. 270.

[3] Marq. 358 foll.; Article 'Sibyllini libri' in *Dict. of Antiquities*, ed. 2.

[4] Livy, 22. 9, 10; 23 30, 31.   [5] Ad *Aen.* 1. 720.

[6] Plut. *de Fort. Rom.* 5. 10; Cic. *Nat. Deor.* 2. 61. Aust (*de Aedibus sacris*, p. 19) puts it in B. C. 115, in Scaurus' consulship.

passages in Ovid and Festus[1], that both before and after the day of the true Vestalia there were days set apart for the cult of the goddess, which were *nefasti* and also *religiosi*[2]. Ovid's lines are worth quoting; he consults the Flaminica Dialis[3] about the marriage of his daughter:

> Tum mihi post sacras monstratur Iunius idus
> Utilis et nuptis, utilis esse viris,
> Primaque pars huius thalamis aliena repeita est,
> Nam mihi sic coniunx sancta Dialis ait;
> 'Donec ab Iliaca placidus purgamina Vesta
> Detulerit flavis in mare Thybris aquis,
> Non mihi detonsos crines depectere buxo,
> Non ungues ferro subsecuisse licet,
> Non tetigisse virum, quamvis Iovis ille sacerdos,
> Quamvis perpetua sit mihi lege datus.
> Tu quoque ne propera. Melius tua filia nubet
> Ignea cum pura Vesta nitebit humo.'

What is the meaning of this singular aspect of the Vesta-cult? Why should these days be so ill-omened or so sacred that during them marriages might not be celebrated, and the priestess of Jupiter might not hold any intercourse with her husband, cut her hair, or pare her nails? And what is the explanation of the annotation Q[uando] St[ercus] D[elatum] F[as][4], which on the 15th indicated the breaking of the spell, and a return to ordinary ways of life? Before attempting to answer these questions, it will be as well to say a few words about the nature and probable origin of the worship of Vesta. Owing to the remarkable vitality and purity of this cult throughout the whole of Roman history, we do not meet here with those baffling obscurities which so often beset us in dealing with deities that had lost all life and shape when Roman scholars began to investigate them. And yet we know that we are here in the presence of rites and ideas of immemorial antiquity.

---

[1] Ovid, *Fasti*, 6. 219 foll.; Festus, 250, s. v. *Penus*: '[Penus vo]catur locus intimus in aede Vestae, tegetibus saeptus, qui certis diebus circa Vestalia aperitur. Ii dies religiosi habentur.'

[2] For the meanings of *nefastus* and *religiosus* see Introduction, p. 9; Marq. 291.

[3] No doubt this was done, and the lines composed, in order to please Augustus and reflect the revival of the old *religio*.

[4] Varro, *L. L.* 6. 32.

In an article of great interest in the *Journal of Philology*
for 1885 [1], Mr. J. G. Frazer first placed the origin of the cult
in a clear light for English scholars. By comparing it with
similar practices of existing peoples still in a primitive condition of life, he made apparent the real germ of the institution
of the Vestal Virgins. Helbig, in his *Italiker in der Poebene* [2],
had already recognized that germ in *the necessity of keeping
one fire always alight in each settlement*, so that its members
could at any time supply themselves with the flame, then
so hard to procure at a moment's notice; and Mr. Frazer
had only to go one step further, and show that the task
of keeping this fire alight was that of the daughters of the
chief. This step he was able to take, supported by evidence
from Damaraland in South Africa, where the priestess of the
perpetual fire is the chief's daughter ; quoting also the following
example from Calabria in Southern Italy : 'At the present day
the fire in a Calabrian peasant's house is never (except after
a death) allowed to die quite out, even in the heat of summer ;
it is a bad omen if it should chance to be extinguished, and
the girls of the house, whose special care it is to keep at least
a single brand burning on the hearth, are sadly dismayed
at such a mishap.' The evidence of the Roman *ius sacrum*
quite confirms this modern evidence ; the Vestals were under
the patria potestas of the pontifex maximus, who represented
in republican times the legal powers of the Rex, and from this
fact we may safely argue that they had once been the daughters
of the primitive chief. The *flamines* too, or *kindlers*, as being
under the potestas of the pontifex, may be taken as representing
the sons of the primitive household [3]. But from various
reasons [4] the duties of the *flamines* became obsolete or obscure ;
while those of the Vestals remained to give us an almost
perfect picture of life in the household of the oldest Latins.

From the first, no doubt, the tending of the fire was in some
sense a religious service, and the flame a sacred flame [5]. There

---

[1] Vol. xiv, No. 28   [2] p. 53.
[3] Marq. 250. In the Andaman Islands both sons and daughters take
part in the work of maintaining the fires (Man's *Andaman Islands*, quoted
by Mr. Frazer, op. cit. p. 153).
[4] See my article 'Sacerdos' in *Dict. of Antiquities*, ed. 2.
[5] Vesta herself was originally simply the fire on the hearth (Frazer,
op. cit. 152). Note that the flame was obtained afresh each year on March 1,

must have been many stages of growth from this beginning to the fully developed Vesta of the Republic and Empire; yet we can see that the lines of development were singularly simple and consistent. The sacred fire for example was maintained in the aedes Vestae, adjoining the king's house [1] (regia); and the penus Vestae, which must originally have contained the stores on which the family depended for their sustenance, was always believed to preserve the most sacred and valuable objects possessed by the State [2].

We return to the Vestalia, of which the ritual was as follows. On June 7, the penus Vestae, which was shut all the rest of the year, and to which no man but the pontifex maximus had at any time right of entry, was thrown open to all matrons. During the seven following days they crowded to it barefoot [3]. Ovid relates his own experience [4]:

> Forte revertebar festis Vestalibus illa
> Qua nova Romano nunc via iuncta foro est.
> Huc pede matronam vidi descendere nudo:
> Obstipui tacitus sustinuique gradum.

The object of this was perhaps to pray for a blessing on the household. On plain and old-fashioned ware offerings of food were carried into the temple: the Vestals themselves offered the sacred cakes made of the first ears of corn plucked, as we saw, in the early days of May [5]; bakers and millers kept holiday, all mills were garlanded, and donkeys decorated with wreaths and cakes [6].

> Ecce coronatis panis dependet asellis
> Et velant scabras florida serta molas.

On June 15 the temple (aedes, not templum) was swept and the refuse taken away and either thrown into the Tiber

even in historical times, by the primitive method of the friction of the wood of a 'lucky' tree (Festus, 106), or from the sun's rays. We are not told which priest performed this rite.

[1] Middleton, Rome in 1885, p. 181 foll.

[2] This belief, and the nature of the treasures, are fully discussed by Marquardt, p. 251, with additions by Wissowa.

[3] Cp. Petronius, Sat. 44 (of the aquaelicium).

[4] Fasti, 6. 395 foll.   [5] Above, p. 110.

[6] As the beast that usually worked in mills? There is a Pompeian painting of this scene (Gerhard, Ant. Bild. pl. 62).

or deposited in some particular spot [1]. Then the *dies nefasti* came to an end; and the 15th itself became *fastus* as soon as the last act of cleansing had been duly performed: 'Quando stercus delatum fas.'

In this account of the ritual of these days, two features claim special attention: (1) the duties of the Vestals in connexion with the provision of food; (2) the fact that the days were *religiosi*, as is illustrated by the prohibition of marriage and the mourning of the Flaminica Dialis. That these two features were in some way connected seems proved by the cessation of the mourning when the penus Vestae was once more closed.

1. It needs but little investigation to discover that, though the germ of the cult was doubtless the perpetual fire in the king's house, the cult itself was by no means confined to attendance on the fire; and this was so probably from the very first. The king's daughters fetched the water from the spring, both for sacred and domestic purposes; and this duty was kept up throughout Roman history, for water was never 'laid on' to the house of the Vestals, but carried from a sacred fountain [2]. They also crushed the corn with pestle and mortar, and prepared the cakes for the use of the family—duties which survived in all their pristine simplicity in the preparation of the *mola salsa* in the early days of May [3]; and they swept the house, as the Vestals afterwards continued to cleanse the penus Vestae, on June 15. The penus, or store-closet of the house, was under their charge; on the state

[1] Varro, *L. L.* 6. 32 'Dies qui vocatur Q. St. D. F. ab eo appellatur quod eo die ex aede Vestae stercus everritur et per Capitolinum clivum in locum defertur certum.' It is Ovid who tells us it was thrown into the Tiber (*Fasti*, 6. 713).

[2] Jordan, *Tempel der Vesta*, p. 63.

[3] The crushing of the grain no doubt comes down from a time when there were no mills (Helbig, *Italiker in der Poebene*, 17 and 72). The preparation of the cakes was also peculiar, and even that of the salt which was used in them (Festus, 159; cp. Serv. *Ecl.* 8. 82). The latter passage is the *locus classicus* for all these duties: 'Virgines Vestales tres maximae ex nonis Maiis ad pridie Idus Maias alternis diebus (i. e. on 7th, 9th, 11th?) spicas adoreas in corbibus messuariis ponunt, easque spicas ipsae virgines torrent, pinsunt, molunt, atque ita molitum condunt. Ex eo farre virgines ter in anno molam faciunt, Lupercalibus, Vestalibus, Idibus Septembribus, adiecto sale cocto et sale duro.' For examples of the primitive method of cooking see Miss Kingsley's *Travels in West Africa*, p. 208; and Sir Joseph Banks's *Journal* (ed. Hooker), p. 137.

of its contents the family depended for its comfort and prosperity, and from the very outset it must have had a kind
of sacred character[1]. The close connexion of Vesta and her
ministrants with the simple materials and processes of the
house and the farm is thus quite plain ; and we may trace it in
every rite in which they took any part. The Fordicidia and
the Parilia in April were directly concerned with the flocks
and herds of the community ; in May the festival of the Bona
Dea and the mysterious ceremony of the Argei point to the
season of peril during the ripening of the crops. After the
Vestalia the Vestals were present at the Consualia and
the festival of Ops Consiva in August, which, as we shall see,
were probably harvest festivals ; and on the Ides of October
the blood of the 'October horse' was deposited in their care
for use at the Fordicidia as a charm for fertility. So constant
is the connexion of Vesta with the fruits of the earth, that
it is not surprising that some Roman scholars[2] should have
considered her an earth goddess ; especially as, in a volcanic
region, the proper home of fire would be thought to be beneath
the earth. But such explanations, and also the views of
modern scholars who have sought to find in Vesta a deity
of abstract ideas, such as 'the nourishing element in the fire[3]',
are really superfluous. The associations which grew up
around the sacred hearth-fire can all be traced to the original
germ, if it be borne in mind that the fire, the provision-store,
and the protecting deities of that store, were all placed together
in the centre of the house, and that all domestic operations,
sacrificial or culinary, took place at or by means of, the
necessary fire. 'What is home but another word for cooking?'

---

[1] *Penus* means, in the first instance, food. Cic. *Nat. Deorum*, 2. 68 'Est
omne quo vescuntur homines penus.' Hence it came to mean the store-
closet in the centre of the house, of which the Penates were the guardian
spirits. Its sacred character is indicated in a passage of Columella
(*R. R.* 12. 4 ; and see my paper on the *toga praetexta* of Roman children,
in *Classical Review*, Oct. 1896).

[2] Varro, ap. S. Aug. *de Civ.* 7. 24 ; cp. 7. 16. Ovid, *Fasti*, 6. 267, writes,
'Vesta eadem quae terra,' but more correctly in 291, 'Nec tu aliud Vestam
quam vivam intellige flammam.' Some moderns derive Vesta from root
vas = 'dwelling,' and make her the earth in special relation to the
dwelling ; e. g. O. Gilbert, i. 348 note.

[3] Preuner, *Hestia-Vesta*, p. 221 'Gottheit des Feuers, sofern religiöse,
ethische Ideen sich in demselben abspiegeln, nicht des Feuers als blossen
Elements.' This is surely turning the question upside down.

Nor must we forget that the living fire was for primitive man a mysterious thing, and invested from the first with divine attributes [1].

2. The fact that from the 5th to the 15th the days were not only *nefasti* but also *religiosi* is not easy to explain. It is true that in two other months, February and April, we find a parallel series of *dies nefasti* in the first half of the month; in February it extended from the Kalends to the Lupercalia (15th), and in April from the Nones to the Vinalia (23rd) [2]. But these days in February and April were *nefasti* in the ordinary sense of the word, i. e. the cessation of judicial business, and we are not told of them that they were also *religiosi*, or that the Flaminica Dialis lay during them under any special restrictions, as in the days we are speaking of. On the other hand, we find to our surprise that the other days on which this priestess was forbidden to comb hair or cut nails were not even *nefasti* in the ordinary sense, viz. those of the 'moving' of the *ancilia* and of the ceremony of the Argei [3] : so that we are baffled at every point in looking for a solution to the calendar.

But there is one fact that is quite clear, namely, that the *tempus nefastum* was in some way or other the result of the purification of the aedes Vestae, since it ceased at the moment the last act of cleansing was completed. Now it does seem to be the case that among some peoples living by agriculture but as yet comparatively uncivilized, special importance is attached to the days immediately before harvest and the gathering of the first-fruits—at which time there is a general cleaning out of house, barns, and all receptacles and utensils, and following upon this a period of rejoicing. Mr. Frazer, in his *Golden Bough* has collected some examples of this practice, though he has not brought them together under one head or given them a single explanation. The most striking, and at the same time the best attested, example is as follows [4] :

---

[1] Tylor, *Prim. Cult.* ii. 251 ; Grimm, *German Mythology* (Eng. trans.), p. 601 foll.

[2] In July also the days were *nefasti* from the Kalends to the 9th ; but to the meaning of this we have no clue whatever.

[3] See above, p. 115.

[4] *G. B.* ii. 75. In an appendix (p. 373 foll. and esp. 382) will be found some other examples of the same type of ritual. Cp. also ii. 176 (from Punjaub), which example, however, does not seem in any way connected

'Among the Creek Indians of North America, the *busk*, or festival of firstfruits, was the chief ceremony of the year. It was held in July or August, when the corn was ripe, and marked the end of the old year and the beginning of the new one. Before it took place none of the Indians would eat or even handle any of the new harvest. . . . Before celebrating the Busk, the people provided themselves with new clothes and new household utensils and furniture; they collected their old clothes and rubbish, together with all the remaining grain and other old provisions, cast them together in one common heap and consumed them with fire. As a preparation for the ceremony all the fires in the village were extinguished, and the ashes swept clean away. In particular the hearth or altar of the temple was dug up, and the ashes carried out. . . . Meanwhile the women at home were cleaning out their houses, renewing the old hearths, and scouring all the cooking vessels that they might be ready to receive the new fire and the new fruits. The public or sacred square was carefully swept of even the smallest crumbs of previous feasts, for fear of polluting the first-fruit offerings. Also every vessel that had contained any food during the expiring year was removed from the temple before sunset.' A general fast followed, we are told; 'and when the sun was declining from the meridian, all the people were commanded by the voice of a crier to stay within doors, to do no bad act, and to be sure to extinguish and throw away every spark of the old fire. Universal silence now reigned. Then the high priest made the new fire by the friction of two pieces of wood, and placed it on the altar under the green arbour. This new fire was believed to atone for all past crimes except murder. Then a basket of new fruits was brought; the high priest took out a little of each sort of fruit, rubbed it with bear's oil, and offered it together with some flesh to the bountiful spirit of fire as a first-fruit offering and an annual oblation for sin. . . . Finally the chief priest made a speech, exhorting the people to observe their old rites and customs, announcing that the new divine fire had purged away the sins of the past year, and earnestly warning the women

with harvest. But the practice of the Creek Indians is so unusually well attested that it deserves special attention. It is described by no less than four independent authorities (see Mr. Frazer's note on p. 76).

that if any of them had not extinguished the old fire, or had contracted any impurity, they must forthwith depart lest the divine fire should spoil both them and the people.'

The four chief points in this very interesting account are, (1) the extremely solemn and critical character of the whole ceremonial, as indicated in the general fast; (2) the idea of the necessity of purification preparatory to the reception of first-fruits, a purification which seems to extend to human beings as well as to houses, receptacles, and utensils; (3) the renewal of the sacred fire, which was coincident with the beginning of a new year; (4) the solemn reception of the first-fruits. Comparing these with Roman usage, we notice that the first two are fully represented at the Vestalia, the one by the religious character of the days, and the mourning of the Flaminica Dialis, the other by the cleansing of the penus Vestae, and the careful removal of all its refuse. The third is represented, not at the Vestalia, but at the beginning of the year on March 1, when the sacred fire was renewed, as we saw, in the primitive fashion by the friction of two pieces of wood, and the temple of Vesta was adorned with fresh laurels, as was the case also with the altar in the American example just quoted. The fourth point is represented neither in March nor June, but rather by the plucking of the first ears of corn by the Vestals before the Ides of May, from which they made the sacred salt-cakes of sacrifice.

Now we need not go the length of assuming that the Roman ceremonies of March, May and June were three parts of one and the same rite which in course of time had been separated and attached to different periods of the year; though this indeed may not be wholly impossible. But we may at least profitably notice that all the four striking features of the Indian ceremony are found in the cult of Vesta, and descended no doubt to the later Romans from an age in which both the crops, the fire and the store-houses were regarded as having much the same sacred character as they had for the Creek Indians.

To me indeed it had seemed probable, even before the publication of Mr. Frazer's *Golden Bough*, that the cleansing of the penus Vestae was nothing but a survival of a general purification of store-houses, barns, utensils, and probably of all the apparatus of farming, including perhaps human beings,

before the completion of the harvest which was now close at
hand. The date of the Vestalia is indeed too early to let us
suppose it to have been a real harvest festival, nor had it any
of the joyous character found in such rites ; and, as we shall
see, the true harvest festivals are to be found in the month of
August. The corn harvest in middle Italy took place in the
latter half of June and in July [1]; and, as is everywhere still
the practice, the festivals proper did not occur until the whole
work of harvesting was done. But at the time of the Vestalia
the crops were certainly ripening ; in May we have already had
the plucking of the first ears by the Vestals, and the *lustratio
segetum* which has been described under the head of Ambarvalia
on May 28.

I must leave to anthropologists the further investigation of
the ideas underlying the ritual we have been examining ; it is
something to have been able to co-ordinate it with rites which
are so well attested as those of the Creek Indians, and which
admit without difficulty of a reasonable interpretation [2].

III Id. Iun. (June 11). N.

MAT[RALIA]. (tusc. ven. maff.)
MATR[I] MATUT[AE]. (ven.)
MATRALIA. (philoc.)

The temple of which this day was apparently the *dies natalis*
dated from the Veientine War, 396 b. c., and was the result of
a vow made by L. Furius Camillus [3]. An earlier temple was
attributed to Servius Tullius ; but it is extremely improbable
that anything more than a *sacellum* or altar existed at such an
early date [4]. The cult of Mater Matuta was widely extended in
Italy, and clearly of genuine and ancient Italian origin ; she
can be separated with certainty from the Greek goddess
Leucothea with whom Ovid mixes her up, and from whom she
derived a connexion with harbours which did not originally

---

[1] Nissen, *Landeskunde*, 399.
[2] The whole of Mr. Frazer's section on the sacramental eating of new
crops should be read in connexion with the Vestalia.
[3] Aust, *de Aedibus sacris*, p. 7 ; Liv. 5. 19 and 23. The temple was in
the Forum boarium, near the Circus maximus.
[4] Wissowa in *Myth. Lex.* s. v. Mater Matuta, 2463.

belong to her[1]. The evidence for the wide spread of her cult consists of (1) two extremely old inscriptions from Pisaurum in Umbria, of which Mommsen observes, 'lingua meram vetustatem spirat'[2]; (2) certain inscriptions and passages of Livy which prove that her worship existed among the Volsci, in Campania, and at Praeneste[3]. At Satricum she was apparently the chief deity of the place and probably also at Pyrgi, the port of Caere in Etruria[4]. The cult seems to have had some marked peculiarities, of which one or two fragments have come down to us. Only the wife of a first marriage could deck the image of the goddess[5]; no female slaves were allowed in the temple except one, who was also driven out of it with a box on the ear, apparently as a yearly recurring memorial of the rule[6]; the sacred cakes offered were cooked in old-fashioned earthenware[7]; and, lastly, the women are said to have prayed to this goddess for their nephews and nieces in the first place, and for their own children only in the second[8]. All that can be deduced from these fragments is that the Mater Matuta was an ancient deity of matrons, and perhaps of the same type as other deities of women such as Carmenta, Fortuna, and Bona Dea[9].

---

[1] Ovid, *Fasti*, 6. 473 foll.; Cic. *Nat. Deor.* 3. 48; *Tusc.* 1. 28. Plutarch (*Quaest. Rom.* 16. 1) noted a likeness between her cult and that of Leucothea in his own city of Chaeroneia; an interesting passage, though quite inconclusive as to the Greek origin of Mater Matuta. Plutarch, like Servius (*Aen.* 5. 241) and others, has adopted Ovid's legend of Ino by way of explanation of the identity of Leucothea and Matuta. Merkel (*Fasti*, clxxxiv) believed the cult to be wholly Greek; Bouché-Leclercq (*Hist. de Divination*, iv. 147) follows Klausen in identifying Mater Matuta with Tethys (cf. Plut. *Rom.* 2) and with the deity of the oracle at Pyrgi. But see Wesseling on Diod. Sic. 15, p. 337; and Strabo, Bk. 5, p. 345.

[2] *C. I. L.* i. 176, 177.   [3] Liv. 6. 33. 4; Wissowa, *Lex.* 2462.

[4] Diod. Sic. 15. 14, p. 337, and Wesseling's note. The temple at Pyrgi was an important one, and rich enough to be plundered by Dionysius I of Syracuse. But it must be admitted that the identification of the deity of Pyrgi with Mater Matuta is not absolutely certain. Strabo, l. c., calls her Eileithyia, Aristotle (*Oecon.* 1349 b) Leucothea; and it is thought that Mater Matuta alone combines the characteristics of these two. If, however, the goddess of Pyrgi was the deity of the oracle, she might almost as well have been a Fortuna, like those of Antium and Praeneste.

[5] Tertullian, *de Monogam.* 17.

[6] Ovid, *Fasti*, 6. 481, with Plut. *Q. R.* 16; *Camill.* 5.

[7] Varro, *L. L.* 5. 106. Ovid (482) writes of *liba tosta*, i. e. cakes cooked in pans rather than baked, like the *mola salsa*. See above, p. 149; and cp. Ovid, 532 'in subito cocta foco.'   [8] Plut. ll. cc.; Ovid, 559 foll.

[9] See below on Jan. 11. I cannot explain the rule that a woman prayed for nephews and nieces before her own children, which is peculiar to this cult.

The best modern authorities explain her as a goddess of the dawn's light and of child-birth, and see a parallel in Juno Lucina [1]; and Mommsen has pointed out that the dawn was thought to be the lucky time for birth, and that the Roman names Lucius and Manius have their origin in this belief [2]. Lucretius shows us that in his day Mater Matuta was certainly associated with the dawn [3]:

> roseam Matuta per oras
> Aetheris auroram differt et lumina pandit.

We should, however, be glad to be more certain that Matuta was originally a substantive meaning dawn or morning. Verrius Flaccus [4] seems to have believed that the words *mane, maturus, matuta, manes,* and *mānus,* all had the meaning of 'good' contained in them; so that Mater Matuta might after all be only another form of the Bona Dea, who is also specially a woman's deity. But this cult was not preserved, like that of Vesta, by being taken up into the essential life of the State, and we are no longer able to discern its meaning with any approach to certainty.

It is noticeable that this day was, according to Ovid [5], the dedication of a temple of Fortuna, also *in foro boario*: but no immediate connexion can be discovered between this deity and Mater Matuta. This temple was remarkable as containing a wooden statue, veiled in drapery, which was popularly believed to represent Servius Tullius [6], of whose connexion with Fortuna we shall have more to say further on. No one, however, really knew what the statue was; Varro and Pliny [7] write of one of Fortuna herself which was heavily draped, and may have been the one in this temple. Pliny says that the statue of Fortuna was covered with the *togae praetextae* of Servius Tullius, which lasted intact down to the death of Seianus; and

---

[1] Preller, i. 322; Wissowa in *Lex.*

[2] *R. H.* (Eng. trans.) i. 162. [3] Lucr. 5. 654.

[4] Paulus, 122 'Matrem Matutam antiqui ob bonitatem appellabant, et maturum idoneum usui,' &c. See also Curtius, *Gk. Etym.* i. 408.

[5] *Fasti,* 6. 569 foll.; 625 foll.: cp. Dionysius, 4. 40. Ovid has three fanciful explanations of the draping.

[6] Ovid, l. c.; Dionys. 4. 40.

[7] Varro ap. Nonium, p. 189; Plin. *N. H.* 8. 194, 197. See Schwegler, *R. G.* i. 712, note 3, and a full discussion in *Lex.* by R. Peter, s. v. Fortuna, p. 1509.

it is singular that Seianus himself is said to have possessed
a statue of Fortuna which dated from the time of Servius[1],
and which turned its face away from him just before his fall.
Seianus was of Etruscan descent, we may remember; Servius
Tullius, or Mastarna, was certainly Etruscan; and among
Etruscan deities we find certain shrouded gods[2]. These facts
seem to suggest that the statue (or statues, if we cannot refer
all the passages above quoted to one statue) came from Etruria,
and was on that account a mystery both to the learned and the
ignorant at Rome. To us it must also remain unexplained[3].

Id. Iun. (June 13). NP.

FERIAE IOVI. (VEN.)
IOVI. (TUSC.)

To these notes in the calendars we may add a few lines
from Ovid :

> Idibus Invicto sunt data templa Iovi.
> Et iam Quinquatrus iubeor narrare minores:
> Nunc ades o coeptis, flava Minerva, meis.
> Cur vagus incedit tota tibicen in urbe ?
> Quid sibi personae, quid stola longa volunt ?

All Ides, as we have seen, were sacred to Jupiter; they are
so noted in the surviving calendars in May, June, August,
September, October and November, and were probably originally so noted in all the months[4]. On this day the *collegium*
or guild of the tibicines feasted in the temple of Jupiter

---

[1] Dio Cassius, 58. 7.

[2] Seneca, *Q. N.* 2. 41 ; Müller-Deecke, *Etrusker*, ii. 83 ; Dennis, *Etruria*, i,
Introduction lvi. The passage of Seneca is a very curious one about the
Etruscan lightning-lore. O. Müller guesses that the *di involuti* were Fates
(*Schicksalsgottheiten*), which would suit Fortuna (cp. Hor. *Od.* 1. 35).

[3] There is just a possibility that it was confused with a statue of
Pudicitia, also *in foro boario*, and also said to have been veiled (Festus,
242). Varro, l. c., calls the goddess of the statue, Fortuna Virgo, and
Preller suggested that she was identical with Pudicitia. The lines of
Ovid seem to favour this view (*Fasti*, 6. 617 foll.) :

> Veste data tegitur. Vetat hanc Fortuna moveri
> Et sic e templo est ipsa locuta suo ;
> 'Ore revelato qua primum luce patebit
> Servius, haec positi prima pudoris erit.
> Parcite, matronae, vetitas attingere vestes :
> Sollemni satis est voce movere preces.'

[4] Mommsen in *C. I. L.* i.[2] 298.

Capitolinus [1]. The temple referred to by Ovid of Jupiter
Invictus as having been dedicated on this day may possibly
have been one of two mentioned by Livy as dedicated on the
Capitol in B. C. 192 [2] ; but the coincidence of a dedication-day
with the Ides may perhaps suggest a higher antiquity [3].

For the right meaning and derivation of the word Quinquatrus the reader is referred to what has been already said
under March 19. June 13 was usually called Quinquatrus
minusculae, not because it was really Quinquatrus (i. e. five
days after the Ides), but because through the feast of the
tibicines it was associated with their patron Minerva [4], in
whose temple on the Aventine they met, apparently before
they set out on the revelling procession to which Ovid refers [5].
Varro makes this clear when he writes 'Quinquatrus minusculae dictae Iuniae Idus *ab similitudine* maiorum' [6], i. e. it was
not really Quinquatrus, but was popularly so called because
the other festival of Minerva and her followers bore that
name. Verrius Flaccus was equally explicit on the point :
'Minusculae Quinquatrus appellantur quod is dies festus est
tibicinum, qui colunt Minervam cuius deae proprie festus dies
est Quinquatrus mense Martio' [7].

The revelry of the tibicines, during which they wore the
masks and long robes mentioned by Ovid, was explained by
a story which the poet goes on to tell, and which is told
also by Livy and by Plutarch with some variations [8] ; how
they fled to Tibur in anger at being deprived by Appius

---

[1] Livy, 9. 30 ; Val. Max. 2. 5. 4 ; Varro, *L. L.* 6. 17. Cp. *C. I. L.* vi. 3696
[Magistri] quinq(uennales) [collegi] teib(icinum) Rom(anorum) qui s(acris)
p(ublicis) p(raesto) s(unt) Iov(i) Epul(oni) s(acrum).

[2] So Preller, i. 198.

[3] Aust, in *Lex.* s. v. Iuppiter, 680. Both here and in his work *de
Aedibus sacris*, this scholar declines to distinguish between Iup. Invictus
and Iup. Victor.

[4] For Minerva as the patron of all such guilds see Wissowa in *Lex.*
s. v. Minerva, 2984 foll.

[5] Varro, *L. L.* 6. 17. There were three days of revelry, according to
Livy (9. 30): did they meet in this temple on each day? The 13th was
the day of the *epulum* ; which the other days were we do not know.

[6] *L. L.* 6. 17.

[7] Festus, 149, s. v. minusculae. Cf Ovid, *Fasti*, 6. 695.

[8] Livy, l. c. Plutarch, *Quaest. Rom.* 55, who confuses two Appii Claudii,
and refers the story to the Decemvir instead of to the Censor of 311 B.C.
Livy omits the very Roman trait (Ov. 673 foll.) of the *libertus* feigning to
be surprised by his *patronus*.

Claudius the censor of their feast in the Capitol : how they were badly missed at Rome, tricked and made drunk by a freedman at Tibur, and sent home unconscious on a big waggon. The story is genuinely Roman in its rudeness and in the rough humour which Ovid fully appreciates ; the favourite feature of a secession is seen in it, and also the peaceful settlement of difficulties by compromise and contract. I see no reason why it should not be the echo of an actual event, though in detail it is obviously intended to explain the masks and the long robes. These are to be seen represented on a coin of the gens Plautia [1], to which the fierce censor's milder colleague belonged, who negotiated the return of the truants. Plutarch calls the ' stolae longae' women's clothes ; but it is more natural to suppose that they were simply the dress of Etruscan pipe-players of the olden time [2].

The story well shows the universal use of the *tibia* in all sacred rites ; the tibicines were indispensable, and had to be got back from Tibur by fair means or foul. As Ovid says :

> Cantabat fanis, cantabat tibia ludis,
> Cantabat maestis tibia funeribus.

The instrument was probably indigenous in Italy, and the only indigenous one of which we know. ' The word *tibia*,' says Professor Nettleship [3], ' is purely Italian, and has, so far as I can find, no parallel in the cognate languages.' Müller, in his work on the Etruscans, does indeed assume that the Roman tibicines were of Etruscan origin, which would leave the Romans without any musical instrument of their own. The probability may rather be that it was the general instrument of old Italy, specially cultivated by the one Italian race endowed with anything like an artistic temperament.

---

[1] Cohen, *Méd. Pl.* 33 ; Borghesi, *Op.* i. 201 (quoted by Marq. 577).

[2] Müller-Deecke, *Etrusker*, ii. 202.

[3] *Journal of Philology*, vol. xi. p. 189. It was a short pipe played with a reed, and no doubt almost the same thing as the short rough oboes which are still favourites in Italy, and which are still sometimes played two at a time in the mouth as of old. Their antiquity is vouched for by the law of the Twelve Tables, which limited the players at a funeral to ten. See Professor Anderson's article ' tibia ' in *Dict. of Ant.* (ed. 2).

XII KAL. IUN. (JUNE 20). C.

SUMMAN[O] AD CIRC[UM] MAXIM[UM]. (VEN. ESQ. AMIT.)

To this note may be added that of Ovid [1]:

> Reddita, quisquis is est, Summano templa feruntur,
> Tum cum Romanis, Pyrrhe, timendus eras.

The date of the foundation of the temple of Summanus was probably between 278 and 275 B.C. [2]; the foundation was the result of the destruction by lightning, no doubt at night, of a figure of Jupiter on the Capitol [3]. Who was this Summanus? Ovid's language, *quisquis is est*, shows that even in his time this god, like Semo Sancus, Soranus, and others, had been fairly shouldered out of the course by more important or pushing deities. In the fourth century A.D. S. Augustine [4], well read in the works of Varro and the Roman antiquarians, could write as follows: 'Sicut enim apud ipsos legitur, Romani veteres nescio quem Summanum, cui nocturna fulmina tribuebant, coluerunt magis quam Iovem—sed postquam Iovi templum insigne ac sublime constructum est, propter aedis dignitatem sic ad eum multitudo confluxit, ut vix inveniatur, qui Summani nomen, quod audire iam non potest, se saltem legisse meminerit.' In spite of the decay and disappearance of this god we may believe that the Christian Father has preserved the correct tradition as to his nature when he tells us that he was the wielder of the lightning *of the night*, or in other words a nocturnal Jupiter. We do in fact find a much earlier statement to the same effect traceable to Verrius Flaccus [5]. Varro also mentions him and classes him with Veiovis, and with the Sabine deities whom he believed to have been brought to Rome by Tatius [6]. There is, however, no need to suppose with Varro that he was Sabine, or with Müller that he was Etruscan [7]; the name is Latin

---

[1] *Fasti*, 6. 731.　　　　　　　　　[2] Aust, *de Aedibus sacris*, p. 13.

[3] Not to be confused, as in Livy, *Epit.* 14, with a statue of Summanus himself on the same temple (in fastigio Iovis: Cicero, *Div.* I. 10).

[4] *de Civ. Dei*, 4. 23.

[5] Festus, 229, s.v. Proversum fulgor: 'Quod diurna Iovis, nocturna Summani fulgura habentur.' (Cp. Pliny, *N. H.* 2. 52.) An interesting inscription (*C. I. L.* vi. 206) runs, 'Summanium fulgus conditum,' i.e. 'a bolt which fell before dawn was buried here.'

[6] *L. L.* 5. 74.　　　　　　　　　[7] Müller-Deecke, *Etrusker*, ii. 60.

and probably = Submanus, i. e. the god who sends the lightning before the dawn.

It is interesting to find the wheel symbol here again, as is noticed by Gaidoz in his *Studies of Gallic Mythology* [1]. We can hardly doubt that the Summanalia which Festus explains as 'liba farinacea in modum rotae ficta ,' were cakes offered or eaten on this day : it is hard to see what other connexion they could have had. Mr. Arthur Evans has some interesting remarks [3] on what seem to be moulds for making religious cakes of this kind, found at Tarentum ; they are decorated, not only with the wheel or cross, but with many curious symbols. 'It is characteristic,' he writes, 'in a whole class of religious cakes that they are impressed with a wheel or cross, and in other cases divided into segments as if to facilitate distribution. This symbolical division seems to connect itself *with the worship of the ancestral fire* rather than with any solar cult. In a modi-fied form they are still familiar to us as "hot-cross buns."' Summanus, however, does not seem to have had anything to do with the ancestral fire.

VIII KAL. QUINCT. (JUNE 24). C.

FORTI FORTUNAE TRANS TIBER[IM] AD MILLIAR[IUM] PRIM[UM] ET
    SEXT[UM]. (AMIT.)
FORTIS FORTUNAE. (VEN. PHILOC.)
SACRUM FORTIS FORTUNAE. (RUST.)

Ovid writes of this day as follows [4]:

> Ite, deam laeti Fortem celebrate, Quirites!
>   In Tiberis ripa munera regis habet.
> Pars pede, pars etiam celeri decurrite cymba,
>   Nec pudeat potos inde redire domum.
> Ferte coronatae iuvenum convivia lintres :
>   Multaque per medias vina bibantur aquas.
> Plebs colit hanc, quia, qui posuit, de plebe fuisse
>   Fertur, et ex humili sceptra tulisse loco.
> Convenit et servis ; serva quia Tullius ortus
>   Constituit dubiae templa propinqua deae.

---

[1] *Études de Mythologie Gauloise*, i. p. 92. M. Gaidoz looks on these wheel-cakes as 'emblematic of Summanus' as a god of sun and sky.
[2] Festus, p. 348. The MS. has 'finctae.'
[3] *Journal of Hellenic Studies*, vol. vii, No. 1 (1886), p. 44 foll.
[4] *Fasti*, 6. 775 foll.

H. Peter, in his additional notes to Ovid's *Fasti*[1], has one so lucid on the subject of the temples of Fors Fortuna mentioned in this passage that I cannot do better than reproduce it. 'We find three temples of the goddess mentioned, all of which lay on the further side of the Tiber. The first was that of Servius Tullius mentioned by Varro in the following passage[2]: "Dies Fortis Fortunae appellatus ab Servio Tullio rege, quod is fanum Fortis Fortunae secundum Tiberim extra urbem Romam dedicavit Iunio mense." The second is one stated by Livy[3] to have been built by the consul Spurius Carvilius in 460 B. C. near the temple of Servius. The third is mentioned by Tacitus[4] as having been dedicated at the end of the year 17 A. D. by Tiberius, also on the further side of the Tiber in the gardens of Caesar. Of these three temples the third does not concern us in dealing with Ovid's lines, because it was completed and dedicated long after the composition of the sixth book of the *Fasti*, perhaps at a time when Ovid was already dead; we have to do only with the first two. Now we find in the *Fasti* of Amiternum[5] the following note on the 24th of June: "Forti Fortunae trans Tiberim ad milliarium primum et sextum"; and this taken together with Ovid suggests that either besides the temple of Carvilius there were two temples of Fors Fortuna attributed to Servius, or (and this appears to me more probable) the temple of Carvilius itself was taken for a foundation of Servius as it had the same dedication-day and was in the same locality. In this way the difficulties may be solved.' I am disposed to accept the second suggestion of Peter's; for, as Mommsen has remarked[6], it is quite according to Roman usage that Carvilius should have placed his temple close to a much more ancient *fanum* of the same deity; i. e. the principle of the locality of cults often held good through many centuries.

Many cults of Fortuna were referred to Servius Tullius, but especially this one, because, as Ovid says, it was particularly a festival of the plebs of which he was the traditional hero; and also because it was open to slaves, a fact which was naturally connected with the supposed servile birth of this

[1] p. 104.
[3] Livy, 10. 46. 17.
[5] See above, the heading of this section.
[2] *L. L.* 61. 7.
[4] *Ann.* 2. 41.
[6] *C. I. L.* 320.

king. The jollity and perhaps looseness of the occasion seemed to indicate a connexion between the lower stratum of population and the worship of Fortuna: 'On foot and in boats,' says Ovid, 'the people enjoyed themselves even to the extent of getting drunk.' We are reminded in fact of the plebeian license of the festival of Anna Perenna in March [1]. It is perhaps worth noting that on June 18 the calendar of Philocalus has the note *Annae Sacrum*, which unluckily finds no corroboration from any other source. Whether it was an early popular cult, whether it was connected in any way with that of Fors Fortuna, and whether both or either of them had any immediate relation to the summer solstice, are questions admitting apparently of no solution.

It has rarely happened that any Roman cult has been discussed at length in the English language, especially by scholars of unquestionable learning and resource. But on the subject of Fortuna, and Fors Fortuna, an interesting paper appeared some years ago by Prof. Max Müller in his volume entitled *Biographies of Words* [2], which I have been at great pains to weigh carefully. The skill and lucidity with which the Professor's arguments are, as usual, presented, make this an unusually pleasant task.

He starts, we must note, with a method which in dealing with Italian deities has been justly and emphatically condemned [3]; he begins with an etymology in order to discover the nature of the deity, and goes on to support this by selecting a few features from the various forms of the cult. This method will not of course be dangerous, if the etymology be absolutely certain; and absolute certainty, so far as our present knowledge reaches, is indeed what the Professor claims for his. Though we may doubt whether the science of Comparative Philology is as yet old and sure enough to justify us in violating a useful principle in order to pay our first attentions to its results, we may waive this scruple for the present and take the etymology in this case at the outset.

The Professor alludes to the well-known and universally accepted derivation of Fors and Fortuna from *ferre*, but rejects

[1] See above, p. 50. [2] ch. i.
[3] Marquardt, p. 2.

it: 'I appeal to those who have studied the biographies of similar Latin words, whether they do not feel some misgiving about so vague and abstract a goddess as "Dea quae fert," the goddess who brings.' But feeling the difficulty that Fortuna may not indeed have been originally a deity at all, but an abstract noun which became a deity, like Fides, Spes, &c., in which case his objection to the derivation from *ferre* would not apply, he hastens to remove it by trying to show from the early credentials of Fortuna, that she did not belong to this latter class, but has characteristics which were undoubtedly heaven-born. The process therefore was this: the ordinary etymology, though quite possible, is vague and does not seem to lead to anything; is there another to be discovered, which will fulfil philological requirements and also tell us something new about Fortuna? And are there any features to be found in the cult which will bear out the new etymology when it is discovered?

He then goes on to derive the word from the Sanskrit root HAER, 'to glow,' from which many names expressive of the light of day have come: 'From this too comes the Greek Χάρις with the Χάριτες, the goddess of morning; and from this we may safely derive *fors, fortis*, taking it either as a mere contraction, or a new derivative, corresponding to what in Sanskrit would be *Har-ti*, and would mean the brightness of the day, the Fortuna *huiusce diei.*'

So much for the etymological argument; on which we need only remark, (1) that while it may be perfectly possible in itself, it does not impugn the possibility of the older derivation; (2) that it introduces an idea 'bright,' hardly less vague and unsubstantial than that conveyed by 'the thin and unmeaning name' *she who brings or carries away.* When, indeed, the Professor goes on, by means of this etymology, to trace Fortuna to a concrete thing, viz. the dawn, he is really making a jump which the etymology does not specifically justify. All he can say is that it would be 'a most natural name for the brightest of all goddesses, the dawn, the morning, the day.'

He looks, however, for further justification of the etymology to the cult and mythology of Fortuna. From among her many cult-names he selects two or three which seem suitable. The first of these is Fortuna *huiusce diei*. This Fortuna was, he tells us, like the Ushas of the Veda, 'the bright light of each day, very much like what we might call "Good morning."' But as a matter of fact all we know of this Fortuna is that Aemilius Paullus, the victor of Pydna, vowed a temple to her in which he dedicated certain statues[1]; that Catulus, the hero of Vercellae, may have repaired or rebuilt it, and that on July 30, the day of the latter battle, there was a sacrifice at this temple[2]. What-ever therefore was the origin of this cult (and it may date no further back than Pydna) it seems to have been specially concerned, as its name implies, with the events of particular famous days. It is pure guesswork to imagine that its connexion with such days may have arisen from an older meaning, viz. the *bright light of each day*. Nothing is more natural than the *huiusce diei*, if we believe that this Fortuna simply represented chance, that inexplicable power which appealed so strongly to the later sceptical and Graecized Roman, and which we see in the majority of cult-names by which Fortuna was known in the later Republic. The advocate of the dawn-theory, on the other hand, has to account for the total loss in the popular belief of the nature-meaning of the epithet and cult—a loss which is indeed quite possible, but one which must necessarily make the theory less obvious and acceptable than the ordinary one.

Secondly, the Professor points out, that on June 11, the day of the Matralia, Fortuna was worshipped coincidently with Mater Matuta—the latter being, as he assumes beyond doubt, a dawn-goddess. But we have already seen that this as-sumption is not a very certain one[3]; and we may now add that the coincident worship must simply mean that two temples had the same dedication-day, which may be merely accidental[4].

But the chief argument is based on the cult of Fortuna Primigenia, 'the first-born of the gods,' as he translates the word, in accordance with a recent elaborate investigation of its

---

[1] Pliny, *N. H.* 34. 54.
[2] Plut. *Marius*, 26; Pliny, l.c. I follow Aust, *de Aedibus sacris*, p. 26.
[3] Above, p. 156.
[4] Ovid is the only authority for the worship of Fortuna on June 11 (*Fasti*, 6. 569); it is not mentioned in the calendars (Tusc. Ven. Maff.) which have notes surviving for this day.

meaning[1]. This cult does indeed show very curious and interesting characters. It belonged originally to Praeneste, where Fortuna was the presiding deity of an ancient and famous oracle. Here have been found inscriptions to Fortuna, 'DIOVO[S] FILEA[I] PRIMOGENIA[I],' the first-born daughter of Jupiter[2]. Here also, strange to say, Cicero describes[3] an enclosure sacred to Jupiter Puer, who was represented there with Juno as sitting in the lap of Fortuna 'mammam appetens.' This very naturally attracted Prof. Max Müller's keenest attention, and he had no difficulty in finding his explanation : Fortuna is 'the first-born of all the bright powers of the sky, and the daughter of the sky ; but likewise from another point of view the mother of the daily sun who is the bright child she carries in her arms.' This is charming ; but it is the language and thought, not of ancient Italians, but of Vedic poets. The great Latin scholar, who had for years been soaking his mind in Italian antiquities, will hardly venture on an explanation at all : 'haud ignarus quid deceat eum qui Aboriginum regiones attingat[4].'

I shall have occasion later on[5] to say something of this very interesting and mysterious cult at Praeneste. At present I must be content with pointing out that it is altogether unsafe to regard it as representative of any general ideas of ancient Italian religion. As Italian archaeologists are aware, Praeneste was a city in which Etruscan and Greek influences are most distinctly traceable, and in which foreign deities and myths seem to have become mixed up with native ones, to the extreme bewilderment of the careful inquirer[6]. We may accept the Professor's explanation of it with all respect as a most interesting hypothesis, but as no more than a hypothesis which needs much more information than we as yet possess to render it even a probable one.

By his own account the Professor would not have been led so far afield for an explanation of Fortuna if he had not been struck by the apparent difficulty involved in such a goddess

---

[1] By H. Jordan, *Symbolae ad historiam religionum Italicarum alterae* (Königsberg, 1885). See also R. Peter, in *Lex.* s. v. Fortuna, 1542, and Aust, *Lex.* s. v. Iuppiter, 647.

[2] *C. I. L.* xiv. 2863.   [3] *de Div.* 2. 41. 85.

[4] Jordan, op. cit. p. 12.   [5] See below, p. 223 foll., under Sept. 13.

[6] Fernique, *Étude sur Préneste*, pp. 8 and 139 foll.

as 'she who brings.' Towards the removal of this difficulty, however, the late Mr. Vigfusson did something in a letter to the *Academy* of March 17, 1888[1]. He equated Fors and Fortuna with the Icelandic *buror*, from a verb having quite as wide and general a meaning as *fero*, and being its etymological equivalent. 'There is a department of its meanings,' he tells us, 'through which runs the notion of an invisible, passive, sudden, involuntary, chance agency'; and another, in which *bera* means to give birth, and produces a noun meaning birth, and so lucky birth, honour, &c. The two ideas come together in the Norse notion of the Norns who presided at the birth of each child, shaping at that hour the child's fortune[2].

It is rather to the ideas of peoples like the early Teutons and Celts that we must look for mental conditions resembling those of the early Italians, than to the highly developed poetical mythology of the Vedas; and it is in the direction which Mr. Vigfusson pointed out that I think we should search for the oldest Italian ideas of Fortuna and for the causes which led to her popularity and development. In a valuable paper, to which I shall have occasion to refer again, Prof. Nettleship[3] suggested that Carmenta (or Carmentes) may be explained with S. Augustine[4] as the goddess or prophetess who tells the fortunes of the children, and that this was the reason why she was especially worshipped by matrons, like Mater Matuta, Fortuna and others. The Carmentes were in fact the Norns of Italy. Such a practical need as the desire to know your child's fortunes would be quite in harmony with what we know of the old Italian character; and I think it far from impossible that Fortuna, as an oracular deity in Italy, may have been originally a conception of the same kind. perhaps not only a prophetess as regards the children, but also of the good luck of the mother in childbirth. Perhaps the most striking fact in her multifarious cults is the predominance in them of women as worshippers. Of the very Fortuna Primogenia of whom we have been speaking Cicero tells us

---

[1] See also his previous letter of March 3.
[2] He held 'birth' and 'fortune' to be words etymologically related. Cp. a communication from Prof. Kluge in the same number of the *Academy*.
[3] *Journal of Philology*, vol. xi. 178; *Studies in Latin Literature*, p. 60.
[4] *de Civ. Dei*, 4. 11. Cp. Serv. *Aen.* 8. 336.

that her ancient home at Praeneste was the object of the special devotion of mothers [1]. The same was the case with Fortuna Virilis, Muliebris, Mammosa, and others.

If we look at her in this light, there is really no difficulty in understanding why what seems to us at first sight a very vague conception, 'the goddess who brings,' should not have meant something very real and concrete to the early Italian mind. And again, if that be so, if Fortuna be once recognized as a great power in ways which touched these essential and practical needs of human nature, we may feel less astonishment at finding her represented either as the daughter or the mother of Jupiter. Such representation could indeed hardly have been the work of really primitive Italians; it arose, one may conjecture, if not from some confusion which we cannot now unravel, from the fame of the oracle—one of the very few in Italy—and the consequent fame of the goddess whose name came to be attached to that oracle. Or, as Jordan seems to think, it may have been the vicinity of the rock-oracle to the temple of Jupiter which gave rise to the connexion between the two in popular belief; a belief which was expressed in terms of relationship, perhaps under Greek influence, but certainly in a manner for the most part absent from the unmythological Italian religion. Why indeed in the same place she should be mother as well as daughter of Jupiter (if Cicero be accurate in his account, which is perhaps not quite certain) may well puzzle us all. Those who cannot do without an explanation may accept that of Prof. Max Müller, if they can also accept his etymology. Those who have acquired what Mommsen has called the 'difficillima ars nesciendi,' will be content with Jordan's cautious remark, 'Non desunt vestigia divinum numen Italis notum fuisse deis deabusve omnibus et hoc ipso in quo vivimus mundo antiquius [2].'

But Fortuna has not only been conjectured to be a deity of the dawn; she has been made out to be both a moon-goddess and a sun-goddess. For her origin in the moon there

---

[1] l. c. 'Castissime colitur a matribus.' One of the ancient inscriptions from Praeneste (C. I. L. xi. 2863) is a dedication 'nationu cratia' = *nationis gratia*, which may surely mean 'in gratitude for childbirth,' though Mommsen would refer it to cattle, on the ground of a gloss of Festus (p. 167).

[2] Jordan, op. cit. p. 12.

is really nothing of any weight to be urged; the advocate
of this view is one of the least judicious of German specialists,
and his arguments need not detain us[1]. But for her connexion
with the sun there is something more to be said.

The dedication day of the temple of Fors Fortuna was
exactly at the summer solstice. It is now St. John the
Baptist's day, and one on which a great variety of curious local
customs, some of which still survive, regularly occur; and
especially the midsummer fires which were until recently
so common in our own islands. Attention has often been
drawn to the fondness for parallelism which prompted the
early Christians to place the birth of Christ at the winter
solstice, when the days begin to grow longer, and that of the
Baptist—for June 24 is his reputed birthday as well as festival
—at the summer solstice when they begin to shorten; following
the text, 'He must increase and I must decrease[2].' Certainly
the sun is an object of special regard at all midsummer
festivals, and is supposed to be often symbolized in them
by a wheel, which is set on fire and in many cases rolled down
a hill[3]. Now the wheel is of course a symbol in the cult
of Fortuna, and is sometimes found in Italian representations
of her, though not so regularly as the cornucopia and the
ship's rudder which almost invariably accompany her[4].
Putting this in conjunction with the date of the festival
of Fors Fortuna, the Celtic scholar Gaidoz has concluded that
Fortuna was ultimately a solar deity[5]. The solar origin of
the symbol was, he thinks, quite forgotten; but the wheel,
or the globe which sometimes replaces it, was certainly at one
time solar, and perhaps came from Assyria. If so (he
concludes), the earliest form of Fortuna must have been
a female double of the sun.

---

[1] O. Gilbert, *Gesch. u. Topogr. der Stadt Rom*, ii. 260 foll.

[2] St. John, iii. 30; St. Augustine, Sermo xii in Nativitate Domini: 'In
nativitate Christi dies crescit, in Johannis nativitate decrescit. Profectum
plane facit dies, quum mundi Salvator oritur; defectum patitur quum
ultimus prophetarum nascitur.'

[3] See many examples in *The Golden Bough*, ii. 258 foll., and Brand's
Popular Antiquities, p. 306.

[4] See R. Peter, in *Lex.*, s.v. Fortuna, 1506.

[5] *Études de Myth. Gaul.* i. 56 foll. On p. 58 we find, 'La Fortune nous
paraît donc sortir, par l'intermédiaire d'une image, d'une divinité du
soleil.'

All hints are useful in Roman antiquities, and something may yet be made of this. But it cannot be accepted until we are sure of the history and descent of this symbol in the representations of Fortuna ; it is far from impossible that the wheel or globe may in this case have nothing more to do with the sun than the rudder which always accompanies it. In any case it can hardly be doubted that it is not of Italian origin ; it is found, e. g. also in the cult of Nemesis, who, like Tyche, Eilithyia, and Leucothea, is probably responsible for much variation and confusion in the worship of Italian female deities [1]. As to the other fact adduced by Gaidoz, viz. the date of the festival, it is certainly striking, and must be given its full weight. It is surprising that Prof. Max Müller has made no use of it. But we must be on our guard. It is remarkable that we find in the Roman calendars no other evidence that the Romans attached the same importance to the summer solstice as some other peoples ; the Roman summer festivals are concerned, in accordance with the true Italian spirit, much more with the operations of man in dealing with nature than with the phenomena of nature taken by themselves. It is perhaps better to avoid a hasty conclusion that this festival of Fors Fortuna was on the 24th because the 24th was the end of the solstice, and rather to allow the equal probability that it was fixed then because harvest was going on. Columella seems to be alluding to it in the following lines [2] :

> Sed cum maturis flavebit messis aristis
> Allia cum cepis, cereale papaver anetho
> Iungite, dumque virent, nexos deferte maniplos,
> Et celebres Fortis Fortunae dicite laudes
> Mercibus exactis, hilaresque recurrite in hortos.

The power of Fortuna as a deity of chance would be as important for the perils of harvest as for those of childbirth ; and it is in this connexion that the Italians understood the

---

[1] For the history of these symbols in Greek cults, and especially that of Tyche, see a paper by Prof. Gardner in *Journal of Hellenic Studies,* vol. ix. p. 78, on 'Countries and Cities in ancient art.' The rudder seems to connect Fortuna with sea-faring ; it is often accompanied by a ship's prow (R. Peter, *Lex.* 1507) ; in connexion with which we may notice that even in Italy her cult is rarely found far from the sea. Cp. Horace, *Od.* i. 35, 6 'dominam aequoris.'

[2] 10. 311 foll. ; Marq. 578.

meaning of that cornucopia which is perhaps her most constant symbol in art [1].

Lastly, there is a formidable question, which may easily lead the unwary into endless complications, and on which I shall only touch very briefly. How are we to explain the legendary connexion between the cult of Fortuna and Servius Tullius? That king, the so-called second founder of Rome, was said, as we have seen, to have erected more than one sanctuary to Fortuna, and was even believed to have had illicit dealings with the goddess herself [2]. The dedication-day of Fors Fortuna was said to have been selected by him, and, as Ovid describes it, was a festival of the poorer kind of people, who thus kept up the custom initiated by the popular friend of the plebs.

Since the Etruscan origin of Servius Tullius has been placed beyond a doubt by the discovery of the famous tomb at Vulci, with the paintings of Cales Vibenna released from his bonds by Mastarna [3], which has thus confirmed the Etruscan tradition of the identity of Mastarna and Servius preserved by the emperor Claudius in his famous speech [4], it would seem that we may consider it as highly probable that if Servius did really institute the cult of Fortuna at Rome, that cult came with him from Etruria. This by no means compels us to look on Fortuna as an Etruscan deity only; but it seems to be a fact that there was an Etruscan goddess who was recognized by the Romans as the equivalent of their Fortuna [5]. This was Nortia, a great deity at Volsinii, as is fully proved by the remains found there [6]; and we may note that the city was near to and in close alliance with Vulci, where the tomb was found containing the paintings just alluded to. Seianus, a native of Volsinii [7], was supposed to be under the protection of this deity, and, as we have already seen, to possess an ancient statue of her.

---

[1] R. Peter, *Lex.* 1505. She is also often represented with a *modius*, and with ears of corn. Cp. Horace, l.c. (of the Fortuna of Antium): 'Te pauper ambit sollicita prece Ruris colonus.'

[2] Ovid, *Fasti*, 6. 573 foll. Schwegler, *R. G.* i. 711 foll.; Preller, ii. 180.

[3] Dennis, *Cities and Cemeteries of Etruria*, vol. ii. p. 506; Gardthausen, 'Mastarna,' figures the painting (plate i).

[4] Tac. *Ann.* 11. 24; the fragments of the original speech are printed from the inscription at Lyons in Mr. Furneaux's *Annals of Tacitus*, vol. ii. p. 210.

[5] Juvenal, 10. 74, and note of the Scholiast.

[6] Müller-Deecke, *Etrusker*, ii. 52; Dennis, *Cit. and Cem.* ii. 24.

[7] Juvenal, l. c.

In her temple a nail was driven every year as in the temple of Jupiter Capitolinus [1], and hence some have concluded that she was a goddess of time. It cannot, however, be regarded as certain whether this nail-driving was originally symbolical only, or at all, of time; it may quite as well remind us of the famous Fortuna of Antium and the 'clavos trabales' of Horace's Ode [2]. However this may be, it is a fair guess, though it must be made with hesitation, that the Fortuna of Servius was the equivalent of this Nortia, to whom the Roman plebs gave a name with which they were in some way already familiar. Mastarna continued to worship his native deity after he was settled in Rome; and the plebs continued to revere her, not because of his luck, which was indeed imperfect, but simply because she was his protectress [3]. If we try to get beyond this we lose our footing; and even this is only conjecture, though based upon evidence which is not entirely without weight.

[1] See below on Sept. 13, p. 234. .
[2] Müller-Deecke, ii. 308. Gaidoz, op. cit. p. 56, on the connexion between Fortuna, Necessitas, and Nemesis.
[3] Gerhard, *Agathodaemon*, p. 30, has other explanations.

MENSIS QUINCTILIS.

THE festivals of this month are so exceedingly obscure that it seems hopeless to try to connect them in any definite way with the operations either of nature or of man. We know that this was the time when the sun's heat became oppressive and dangerous ; statistics show at the ·present day that the rate of mortality rises at Rome to its greatest height in July and August, as indeed is the case in southern latitudes generally. We know also that harvest of various kinds was going on in this month: ' Quarto intervallo inter solstitium et caniculam plerique messem faciunt,' writes Varro (*R. R.* 1. 32). We should have expected that the unhealthy season and the harvest would have left their mark on the calendar ; but in the scantiness of our information we can find very few traces of their influence. We here lose the company of Ovid, who might, in spite of his inevitable ignorance, have incidentally thrown some ray of light upon the darkness ; but it is clear that even Varro and Verrius knew hardly anything of the almost obsolete festivals of this month. The Poplifugia, the Lucaria, the Neptunalia, and the Furrinalia, had all at one time been great festivals, for they are marked in large capitals in the ancient calendars ; but they had no more meaning for the Roman of Varro's time than the lesser saints'-days of our calendar have for the ordinary Englishman of to-day. The ludi Apollinares, of much later date, which always maintained their interest, did not fall upon the days of any of these festivals, or obliterate them in the minds of the people ; they must have decayed from pure inanition—want of practical correlation with the life and interests of a great city.

III Non. Quinct. (July 5).   NP.

POPLIF[UGIA].   (MAFF. AMIT. ANT.)
FERIAE IOVI.   (AMIT.)

The note 'feriae Iovi' in the calendar of Amiternum is
confirmed in a curious way, by a statement of Dio Cassius [1],
who says that in B.C. 42 the Senate passed a decree that Caesar's
birthday should be celebrated on this day [2], and that any one
who refused to take part in the celebration should be 'sacer
Iovi et Divo Iulio.'   But we know far too little of the rites of
this day to enable us to make even a guess at the meaning
of its connexion with Jupiter.   It is just worth noting that two
days later we find a festival of Juno, the Nonae Caprotinae;
the two days may have had some connexion with each other,
being separated by an interval of one day, as is the case with
the three days of the Lemuria, the two days of the Lucaria
in this month, and in other instances [3]; and their rites were
explained by two parts of the same aetiological story—viz.
that the Romans fled before the Fidenates on the 5th, and
in turn defeated them on the 7th [4].   But we are quite in the
dark as to the meaning of such a connexion, if such there was.
Nor can we explain the singular fact that this is the only festival
in the whole year, marked in large capitals in the calendars,
which falls *before the Nones* [5].

There is hardly a word in the whole calendar the meaning
of which is so entirely unknown to us as this word Poplifugia.
Of the parallel one, the Regifugium in February, something
can be made out, as we shall see [6]; and it is not unlikely that
the ritualistic meaning concealed in both may be much the
same.   But all attempts to find a definite explanation for
Poplifugia have so far been fruitless, with the single exception

---

[1] Bk. 47. 18.   We owe the reference to Merkel, *Praef. in Ovidii Fastos*, clix.
[2] His real birthday seems to have been the 12th, which was already
occupied by the ludi Apollinares.
[3] Mommsen in *C. I. L.* 321 (on July 7).
[4] Varro, *L. L.* 6. 18; Marq. 325.
[5] See Introduction, p. 7.   This anomaly led Huschke to the inadmissible supposition that this was the single addition made to the calendar of
Numa in the republican period.   He accepts Varro's explanatory story,
Röm. Jahr, p. 224.
[6] See below, p. 327.

perhaps of that of Schwegler [1], who himself made the serious blunder of confounding this day with the Nonae Caprotinae. It is true that the two days and their rites were confused even in antiquity, but only by late writers [2]; the calendars, on the other hand, are perfectly plain, and so is Varro [3], who proceeds from the one to the other in a way that can leave no doubt that he understood them as distinct.

The simple fact is that the meaning of the word Poplifugia had wholly vanished when the calendar began to be studied. Ingenuity and fancy, as usual, took the place of knowledge, and two legends were the result—the one connecting the word with the flight of the Romans from an army of their neighbours of Fidenae, after the retirement of the Gauls from the city [4]; the other interpreting it as a memorial of the flight of the people after the disappearance of Romulus in the darkness of an eclipse or sudden tempest [5]. The first of these legends may be dismissed at once; the large capitals in which the name Poplifugia appears in the fragments of the three calendars which preserve it, are sufficient evidence that it must have been far older than the Gallic invasion [6]. The second legend might suggest that the story itself of the death of Romulus had grown out of some religious rite performed at this time of year; and it was indeed traditionally connected with the Nones of this month [7]. But that day is unluckily not the day of the Poplifugia, which it is hardly possible to connect with the disappearance of Romulus. There may, however, have been a connexion between the rites of the two days, as has been pointed out above; and this being so, it is worth while to notice a suggestion made by Schwegler, in spite of the fact that he confused the two days together. He saw that the disappearance of Romulus was said to have occurred while he was holding a *lustratio* of the citizens [8], and concluded that

---

[1] *R. G.* i. 532 : see Mommsen's criticism in *C. I. L* 321 f.

[2] Macrob. 6. 11. 36 ; Plut. *Rom.* 29, *Camill.* 33. See also O. Müller's note on Varro, *L. L.* 6. 18.　　　　　　　　　　　[3] *L. L.* 6. 18.

[4] This is Varro's account ; the Etruscans are a variant in Macrobius, l. c.

[5] Dionys. 2. 56 ; Plut. *Rom.* 29. See Lewis, *Credibility of Early Roman History,* i. 430.

[6] Introduction, p. 15.　　　　　　　[7] Cic. *de Rep.* 1. 16 ; Plut. *Rom.* 27.

[8] Liv. 1. 16 'Ad exercitum recensendum.' Lustratio came to be the word for a review of troops because this was preceded by a religious *lustratio populi.*

the Poplifugia may have been an ancient rite of lustration—
an idea which other writers have been content to follow without
always giving him the credit of it [1].

Such a rite may very well be indicated by the following
sentence of Varro [2]—the only one which gives us any solid
information on the question : *Aliquot huius diei vestigia fugae in
sacris apparent, de quibus rebus antiquitatum libri plura referunt.*
It seems not unreasonable to guess that the rite was one of
those in which the priest, or in this case, as it would seem, the
people also, fled from the spot after the sacrifice had been
concluded.   As the slayer of the ox at the Athenian Bouphonia
(which curiously enough took place just at this same time
of year) fled as one guilty of blood, so it may possibly have
been that priest and people at Rome fled after some similar
sacrifice, and for the same reason [3].   Or it may have been that
they fled from the victim as a scapegoat which was destined to
carry away from the city some pollution or pestilence.   It is
interesting to find at Iguvium in Umbria some 'vestigia fugae,'
not of the people, indeed, but of victims, at a *lustratio populi*
which seems to have had some object of this kind [4].   Heifers
were put to flight, then caught and killed, apparently in order
to carry off evils from the city [5], as well as to represent and
secure the defeat of its enemies.   Such performances seem
especially apt to occur at sickly seasons [6]; and as the unhealthy
season began at Rome in July [7], it is just possible that the
Poplifugia was a ceremony of this class.

Non. Quinct. (July 7).   N.

This day does not appear as a festival in the old calendars ;
but the late one of Silvius [8] notes it as *Ancillarum Feriae*, or

---

[1] e. g. Gilbert, i. 290 ; Marq. 325.

[2] *L. L.* 6. 18.   Details have vanished with the great work here quoted,
the *Antiquitates divinae.*

[3] Schwegler suggested the parallel, i. 534, note 20.   For the Bouphonia
see especially Mannhardt, *Myth. Forsch.* 68.   For other such rites, Lobeck,
Aglaophamus, 679, 680.   [4] Bücheler, *Umbrica*, 114.

[5] The idea of the scapegoat was certainly not unknown in Italy ;
Bücheler quotes Serv. (*Aen.* 2. 140) 'Ludos Taureos a Sabinis propter pesti-
lentiam institutos dicunt, *ut lues publica in has hostias verteretur.*'   See on
the Regifugium, below, p. 328.

[6] See examples in Frazer, *Golden Bough*, ii. 160 foll.   The one from the
Key Islands is interesting as including a flight of the people.

[7] Nissen, *Landeskunde*, 406.   [8] *C. I. L.* p. 269.

Feast of Handmaids, and adds the explanatory story which is found also in Plutarch and Macrobius[1]. The victorious Fidenates having demanded the surrender of the wives of the Romans, the latter made over to them their *ancillae*, dressed in their mistresses' robes, by the advice of a certain Philotis, or Tutula[2], one of the handmaids. Ausonius alludes to the custom that gave rise to the story:

> Festa Caprotinis memorabo celebria Nonis
> Cum stola matronis dempta teget famulas[3].

Plutarch also tells us that on this day the *ancillae* not only wore the matron's dress, but had license for what may be described as a game of romps; they beat each other, threw stones at each other, and scoffed at the passers by[4].

This last point supplies us with a possible clue both to the origin of the custom and the explanatory legend. One of the most frequent customs at harvest-time used to be, and still is in some places, for the harvesters to mock at, and even to use roughly, any stranger who appears on the field; frequently he is tied up with straw, even by the women binding the sheaves, and only released on promise of money, brandy, &c.; or he is ducked in water, or half-buried, or in pretence beheaded[5]. The stranger in such cases is explained as representing the spirit of the corn; the examples collected by Mannhardt and Mr. Frazer seem fairly conclusive on this point[6]. The wearing of the matron's dress also seems to be a combination of the familiar practices of the winter Saturnalia with harvest customs, which in various forms is by no means uncommon[7], though I have not found a case of exchange of dress after harvest.

[1] Macrob. i. 11. 36; Plut. *Camill.* 33.
[2] Aug. *de Civ. Dei*, 4. 8.   [3] *de Feriis*, 9.
[4] The last point is in *Camill.* 33-6: cp. *Rom.* 29. 6.
[5] The bearing of these customs on the Nonae Caprotinae, and on the Greek story of Lityerses, was suggested by Mannhardt, *Myth. Forsch.* 32. Mr. Frazer gives a useful collection of examples, *G. B.* ii. 363 foll. The custom survives in Derbyshire (so I am told by Mr. S. B. Smith, Scholar of Lincoln College), but only in the form of making the stranger 'pay his footing.'   [6] *G. B.* i. 381.
[7] It was the custom, says Macrobius (i. 10) 'ut patres familiarum, frugibus et fructibus iam coactis, passim cum servis vescerentur, cum quibus patientiam laboris in colendo rure toleraverant.' The old English harvest- or mell-supper, had all the characteristics of Saturnalia (Brand, *Pop. Antiq.* 337 foll.).

Thus it would seem possible that we have here a relic of Italian harvest-custom ; and this is confirmed by the statement of Tertullian that there was on this day a sacrifice to the harvest-god Consus[1], at his underground altar in the Circus Maximus, of which we shall have more to say under Aug. 21 (Consualia). It is worth noting here that just as the legend of the Rape of the Sabines was connected with the Consualia[2], so the analogous story of the demand of the Fidenates for Roman women is associated with the *Ancillarum Feriae*, and the day of the sacrifice to Consus. This not only serves to connect together the two days of Consus-worship, but suggests that harvest was a favourable opportunity for the practice of capturing wives in primitive Italy, when the women were out in the fields, and might be carried off by a sudden incursion.

This day was also known as Nonae Caprotinae, because the women, presumably those who had been helping at the harvest, both bond and free[3], sacrificed to Juno Caprotina under a wild fig-tree (caprificus) in the Campus Martius[4]. Juno Caprotina was a Latin goddess, of great renown at Falerii[5], where the goat from which she took her name appears in the legend of her cult. The character of Juno as the representative of the female principle of human life[6] suits well enough with the prominence of women both in the customs and legends connected with the day ; and the fig-tree with its milky juice, which was used, according to Macrobius, in the sacrifice to Juno instead of milk, has also its significance[7]. Varro adds that a rod (virga) was also cut from this tree[8], without telling

---

[1] Tertullian, *de Spect.* 5.   [2] See below, p. 208.

[3] This point—the union of free- and bond-women in the sacrifice—seems to prove that Nonae Caprotinae and ancillarum feriae were only two names for the same thing. Macrobius connects the legend of the latter with the rite of the former (i. 11. 36).

[4] Plut. *Rom.* 29. Varro, *L. L.* 6. 18 writes 'in Latio.'

[5] Deecke, *Die Falisker*, 89; Roscher, in *Lex.* s. v. Juno, p. 599.

[6] See above, p. 143.

[7] One naturally compares the ficus Ruminalis and the foundation-legend of Rome.

[8] It is curious that the practice in husbandry called *caprificatio*, or the introduction of branches of the wild tree among those of the cultivated fig to make it ripen (Plin. *N. H.* 15. 79 ; Colum. 11. 2) took place in July ; and it strikes me as just possible that there may have been a connexion between it and the Nonae Caprotinae.

us for what purpose it was used ; and it has been ingeniously conjectured that it was with this that the handmaids beat each other, as Plutarch describes, to produce fertility, just as at the Lupercalia the women were beaten with strips cut from the skins of the victims (amiculum Junonis). But this is mere conjecture, and Varro's statement is too indefinite to be pressed [1].

VIII ID. QUINCT. (JULY 8). N.

'Piso ait vitulam victoriam nominari, cuius rei hoc argumentum profert, quod postridie nonas Iulias re bene gesta, cum pridie populus a Tuscis in fugam versus sit (unde Populifugia vocantur), post victoriam certis sacrificiis fiat *vitulatio* [2].'

I must be content with quoting this passage, and without comment ; it will suffice to show that the meaning of the word 'vitulatio' was entirely unknown to Roman scholars. Why they should not have connected it with *vitulus* I know not : we may remember that in the Iguvian ritual *vituli* seem to have performed the function of scapegoats [3]. If the vitulatio is in any way to be connected with the Poplifugia, as it was indeed in the legend as given by Macrobius above, it may be worth while to remember that that day is marked in one calendar as ' feriae Iovi,' and that the *vitulus* (heifer) was the special victim of Jupiter [4].

PRID. NON. QUINCT.—III ID. QUINCT. (JULY 6–13).
LUDI APOLLINARES.

All these days are marked ' ludi ' in Maff. Amit. Ant. ; the 6th ' ludi Apoll[ini],' and the 13th 'ludi in circo.'

These games [5] were instituted in 212 B. C., for a single occasion only, at the most dangerous period of the war with Hannibal, when he had taken Tarentum and invaded Campania. Recourse was had to the Sibylline books and to the Italian oracles of Marcius, and the latter answered as follows [6] :

---

[1] Mannhardt, *Myth. Forsch.* l. c.
[2] Macrob. 3. 2. 11 and 14.   Macrobius also quotes Varro in the 15th book of his *Res Divinae* ' Quod pontifex in sacris quibusdam vitulari soleat, quod Graeci παιανίζειν vocant.'   Perhaps we may compare *visceratio* : Serv. Aen. 5. 215.
[3] Above, p. 176.
[5] See Marq. 384, and *Lex.* s. v. Apollo 447.
[4] Marq. 170.
[6] Liv. 25. 12.

'Hostes Romani si expellere voltis, vomicamque quae gentium venit longe, Apollini vovendos censeo ludos, qui quotannis Apollini fiant,' &c. The games were held, as we may suppose, on the analogy of the ludi plebeii, originally on the 13th day of the month[1], and were, in course of time, extended backwards till in the Julian calendar we find them lasting from the 6th to the 13th. They had a Greek character from the first; they were superintended by the Decemviri sacris faciundis, who consulted the Sibylline books and organized the ritual of foreign cults; and they included scenic shows, after the Greek fashion, as well as chariot races[2].

It was matter of dispute whether in this year, 212, Apollo was expected to show his favour to Rome as a conqueror of her foe or as an averter of pestilence in the summer heats; both functions were within his range. But in 208 we are told that the ludi were renewed by a lex, made permanent, and fixed for July 13 in consequence of a pestilence[3]; and we may fairly assume that this was, in part at least, the cause of their institution four years earlier. What little we know of the traditions of Apollo-worship at Rome points in the same direction. His oldest temple in the Flaminian fields, where, according to Livy, a still more ancient shrine once stood[4], was vowed in 432 B.C. in consequence of a pestilence; and the god had also the cult-title Medicus[5]. The next occasion on which we meet with the cult is that of the first institution of a lectisternium in 397 B.C., Livy's account of which is worth condensing[6]. That year was remarkable for an extremely cold

[1] The MSS. of Livy (27. 23) have a. d. iii Nonas, no doubt in error for a. d. iii Idus. Merkel, Praef. xxviii.; Mommsen, C. I. L. 321.

[2] Liv. 25. 12; 26. 33; Festus, 326; Cic. Brutus, 20, 78, whence it appears that Ennius produced his Thyestes at these ludi. Cp. the story in Macrob. 1. 17. 25.

[3] Liv. 27. 23.

[4] Liv. 3. 63. This older shrine Livy calls Apollinar. The temple that followed it was the only Apollo-temple in Rome till Augustus built one on the Palatine after Actium; this is clear from Asconius, p. 81 (ad Cic. in toga candida), quoted by Aust, de Aedibus sacris, 7. It was outside the Porta Carmentalis, near the Circus Flaminius. A still more ancient Apollinar is assumed by some to have existed on the Quirinal; but it rests on an uncertain emendation of O. Müller in Varro, L. L. 5. 52.

[5] Liv. 40. 51. The Romans seem originally to have called the god Apello, and connected the name with pellere. Paulus, 22; Macrob. 1. 17. 15.

[6] Liv. 5. 13.

winter, which was followed by an equally unhealthy summer, destructive to all kinds of animals. As the cause of this pestilence could not be discovered, the Sibylline books were consulted ; the result of which was the introduction of a *lectisternium*, at which three couches were laid out with great magnificence, on which reposed Apollo and Latona, Diana and Hercules, Mercurius and Neptunus, whose favour the people besought for eight days.

The cult of Apollo, though thus introduced in its full magnificence at Rome in historical times, was ' so old in Italy as almost to give the impression of being indigenous[1].' Tradition ascribed to Tarquinius Superbus the introduction from Cumae of the Sibylline oracles, which were intimately connected with Apollo-worship ; and that Etruscan king may well have been familiar with the Greek god, who was well known in Etruria as *Aplu*[2], and who was worshipped at Caere, the home of the Tarquinian family, which city had a 'treasury' at Delphi[3]. The Romans themselves, according to a tradition which is by no means improbable, had very early dealings with the Delphic oracle.

It does not seem certain that Apollo displaced any other deity when transplanted to Rome. It has been thought that the obscure Veiovis became clothed with some of Apollo's characteristics, but this is extremely doubtful[4]. The mysterious deity of Soracte, *Soranus*, is called Apollo by Virgil[5] ; this, however, is not a true displacement, like that, e. g., of the ancient Ceres by the characteristics of Demeter, but merely a poetical substitution of a familiar name for an unfamiliar one which was unquestionably old Italian.

It does not seem probable that in the Republican period the cult of Apollo had any special influence, either religious or ethical, for the Roman people generally. It was a priestly experiment—a new physician was called in at perilous times, according to the fashion of the Roman oligarchy, either to give advice by his oracles, or to receive honours for his benefits as ἀλεξίκακος. It is in the age of Augustus that the cult begins to

---

[1] *Lex.* s. v. Apollo, 446.   [2] Müller-Deecke, *Etrusker*, ii. 69.
[3] Strabo, p. 214 ; Herodotus, I. 167.
[4] Jordan on Preller, i. 265.
[5] *Aen.* II. 785 'Summe deum, sancti custos Soractis Apollo,' &c.

be important; the family of the Caesars was said to have had
an ancient connexion with it[1], and after the victory at Actium,
where a temple of Apollo stood on the promontory, Augustus
not only enlarged and adorned this one, but built another on
the Palatine, near his own house, to Apollo Palatinus. But
for the 'Apollinism' of Augustus, and for the important part
played by the god in the *ludi saeculares* of B. C. 17, I must refer
the reader to other works[2].

XIV KAL. SEXT. (JULY 19). N̄P.

LUCAR[IA]. (MAFF. AMIT.)

XII KAL. SEXT. (JULY 21). N̄P.

LUCAR[IA]. (MAFF. AMIT.)

Here, as in the next two festivals we have to consider, we
are but 'dipping buckets into empty wells.' The ritual, and
therefore the original meaning of this festival, is wholly lost
to us, as indeed it was to the Romans of Varro's time. Varro,
in his list of festivals, does not even mention this one; but it
is possible that some words have here dropped out of his text[3].
The only light we have comes at second-hand from Verrius
Flaccus[4]. 'Lucaria festa in luco colebant Romani, qui per-
magnus inter viam Salariam et Tiberim fuit, pro eo, quod victi
a Gallis fugientes[5] e praelio ibi se occultaverint.' This passage

---

[1] Serv. *Aen.* 10. 316 'Omnes qui secto matris ventre procreantur, ideo
sunt Apollini consecrati, quia deus medicinae est, per quam lucem sorti-
untur. Unde Aesculapius eius fingitur filius: ita enim eum [esse] pro-
creatum supra (7. 761) diximus. Caesarum etiam familia ideo sacra
retinebat Apollinis, quia qui primus de eorum familia fuit, exsecto matris
ventre natus est. Unde etiam Caesar dictus est.'

[2] A concise account by Roscher, *Lex.* s. v. Apollo 448 ; Boissier, *Religion
Romaine*, i. 96 foll. ; Gardthausen, *Augustus*, vol. ii, p. 873. For the *ludi
saeculares* see especially Mommsen's edition of the great but mutilated
inscription recently discovered in the Campus Martius (*Eph. Epigr.* viii.
1 foll.) ; Diels, *Sibyllin. Blätter*, p. 109 foll. ; and the *Carmen Saeculare* of
Horace, with the commentaries of Orelli and Wickham.

[3] *L. L.* 6. 18 fin. and 19 init.

[4] Festus. 119. s. v. Lucaria.

[5] The battle of the Allia was fought on the 18th, the day before the first
Lucaria. This no doubt suggested the legend connecting the two, especially as the Via Salaria, near which was the grove of the festival, crossed
the battle-field some ten miles north of Rome.

reminds us of the story explanatory of the Poplifugia, and might suggest, as in that case, an expiatory sacrifice and flight of the people from a scapegoat destined to carry away disease. But here we know of no *vestigia fugae* in the cult, such as Varro tells us were apparent at the Poplifugia.

The only possible guess we can make must rest on the name itself, taken together with what Festus tells us of the great wood once existing between the Via Salaria and the Tiber, in which the festival was held—a wood which no doubt occupied the Pincian hill, and the region afterwards laid out in gardens by Lucullus, Pompeius, and Sallust the historian. Lucaria is formed from *lucar* as Lemuria from *lemur*; and *lucar*, though in later times it meant 'the sum disbursed from the *aerarium* for the games[1],' drawn probably from the receipts of the sacred groves, may also at one time itself have meant a grove. An inscription from the Latin colony of Luceria shows us *lucar* in this sense[2]:

IN · HOCE · LUCARID · STIRCUS · NE · IS · FUNDATID, &c.

Now there can be no doubt about the great importance of woods, or rather of clearings in them, in the ancient Italian religion. '*Nemus* and *lucus*,' says Preller[3], 'like so many other words, remind us of the old Italian life of woodland and clearing. *Nemus* is a pasturage, *lucus* a "light" or clearing[4], in the forest, where men settled and immediately began to look to the interests of the spirits of the woodland, and especially of Silvanus, who is at once the god of the wild life of the woodland and of the settler in the forest—the backwoodsman.' The woods left standing as civilization and agriculture advanced continued to be the abodes of *numina*, not only of the great Jupiter, who, as we shall see, was worshipped in groves all over Italy[5], and of Diana, who at Aricia bore the title of Nemorensis, but of innumerable spirits of the old worship,

---

[1] See Friedländer in Marq. 487 ; Plutarch, *Q. R.* 88.

[2] Mommsen in *Ephemeris Epigraphica*, ii. 205.

[3] i. 111 ; Liv. 24. 3 ; Cato, ap. Priscian, 629. Much useful matter bearing on *luci* as used for boundaries, *asyla*, markets, &c., will be found in Rudorff, *Gromatici Veteres*, ii. 260.

[4] 'Light' is not uncommon in England for a 'ride' or clearing in a wood.

[5] Below, pp. 222, and 228.

Fauni, Silvani, and other manifestations of the idea most definitely conceived in the great god Mars[1]. But men could not of course know for certain what spirits dwelt in a wood, whose anger might be roused by intrusion or tree-felling; and old Cato, among his many prescriptions, material and religious, gives one in the form of an invocation to such unknown deities if an intrusion had to be made. It is worth quoting, and runs as follows[2]: 'Lucum conlucare Romano more sic oportet. Porco piaculo facito. Sic verba concipito: Si Deus, si Dea es, quoium illud sacrum est, uti tibi ius siet porco piaculo facere, illiusce sacri coercendi ergo. Harumce rerum ergo, sive ego, sive quis iussu meo fecerit, uti id recte factum siet. Eius rei ergo te hoc porco piaculo immolando bonas preces precor, uti sies volens propitius mihi, domo familiaeque meae, liberisque meis. Harumce rerum ergo macte hoc porco piaculo immolando esto.'

Applying these facts to the problem of the Lucaria, though necessarily with hesitation, and remembering the position of the wood and the date of the festival, we may perhaps arrive at the following conclusion; that this was a propitiatory worship offered to the deities inhabiting the woods which bordered on the cultivated Roman ager. The time when the corn was being gathered in, and the men and women were in the fields, would be by no means unsuitable for such propitiation. It need not have been addressed to any special deity, any more than that of Cato, or as I believe, the ritual of the Lupercalia[3]; it belonged to the most primitive of Roman rites, and partly for that reason, partly also from the absorption of land by large private owners[4], it fell into desuetude. The grove of the Fratres Arvales and the decay of their cult (also

---

[1] On the whole subject of the religious ideas arising from the first cultivation of land in a wild district I know nothing more instructive than Robertson Smith's remarks in *Religion of the Semites*, Lecture iii.; I have often thought that they throw some light on the origin of Mars and kindred numina. The most ancient settlements in central Italy are now found to be on the tops of hills, probably once forest-clad (see Von Duhn's paper on recent excavations, *Journal of Hellenic Studies*, 1896, p. 125). For a curious survival of the feeling about woods and hill-tops in Bengal, see Crooke, *Religion, &c., in India*, ii. 87.

[2] *R. R.* 139. For *piacula* of this kind see also Henzen, *Acta Fratr. Arv.* 136 foll.; Marq. 456.　　　　　　　　[3] See below, p. 312.

[4] See a passage in Frontinus (*Grom. Vet.* 1. 56: cp. 2. 263).

addressed to a nameless deity) offers an analogy on the other side of Rome, towards Ostia.

Such a hypothesis seems not unreasonable, though it is based rather on general than particular evidence. It is at any rate better than the wild guessing of one German inquirer, who is always at home when there is no information. Huschke[1] believes that the words *Lucaria* and *Luceres* (the ancient Roman tribe name) are both derived from *lucus* because the Lucaria take place in July, which is the auspication-month of the Luceres. And there are two days of this festival, because the Luceres owed protection both to the Romani and Quirites (Rhamnes and Tities) and therefore worshipped both Janus and Quirinus.

x Kal. Sext. (July 23). NP.

NEPT[UNALIA]. (pinc. maff.),
feriae neptuno. (pinc. allif.)

The early history of Neptunus is a mystery, and we learn hardly anything about him from his festival. We know that it took place in the heat of summer, and that booths or huts made of the foliage of trees were used at it, to keep the sun off the worshippers—and that is all[2]. Neither of these facts suggests a sea-god, such as we are accustomed to see in Neptune; yet they are hardly strong enough to enable us to build on them any other hypothesis as to his character or functions. Nor does his name help us. Though it constantly appears in Etruscan art as the name of a god who has the characteristics of the Greek Poseidon, it is said not to be of genuine Etruscan origin[3]. If this be so, the Etruscans must

---

[1] *Röm. Jahr*, p. 221, and note 81 on p. 222.

[2] Festus, 377 'Umbrae vocantur Neptunalibus casae frondeae pro tabernaculis.' Wissowa (*Lex*. s.v. Neptunus, 202) compares the σκιάδες of the Spartan Carneia (also in the heat of summer), described in Athenaeus, 4. 141 F.

[3] Müller-Deecke, *Etrusker*, ii. 54, with Deecke's note 51 b. The Etruscan forms are Nethunus and Nethuns. The form of the word is adjectival like Portunus, &c.; but what is the etymology of the first syllable? We are reminded of course of Nepe or Nepete, an inland town near Falerii; and to this district the cult seems specially to have belonged. Messapus, 'Neptunia proles,' leads the Falisci and others to war in Virg. *Aen*. 7. 691, and Halesus, Neptuni filius, was eponymous hero of Falerii (Deecke,

have borrowed it from some people who already used it of a sea-god when the loan was made; but one does not see why this great seafaring people should have gone outside the language of their own religion for a name for their deity of the sea.

In the ancient cult-formulae preserved by Gellius [1], Neptunus is coupled with a female name Salacia; and of this Varro writes 'Salacia Neptuni a salo'—an etymology no doubt suggested by the later identification of Neptunus with Poseidon. Salacia is in my opinion rather to be referred to *salax* ('lustful,' &c.), and, like Nerio Martis [2], to be taken as indicating the virile force of Neptunus as the divine progenitor of a stock [3]. This seems to be confirmed by the fact that this god was known as Neptunus pater, like Mars, Janus, Saturnus, and Jupiter himself [4]; all of whom are associated in cult or legend with the early history of Latin stocks.

When Neptunus first meets us in Roman history, he has already put on the attributes of the Greek Poseidon; this was in B. C. 399, at the first lectisternium, where he is in company with Apollo and Latona, Diana and Hercules, and is specially coupled with Mercurius (= Hermes) [5]. What characteristics of his suggested the identification, either here or in Etruria, we cannot tell. We find no trace of any evidence connecting him with the sea; and the coupling with Hermes need mean no more than that both this god and Poseidon found their way to Rome through the medium of Greek trade.

It has recently been conjectured [6] that the object of both the Lucaria and Neptunalia was to avert the heat and drought

---

Falisker, 103). There is no known connexion of Neptunus with any coast town.

[1] 13. 23. 2 : cp. Varro, *L. L.* 5. 72.

[2] See above, p. 60.

[3] Cp. Serv. *Aen.* 5. 724 '(Venus) dicitur et Salacia, quae proprie meretricum dea appellata est a veteribus.'

[4] Gell. 5. 12 ; Henzen, *Act. Fratr. Arv.* 124. Wissowa, in his article 'Neptunus,' goes too far, as it seems to me, when he asserts that the 'pater' belonged to all deities of the oldest religion. See below, p. 220.

[5] Liv. 5. 13. 6 ; Dionys. 12. 9. Wissowa, *Lex.* s. v. Nept. 203, for his further history as Poseidon.

[6] Wissowa in *Lex.* l. c. I doubt if much can be made of the argument that the Neptunalia on the 23rd is necessarily connected with the Lucaria on the 17th and 19th—i. e. three alternate days, like the three days of the Lemuria in May.

of July, and to propitiate the deities of water and springs, of whom Neptunus (judging from his identification with Poseidon) may possibly have been one; but this is no more than a vague guess, which its author only puts forward 'with all reserve.'

VIII KAL. SEXT. (JULY 25). NP.

FURR[INALIA]. (PINC. ALLIF. MAFF.)
FERIAE FURRINAE. (PINC. ALLIF.)

It seems to be the lesson of the festivals of July that there was an early stage of the Roman religion which had lost all meaning for the Romans themselves when they began to inquire into the history of their own religion. Of this last festival of the month we know no single item in the cult, and therefore have nothing substantial to guide us. It seems almost certain that even Varro and Verrius Flaccus[1] knew nothing of the festival but its name as it stood in the calendar. Nor did they know anything of the goddess Furrina or Furina. Varro is explicit; he says that she was celebrated 'apud antiquos,' for they gave her an annual festival and a flamen, but that in his day there were hardly a dozen Romans who knew either her name or anything about her.

Varro is no doubt right in arguing from the festival and the flamen to the ancient honour in which she was held; and these facts also tend to prove that she was a single deity, and quite distinct from the Furiae with whom the later Romans as well as the Greeks naturally confounded her—an inference which is confirmed by the long *u* indicated by the double *r* in the calendars[2].

There is therefore nothing but the etymology to tell us anything about the goddess, and from this source we cannot expect to learn anything certain. Preller plausibly suggested a connexion with *fur*, *furvus*, and *fuscus*, from a root meaning

---

[1] Varro, *L. L.* 5. 84 'Furinalis (flamen) a Furina quoius etiam in fastis Furinales feriae sunt': cp. 6. 19 'Ei sacra instituta annua et flamen attributus: nunc vix nomen notum paucis.'

[2] See Wissowa's short and sensible note in *Lex.* s. v. Furrina. For the confusion with Furiae, Cic. *de Nat. Deor.* 3. 46; Plut. *C. Gracch.* 17; *Lex.* s. v. Furiae. Jordan, in Preller, ii. 70, is doubtful on the etymological question.

dark or secret; and if this were correct she might be a deity of the under-world or of the darkness. Bücheler in his *Umbrica* [1] suggested a comparison with the Umbrian *furfare=* februare ('to purify'), which will at least serve to show the difficulty of basing conclusions on etymological reasoning. Jordan conjectured that the festival had to do with the averting of dangerous summer heat [2]—a conclusion that is natural enough, but does not seem to rest on any evidence but its date. Lastly, Huschke [3], again in his element, boldly asserts that the Furrinalia served to appease the deities of revenge who hailed from the black region of Vediovis—wrongly confusing Furrina and the Furiae. It will be quite obvious from these instances that it is as hopeless as it is useless to attempt to discover the nature of either goddess or festival by means of etymological reasoning.

[1] p. 71.   [2] In Preller, ii. 121.   [3] *Röm. Jahr*, 221.

MENSIS SEXTILIS.

August is with us the month when the corn-harvest is begun; in Italy it is usually completed in July, and the final harvest-festivals, when all the operations of housing, &c., have been brought to a close, would naturally have fallen for the primitive Roman farmer in the sixth month. The Kalends of Quinctilis would be too early a date for notice to be given of these; some farmers might be behindhand, and so cut off from participation. The Kalends of Sextilis would do well enough; for by the Nones, before which no festival could be held, there would be a general cessation from labour. No other agricultural operations would then for a time be specially incumbent on the farmer[1].

Before the Ides we find no great festival in the old calendar, though the sacrifice on the 12th at the *ara maxima* was without doubt of great antiquity. The list begins with the Portunalia on the 17th; and then follow, with a day's interval between each, the Vinalia Rustica, Consualia, Volcanalia, Opeconsivia, and Volturnalia. The Vinalia had of course nothing to do with harvest, and the character of the Portunalia and Volturnalia is almost unknown; but all the rest may probably have had some relation to the harvesting and safe-keeping of crops, and the one or two scraps of information we possess about the Portunalia bear in the same direction. Deities of fire and water seem to be propitiated at this time, in order to preserve the harvest from disaster by either element. The rites are

---

[1] Varro, *R. R.* I. 33, has only the following: 'Quinto intervallo, inter caniculam et aequinoctium auctumnale oportet stramenta desecari, et acervos construi, aratro offringi, frondem caedi, prata irriₒua iterum secari.'

secret and mysterious, the places of worship not familiar
temples, but the *ara maxima*, the underground altar of Consus,
or the Regia ; which may perhaps account for the comparatively
early neglect and decadence of some of these feasts. We may
also note two other points: first, the rites gather for the most
part in the vicinity of the Aventine, the Circus Maximus, and
the bank of the Tiber ; which in the earliest days must have
been the part of the cultivated land nearest the city[1], or at any
rate that part of it where the crops were stored. Secondly,
there is a faint trace of commerce and connexion between
Rome and her neighbours—Latins and Sabines—both in the
rites and legends of this month, which may perhaps point to
an intercourse, whether friendly or hostile, brought about by
the freedom and festivities of harvest time.

Non. Sext. (Aug. 5). F. (NP. ant.)

SALUTI IN COLLE QUIRINALE SACRIFICIUM PUBLICUM.   (VALL.)
SALUTI IN COLLE.   (AMIT. ANT.)
NATALIS SALUTIS.   (PHILOC.)

The date of the foundation of the temple of Salus was 302 B.C.,
during the Samnite wars[2].   The cult was probably not wholly
new.   The *Augurium Salutis*, which we know through its
revival by Augustus, was an ancient religious performance at
the beginning of each year, or at the accession of new consuls,
which involved, first the ascertaining whether prayers would
be acceptable to the gods, and secondly the offering of such
prayers on an auspicious day[3].   Two very old inscriptions also
suggest that the cult was well distributed in Italy at an early
period[4].   Such impersonations of abstract ideas as Salus, Concordia, Pax, Spes, &c., do not belong to the oldest stage of
religion, but were no doubt of pontifical origin, i. e. belonged
to the later monarchy or early republic[5].   We need not suppose

---

[1] This is the natural position for the *ager* of the oldest community on
the Palatine. The Campus Martius was believed to have been 'king's
land' of the later developed city (Liv. 2. 5).

[2] Liv. 10. 1. 9; Aust, *de Aedibus sacris*, p. 10.

[3] Marq. 377 ; Dio Cass. 37. 24 and 25 ; Tac. *Ann.* 12. 23.

[4] *C. I. L.* i. 49 and 179.

[5] See Preller, ii. 228; and article 'Sacerdos' in *Dict. of Antiquities*, new
edition.

that they were due to the importation of Greek cults and ideas, though in some cases they became eventually overlaid with these. They were generated by the same process as the gods of the Indigitamenta[1]—being in fact an application to the life of the state of that peculiarly Roman type of religious thought which conceived a distinct *numen* as presiding over every act and suffering of the individual. This again, as I believe, in its product the Indigitamenta, was an artificial priestly exaggeration of a very primitive tendency to see a world of nameless spirits surrounding and influencing all human life.

The history of the temple is interesting[2]. Not long after its dedication its walls were painted by Gaius Fabius, consul in 269 B.C., whose descendants, among them the historian, bore the name of Pictor, in commemoration of a feat so singular for a Roman of that age[3]. It was struck by lightning no less than four times, and burnt down in the reign of Claudius. Livy[4] tells us that in 180 B.C., by order of the decemviri a supplicatio was held, in consequence of a severe pestilence, in honour of Apollo, Aesculapius, and Salus ; which shows plainly that the goddess was already being transformed into the likeness of the Greek Ὑγίεια, and associated rather with public health than with public wealth in the most general sense of the word.

vi Id. Sext. (Aug. 9). F. (allif.) N͆P. (amit. maff. etc.)

SOLI INDIGITI IN COLLE QUIRINALE. (amit. allif.)
SOL[IS] INDIGITIS IN COLLE QUIRINALE SACRIFICIUM PUBLICUM. (vall.)

There was an ancient worship of Sol on the Quirinal, which was believed to be of Sabine origin. A *Solis pulvinar* close to the temple of Quirinus is mentioned, and the Gens Aurelia was said to have had charge of the cult[5].

---

[1] On this difficult subject see *Dict. of Antiquities*, s. v. Indigitamenta ; and the long and exhaustive article by R. Peter in Roscher's *Lexicon* (which is, however, badly written, and in some respects, I think, misleading).
[2] See the valuable summary of Aust (in ten lines).
[3] Plin. *N. H.* 35. 19. [4] 40. 19.
[5] Paulus, 23 ; Quintil. 1. 7. 12 ; Varro, *L. L.* 5. 52 (from the 'sacra Argeorum'), if we read ' adversum Solis pulvinar cis aedem Salutis.' The

But the Sol of August 9 is called in the calendars *Sol Indiges.* What are we to understand by this word, which appears in the names Di Indigetes, Jupiter Indiges, or Indigetes simply ? The Roman scholars themselves were not agreed on the point ; the general opinion was that it meant ' of or belonging to a certain place,' i. e. fixed there by origin and protecting it[1]. This view has also been generally adopted, on etymological or other grounds, by modern writers, including Preller[2]. Recently a somewhat different explanation has been put forward in the *Mythological Lexicon,* suggested by Reifferscheid in his lectures at Breslau. According to this view, *Indiges* (from *indu* and root *ag* in *agere*) was a deity working in a particular act, business, place, &c., of men's activity, and in no other ; it is of pontifical origin, like its cognate *indigitamenta,* and is therefore not a survival from the oldest religious forms[3].

The second of these explanations does not seem to help us to understand what was meant by Sol Indiges ; and its exponent in the *Lexicon,* in order to explain this, falls back on an ingenious suggestion made long ago by Preller. In dealing with Sol Indiges, Preller explained Indiges as = *index,* and conjectured that the name was not given to Sol until after the eclipse which foretold the death of Caesar, comparing the lines of Virgil (*Georg.* 1. 463 foll.) :

> Sol tibi signa dabit. Solem quis dicere falsum
> Audeat ? ille etiam caecos instare tumultus
> Saepe monet, fraudemque et operta tumescere bella.
> Ille etiam exstincto miseratus Caesare Romam :
> Cum caput obscura nitidum ferrugine texit,
> Impiaque aeternam timuerunt saecula noctem.

Preller may be right ; and if he were, we should have no further trouble in this case. In the pre-Julian calendar, on this hypothesis, the word Indiges was absent. This is also the opinion of the last scholar who, so far as I know, has touched

---

name is said to be connected with the Umbrian and Etruscan god of light, Usil, a word thought to be recognizable in Aurelius (= Auselius, Varro, l. c.), and in the Ozeul of the Salian hymn (Wordsworth, *Fragments and Specimens of Early Latin,* p. 564 foll.).

[1] So e. g. Virgil, *Georg.* 1. 498 ' Di patrii indigites et Romule Vestaque Mater.' Peter, in *Lex.* s. v. Indigitamenta, 132.

[2] i. 325. [3] *Lex.* s. v. Indigitamenta, 137.

the question ; but Wissowa[1], with reason as I think, reverts to the first explanation given above of the word Indiges ('of or belonging to a certain place'), and believes that the word, when added to Sol in the Julian calendar, was simply meant to distinguish the real indigenous Sun-god from foreign solar deities.

PRID. ID. SEXT. (AUG. 12). C.

HERCULI INVICTO AD CIRCUM MAXIM[UM]. (ALLIF. AMIT.)
[HERCULI MAGNO CUSTODI IN CIRCO FLAMIN'IO] (VALL.) is generally taken as a confusion with June 4[2].]

This is the only day to which we can ascribe, on the evidence of the calendars, the yearly rites of the *ara maxima,* and of the *aedes Herculis* in the Forum boarium. These two shrines were close together ; the former just at the entrance of the Circus maximus, the latter, as has been made clear by a long series of researches, a little to the north-east of it[3]. We are led to suppose that the two must have been closely connected in the cult, though we are not explicitly informed on the point.

The *round* temple indicates a very ancient worship, as in the case of the aedes Vestae, and the legends confirm this. The story of Hercules and Cacus, the foundation-legend of the cult, whatever be its origin, shows a priesthood of two ancient patrician families, the Potitii and Pinarii[4]. Appius Claudius, the censor of 312 B.C., is said to have bribed the Potitii, the chief celebrants, to hand over their duties to public slaves[5] ; but in the yearly rites, consisting chiefly in the sacrifice of a heifer, these were presided over by the praetor urbanus, whose connexion with the cult is attested by inscriptions[6]. That there was at one time a reconstruction of the cult,

---

[1] Wissowa, *de Romanorum Indigetibus et Novensidibus* (Marburg, 1892).

[2] Merkel, *Praef. in Ov. Fastos,* cxxxv ; Mommsen, *C. I. L.* 324.

[3] *Lex.* s. v. Hercules, 2903 foll., where R. Peter has summarized and criticized all the various opinions.

[4] Liv. I. 7.

[5] Dionys. I. 40, who says that the duties were performed by slaves in his day. See *Lex.* 2925 for a long list of conjectures about this part of the legend. The Potitii never occur in inscriptions ; and I think with Jordan (Preller, ii. 291) that the name is imaginary, invented to account for the functions of the slaves.

[6] *C. I. L.* vi. 312-319, found on the site of the *aedes.*

especially in the direction of Greek usage, seems indeed probable; for the praetor wore a laurel wreath and sacrificed with his head uncovered after the Greek fashion [1]. But there is enough about it that was genuine Roman to prove that the foundation-legend had some of its roots in an ancient cult; e. g. at the sacred meal which followed the previous sacrifice in the evening, the worshippers did not lie down but sat, as was the most ancient practice both in Greece and Italy [2]. Women were excluded, which is in keeping with the Italian conception of Hercules as Genius, or the deity of masculine activity [3]. The sacrifice was followed by a meal on the remainder, which was perhaps an old practice in Italy, as in Greece. In this feature, as in two others, we have a very interesting parallel with this cult, which does not seem to have been noticed, in the prescription given by Cato for the invocation of Mars on behalf of the farmer's cattle [4]. After prescribing the material of the offering to Mars Silvanus, he goes on as follows: 'Eam rem divinam *vel servus, vel liber licebit faciat.* Ubi res divina facta erit, *statim ibidem consumito. Mulier ad eam rem divinam ne adsit,* neve videat quomodo fiat. Hoc votum in annos singulos, si voles, licebit vovere.' Here we have the eating of the remainder [5], the exclusion of women, and the participation in the cult by slaves; the exclusion of women is very curious in this case, and seems to show that such a practice was not confined to worships of a sexual character. It is also worth noting that just as Cato's formula invokes Mars Silvanus, so in Virgil's description of the cult of the *ara maxima* [6], we find one special feature of Mars-worship, namely the presence of the *Salii* [7]. It is hardly possible to suppose that Virgil here was guilty of a wilful confusion: is it possible, then, that in this cult some

---

[1] Macrob. 3. 12. 2; Varro, *L. L* 6. 15. The uncovered head also occurs in the cult of Saturnus; and R. Peter argues that the custom may after all be old-Italian (*Lex.* 2928).

[2] Marquardt, *Privatalterthümer*, vol. i, p. 291.

[3] See above, p. 142 foll. Plut. *Qu. Rom.* 60; Macrob. 1. 12. 38. In *Q. R.* 90 Plutarch notes that no other god might be mentioned at the sacrifice, and no dog might be admitted.

[4] *de Re Rustica*, 83.

[5] The word was *profanatum*, opposed to *polluctum* (see Marq. 149).

[6] *Aen.* 8. 281 foll.

[7] Salii are found in the cult of Hercules also at Tibur: Macrob. 3. 12. 7. See a note of Jordan in Preller, i. 352.

form of Mars is hidden behind Hercules, and that the Hercules of the *ara maxima* is not the Genius after all, as modern scholars have persuaded themselves?

But what marks out this curious cult more especially from all others is the practice of offering on the *ara maxima* 'decumae' or tithes, of booty, commercial gains, sudden windfalls, and so on [1]. The custom seems to be peculiar to this cult, though it is proved by inscriptions of Hercules-cults elsewhere in Italy— e. g. at Sora near Arpinum, at Reate, Tibur, Capua and else- where [2]. But these inscriptions, old as some of them are, cannot prove that the practice they attest was not ultimately derived from Rome. At Rome, indeed, there is no question about it; it is abundantly proved by literary allusions, as well as by fragments of divine law [3]. Was it an urban survival from an old Italian rural custom, or was it an importation from elsewhere?

In favour of the first of these explanations is the fact that the offering of *first-fruits* was common, if not universal, in rural Italy [4]. They are not, indeed, known to have been offered specially to Hercules; but the date, Aug. 12, of the sacrifice at Rome might suggest an original offering of the first- fruits of the Roman ager, before the growth of the city had pushed agriculture to some distance away. Now first-fruits are the oldest form of tribute to a god as 'the lord of the land,' developing in due time into fixed tithes as temple-ritual becomes more elaborate and expensive [5]. In their primitive form they are found in all parts of the world, as Mr. Frazer has shown us in an appendix to the second volume of his *Golden Bough* [6]. It is certainly possible that in this way the August cult of the *ara maxima* may be connected with the general character of the August festivals; that the offering of the first-fruits of harvest gave way to a regulated system of tithes [7], of which

---

[1] *Lex.* 2931 foll.; *C. I. L.* i. 149 foll.
[2] The examples are collected by R. Peter in *Lex.* 2935.
[3] Festus, 253, s. v. pollucere merces; Plut. *Qu. Rom.* 18; *Vita Sullae*, 35; *Crassi*, 2; *Lex.* 2032 foll.
[4] Marq. 469; Festus, p. 318, s. v. sacrima.
[5] Robertson Smith, *Religion of the Semites*, p. 233.
[6] *G. B.* ii. 373 foll.
[7] In the legend Hercules gave a tenth part of his booty to the inhabitants of the place (Dionys 1. 40).

we find a survival in the offerings of the tenth part of their booty by great generals like Sulla and Crassus. As the city grew, and agriculture became less prominent than military and mercantile pursuits, the practice passed into a form adapted to these—i. e. the *decumae* of military booty or mercantile gain [1].

But there is another possibility which must at least be suggested. The myth attached to the *ara maxima* and the Aventine, that of Hercules and Cacus, stands alone among Italian stories, as the system of tithe-giving does among Italian practices. We may be certain that the practice did not spring from the myth; rather that an addition was made to the myth, when Hercules was described as giving the tenth of his booty, in order to explain an unusual practice. Yet myth and practice stand in the closest relation to each other, and the strange thing about each is that it is unlike its Italian kindred.

Of late years it has become the fashion to claim the myth as genuine Italian, in spite of its Graeco-Oriental character, on the evidence of comparative mythology [2] : but no explanation is forthcoming of its unique character among Italian myths, all of which have a marked practical tendency, and a relation to some human institution such as the foundation of a city. They are legends of human beings and practices : this is an elemental myth familiar in different forms to the Eastern mind. Again, the Hercules of the myth has nothing in common with the genuine Italian Hercules, whom we may now accept as = genius, or the masculine principle—as may be seen from the sorry lameness of the attempt to harmonize the two [3]. Beyond doubt there was an Italian spirit or deity to whom the name Hercules was attached : but there is no need to force all the forms of Hercules that meet us into exact connexion with the genuine one. We have seen above that the Hercules of the *ara maxima* may possibly have concealed Mars himself, in his original form of a deity of cattle, pasture, and clearings. But there is yet another possible explanation of this tangled problem.

The Roman form of the Cacus-myth, in which Cacus steals

[1] See Mommsen in *C. I. L.* i. 150.
[2] e. g. in Bréal, *Hercule et Cacus.*
[3] See *Lex.* 2286 (R. Peter, quoting Reifferscheid).

the cattle from Hercules, and tries to conceal his theft by
dragging them backwards into his cave by their tails, has
recently been found in Sicily depicted on a painted vase,
whither, as Professor Gardner has suggested, it may have been
brought by way of Cyprus by Phoenician traders[1]; and the
inference of so cautious an archaeologist is, apparently, that
the myth may have found its way from Sicily to the Tiber.
Nothing can be more probable; for it is certain that even
before the eighth century B.C. the whole western coast of
Italy was open first to Phoenician trade and then to Greek.
And we are interested to find that the only other traces of the
myth to be found in Italy are located in places which would
be open to the same influence. From Capua we have a bronze
vase on which is depicted what seems to be the punishment of
Cacus by Hercules[2]; and a fragment of the annalist Gellius
gives a story connecting Cacus with Campania, Etruria, and
the East[3]. At Tibur also, which claimed a Greek origin,
there is a faint trace of the myth in an inscription[4].

Now assuming for a moment that the myth was thus
imported, is it impossible that the anomalies of the cult should
be foreign also? That one of them at least which stands out
most prominently is a peculiarly Semitic institution; tithe-
giving in its systematized form is found in the service of that
Melcarth who so often appears in Hellas as Herakles[5]. The
coincidence at the Aventine of the name, the myth, and the
practice, is too striking to be entirely passed over—especially
if we cannot find certain evidence of a pure Italian origin, and
if we *do* find traces of all three where Phoenicians and Greeks
are known to have been. We may take it as not impossible
that the *ara maxima* was older than the traditional foundation
of Rome, and that its cult was originally not that of the
characteristic Italian Hercules, but of an adventitious deity
established there by foreign adventurers.

---

[1] *Journal of Hellenic Studies*, vol. xiii. 73. Professor Gardner is inclined to
consider the myth as Phoenician rather than Greek, and attached to the
Phoenician Melcarth = Herakles. The vase is in the Ashmolean Museum,
and was found by the Keeper, Mr. Arthur Evans.

[2] *Mon. dell' Inst.* v. 25. But the character of the vase is archaic Ionian,
as Prof. Gardner tells me; *Lex.* 2275.

[3] H. Peter, *Fragmenta Hist. Rom.* p. 166 (= Solinus, i. 7).

[4] *C. I. L.* xiv. 3555; *Lex.* 2278.

[5] Robertson Smith, op. cit. pp. 228 foll., and additional note F.

ID. SEXT. (AUG. 13). NP.

FER͜IAE] IOVI.   (AMIT. ALLIF.)
DIANAE IN AVENTINO.   (AMIT. VALL. ANT. ALLIF.)
SACRUM DEANAE. (RUST.)   NATALIS DIANES. (PHILOC.)
VORTUMNO IN AVENTINO.   (AMIT. ALLIF.)
HERC͜ULI] INVICTO AD PORTAM TRIGEMINAM.   (ALLIF.)
CASTORI POLLUCI IN CIRCO FLAMINIO.   (AMIT. ALLIF.)
FLORAE AD C͜IRCUM] MAXIMUM.   (ALLIF.)

All Ides, as we have seen, were sacred to Jupiter; and it does not seem that there is here any further significance in the note 'feriae Iovi.' Though there was a conjunction here of many cults, this day was best known as that of the dedication of the temple of Diana on the Aventine, which was traditionally ascribed to Servius Tullius. There are interesting features in this cult, and indeed in the worship of this goddess throughout Latium and Italy. For the most famous of all her cults, that of Aricia[1], I need only refer to Mr. Frazer's *Golden Bough*—the most elaborate and convincing examination of any ancient worship that has yet appeared. Of the goddess in general it will be sufficient to say here that whatever be the etymology of her name or the earliest conception of her nature—and both are very far from certain—she was for the old Latins second only to Jupiter Latiaris in the power she exercised of uniting communities together and so working in the cause of civilization. This was the case with the cult on the Aventine, as it was also with that at Aricia[2].

About the political origin of the temple on the Aventine tradition was explicit[3]. Livy says that Servius Tullius persuaded the chiefs of the Latins to build a temple of Diana in conjunction with the Romans; and Varro calls it 'commune Latinorum Dianae templum.' The 'lex templi,' or ordinance for the common worship of Romans and Latins, was seen by Dionysius—so he declares—written in Greek characters and

---

[1] The day of the festival at Aricia is thought to have been also Aug. 13 (*Lex.* s. v. Diana, 1006).

[2] Beloch, *Italischer Bund*, 180; Cato (ap. Priscian, 7. 337, ed. Jordan, p. 41) gives the names of the towns united in and by the Arician cult—Aricia, Tusculum, Lanuvium, Laurentum, Cora, Tibur, Pometia, Ardea.

[3] Liv. 1. 45 Dionys. 4. 26; Varro, *L. L.* 5. 43.

preserved in the temple[1]. The horns of a cow[2], hung up in front of this temple, gave rise to legends, one of which is preserved by Livy, and seems to bring the Sabines also into the connexion. This temple was, then, from the beginning in some sense extra-Roman, i. e. did not belong to the purely Roman gentile worship. And it had other characteristics of the same kind; it was specially connected with the Plebs and with slaves, and as, in the case of the neighbouring temple at Ceres, there was a Greek character in the cult from the beginning.

I. *The Connexion with the Plebs.* The position on the Aventine would of itself be some evidence of a non-patrician origin; so also the traditional ascription to Servius Tullius as the founder. More direct evidence seems wanting[3], but it is not impossible that the temple marks a settlement of Latins in this part of the city.

II. *The Connexion with Slaves.* The day was a holiday for slaves[4], perhaps after the work of harvest. There was one other Latin goddess, Feronia, who was especially beloved by emancipated slaves[5]; and as Feronia was a deity both of markets and harvests, there is something to be said for the suggestion[6] that both slave holidays and slave emancipation would find a natural place on occasions of this kind. It would seem also that this temple was an asylum for runaway or criminal slaves—a fact which slips out in Festus' curious reproduction of a gloss of Verrius Flaccus[7]: 'Servorum dies festus vulgo existimatur Idus Aug., quod eo die Servius Tullius, natus servus, aedem Dianae dedicaverit in Aventino, cuius tutelae sint cervi, a quo celeritate fugitivos vocent servos.' The stag, as the favourite beast of Diana, may

---

[1] Dionys. l. c. See Jordan, *Krit. Beiträge*, 253.

[2] So Liv l. c.: other temples of Diana had deers' horns, according to Plutarch, *Q. R.* 4. The cow was Diana's favourite victim (Marq. 361); but we cannot be sure that this was not a feature borrowed from the cult of Artemis (Farnell, *Greek Cults*, ii. 592).

[3] The passages from Livy quoted by Steuding (*Lex.* 1008) are hardly to the point, as the cult is not mentioned in them.

[4] Plut. *Q. R.* 100.

[5] Serv. *Aen.* 8. 564 : cp. Liv. 22. 1, 26. 11.

[6] Mannhardt, *A. W. F.* 328 foll.

[7] Festus, 343, 'Servorum dies.'

perhaps have a Greek origin; but the inference from the false etymology remains the same.

III. *The Greek Character in the Cult.* As in the case of Ceres, the temple-foundations of this age might naturally have a Greek character, owing to the foreign relations of the Etruscan dynasty in Rome [1]. We have already noticed the lex templi, said to have been written in Greek characters. It is a still more striking fact that there was in this temple a ξόανον, or wooden statue of Diana, closely resembling that of Artemis at Massilia, which was itself derived from the famous temple at Ephesus [2]. The transference to Diana of the characteristics of Artemis was no doubt quite natural and easy; for, hard as it is to distinguish the Greek and Italian elements in the cult, we know enough of some at least of the latter to be sure that they would easily lend themselves to a Greek transformation. This transformation must have begun at a very early period, for in B. C. 398 we find Diana already associated with Apollo and Latona, in the first *lectisternium* celebrated at Rome, where she certainly represented Artemis [3].

On the whole this temple and its cult seem a kind of anticipation of the great temple on the Capitol, in marking an advance. in the progress of Rome from the narrow life of a small city-state to a position of influence in Western Italy. The advance of the Plebs, the emancipation of slaves, the new relations with Latin cities, and the introduction of Greek religious ideas are all reflected here. New threads are being woven into the tissue of Roman social and political life.

The close relation of Diana to human life is not very difficult to explain. Like Fortuna, Juno Lucina, Bona Dea, and others, she was a special object of the worship of women; she assisted the married woman at childbirth [4]; and on this day the Roman

---

[1] See above, p. 75.

[2] Strabo, Bk. 4, p. 180; Farnell, *Greek Cults*, ii. 529 and 552.

[3] Liv. 5. 13 : Apollo and Latona, Diana and Hercules, Mercurius and Neptunus.

[4] *Lex.* 1007. The excavations at Nemi have produced several votive offerings in terra-cotta of women with children in their arms. Cp. Ovid, *Fasti*, 3. 269. Plutarch tells us (*Q. R.* 3) that men were excluded from a shrine of Diana in the Vicus Patricius; but of this nothing further is known.

women made a special point of washing their heads[1]—an unusual performance, perhaps, which has been explained by reference to the sanctity of the head among primitive peoples[2]. But Diana, like Silvanus, with whom she is found in connexion[3], was no doubt originally a spirit of holy trees and woods, i. e. of wild life generally, who became gradually reclaimed and brought into friendly and useful relations with the Italian farmer, his wife, and his cattle[4].

This was also the *dies natalis* of another temple on the Aventine, that of Vortumnus, which was dedicated in B. C. 264 by the consul M. Fulvius Flaccus[5]. About the character of this god there is fortunately no doubt. Literature here comes to our aid, as it too rarely does: Propertius[6] describes him elaborately as presiding over gardens and fruit, and Ovid[7] tells a picturesque story of his love for Pomona the fruit-goddess, whose antiquity at Rome is proved by the fact that she had a flamen of her own[8]. The date, August 13, when the fruit would be ripe, suits well enough with all we know of Vortumnus.

The god had a bronze statue in the Vicus Tuscus, and perhaps for that reason was believed to have come to Rome from Etruria[9]. But his name, like Picumnus, is beyond doubt Latin, and may be supposed to indicate the turn or change in the year at the fruit-season[10]; and if he really was an immigrant, which is possible, his original cult in Etruria was not Etruscan proper, but old Italian.

Three other dedications are mentioned in the calendars as occurring on Aug. 13: to Hercules invictus ad portam trige-

---

[1] Plut. *Q. R.* 100; Jevons, *Introduction*, p. lxviii.

[2] Frazer, *Golden Bough*, i. 187.

[3] *C. I. L.* vi. 656, 658.

[4] Frazer, *G. B.* i. 105: cp. Robertson Smith, *Religion of the Semites*, p. 128 foll. Serv. *Georg.* 3. 332 'Ut omnis quercus Iovi est consecrata, et omnis *lucus* Dianae.' (Hor. *Od.* 1. 21.) The reclaiming of Diana from the woodland to the homestead is curiously illustrated by an inscription from Aricia (Wilmanns, *Exempla*, 1767) in which she is identified with Vesta.

[5] Aust, *de Aedibus sacris*, p. 15. [6] 5. (4.) 2.

[7] *Metaph.* 14. 623 foll.; Preller, i. 451.

[8] Varro, *L. L.* 7. 45. A god Pomonus (gen. Puemones) occurs in the Iguvian ritual (Bücheler, *Umbrica*, 158) who may have been identical with Vortumnus.

[9] Varro, *L. L.* 5. 46.

[10] Preller, i. 452, and Jordan's note.

minam; to Castor and Pollax in circo Flaminio; and to Flora
ad circum maximum. Of these cults nothing of special interest
is known, and the deities are treated of in other parts of this
work.

XVI KAL. SEPT. (AUG. 17). NP.

PORT[UNALIA]. (MAFF. AMIT. VALL.)
TIBERINALIA. (PHILOC.)
FERIAE PORTUNO. (AMIT. ANT.)
PORTUNO AD PONTEM AEMILIUM. (AMIT. VALL. ALLIF.)
IANO AD THEATRUM MARCELLI. (VALL. ALLIF.)

Who was Portunus, and why was his festival in August?
Why was it at the Pons Aemilius, and where was that bridge?
Can any connexion be found between this and the other August
rites? These questions cannot be answered satisfactorily; the
scraps of evidence are too few and too doubtful. We have
here to do with another ancient deity, who survives in the
calendars only, and in the solitary record that he had a special
flamen. This flamen might be a plebeian[1], which seems to
suit with the character of other cults in the district by the
Tiber, and may perhaps point to a somewhat later origin than
that of the most ancient city worships.

There are but two or three texts which help us to make an
uncertain guess at the nature of Portunus. Varro[2] wrote
'Portunalia et Portuno, quoi eo die aedes in portu Tiberino
facta et feriae institutae.' Mommsen takes the *portus* here as
meaning Ostia at the mouth of the Tiber, and imagines a yearly
procession thither from Rome on this day[3]. This of course is
pure hypothesis; but if, as he insists, *portus* is rarely or never
used for a city wharf on a river such as that at Rome, we may

---

[1] Festus, 217, s. v. persillum. All we know of his duties is that he
'unguit arma Quirini'; the word for the oil or grease he used was 'persillum.' Quirinus had his own flamen, who might be supposed to do this
office for him; hence Marq. (328 note) inferred that the god in this case
was a form of Janus, Janus Quirinus. But there is no other sound evidence for a Janus Quirinus, though Janus and Portunus may be closely
connected.

[2] *L. L.* 6. 19.

[3] *C I. L.* 325. He thinks that the *atria Tiberina* mentioned by Ovid
(*Fasti*, 4. 329) were a station on the route of the procession.

perhaps accept it provisionally; but in doing so we have to yield another point to Mommsen, viz. the identity of Portunus and Tiberinus. In the very late calendar of Philocalus this day is called Tiberinalia, and from this Mommsen infers the identity of the two deities [1].

But it may be that the original Portunus had no immediate connexion either with river or harbour. We find a curious but mutilated note in the Veronese commentary on Virgil [2]: ' Portunus, ut Varro ait, deus portuum portarumque praeses. Quare huius dies festus Portunalia, qua apud veteres claves in focum add. . . . mare institutum.' Huschke [3] here conjectured ' addere et infumare,' and inferred that we should see in Portunus the god of the gates and keys which secured the stock of corn, &c., in storehouses. Wild as this writer's conjectures usually are, in this case it seems to me possible that he has hit the mark. If the words 'claves in focum' are genuine, as they seem to be, we can hardly avoid the conclusion that something was done to keys on this day; perhaps the old keys of very hard wood were held in the fire to harden them afresh [4]. It is worth noting that according to Verrius [5] Portunus was supposed 'clavim manu tenere et deus esse portarum.' This would suit very well with harvest-time, when barns and storehouses would be repaired and their gates and fastenings looked to — more especially as it is not unlikely that the word *portus* originally meant a safe place of any kind, and only as civilization advanced became specially appropriated to harbours [6]. This appropriation may have come about through the medium of storehouses near the Tiber; and it was long ago suggested by Jordan that these were under the particular care of Portunus [7].

[1] Mommsen has not convinced other scholars, e. g. Jordan on Preller, ii. 133, and Marq. 328, who points out that if Volturnus is an old name for the Tiber, that river-god was already provided with a flamen (Volturnalis\, and a festival in this month (see below on Volturnalia). I am disposed to think that Mommsen's critics have the best of the argument.

[2] On *Aen.* 5. 241.

[3] *Röm. Jahr*, p. 250. Jordan restored the passage thus : 'Quo apud veteres aedes in portu et feriae institutae' (Preller, i. 178 note).

[4] See Marquardt, *Privatalterthümer*, p. 226.

[5] Paulus, 56.

[6] In Festus, 233, *portus* is said to have been used for a house in the Twelve Tables.

[7] *Topogr.* i. 430 ; Marq. agrees (327 note).

If Portunus were really a god of keys and doors and store-houses, it would be natural to look for some close relation between him and Janus.   But what can be adduced in favour of such a relation does not amount to much [1] ; and it may have been merely by accident that this was the dedication-day of a temple of Janus 'ad theatrum Marcelli' [2].

XIV KAL. SEPT. (AUG. 19). F P. (MAFF. AMIT.) F.
(ANT. ALLIF.) N̶P. (VALL.[3])

VIN[ALIA]. (MAFF. VALL. AMIT. ETC.)
FERIAE IOVI. (ALLIF.)
VENERI AD CIRCUM MAXIMUM. (VALL.)

The 'Aedes Veneris ad Circum Maximum' alluded to in the *Fasti Vallcnses* was dedicated in 295 B. C., and the building was begun at the expense of certain matrons who were fined for adultery [4].   As has been already explained, no early con-nexion can be proved between Venus and wine or the vintage [5] ; though both August 19 and April 23, the days of the two Vinalia, were dedication-days of temples of the goddess.

The difficult question of the two festivals called Vinalia has been touched upon under April 23.   The one in August was known as Vinalia Rustica [6], and might naturally be supposed to be concerned with the ripening grapes.   It has been con-jectured [7] that it was on this day, which one calendar marks as a festival of Jupiter, that the Flamen Dialis performed the *auspicatio vindemiae*, i. e. plucked the first grapes, and prayed and sacrificed for the safety of the whole crop [8].   If it be

---

[1]. Preller, i. 177.

[2] It was a late foundation, vowed by C. Duilius in the First Punic War (B. C. 260).   When rebuilt by Tiberius (Tac. *Ann.* 2. 49) the dedication-day became Oct. 18.   See Aust, *de Aedibus sacris*, p. 18.

[3] See above on April 23, p. 85.

[4] Livy, 10. 31 ; Aust, *de Aedibus sacris*, p. 12.

[5] See above, p. 86.   [6] Paulus, 264.

[7] Preller, i. 196 ; Marq. 333 note.

[8] Varro, *L. L.* 6. 16 ' Vinalia a vino ; Hic dies Iovis, non Veneris ; huius rei cura non levis in Latio ; nam aliquot locis vindemiae primum a sacer-dotibus publicae fiebant, ut Romae etiam nunc ; nam flamen Dialis auspi-catur vindemiam, et ut iussit vinum legere, agna Iovi facit, inter quoius exta caesa et porrecta flamen primus vinum legit.'   But this note, coming between others on the Cerialia and Robigalia, clearly refers to April 23.

argued that August 23 was too early a date for such a rite, since the vintage was never earlier than the middle of September, we may remember that the Vestal Virgins plucked the first ears of corn as early as the first half of May for the purpose of making sacred cakes, some weeks before the actual harvest [1].

But it is certainly possible that both Vinalia have to do with wine, and not with the vintage. Festus says that this day was a festival because the new wine was then first brought into the city [2]; and this does not conflict with Varro [3], who tells us that on this day *fiunt feriati olitores*—for it would naturally be a day of rejoicing for the growers. Mommsen, with some reason, refers these passages to the later custom of not opening the wine of the last vintage for a year [4], in which case the year must be understood roughly as from October to August. He would, in fact, explain this second Vinalia as instituted when this later and more luxurious custom arose, the old rule of a six months' period surviving in the April ceremony. If we ask why the August Vinalia are called Rustica, Mommsen answers that the country growers were now at liberty to bring in their wine.

It is difficult to decide between these conflicting views. When an authority like Mommsen bids us beware of connecting the Vinalia Rustica with the *auspicatio vindemiae*, we feel that it is at our peril that we differ from him. He is evidently quite unable to look upon such a date as August 19 as in any way associated with the vintage which followed some weeks later. Yet I cannot help thinking that this association is by no means impossible ; for the grapes would by this time be fully formed on the vines, and the next few weeks would be an anxious time for the growers [5]. Ceremonies like that of the

---

and the latter part of it must be taken as simply explaining 'huius rei cura non levis' without reference to a particular day.

[1] See above, p. 110.   [2] p. 264.

[3] *L. L.* 6. 20. The passage in 6. 16, quoted above, ends thus : 'In Tus-culanis hortis (sortis in MS.) est scriptum : Vinum novum ne vehatur in urbem antequam Vinalia calentur,' which may refer to a notice put up in the vineyards. Another reading is ' sacris.'

[4] *C. I. L.* 316 and 326 ; Varro, *R. R.* 1. 65.

[5] Cf. Pliny, *N. H.* 18. 284 'Tria namque tempora fructibus metuebant, propter quod instituerunt ferias diesque festos, Robigalia, Floralia, Vinalia.' I do not see why the Vinalia here should not be the Vinalia Rustica.

Auspicatio, intended to avert from crops the perils of storm or disease, are known sometimes to take place when the crops are still unripe. I have already alluded to the proceedings of the Vestals in May. Mr. Frazer, in an Appendix to his *Golden Bough*[1], gives a curious instance of this kind from Tonga in the Pacific Ocean, where what we may call the auspicatio of the Yam-crop took place before the whole crop was fit for gathering. It was celebrated 'just before the yams in general are arrived at a state of maturity; those which are used in this ceremony being planted sooner than others, and consequently they are the firstfruits of the yam season. The object of this offering is to ensure the protection of the gods, that their favour may be extended to the welfare of the nation generally and in particular to the productions of the earth, of which yams are the most important.'

XII KAL. SEPT. (AUG. 21). NP.

CONS[UALIA]. (PINC. MAFF. VALL. ETC.)
CONSO IN AVENTINO SACRIFICIUM. (VALL.)

There was a second festival of Consus on Dec. 15; but the note 'Conso in Aventino' there appears three days earlier, Dec. 12. The temple on the Aventine was a comparatively late foundation[2]; but as the cult of this old god became gradually obscured, it seems to have been confused with the most ancient centre of Consus-worship, the underground altar in the Circus maximus, 'ad primas metas'[3]. It is with this latter that we must connect the two Consualia. What the altar was like we do not exactly know; it was only uncovered on the festival days. Dionysius calls it a τέμενος, Servius a 'templum sub tecto'; and Tertullian, who explicitly says that it was 'sub terra,' asserts that there was engraved on it the following inscription: 'Consus consilio, Mars duello, Lares coillo[4] potentes.' Wissowa remarks that this statement 'is not

Cp. Virg. *Georg.* 2. 419 'Et iam maturis metuendus Iuppiter uvis.' Hartmann, *Röm. Kal.* 137 foll.
[1] Vol. ii. 379.　　　　[2] B. c. 272 (Festus, 209; Aust, p. 14).
[3] For this altar, Tertull. *Spect.* 5 and 8; Dionys. 1. 33; Tac. *Ann.* 12. 24; Serv. *Aen.* 8. 636.
[4] No correction of this word seems satisfactory: see Mommsen, *C. I. L.* 326.

free from suspicion'; and we may take it as pretty certain that if it was really there it was not very ancient. The false etymology of Consus, and the connexion of Mars with war, both show the hand of some comparatively late interpreter of religion; and the form of the inscription, nominative and descriptive, is most suspiciously abnormal.

For the true etymology of Consus we are, strange to say, hardly in doubt; and it helps us to conjecture the real origin of this curious altar. Consus is connected with 'condeie'[1], and may be interpreted as the god of the stored-up harvest; the buried altar will thus be a reminiscence of the very ancient practice—sometimes of late suggested as worth reviving for hay – of storing the corn underground[2]. Or if this practice cannot be proved of ancient Italy, we may aptly remember that sacrifices to chthonic deities were sometimes buried; a practice which may in earliest times have given rise to the connexion of such gods with wealth—when agricultural produce rather than the precious metals was the common form of wealth[3]. Or again we may combine the two interpretations, and guess that the corn stored up underground was conceived as in some sense sacrificed to the chthonic deities.

If these views of the altar are correct, we might naturally infer that the Consualia in August was a harvest festival of some kind. Plutarch[4] asks why at the Consualia horses and asses have a holiday and are decked out with flowers; and such a custom would suit excellently with harvest-home. Unluckily in the only trace of this custom preserved in the calendars, it is attributed to the December festival, and is so mutilated as to be useless for detail[5].

---

[1] Wissowa, *Lex.* s. v. Consus, 926.
[2] Suggested by Mommsen, *C. I. L.* 326, and accepted by Wissowa. Unluckily Columella (r. 6), in alluding to the practice, says nothing of its occurrence in Italy. The alternative explanation was suggested to me by Robertson Smith (*Religion of the Semites,* 107) : see also a note in Müller-Deecke, *Etrusker,* ii. 100 ; and below on Terminalia (p. 325).
[3] The underground altar of Dis Pater in the Campus Martius, at which the ludi saeculares were in part celebrated (Zosimus, 2. 1), may have had a like origin.
[4] *Qu. Rom.* 40 : cf. Dionys. 1. 33.
[5] Fast. Praen. ; *C. I. L.* 237.

FERIAE CONSO EQUI ET [MULI FLORIBUS CORONANTUR].
QUOD IN EIUS TU[TELA SUNT].
[ITA]QUE REX EQUO [VECTUS].

The amplifications here are Mommsen's, the first two based
on Plutarch's statement.   It is a difficulty, as regards the first,
that the middle of December would be a bad time for flowers:
perhaps this did not occur to the great scholar.   I would
suggest that either Verrius' note is here accidentally misplaced,
or that the lacunae must be filled up differently.   In any case
I do not think we need fear to refer Plutarch's passage to the
Consualia of August, and therefore to harvest rejoicings on
that day.

The connexion of the Consus-cult with horses was so
obvious as to give rise eventually to the identification of the
god with Poseidon Hippios.   It is certain that there were
horse-races in the Circus maximus at one of the two Consualia,
and as Dionysius [1] connects them with the day of the Rape of
the Sabines, which Plutarch puts in August, we may be fairly
sure that they took place at the August festival.   Mules also
raced—according to Festus [2], because they were said to be the
most ancient beasts of burden.   This looks like a harvest
festival, and may carry us back to the most primitive agricultural society and explain the origin of the Circus maximus ;
for the only other horse-races known to us from the old calendar
were those of Mars in the Campus Martius on Feb. 27 and
March 13 [3].   We may suppose that when the work of harvest
was done, the farmers and labourers enjoyed themselves in
this way and laid the foundation for a great Roman social
institution [4].

Once more, it is not impossible that in the legendary connexion of the Rape of the Sabine women with the Consualia [5]
we may see a reflection of the jollity and license which accompanies the completion of harvest among so many peoples.

[1] 2. 31, where he says that they were kept up in his own day : cf. Strabo,
Bk. 5. 3. 2.   [2] p. 148.
[3] Friedländer in Marq. 482.   For the connexion of games with harvest
see Mannhardt. *Myth. Forsch.* 172 foll.
[4] Varro (ap. Non. p. 13) quotes an old verse which seems to the point
here : ' Sibi pastores ludo faciunt coriis consualia.'
[5] Varro, *L. L.* 6. 20 ; Serv. *Aen.* 8. 636 ; Dionys. 2. 31 ; Cic. *Rep.* 2. 12.

Romulus was said to have attracted the Sabines by the first celebration of the Consualia. Is it not possible that the meeting of neighbouring communities on a festive occasion of this kind may have been a favourable opportunity for capturing new wives[1]? The sexual license common on such occasions has been abundantly illustrated by Mr. Frazer in his *Golden Bough*[2].

Before leaving the Consualia we may just remark that Consus had no flamen of his own, in spite of his undoubted antiquity; doubtless because his altar was underground, and only opened once or perhaps twice a year. On August 21 his sacrifice was performed, says Tertullian[3], by the Flamen Quirinalis in the presence of the Vestals. This flamen seems to have had a special relation to the corn-crops, for it was he who also sacrificed a dog to Robigus on April 25[4], to avert the mildew from them; and thus we get one more confirmation from the cult of the view taken as to the agricultural origin of the Consualia.

x Kal. Sept. (Aug. 23). N̄.

VOLCANALIA. (PINC. MAFF. VALL. ETC.)
VOLCANO IN CIRCO FLAMINIO. (VALL.)
VOLCANO. (PINC.)
(A mutilated fragment of the calendar of the Fratres Arvales gives QUIR[INO] IN COLLE, VOLK[ANO] IN COMIT[IO], OPI OPI-FER[AE] IN . . . , [NYMP]HIS (?) IN CAMPO).

Of the cult of this day, apart from the extracts from the calendars, we know nothing, except that the heads of Roman families threw into the fire certain small fish with scales, which were to be had from the Tiber fishermen at the 'area Volcani'[5]. We cannot explain this; but it reminds us of the fish called *maena*, with magical properties, which the old

---

[1] See above, p. 178. [2] Vol. ii. 171 foll., 372 foll.
[3] *de Spect.* 8. [4] See above, p. 89; Ovid, *Fasti*, 4. 908.
[5] Festus, p. 210, s. v. piscatorii ludi (Varro, *L. L.* 6 20). The latter uses the word 'animalia,' and does not mention fish. The fish were apparently sacrificed at the domestic hearth; but it is doubtful whether Volcanus was ever a deity of the hearth-fire (see Schwegler, *R. G.* i. 714; Wissowa, *de Feriis*, xiv).

woman offered to Tacita and the ghost-world at the Parentalia[1]. Fish-sacrifices were rare ; and if in one rite fish are used to propitiate the inhabitants of the underworld, they seem not inappropriate in another of which the object is apparently to propitiate the fire-god, who in a volcanic country like that of Rome must surely be a chthonic deity.

The antiquity of the cult of Volcanus is shown by the fact that there was a Flamen Volcanalis[2], who on May 1 sacrificed to Maia, the equivalent, as we saw, of Bona Dea, Terra, &c. With Volcanus we may remember that Maia was coupled in the old prayer formula preserved by Gellius (13. 23)—*Maia Volcani.* From these faint indications Preller[3] conjectured that the original notion of Volcanus was that of a favouring nature-spirit, perhaps of the warmth and fertilizing power of the earth.   However this may be, in later times, under influences which can only be guessed at, he became a hostile fire-god, hard to keep under control.   Of this aspect of him Wissowa has written concisely at the conclusion of his little treatise *de Feriis.*   He suggests that the appearance of the nymphs[4] in the rites of this day indicates the use of water in conflagrations, and that Ops Opifera was perhaps invoked to protect her own storehouses.   The name Volcanus became a poetical word for devouring fire as early as the time of Ennius, and is familiar to us in this sense in Virgil[5].   After the great fire at Rome in Nero's time a new altar was erected to Volcanus by Domitian, at which (and at all Volcanalia) on this day a red calf and a boar were offered for sacrifice[6].   At Ostia the cult became celebrated; there was an 'aedes' and a 'pontifex Volcani' and a 'praetor sacris Volcani faciundis.'   In August the storehouses at Ostia would be full of new grain arrived from Sicily, Africa, and Egypt, and in that hot month would be especially in danger from fire ; an elaborate cult of Volcanus the fire-god was therefore at this place particularly desirable.

---

[1] See below, p. 309 ; Ovid, *Fasti,* 2. 571 foll.

[2] See above on May 23, p. 123 ; Varro, *L. L.* 5. 84 ; Macrob. 1. 12. 18 ; *C. I. L.* vi. 1628.

[3] ii. 149.

[4] In the mutilated note in Fast. Praen. given above.   For Wissowa's views as to the mistake of supposing Volcanus to have been a god of smiths, see above, p. 123 (May 23).

[5] Ennius, *Fragm.* 5. 477 ; Virg. *Aen.* 5. 662.   [6] *C. I. L.* vi. 826.

The aedes Volcani in circo Flaminio was dedicated before 215 B.C.; the exact date is not known[1]. Its position was explained by Vitruvius[2] as having the object of keeping conflagrations away from the city. Mr. Jevons, in his Introduction to a translation of Plutarch's *Quaestiones Romanae*[3], has argued from this position, outside the pomoerium, and from a doubtful etymology, that the cult of Volcanus was a foreign introduction; but the position of the temple is no argument, as has been well shown by Aust[4], and the chief area Volcani, or Volcanal, was in the Comitium, in the heart of the city[5].

IX KAL. SEPT. (AUG. 24). MUNDUS PATET.

This does not appear in the calendars. We learn from Festus[6] that on this day, on Oct. 5, and Nov. 8, the 'mundus' was open. This mundus was a round pit on the Palatine, the centre of Roma quadrata[7]—the concave hollow being perhaps supposed to correspond to the concave sky above[8]. It was closed, so it was popularly believed, by a 'lapis manalis' (Festus s. v.). When this was removed, on the three days there was supposed to be free egress for the denizens of the underworld[9].

I am much inclined to see in this last idea a later Graeco-Etruscan accretion upon a very simple original fact. O. Müller long ago suggested this—pointing out that in Plutarch's description of the foundation of Roma quadrata the casting into the trench of first-fruits of all necessaries of life gives us a clue to the original meaning of the mundus. If we suppose

---

[1] Liv. 24. 10. 9.   [2] Vitruv. 1. 7. 1.

[3] *Roman Questions*, xviii.   [4] *de Aedibus sacris*, p. 47 foll.

[5] What this was we do not really know: there were several of them (Preller, ii. 150).

[6] Fest. 154, from Ateius Capito; Macrob. 1. 16. 17.

[7] Plut. *Rom.* 11; Ovid, *Fasti*, 4. 821. Plutarch wrongly describes it as being in the Comitium.

[8] This seems to be meant by Cato's words quoted by Festus, l. c. ' Mundo nomen impositum est ab eo mundo quod supra nos est. . . eius inferiorem partem veluti consecratam dis Manibus clausam omni tempore nisi his diebus (i. e. the three above mentioned) maiores c[ensuerunt habendam], quos dies etiam religiosos iudicaverunt.'

[9] Fest. 128. So Varro, ap. Macrob. 1. 16. 18 'Mundus cum patet, deorum tristium atque inferum ianua patet.' *Lex.* s. v. Dis Pater, 1184; Preller, ii. 68.

that it was the *penus* of the new city—a sacred place, of course—
used for storing grain, we can see why it should be open on
Aug. 24 [1]. Nor is it difficult to understand why, when the
original use and meaning had vanished, the Graeco-Etruscan
doctrine of the underworld should be engrafted on this simple
Roman stem. Dis and Proserpina claim the mundus : it is
' ianua Orci,' ' faux Plutonis '[2]—ideas familiar to Romans who
had come under the spell of Etruscan religious beliefs.

VIII KAL. SEPT. (AUG. 25). N̄.

OPIC[ONSIVIA]. (ALLIF. MAFF. VALL.)

OPICID. (PINC.) The last two letters must be a cutter's
error.

FERIAE OPI ; OPI CONSIV. IN REGIA. (ARV.) The last four
words seem to belong to Aug. 26 (see Mommsen ad loc.).

This festival follows that of Consus after an interval of three
days ; and Wissowa [3] has pointed out that in December the
same interval occurs between the Consualia (15th) and the
Opalia (19th). This and the epithet or cognomen Consiva,
which is fully attested [4], led him to fancy that Ops was the
wife of Consus, and not the wife of Saturnus, as has been
generally supposed both in ancient and modern times [5]. We
may agree with him that there is no real evidence for any
primitive connexion of Saturnus and Ops of this kind ; as far
as we can tell the idea was adopted from the relation of Cronos
and Rhea. But there was no need to find any husband for
Ops ; the name Consiva need imply no such relation, any more
than Lua Saturni, Moles Martis, Maia Volcani, and the rest [6], or
the Tursa Iovia of the Iguvian inscription so often quoted.
Both adjectival and genitive forms are in my view no more

---

[1] Müller-Deecke, *Etrusker*, ii. 100. Plutarch is explicit : ἀπαρχαί τε πάντων,
ὅσοις νόμῳ μὲν ὡς καλοῖς ἐχρῶντο, φύσει δὲ ὡς ἀναγκαίοις, ἀπετέθησαν ἐνταῦθα.
See above on the Consualia for the practice of burying grain, &c.

[2] Macrob. I. 16. 17. For similar ideas in Greece see A. Mommsen,
Heortologie, 345 foll.

[3] *de Feriis*, vi.   [4] Varro, *L. L.* 6. 21 ; Festus, 187.

[5] Varro, *L. L.* 5. 57 and 64 ; Festus, 186 ; Macrob. I. 10. 19. So Preller,
ii. 20. The keen-sighted Ambrosch had, I think, a doubt about it (*Studien*,
149), and about the conjugal tie generally among Italian deities. See his
note on p. 149.

[6] Gell. 13. 23. Ops Toitesia (if the reading be right) of the Esquiline vase
(Jordan in Preller, ii. 22) may be a combination of this kind (toitesia, conn.
tutus ?) : cf. Ops opifera.

than examples of the old Italian instinct for covering as much
ground as possible in invoking supernatural powers[1]; and
this is again a result of the indistinctness with which those
powers were conceived, in regard both to their nature and
function. A distinct specialization of function was, I am
convinced, the later work of the pontifices. Ops and Consus
are obviously closely related; and Wissowa is probably right
in treating the one as a deity 'messis condendae,' and the other
as representing the 'opima frugum copia quae horreis conditur.'
But when he goes further than this, his arguments ring
hollow[2].

Of the ritual of the Opiconsivia we know only what Varro
tells us[3]: 'Opeconsiva dies ab dea Ope Consiva, quoius in Regia
sacrarium, quod ideo actum (so MSS.) ut eo praeter Virgines
Vestales et sacerdotem publicum introeat nemo.' Many conjectures have been made for the correction of 'quod ideo
actum'[4]; but the real value of the passage does not depend on
these words. The Regia is the king's house, and represents
that of the ancient head of the family: the sacrarium Opis was
surely then the sacred *penus* of that house—the treasury of the
fruits of the earth on which the family subsisted. It suits
admirably with this view that, as Varro says, only the Vestals
and a 'publicus sacerdos' were allowed to enter it—i. e. the
form was retained from remote antiquity that the daughters of
the house were in charge of it[5]—the master of the house being
here represented by the sacerdos—the rex sacrorum or a
pontifex. In this connexion it is worth while to quote
a passage of Columella[6] which seems to be derived from some
ancient practice of the rural household: 'Ne contractentur
pocula vel *cibi* nisi aut ab impube aut certe abstinentissimo
rebus venereis, quibus si fuerit operatus vel vir vel femina

[1] Wissowa himself goes so far as to say that male and female divinities
were joined together 'non per iustum matrimonium sed ex officiorum
adfinitate,' op. cit. vi.

[2] Op. cit. vii.; Mommsen, *C. I. L.* 327 declines to follow him here.

[3] *L. L.* 6. 20. The MSS. read Ope Consiva: so Mommsen in *C. I. L.* 327.
Wissowa adopts the other form.

[4] See Mommsen, l. c., and Marquardt, 212.

[5] See on Vestalia above, p. 147, and Marq. 251.

[6] Colum. 12 4. Cited in De-Marchi, *Il Culto privato di Roma Antica* (Milan,
1896), p. 56. See my paper in *Classical Review* for Oct. 1896: vol. x.
p. 317 foll.

debere eos flumine aut perenni aqua priusquam penora con-
tingant ablui. Propter quod his necessarium esse pueri vel
virginis ministerium, per quos promantur quae usus postula-
verit.'

vi Kal. Sept. (Aug. 27). N̂P.

VOLT[URNALIA]. (ALLIF. MAFF. VALL.)
FERIAE VOLTURNO. (ARV. INTER ADDITA POSTERIORA.)
VOLTURNO FLUMINI SACRIFICIUM. (VALL.)

Of this very ancient and perhaps obsolete rite nothing seems
to have been known to the later Latin scholars, or they did
not think it worth comment. Varro mentions a Flamen
Volturnalis, but tells us nothing about him. From the occurrence of the name for a river in Campania it may be guessed
that the god in this case was a river also ; and if so, it must
be the Tiber. This is Mommsen's conclusion, and the only
difficulty he finds in it is that (in his view) Portunus is also the
Tiber[1]. Why did he not see that the same river-god, even if
bearing different names, could hardly have two flamines ?
I am content to see in Volturnus an old name for the Tiber,
signifying the winding snake-like river[2], and in Portunus
a god of storehouses, as I have explained above.

Here, then, we perhaps have a trace of the lost cult of the
Tiber, which assuredly must have existed in the earliest times—
and the *flamen* is the proof of its permanent importance.
When the name was changed to Tiber we do not know, nor
whether 'Albula' marks an intermediate stage between the
two ; but that this was the work of the pontifices seems likely
from Servius[3], who writes 'Tiberinus . . . a pontificibus indigitari solet.' Of a god Tiberinus there is no single early
record.

It should just be mentioned that Jordan[4], relying on
Lucretius, 5. 745, thought it probable that Volturnus might
be a god of whirlwinds ; and Huschke[5] has an even wilder
suggestion, which need not here be mentioned.

---

[1] *C. I. L.* 327.   [2] Preller, ii. 142.   [3] *Aen.* 8. 330.
[4] In Preller, ii. 143. In the passage of Lucretius Volturnus is coupled
with Auster : 'Inde aliae tempestates ventique secuntur, Altitonam Volturnus et Auster fulmine pollens.' Columella (11. 2. 65) says that some
people use the name for the east wind (cp. Liv. 22. 43).
[5] *Röm. Jahr*, 251.

MENSIS SEPTEMBER.

THE Calendar of this month is almost a blank. Only the Kalends, Nones and Ides are marked in the large letters with which we have become familiar; no other festival is here associated with a special deity. But the greater part of the month is occupied with the ludi Romani (5th to 19th)[1], and the 13th (Ides), as we know from two Calendars, was not only, like all Ides, sacred to Jupiter, but was distinguished as the day of the famous 'epulum Jovis,' and also as the *dies natalis* of the great Capitoline temple.

The explanation of the absence of great festivals in this month is comparatively simple. September was for the Italian farmer, and therefore for the primitive Roman agricultural community, a period of comparative rest from urgent labour and from religious duties; for no operations were then going on which called for the invocation of special deities to favour and protect. A glance at the rustic calendars will show this well enough[2]. The *messes* which figure in July and August have come to an end, and the vintage does not appear until October. There is of course work to be done, as always, but it is the easy work of the garden and orchard. 'Dolia picantur: poma legunt: arborum oblaqueatio.' Varro, who divides the year for agricultural purposes into eight irregular periods, has little to say of the fifth of these, i. e. that which preceded the autumn equinox. 'Quinto intervallo inter cani-

---

[1] This represents the length which the ludi had attained in Cicero's time (*Verr.* i. 10. 31). September 4 was probably added after Caesar's death (Mommsen in *C. I. L.* 328).

[2] *C. I. L.* 281.

culam et aequinoctium autumnale oportet stramenta desecari, et acervos construi, aratro offringi, frondem caedi, prata irrigua iterum secari[1].'

This was also the time when military work would be coming to an end. In early times there were of course no lengthy campaigns; and such fighting as there was, the object of which would be to destroy your enemies' crops and harvest, would as a rule be over in August. Even in later times, when campaigns were longer, the same would usually be the case; and the performance of vows made by the generals in the field, and also their vacation of office, would naturally fall in this month. We find, in fact, that the ludi which occupied so large a number of September days, had their origin in the performance of the *vota* of kings or consuls after the close of the wars[2]; and we have evidence that the Ides of September was the day on which the earliest consuls laid down their office[3]. There was, in fact, every opportunity for a lengthened time of ease; the people were at leisure and in good temper after harvest and victory; even the horses which took part in the games were home from war service or resting from their labours on the farm[4].

It is not strictly within the scope of this work to describe the ludi Romani, which in their fully organized form were of comparatively late date; but their close connexion with the cult of Jupiter affords an opportunity for some remarks on that most imposing of all the Roman worships.

The ludi Romani came in course of time, as has been said above, to extend from the 5th to the 19th; they spread out in fact on each side of the Ides[5], the day on which took place the 'epulum Jovis' in the Capitoline temple. As this day was also

[1] *R. R.* I. 33.
[2] See Mommsen's masterly essay in his *Römische Forschungen*, vol. ii. p. 42 foll. Aust, in *Myth. Lex.* s.v. Iuppiter, 732.
[3] Mommsen, *Röm. Chronol.* 86 foll.
[4] The 'equorum probatio,' preliminary to the races in the circus, took place on the day after the Ides : see above, p. 27.
[5] Mommsen (*C. I. L.* 328, and *Röm. Forsch.* ii. 43 foll.) points out that the real centre-point and original day of the ludi proper was the day of the great procession (pompa) from the Capitol to the Circus maximus ; and that this was probably the 15th, two days after the epulum, because the 14th, being *postriduanus*, was unlucky, and that day was also occupied by the 'equorum probatio.' (See Fasti Sab., Maff., Vall., Amit. and Antiat.)

the *dies natalis* of the same temple, and that on which the nail was driven into the wall of the cella Jovis[1], we have a very close connexion between the ludi and the cult of Jupiter. The link is to be found in the fact that in the *ludi votivi*, which were developed into ludi Romani, the vows were made and paid to the supreme god of the State[2]. We have from a later time the formula of such a vow preserved by Livy[3]. 'Si duellum quod cum rege Antiocho sumi populus iussit id ex sententia senatus populique Romani confectum erit, tum tibi, Iuppiter, populus Romanus ludos magnos dies decem continuos faciet, donaque ad omnia pulvinaria dabuntur de pecunia, quantam senatus decreverit: quisquis magistratus eos ludos quando ubique faxit, hi ludi recte facti donaque data recte sunto.'

The epulum Jovis, thus occurring in the middle of the ludi, is believed by some writers to have originally belonged to the Ides of November and to the ludi plebeii, as it does not happen to be alluded to by Livy in connexion with the ludi Romani, and our first notice of it in September is in the Augustan calendars[4]. But it is surely earlier than B.C. 230, the received date of the ludi plebeii, and of the circus Flaminius in which they took place. We may agree with the latest investigator of the Jupiter-cult that the origin of the epulum is to be looked for in a form of thanksgiving to Jupiter for the preservation of the state from the perils of the war season, and that no better day could be found for it than the foundation-day of the Capitoline temple[5]. This epulum was one of the most singular and striking scenes in Roman public life. It began with a sacrifice; the victim is not mentioned, but was no doubt a heifer, and probably a white

---

[1] See below, p. 234. For the *dies natalis*, see Aust, in *Lex.* s.v. Iuppiter, p. 707 ; Plutarch, *Poplic.* 14.

[2] Mommsen, *Röm. Forsch.* l. c.

[3] Livy, 36. 2. 3. The passage refers to *ludi magni*, i. e. *special* votive games, vowed after the fixed organization of the ludi Romani ; but it is none the less illustrative of the latter, as they originated in votive games.

[4] So Marq. 349 and note ; Mommsen in *C. I. L.* 329, 335. I follow Aust, *Lex.* s.v. Iuppiter, 732. The 'epulum Minervae' of the rustic calendars is but slender evidence for an ancient and special connexion of the goddess with this day ; but Mommsen thinks that the epulum 'magis Minervae quam Iovis fuisse.'

[5] Aust, l. c.

one[1]. Then took place the epulum proper[2], which the three
deities of the Capitol seem to have shared in visible form with
the magistrates and senate. The images of the gods were
decked out as for a feast, and the face of Jupiter painted red
with *minium*, like that of the triumphator. Jupiter had
a couch, and Juno and Minerva each a sella, and the meal
went on in their presence[3].

Now an investigator of the Roman religious system is here
confronted with a difficult problem. Was this simply a Greek
practice like that of the lectisternium, and one which began
with the Etruscan dynasty and the foundation of the Capitoline
temple with its triad of deities? Or is it possible that in the
cult of the Roman Jupiter there was of old a common feast of
some kind, shared by gods and worshippers, on which this
gorgeous ritual was eventually grafted?

Marquardt has gone so far as to separate the epulum Jovis
altogether from the lectisternia, and apparently also from the
inundation of Greek influence[4]. It answers rather, he says,
to such domestic rites as the offering to Jupiter Dapalis
described thus by Cato in the *De Re Rustica*[5] : 'Dapem hoc
modo fieri oportet. Iovi dapali culignam vini quantum vis
polluceto. Eo die feriae bubus et bubulcis, et qui dapem
facient. Cum pollucere oportebit, sic facies. Iupiter dapalis,
quod tibi fieri oportet, in domo familia mea culignam vini
dapi, eius rei ergo macte hac illace dape pollucenda esto.
Manus interluito. Postea vinum sumito. Iupiter dapalis,
macte istace dape pollucenda esto. Macte vino inferio esto.
Vestae, si voles, dato[6]. Daps Iovi assaria pecuina, urna vini
Iovis caste.'

---

[1] Aust, *Lex.* s. v. Iuppiter, 670, 735.

[2] In Capitolio (Gellius, 12. 8. 2 ; Liv. 38. 57. 5). For the collegium of
epulones, which from 196 B. C. had charge of this and other public feasts,
see Marq. 347 foll.

[3] Val. Max. 2. 1. 2 ; Plin. *N. H.* 33. 111 ; Aust, l. c. ; Preller, i. 120.

[4] Marq. 348.

[5] *R. R.* 132. Festus (68) explains daps as 'res divina quae fiebat aut
hiberna semente aut verna,' and Cato directs the farmer to begin to sow
after the ceremony he describes. I do not clearly understand whether
Marquardt intended also to connect the epulum Jovis of Nov. 13 with the
autumn sowing.

[6] I am unable to offer any explanation of these words, though half
inclined to suspect that Vesta was the original deity of this rite of the
farm, and that Jupiter and the wine-offering are later intrusions.

I confess that I do not see wherein lies the point of the comparison of this passage with the ceremony of the epulum; and Marquardt himself does not attempt to elaborate it. There is no mention here of a visible presence of Jupiter in the form of an image, which is the one striking feature of the epulum. Marquardt, as it seems to me, might better have adduced some example from old Italian usage of the *belief* that the gods were spiritually present at a common religious meal—a belief on which might easily be engrafted the practice of presenting them there in actual iconic form. Ovid, for example, writes thus of the cult of the Sabine Vacuna[1]:

> Ante focos olim scamnis considere longis
>   Mos erat, *et mensae credere adesse deos.*
> Nunc quoque cum fiunt antiquae sacra Vacunae,
>   Ante Vacunales stantque sedentque focos.

Or again in the sacra of the curiae, if Dionysius reports them rightly[2], we find a clear case of a common meal in which the gods took part. He tells us that he saw tables in the 'sacred houses' of the curiae spread for the gods with simple food in very primitive earthenware dishes. He does not mention the presence of any images of the gods, but it is probable from his interesting description that each curia partook with its gods of a common meal of a religious character, and one not likely to have come under Greek influence[3].

This last example may suggest a hypothesis which is at least not likely to do any serious harm. Let it be remembered that each curia was a constituent part of the whole Roman community. We might naturally expect to find a common religious meal of the same kind in which the *whole* state took part through its magistrates and senate. This is just what we do find in the epulum Jovis, though the character of its ceremonial is different; and it is certainly possible that this epulum had its origin in a feast like that which Dionysius saw, but one which afterwards underwent vital changes at the

---

[1] *Fasti*, 6. 307. For Vacuna see Preller, i. 408.

[2] Bk. 2. 23 (cp. 2. 50); Marq. 195 foll. For a comparison of Greek and Roman usage of this kind see de Coulanges, *La Cité antique*, p. 132 foll.

[3] He compares this common meal with those of the πρυτανεῖα of Greek cities, and also with the φιδίτια at Sparta. But it is most unlikely that the practice of the curiae should have had any but a native origin.

hands of the Etruscan dynasty of Roman kings. I am strongly inclined to believe that it was under the influence of these kings that the meal came to take place on the Capitol, and in the temple of Jupiter, Juno, and Minerva, which they intended to be the new centre of the Roman dominion [1]; and to them also I would ascribe the presence at the feast of the three deities in iconic form. It may be that before that critical era in Roman history the epulum took place not on the Capitol but in the Regia, which with the temple of Vesta hard by formed the oldest centre of the united Rome; and that the presence of Jupiter [2] or any other god was there a matter of belief, like that of Vacuna with the Sabines, and not of the actual evidence of eyesight.

But this conjecture is a somewhat bold one; and it seems worth while to take this opportunity of examining more closely into the cult of Jupiter, with the object of determining whether the great god was apt, in any part of Italy but Etruria, to lend himself easily to anthropomorphic ideas and practices [3].

The cult of Jupiter is found throughout Italy under several forms of the same name, with or without the suffix -piter = pater, which, so far as we can guess, points to a conception of the god as protector, if not originator, of a stock. This paternal title, which was applied to other deities also, does not necessarily imply an early advance beyond the 'daemonistic' conception of divine beings; it rather suggests that some one such being had been brought into peculiarly close relations with a particular stock, and does no more than indicate a possibility of further individual development in the future [4].

[1] See cap. 7 of Ambrosch's *Studien*; and cp. cap. 1 on the Regia as the older centre.

[2] I may relegate to a footnote the further conjecture that the original deity of the epulum was Vesta. We know that this Sept. 13 was one of the three days on which the Vestals prepared the *mola salsa* (Serv. *Ecl.* 8. 32). We cannot connect this *mola salsa* with the cult of Jupiter on this day, for the Vestals have no direct connexion with that cult at any period of the year; but it is possible that it was a survival from the time when the common meal took place in the Regia.

[3] See Aust's admirable and exhaustive article on Jupiter in Roscher's *Lexicon*.

[4] Robertson Smith (*Religion of the Semites*, 42 foll.) seems to trace the idea back to an actual physical fatherhood. Mr. Farnell, on the other hand (*Cults of the Greek States*, i. 49), believes that in the case of Zeus it expresses

The 'father' in this case has no wife, though we find the word 'mater' applied to goddesses[1]; Juno is undoubtedly the female principle, but she is not, as has so often been imagined, the wife of Jupiter. The attempt to prove this by arguing from the Flamen Dialis and his wife the Flaminica cannot succeed: the former was the priest of Jupiter, but his wife was not the priestess of Juno[2]. There is indeed a certain mysterious dualism of male and female among the old Italian divinities, as we know from the *locus classicus* in Gellius (*N. A.* 13. 23. 2); but we are not entitled to say that the relation was a conjugal one[3].

Before we proceed to examine traces of the oldest Jupiter in Rome and Latium let us see what survivals are to be found in other parts of Italy.

In Umbria we find Jovis holding the first place among the gods of the great inscription of Iguvium, which beyond doubt retains the primitive features of the cult, though it dates probably from the last century B. C.; and records rites which indicate a fully developed city-life[4]. His cult-titles here are Grabovius, of which the meaning is still uncertain, and Sancius, which brings him into connexion with the Semo Sancus and Dius Fidius of the Romans. The sacrifices and prayers are elaborately recorded, but there is no trace in the ritual of anything approaching to an anthropomorphic conception of the god, unless it be the apparent mention of a temple[5]. No image is mentioned, and there is no sign of a common meal. The titles of the deities too have the common old-Italian fluidity, i.e. the same title belongs to more than one deity[6]. Everything points to a stage of religious thought in which the personality of gods had no distinct place. The

'rather a moral or spiritual idea than any real theological belief concerning physical or human origins.' In Italy, I think, the suffix pater indicates a special connexion with a particular stock, and one rather of guardianship than of actual fatherhood. See above on Neptunalia.

[1] See Jordan's note on Preller, i. 56.

[2] See my paper in *Classical Review*, vol. ix. 474 foll.

[3] Wissowa, *de Feriis*, p. 6, in the true spirit of Italian worship, concludes that it was 'non per iustum matrimonium, sed ex officiorum affinitate.'

[4] Bücheler, *Umbrica*; Bréal, *Les Tables Eugubines.*

[5] *Tab.* 1 B. (Bücheler, p. 2, takes it as a temple or sacellum of *Juno*).

[6] Grabovius is an epithet of Mars; Sancius of Fisius; Jovius or Juvius of more than one deity.

centre-point of the cult seems to be a hill, the *ocris fisius*,
within the town of Iguvium, which reminds us of the habits
of the Greek Zeus and the physical or elemental character—
unanthropomorphized—which seems to belong to that earlier
stage in his worship[1].

It is on a hill also that we find the cult among the
Sabellians. An inscription from Rapino in the land of the
Marrucini tells us of a festal procession in honour of 'Iovia
Ioves patres ocris Tarincris,' i.e. Jovia (Juno?) belonging to
the Jupiter of the hill Tarincris[2].

Among the Oscan peoples the cult-title *Lucetius* is the most
striking fact. Servius[3] says: 'Sane lingua Osca Lucetius est
Iuppiter dictus a luce quam praestare hominibus dicitur.'
The same title is found in the hymn of the Roman Salii[4],
and is evidently connected with *lux*; Jupiter being beyond
doubt the giver of light, whether that of sun or moon. So
Macrobius[5]: 'Nam cum Iovem accipiamus lucis auctorem,
unde et Lucetium Salii in carminibus canunt et Cretenses Δία
τὴν ἡμέραν vocant, ipsi quoque Romani Diespitrem appellant ut
diei patrem. Iure hic dies Iovis fiducia vocatur, cuius lux
non finitur cum solis occasu, sed splendorem diei et noctem
continuat inlustrante luna,' &c. The Ides of all months, i.e.
the days of full moon, were sacred to Jupiter. But in all
ceremonies known to us in which the god appears in this
capacity of his, there is, as we might expect, no trace whatever
of a personal or anthropomorphic conception.

The Etruscan Tina, or Tinia, is now generally identified,
even etymologically, with Jupiter[6]. The attributes of the
two are essentially the same, though one particular side of
the Etruscan god's activity, that of the lightning-wielder, is
specially developed. But Tina is also the protector of cities,
along with Juno and Minerva (Cupra and Menvra); and it is
in connexion with this function of his that we first meet
with a decided tendency towards an anthropomorphic con-

---

[1] Farnell, op. cit. i. 50 and notes.
[2] Mommsen, *Unteritalische Dialekten*, 341 ; *Lex.* 637. The Jupiter *Cacunus*
of *C. I. L.* 6. 371 and 9. 4876 also points to *high places*, and there are other
examples.
[3] *Aen.* 9. 567.   [4] Wordsworth, *Fragments and Specimens*, p. 564.
[5] *Sat.* i. 15. 14.
[6] Deecke, *Etruskische Forschungen*, iv. 79 foll.

ception. Even here, however, the stimulus can hardly be said to have come from Italy. 'The one fact,' says Aust[1], 'which is at present quite clear is that the oldest Etruscan representations of gods can be traced back to Greek models. Tinia was completely identified in costume and attributes with the Greek Zeus by Etruscan artists.' The insignia of Etruscan magistrates were again copied from these, and have survived for us in the costume of the Roman triumphator[2], and in part in the insignia of the curule magistrate, i.e. in sceptrum, sella, toga palmata, &c., and in the smearing of the face of the triumphator with *minium*.

Coming nearer to Rome we find at Falerii, a town subject to Roman and Sabellian as well as Graeco-Etruscan influence, the curious rite of the ἱερὸς γάμος described by Ovid (*Amores*, 3. 13), and found also in many parts of Greece[3]. In this elaborate procession Juno is apparently the bride, but the bridegroom is not mentioned. At Argos, Zeus was the bridegroom, and the inference is an obvious one that Jupiter was the bridegroom at Falerii. But this cannot be proved, and is in fact supported by no real evidence as to the old-Italian relation of the god and goddess. The rite is extremely interesting as pointing to what seems to be an early penetration of Greek religious ideas and practices into the towns of Western Italy; but it has no other bearing on the Jupiter-question, nor are we enlightened by the little else we know of the Falerian Jupiter[4].

But at Praeneste, that remarkable town perched high upon the hills which enclose the Latin Campagna to the north, we find a very remarkable form of the Jupiter-cult, and one which must be mentioned here, puzzling and even inexplicable as it certainly is. The great goddess of Praeneste was Fortuna Primigenia—a cult-title which cannot well mean anything but *first-born*[5]; and that she was, or came to be thought of as, the first-born daughter of Jupiter is placed beyond a doubt by an

---

[1] *Lex.* s. v. Iuppiter, p. 634.

[2] Servius *Ecl.* 10. 27; *Dict. of Antiquities* (ed. 2), s.v. Triumphus.

[3] Farnell, i. 184 foll. See also Dion. Hal. 1. 21. 2; Deecke, *Die Falisker*, p. 88; *Lex.* s.v. Juno, 591; Roscher, *Juno und Hera*, 76.

[4] *Lex.* 643.

[5] H. Jordan, *Symbolae ad historiam religionum Italicarum alterae.* Königsberg, 1885.

inscription of great antiquity first published in 1882 [1]. But this is not the only anomaly in the Jupiter-worship of Praeneste. There was another cult of Fortuna, distinct, apparently, from that of Fortuna Primigenia, in which she took the form not of a daughter but of a mother, and, strange as it may seem, of the mother both of Jupiter and Juno. On this point we have the explicit evidence of Cicero (*de Divinatione*, 2. 85), who says, when speaking of the place where the famous 'sortes' of Praeneste were first found by a certain Numerius Suffustius: 'Is est hodie locus saeptus religiose propter Iovis pueri (sacellum?) qui lactens cum Iunone Fortunae in gremio sedens, castissime colitur a matribus.' Thus we have Fortuna worshipped in the same place as the daughter and as the mother of Jupiter; and nowhere else in Italy can we find a trace of a similar conception of the relations either of these or any other deities. We cannot well reject the evidence of Cicero, utterly unsupported though it be: we must face the difficulty that we have here to account for the occurrence of a Jupiter who is the child of Fortuna and also apparently the brother of Juno, as well as of a Jupiter who is the father of Fortuna.

As regards this last feature, the fatherhood of Jupiter, Jordan says emphatically [2]—and no scholar was more careful in his judgements—that in the whole range of Italian religions 'liberorum procreatio nulla est unquam': and he would understand 'filia' in the inscription quoted above in a metaphorical rather than a physical sense. Yet however we choose to think of it, Mommsen is justified in remarking [3] on the peculiarly anthropomorphic idea of Fortuna (and we may add of Jupiter) at which the Latins of Praeneste must have arrived, in comparison with the character of Italian religion generally.

---

[1] 'Orceria . Numeri . nationu . cratia . Fortuna . Diovo . filei . primocenia . donom dedi' (*C. I. L.* xiv. 2863). There are later inscriptions in which she appears as 'Iovis (or Iovi) puero,' in the sense of female child (*C. I. L.* xiv. 2862, 2868). The subject is discussed by Mommsen in *Hermes* for 1884, p. 455, and by Jordan op. cit. See also *Lex.* s. v. Fortuna, 1542 foll., and s. v. Iuppiter, 648.

[2] *Symbolae*, i. p. 8, and cp. 12. For the apparent parallel in the myth of the birth of Mars see on March 1.

[3] *Hermes*, 1884, p. 455 foll.

Even more singular than this is the sonship of Jupiter and the fact that he appeared together with Juno in the lap of Fortuna 'mammae appetens.' Cicero's language leaves no doubt that there was some work of art at Praeneste in which the three were so represented, or believed to be represented. Yet there are considerations which may suggest that we should hesitate before hastily concluding that all this is a genuine Italian development of genuine Italian ideas.

1. Italy presents us with no real parallel to this child-Jupiter, though in Greece we find many. Jordan has mentioned three possible Italian parallels, but rejected them all: Caeculus Volcani, the legendary founder of Praeneste, Hercules bullatus, and the beardless Veiovis. The attributes of the last-named are explained by a late identification with Apollo[1]; Hercules bullatus is undoubtedly Greek: the story of the birth of Caeculus is a foundation-legend, truly Italian in character, but belonging to a different class of religious ideas from that we are discussing. To these we may add that the *boy-Mars* found on a Praenestine cista is clearly of Etruscan origin, as is shown by Deecke in the *Lexicon*, s. v. Maris.

2. Cicero's statement is not confirmed by any inscription from Praeneste. Those which were formerly thought to refer to *Iupiter Puer*[2] are now proved to belong to Fortuna as *Iovis puer* (= *filia*). It is most singular that Fortuna should be thus styled *Iovis puer* in the same place where Jupiter himself was worshipped as *puer*; still more so that in one inscription (2868) the cutter should have dropped out the 's' in Iovis, so that we actually read *Iovi puero*. It may seem tempting to guess that the name Jupiter Puer arose from a misunderstanding of the word *puer* as applied to Fortuna: but the evidence as it stands supplies no safe ground for this.

3. The fact that Cicero describes a statue is itself suspicious, in the absence of corroborative evidence of any other kind[3]:

---

[1] Gellius, *N. A.* 5. 12; Ovid, *Fasti*, 3. 429 foll.; and see above on May 21. For Hercules, Jordan l. c. and his note on Preller, ii. 298. For Caeculus, Wissowa, in *Lex.* s. v.   [2] *C. I. L.* xiv. 2862 and 2868.

[3] The *tria signa* of Liv. 23. 19, placed 'in aede Fortunae' by M. Anicius after his escape from Hannibal, with a dedication, may possibly have been those of Fortuna and the two babes (Preller, ii. 192, note 1): but this is very doubtful.

for it suggests that the cult may have arisen, and have taken its peculiar form, as a result of the introduction of Greek or Graeco-Etruscan works of art. In Praeneste itself, and in other parts of Latium and of Campania, innumerable terra-cottas have been found [1], of the type of the Greek κουροτρόφος, i. e. a mother, sitting or standing, with a child, and occasionally two children [2] in her lap. These may, indeed, be simply votive offerings, to Fortuna and other deities of childbirth: but such objects may quite well have served as the foundation from which the idea of Fortuna and her infants arose. There is a passage in Servius which seems to me to show a trace of a similar confusion elsewhere in this region of Italy. 'Circa hunc tractum Campaniae colebatur *puer Iuppiter* qui Anxyrus dicebatur quasi ἄνευ ξυροῦ, id est sine novacula: quia barbam nunquam rasisset: et *Iuno virgo* quae Feronia dicebatur [3].' True, the Jupiter of Anxur is a boy or youth [4], not an infant: but the passage serves well to show the fluidity of Italian deities, at any rate in regard to the names attached to them. That this *puer Iuppiter* was originally some other deity, and very possibly a Greek one, I have little doubt: while Juno Virgo, Feronia, Fortuna, Proserpina, all seem to slide into each other in a way which is very bewildering to the investigator [5]. This is no doubt owing to two chief causes—the daemonistic character of the early Italian religion, in which many of the spiritual conceptions were even *unnamed*; and, secondly, the confusion which arose when Greek artistic types were first introduced into Italy. Two currents of religious thought met at this point, perhaps in the eighth and following centuries B. C.; and the result was a whirlpool, in which the deities were tossed about, lost such shape as they possessed, or got inextricably entangled with each other. The French student of Praenestine antiquities writes with reason of 'the negligence with which the Praenestine artists

---

[1] Jordan, *Symbolae*, 10 ; *Lex.* s. v. Fortunae, 1543 ; Fernique, *Étude sur Préneste*, 78.

[2] Gerhard, *Antike Bildwerke*, Tab. iv. no. 1, gives an example : the children here, however, are not babes, and the mother has her arms round their necks. It seems more to resemble the types of Leto with Apollo and Artemis as infants (*Lex.* s. v. Leto, 1973), as Prof. Gardner suggests to me.

[3] Ad *Aen.* 7. 799.   [4] *Lex.* s. v. Iuppiter, 640.

[5] See Fernique, *Étude sur Préneste*, pp. 79–81.

placed the names of divinities and heroes on designs borrowed from Greek models, and often representing a subject which they did not understand [1].'

4. And lastly, there is no doubt that Praeneste, in spite of its lofty position on the hills, was at an early stage of its existence subject to foreign influences, like so many other towns on or near the western coast of central Italy. This has been made certain by works of art found in its oldest tombs [2]. Whether these objects came from Greece, Phoenicia, Carthage, or Etruria, the story they tell is for us the same, and may well make us careful in accepting a statement like that of Cicero's without some hesitation. There was even a Greek foundation-legend of Praeneste, as well as the pure Italian one of Caeculus [3]. Evidence is slowly gathering which points to a certain basis of fact in these foundation-stories— of fact, at least, in so far as they seem to indicate that the transformation of the early Italian community into a city and a centre of civilization was coincident with the era of the introduction of foreign trade.

While, then, we cannot hope as yet to account for the singular anomaly in the Jupiter-cult, which is presented to us at Praeneste, we may at least hesitate to make use of it in answering the main question with which we set out—viz. how far we can find in the cult of the genuine Italian Jupiter any tendency towards an anthropomorphic conception of the god. Before we return to Rome a word is needed about the Latin Jupiter. The Latin festival has already been described [4]: it will be sufficient here to point out that none of its features show any advance towards an anthropomorphic conception of Jupiter Latiaris. The god here is of the same type as at Iguvium, one whose sanctuary—whatever it may originally have been—is in a grove on a hill-top [5], the conspicuous religious centre of the whole Latin stock inhabiting the plain below. Of this stock he is the uniting and protecting deity;

---

[1] Fernique, op. cit. p. 79.
[2] Fernique, 139 foll. Wissowa writes of Praeneste as 'a special point of connexion between Latin and Etruscan culture' (*Lex.* s. v. Mercurius, 2813).
[3] Plutarch, *Parallela*, 41.   [4] See at end of April, p. 95.
[5] Liv. I. 31. 3 'visi etiam audire vocem ingentem ex summi cacuminis luco, ut patrio ritu sacra Albani facerent.'

and when once a year his sacred victim is slain, after offerings have been made to him by the representatives of each member of the league, it is essential that each should also receive (and probably consume through its deputies) a portion of the sacrificial flesh (*carnem petere*). This, the main feature, and other details of the ritual, point to a survival from a very early stage of religious culture, and one that we may fairly call aniconic. The victim, a white heifer, the absence of wine in the libations, and the mention of milk and cheese among the offerings, all suggest an origin in the pastoral age; and it would seem that foreign ideas never really penetrated into this worship of a pastoral race. The objects that have been found during excavations near the site of the ancient temple [1] show that, as in the worship of the Fratres Arvales and in that of the curiae, so here, the most antique type of sacred vessels remained in use. Undoubtedly there was in later times a temple, and also a statue of the god [2]: and it is just possible that, as Niebuhr supposed [3], these were the goal of an ancient Alban triumphal procession, older than the later magnificent rite of the Capitol. But we know *for certain* that the ancient cult here suggests neither gorgeous ritual nor iconic usage. We see nothing but the unadorned practices of a simple cattle-breeding people.

Coming now once more to Rome itself, where of course we have fuller information, fragmentary though it be, we find sufficiently clear indications of an ancient cult of Jupiter showing characteristics of much the same kind as those we have already noticed as being genuine Italian.

In the first place the cult is associated with hills and also with trees. It is found on that part of the Esquiline which was known as lucus Fagutalis or Fagutal: here there was a sacellum Iovis 'in quo fuit fagus arbor quae Iovis (so MSS.) sacra habebatur [4]': and the god himself was called Fagutalis.

[1] e.g. the vases of very primitive make (Henzen, *Acta Fratr. Arv.* 30).

[2] Liv. 27. 11 (B.C. 209).

[3] Niebuhr, *Hist. of Rome*, ii. 37. Strong arguments are urged against this view by Aust, *Lex.* 696.

[4] Paul. Diac. 87. The lucus is mentioned in the corrupt fragments of the Argean itinerary (see on May 15) in Varro, *L. L.* 5. 50 (see Jordan, *Topogr.* ii. 242): where I am inclined to think the real reading is 'Esquiliis cis Iovis lucum fagutalem'; 'Iuppiter Fagutalis' in Plin. *N. H.* 16. 37; a 'vicus Iovis Fagutalis,' *C. I. L.* vi. 452 (110 A. D.).

Not far off on the Viminal, or hill of the osiers, there was also an altar of Jupiter Viminius, which we may suppose to have been ancient[1]. The mysterious Capitolium vetus on the Quirinal may be assumed as telling the same tale, though in historical times the memory of the cult there included Minerva and Juno with Jupiter, i.e. the Etruscan 'Trias.' Lastly, on the Capitol itself was the temple of Jupiter Feretrius, reputed to be the oldest in Rome[2]. It was attributed to Romulus, who, after slaying the king of the Caeninenses, dedicated the first spolia opima on an ancient oak 'pastoribus sacram,' and at the same time ' designavit templo Iovis fines cognomenque addidit deo.' The oak, we may assume, was the original dwelling of the god, and upon it were fixed the arms taken from the conquered enemy as a thank-offering for his aid[3]. In this case we seem to be able to guess the development of the cult from this beginning in the tree-worship of primitive 'pastores.' The next step would be the erection of an altar below the tree, in a small enclosure, i.e. a sacellum of the same kind as those of the Argei or the Sacellum Larum[4]. The third stage would be the building of the aedes known to us in history, which Cornelius Nepos says had fallen into decay in his time, and was rebuilt by Augustus on the suggestion of Atticus. Even this was a very small building, for Dionysius saw the foundations of it and found them only fifteen feet wide. This oldest cult of Jupiter was completely overshadowed by the later one of the Etruscan Trias—the aniconic by the iconic, the pure Italian by the mongrel ritual from Etruria.

That this Jupiter Feretrius[5] was the great Jupiter of pre-Etruscan Rome seems to be proved by his connexion with oaths and treaties, in which he resembles the god of the Latin

---

[1] For Iuppiter Viminius and his ara, Fest. 376.

[2] Liv. 1. 10 ; Dionys. 2. 34 ; Propert. 5. (4.) 10.

[3] For other examples of this practice see Bötticher, *Baumkultus*, pp. 73 and 134 ; Virgil, *Aen.* 10. 423, and Servius, ad loc. ; Statius, *Theb.* 2. 707.

[4] Corn. Nep. *Atticus*, 20; cf. Mommsen, *Res Gestae Divi Augusti*, p. 53 ; Dion. Hal. 2. 34. 4. This is apparently what Livy alludes to in 1. 10, attributing it, after Roman fashion, to Romulus : 'Templum his regionibus, quas modo animo metatus sum, dedico sedem opimis spoliis.' For a discussion of the shape of this temple see Aust, in *Lex.* s. v. Iuppiter, 673. He is inclined to attribute it (679) to the A. Cornelius Cossus who dedicated the second *spolia opima* in B.C. 428 (Liv. 4. 20).

[5] The meaning of the cult-title is obscure ; *Lex.* s. v. Iuppiter, 673.

festival. To him apparently belonged the priestly college of the Fetiales, who played so important a part in the declaring of war and the making of treaties : at any rate it was from his temple that the *lapis silex* and the *sceptrum* were taken which accompanied them on their official journeys[1]. It has been supposed that this *lapis silex* was a symbol of the god himself, like the spear of Mars in the Regia, and other such objects of cult[2]. 'We recognize here the primitive forms of a nature-worship, in which the simple flint was sufficient to bring up in men's minds the idea of the heavenly power of lightning and thunder,' i. e. the flint if struck would emit sparks and remind the beholder of lightning. Unluckily the existence of a stone in this temple as an object of worship is not clearly attested. Servius (*Aen.* 8. 641) says that the Fetials took to using a stone instead of a sword to slay their victims with, 'quod antiquum Iovis signum lapidem silicem *putaverunt* esse.' The learned commentator makes a mistake here which will be obvious to all archaeologists, in putting the age of iron before that of stone ; but it has not been equally clear to scholars that he by no means implies his belief that Jupiter was ever worshipped under the form of a stone. He only says that the Fetials *fancied* that this was so : and the whole passage has an aetiological colouring which should put us on our guard[3]. It is not supported by any other statement or tradition, except an allusion in S. Augustine[4] to a 'lapis Capito-

[1] Paul. Diac. 92 ; Serv. *Aen.* 12. 206.

[2] Aust, in *Lex.* 676 . . The idea is that of Helbig in his *Italiker in der Poebene*, 91 foll. Cp. Schwegler, *Röm. Gesch.* i. 681, and Preller, i. 248 foll. H. Nettleship, *Essays in Latin Literature*, p. 35, and Strachan-Davidson (Polybius, *Prolegomena*, viii) discuss the oath *per Iovem lapidem* usefully. Nettleship saw that the passage of Servius is the only one which 'gives any real support' to the notion that the god was represented by a stone ; and Strachan-Davidson notes the aetiological method of Servius.

[3] Cp. his note on the 'sceptrum' (*Aen.* 12. 206), which he explains as being the substitute for a 'simulacrum' of Jupiter. Was this 'simulacrum' a stone ? If so he would have said so. Obviously he knew little or nothing about these cult-objects.

[4] *de Civ. Dei* 2. 29. S. Augustine couples it with the focus Vestae, as something well known : and this could not be said at that time of any object in the temple of Jupiter Feretrius. The epithet Capitolinus would suit the stone of Terminus far better ; and this is, in fact, made almost certain by Servius' language when speaking of Virgil's ' Capitoli immobile saxum ' (*Aen.* 9. 448), which he identifies with the 'lapidem ipsum Termini.' Doubtless if we could be sure that such a stone existed, we might guess that it was an aerolite (Strachan-Davidson, p. 76, who quotes examples).

linus,' which is surely the stone of Terminus (see below): and by the oath 'per Iovem lapidem,' which has been interpreted by some as meaning 'Jupiter in the form of a stone.' But this interpretation is at least open to grave doubt; and in the absence of clearer evidence for the 'Iuppiter lapis' of the temple it is better to understand the oath as being sworn by the god and also by the stone, 'two distinct aspects of the transaction being run together,' in a way not uncommon in Latin formulae[1].

It only remains to conjecture what the 'silex' or 'lapis' was which the Fetials took from the temple together with the sceptrum. Helbig has attempted to prove that it was not a survival of the stone age, e. g. an axe of stone. Had that been so, he argues, the Roman antiquaries, who were acquainted with such implements[2], would have noticed it: and those who describe the rites of the Fetials would have stated that the stone was artificially sharpened. But this negative argument is not a strong one; and I am rather inclined to agree with the suggestion of Dr. Tylor[3], that it was a stone celt believed to have been a thunder-bolt. There may indeed have been more than one of these kept in the temple, for in B. C. 201 the Fetials who went to Africa took with them *each a stone*[4] (privos lapides silices) along with their 'sagmina,' &c. This fact seems to me to prove that the silices, like the sagmina and sceptrum, were only part of the ritualistic apparatus of the Fetials[5], and not objects in which the god was supposed to be manifested. The idea that he was originally worshipped in the form of a stone may well have arisen from this use of stones in the ritual, especially if those stones were believed to be in some way his handiwork[6]. We may think then of the cult of

[1] So Nettleship, l. c.: and Strachan-Davidson, l. c.
[2] He quotes Plin. *N. H.* 37. 135 'cerauniae nigrae rubentesque et similes securibus.'
[3] Communicated to Mr. Strachan-Davidson, and mentioned by him in a note (op. cit. p. 77). An instance in Retzel, *History of Mankind*, vol. i. p. 175. The other suggestion, that it was a meteoric stone, is also quite possible: for Greek examples, see Schömann, *Griech. Alterthümer*, ii. 171 foll.
[4] Liv. 30. 43.
[5] We may compare the 'orbita' of the cult of Jupiter Sancius at Iguvium : Bücheler, *Umbrica*, 141. See above, p. 139.
[6] It may be as well to say, before leaving the subject, that I certainly agree with Mr. Strachan-Davidson that the ordinary oath, 'per Iovem

Jupiter Feretrius as an example of primitive tree-worship, but we are not justified in going further and finding him also in the form of a stone.

There is yet another stone that may have belonged to the earliest Roman cult of Jupiter, but the connexion is not very certain. 'The (rite of) Aquaelicium,' says Festus [1], 'is when rain is procured (elicitur) by certain methods, as for example when the lapis manalis is carried into the city.' This stone lay by the temple of Mars, outside the Porta Capena; we learn from other passages that it was carried by the pontifices [2], but we are not told what they did with it within the walls. It has been ingeniously suggested that this rain-spell, as we may call it, was a part of the cult of Jupiter Elicius, to whom there was an altar close by under the Aventine [3], the cult-title being identical with the latter part of the word 'aquaelicium [4].' We may agree that the stone had nothing to do with the temple of Mars, which happened to be near it, and also that any such rain-spell as this would be more likely to belong to the cult of Jupiter than of any other deity. The heaven-god, who launches the thunder-bolt, is naturally and almost everywhere also the rain-giver [5]: and that this was one of the functions of Jupiter is fully attested, for later times at least [6].

But it must be confessed that the evidence is very slight [7]: and it is as well here to remember that the further we probe back into old Italian rites, the less distinctly can we expect to be able to connect them with particular deities. The formula

lapidem,' where the swearer throws the stone away from him (described by Polybius, 3. 25), has nothing to do with the ritual of the Fetials.

[1] Festus, p. 2. Cp. 128, where this stone is distinguished from the other, which was the 'ostium Orci.' Serv. *Aen.* 3. 175.

[2] Serv. l. c. Marquardt, and Aust following him, add the matrons with bare feet and the magistrates without their praetexta : but this rests on the authority of Petronius (*Sat.* 44), who surely is not writing of Rome, where the ceremony was only a tradition, to judge by Fest. p. 2.

[3] Varro, *L. L.* 6. 94.

[4] O. Gilbert, ii. 154: adopted by Aust, 658, who adds some slight additional evidence : e. g. the 'Iovem aquam exorabant' of the passage from Petronius.

[5] Tylor, *Prim. Cult.* ii. 235-7 : for the Greek Zeus, Farnell, *Cults,* i. 44 foll.

[6] Preller, i. 190. I cannot say that I find evidence earlier than the passage of Tibullus, 1. 7. 26 (Jupiter Pluvius).

[7] Note that the Flamen Dialis is not mentioned along with the Pontifices by Servius, l. c.

'si deus, si dea es' should always be borne in mind in attempting to connect gods and ceremonies. And this ceremony, like
that of the Argei [1] (which also wants a clearly-conceived deity
as its object), is obviously a survival from a very primitive
class of performances which Mr. Frazer has called acts of
'sympathetic magic [2].' I am indebted to the *Golden Bough* for
a striking parallel to the rite of the lapis manalis, among
many others which more or less resemble it. 'In a Samoan
village a certain stone was carefully housed as the representative of the rain-making god : and in time of drought
his priests carried the stone in procession and dipped it in
a stream [3].' What was done with the lapis manalis we are
not told, but it is pretty plain from the word 'manalis,' and
from the fragments of explanation which have come down to
us from Roman scholars, that it was either the object of some
splashing or pouring, or was itself hollow and was filled with
water which was to be poured out in imitation of the desired
rain [4]. Such rites need not necessarily be connected by us
with the name of a god : and the Jupiter Elicius, with whom
it is sought to connect this one, was always associated by the
Romans not with this obsolete rite, but with the elaborated
science of augury which was in the main Etruscan [5].

But this discussion has already been carried on as far as
the scope of this work permits. It may be completed by any
one who has the patience to work through Aust's exhaustive
article, examining his conclusions with the aid of his abundant
references ; but I doubt if anything will be found, beyond what
I have mentioned, which bears closely on the question with
which we set out. That question was, whether the distinctly
anthropomorphic treatment of Jupiter in the 'epulum Iovis'
could be explained by any native Italian practice in his cult (as

[1] See on May 15.
[2] *Golden Bough*, i. 11 foll. ; Grimm, *Teutonic Mythology*, 595 foll. ; abundant
examples in the works of Mannhardt, see indices.
[3] From *Samoa*, by G. Turner, p. 145.
[4] Compare together Nonius, 547. 10 ; 559. 19 (s. v. trulleum), from
Varro; Festus, 128, s. v. 'manalis lapis,' from Verrius Flaccus. The
suggestion that the stone was hollow is O. Gilbert's.
[5] Aust, *Lex.* 657, who believes the Romans to have been mistaken. The
locus classicus is Ovid, *Fasti*, 3. 285 foll. ; a more rational account in Liv.
1. 20 ; Plin. *N. H.* 2. 140. Note the position of the altar of this Jupiter,
i. e. the Aventine.

Marquardt tried to explain it), or must be referred with Aust to foreign, i. e. Graeco-Etruscan, influence. I am driven to the conclusion that Aust is probably right. There is no real trace in Italy of an indigenous iconic representation of Jupiter. Trees and hills are apparently sacred to him, and possibly stones, though this last is doubtful : we find a sacrificial meal at the Latin festival, but no sign that he takes part in it as an image or statue. Elsewhere, as at Praeneste, peculiar representations of him arouse strong suspicions of foreign iconic influence. I think, on the whole, that the Italian peoples owed the sacred image to foreign works of art : and that the 'epulum Iovis' was introduced from Etruria by the Etruscan dynasty which built the Capitoline temple. It may, indeed, have been engrafted upon an earlier sacrificial meal like that of the feriae Latinae, or that of the curiae, or the rustic one of Jupiter dapalis : but, if so, the meal was one at which the ancient Romans were content to *believe*, as Ovid says, that the gods were present, and did not need, like the Greeks, the evidence of their eyes to help out their belief. Their gods were still aniconic when the wave of foreign ideas broke over them. We may say of the earliest Roman cult of Jupiter what Tacitus asserts of the Germans of his day [1] : 'nec cohibere parietibus deos neque in ullam humani oris speciem adsimulare ex magnitudine caelestium arbitrantur : lucos ac nemora consecrant, deorumque nominibus appellant secretum illud quod sola reverentia vident.'

September 13 was also the day on which, according to Livy [2] and Verrius Flaccus [3], a nail (*clavus*) was driven *annually* by the 'Praetor maximus' into the wall of the cella of Minerva in the Capitoline temple, in obedience to an old lex which was fixed up on the wall of the temple adjoining this same cella. But Mommsen's trenchant criticism [4] of the *locus classicus* for this subject in Livy has made it almost certain that the Roman scholars were here in error : that the ceremony was not an annual one, but took place once in a century, in commemora-

---

[1] *Germania*, 9.   [2] 7. 3.   [3] Festus, 55.
[4] In *Röm. Chronologie*, p. 175 foll. Preller (i. 258) had already seen that the ceremony was a religious one, but believed it to be annual, and used for the reckoning of time.

tion of a vow made in 463 B. C., to commemorate the great pestilence of that year, which carried off both the consuls and several other magistrates [1]: that it had no special connexion with the cult of Jupiter, and was not intended, as is generally supposed, to mark the years as they passed. The nail is really the symbol of Fortuna or Necessitas; the rite was Etruscan, and was also celebrated at Volsinii in the temple of the Etruscan deity of Fate; when brought to Rome it was very naturally located in the great temple of the Etruscan Trias, the religious centre of the Roman state. Originally a dictator was chosen (i. e. Praetor maximus) *clavi figendi causa*; and when the dictatorship was dropped after the Second Punic War, the ceremony was allowed to fall into oblivion. Later on the Roman antiquarians unearthed and misinterpreted it, believing it to have been a yearly rite of which the object was to mark the succession of years. This brief account of Mommsen's view may suffice for the purpose of this work: but the subject is one that might with advantage be reinvestigated.

[1] 'An sich hat der Nagel gewiss mit dem Jahre nichts zu thun, sondern steht in seiner natürlichen und wohlbekannten Bedeutung der Schicksals-festung, in welcher er als Attribut der grausen Nothwendigkeit (saeva Necessitas), der Fortuna, der Atropos bei römischen Schriftstellern und auf italischen Bildwerken begegnet.' Mommsen, op. cit. 179. He alludes, of course, to Horace, *Od.* 1. 35, and 3. 24, and to the Etruscan mirror mentioned by Preller (p. 259): see Gerhard, *Etr. Spiegel*, i. 176. But the interpretation of this mirror, as given by Preller, seems to me very doubtful.

MENSIS OCTOBER.

In the Italy of historical times, the one agricultural feature of this month was the vintage. The rustic calendars mark this with the single word *vindemiae*[1]. The vintage might begin during the last few days of September, but October was its natural time, though it is now somewhat earlier : this point is clear both from Varro and Pliny[2]. But the old calendars have preserved hardly a trace of this ; and in fact the only feast which we can in any way connect with wine-making (the Meditrinalia on the 11th) is obscure in name and its ritual unknown to us. We may infer that the practice of viticulture was a comparatively late introduction ; and this is borne out by such facts as the absence of wine in the ritual of the Latin festival[3], and the words of a *lex regia* (ascribed to Numa) which forbade wine to be sprinkled on a funeral pile[4]. Pliny also expressed a decided opinion that viticulture was *multo serior* : and lately Hehn[5] has traced it to the Italian Greeks on etymological grounds. It can hardly have become a common occupation in Latium before the seventh or possibly even the eighth century B. C.

Probably if Ovid had continued his *Fasti* to the end of the year we might have learnt much of interest about this month : as it is, we have only scraps of information about a very few

---

[1] *C. I. L.* i². 281.

[2] Varro, *R. R.* 1. 34. Pliny, *N. H.* 18. 315 : 'Vindemiam antiqui nunquam existimavere maturam ante aequinoctium, iam passim rapi cerno.' Sec. 319 'Iustum vindemiae tempus ab aequinoctio ad Vergiliarum occasum dies xliii.'

[3] See above, p. 97.

[4] Pliny, *N. H.* 14. 88 'Vino rogum ne respargito.' Cp. 18. 24.

[5] *Kulturpflanzen*, &c., p. 65.

primitive rites, only one of which can be said to be known to us in any detail ; and the interpretation of that one is extremely doubtful.

KAL. OCT. (OCTOBER 1). N.

[FIDEI] IN CAPITOLIO.   TIGILL[O] SOROR[IO] AD COMPITUM
ACILI.   (ARV.)

The sacrifice here indicated to Fides in the Capitol is clearly the one which Livy ascribes to Numa[1]: 'Et soli Fidei sollemne instituit.   Ad id sacrarium flamines bigis, curru arcuato (i.e. 'covered') vehi iussit, manuque ad digitos usque involuta rem divinam facere: significantes fidem tutandam, sedemque eius etiam in dextris sacratam esse.'   Dionysius also mentions the foundation, without alluding to the peculiar ritual, but dwelling on the moral influence of the cult both in public and private life[2].

The personification of a moral idea would hardly seem likely to be as old as Numa ; yet there are points in the ritual which suggest a high antiquity, apart from tradition.   It was the three chief flamines who thus drove to the Capitol—i. e. those of Jupiter, Mars, and Quirinus ; these at least were the three who had been just instituted by Numa (Liv. 1. 20), and to them Livy must be referring.   As has been often pointed out, the presence of flamines at a rite is always evidence of its antiquity; and in this case they may have represented the union of the two communities of Septimontium and Quirinal in a common worship on the Capitol, this central point being represented by the Flamen Dialis.   The curious fact that the right hands of these flamens were wrapped up to the fingers in white cloth is another obvious sign of antiquity, and is explained as meaning that the right hand, which was given to another in pledging one's word, then as now[3], was pure and clean, as was the mind of the pledger[4].   A sacred object, statue or victim, was often

---

[1] 1. 21. Dion. Hal. 2. 75.   The significance of this covered vehicle seems to be unknown.

[2] Many passages might be collected to bear out Dionysius' remarks : the reader may refer to Preller, i. 250 foll.

[3] Pliny, N. H. xi. 250.   So 'dextram fidemque dare.'

[4] Wissowa, in Lex. s.v. Fides, Preller, i. 251.   Serv. Aen. 1. 292 and 8. 636 : but Serv. in the latter note says ' Quia fides tecta esse debet et velata.'

thus wrapped or tied with fillets (*vittae*); and the μύσται in the Eleusinian mysteries seem to have worn a crocus-coloured band on the right hand and right foot[1]. The statue of the goddess in her temple had probably the right hand so covered, if at least we are at liberty so to interpret the words of Horace, 'albo Fides velata panno'[2].

A word about the *tigillum sororium*[3]. What this was, and where it was, can be made out with some certainty; beyond that all is obscure. It was a beam, renewed from time to time, let into the opposite walls of a street which led down from the Carinae to the Vicus Cyprius, now the via del Colosseo[4]. It remained till at least the fourth century A. D. It is now generally explained as a primitive Janus-arch, apparently on the ground that one of the altars below it was to Janus Curiatius[5]. As it seems, however, to have been a single beam, without supports except the street walls[6], I am unable to understand this conclusion; and as the Roman antiquaries never supposed it to be such, we can hardly do so safely. They believed it to be a memorial of the expiation undergone by the legendary Horatius for the murder of his sister. Acquitted by the people on appeal, he had to make religious expiation, and this he did by the erection of an altar to Janus Curiatius, and another to Juno Sororia[7], and by passing under a yoke, which was afterwards represented by the *tigillum*.

We may leave the *tigillum* as really inexplicable, unless we are to accept the suggestion of Roscher[8], that the germ of the legend is to be found in the practice of creeping through a split

---

[1] Libanius, *Decl.* 19; Photius, s. v. κροκοῦν (Bötticher, *Baumkultus*, p. 43) οἱ μύσται ὡς φασὶ κρόκῃ τὴν δεξιὰν χεῖρα καὶ τὸν πόδα ἀναδοῦνται.

[2] Hor. *Od.* 1. 35. 21.

[3] The authorities for this and the altars connected with it are Livy, 1. 26; Dion. Hal. 3. 22; Festus, 297 and Paul. 307; Aur. Vict. 4. 9; *Schol. Bob. ad Cic.* p. 277 Orelli; Lydus *de Mensibus*, 4. 1.

[4] Kiepert u. Huelsen, *Formae urbis Romae antiquae*, p. 92 and map 1; Jordan, *Topogr.* ii. 100.

[5] So Roscher, in *Lex.* s. v. Ianus, 21; Gilbert, *Topogr.* 1. 180, who would make it the 'porta Ianualis' of Macrob. 1. 19. 17, wrongly.

[6] It is always in the singular, e.g. 'Transmisso per viam tigillo,' Livy, l. c. Dionys. writes as if it were originally a *iugum*, i. e. two uprights and a cross-beam, but does not imply that it was so in his day.

[7] The altars are mentioned by Festus, Dionys., and *Schol. Bob.*

[8] *Lex.* s. v. Janus, 21; quoting Grimm, *Deutsche Myth.* (E. T. 1157, with quotation from White's *Selborne*).

tree to get rid of spell or disease. The two altars demand a word.

Livy's language seems to suggest that these were in the care of the gens Horatia [1]: ' Quibusdam piacularibus sacrificiis factis, quae deinde genti Horatiae tradita sunt.' If so, perhaps the whole legend of Horatius, or at any rate its connexion with this spot, arose out of this gentile worship of two deities, of whom the cult-titles were respectively Curiatius and Sororia. The coincidence of Janus and Juno is natural enough ; both were associated with the Kalends [2]. But the original meaning of their cult-titles at the Tigillum remains unknown. All we can say is that the Janus of the *curiae* and the Juno of a sister may certainly have given point to a legend of which the hero was acquitted by the Comitia Curiata for the murder of a sister [3].

3 Non. Oct. (October 5). C.

This was one of the three days on which the *mundus* was open: see on August 24.

Non. Oct. (October 7). F.

IOVI FULGURI, IUNONI CURRITI [4] IN CAMPO. (ARV. PAUL.)

Of these worships in Rome nothing else is known. Iuno Curitis is the goddess of Falerii, whose supposed ἱερὸς γάμος was referred to above [5].

v Id. Oct. (October 11). NP.

MEDITR[INALIA]. (SAB. MAFF. AMIT.)

FERIAE IOVI. (AMIT.)

This was the day on which the new wine was tasted. There is no real evidence of a goddess Meditrina. The account in

---

[1] Marquardt, 584.

[2] Macrob. I. 9. 16 '[Ianum] Iunonium quia non solum mensis Ianuarii sed mensium omnium ingressum tenentem : in dicione autem Iunonis sunt omnes Kalendae.'

[3] This Juno may be the 'Weibliche Genius einer Frau,' as Roscher suggests (s. v. Janus, 22 ; s. v. Juno, 598, he seems to think otherwise). But as she is connected with Janus, I should doubt it. For an explanation of 'Ianus Curiatius' cp. Lydus, l. c. ἔφορος εὐγενῶν.

[4] Curriti Arv. : Q uiriti] Paul. [5] p. 223.

Paulus is as follows: 'Mos erat Latinis populis, quo die quis primum gustaret mustum, dicere ominis gratia "Vetus novum vinum bibo, veteri novo morbo medeor." A quibus verbis etiam Meditrinae deae nomen conceptum, eiusque sacra Meditrinalia dicta sunt[1].' Varro had already given the same account: 'Octobri mense Meditrinalia dies, dictus a medendo, quod Flaccus flamen Martialis dicebat hoc die solitum vinum novum et vetus libari et gustari medicamenti causa: quod facere solent etiam nunc multi quom dicunt: Novum vetus vinum bibo, novo veteri vino morbo medeor.'

Note *a*. A parallel practice of tasting both old and new crops is to be found in the ritual of the Fratres Arvales, who in May 'fruges aridas et virides contigerunt,' i. e. the old grain and the new[2].

Note *b*. The belief that the new wine (*mustum*) was wholesome and non-inebriating is discussed charmingly by Plutarch (*Quaest. Conv.* vii. 1).

Note *c*. Mommsen, *C. I. L.* I[2]. 332, points out that the real deity here concerned was doubtless Jupiter: see under Vinalia, p. 86.

III Id. Oct. (October 13). N.

FONT[INALIA]. (SAB. MAFF. AMIT. MIN. IX.)
FERIAE FONTI. (AMIT.)

All we know of this very ancient festival is contained in a few words of Varro[3]: 'Fontinalia a Fonte, quod is dies feriae eius; ab eo tum et in fontes coronas iaciunt et puteos coronant.'

The holiness of wells and springs is too familiar to need illustration here. The original object of the garlanding was probably to secure abundant water.

It is generally assumed that there was a god Fons or Fontus, to whom this day was sacred. There was a delubrum Fontis[4]; an ara Fonti on the Janiculum[5]; and a porta Fontinalis in the Campus Martius. Fons also appears with Flora, Mater Larum,

[1] Paulus, 123; Varro, *L. L.* 6. 21.
[2] Henzen, *Act. Fr. Arv.* pp. 11, 12, 14.
[3] *L. L.* vi. 22. Cp. Festus, 85.
[4] Cic. *N. D.* iii. 20.
[5] Preller, i. 176.

Summanus, &c., in the ritual of the Fratres Arvales[1]. The case seems to be one of those in which multiplicity passes into a quasi-unity: but Fons did not survive long in the latter stage.

Id. Oct. (Oct. 15). NP.

EQUUS AD NIXAS FIT. (PHILOC.)

No calendar but the late one of Philocalus mentions the undoubtedly primitive rite of horse-sacrifice which took place on this day. Wissowa has tried to explain this difficulty, which meets us elsewhere in the Calendar, e. g. on the Ides of May (Argei), June 1 (festival of Carna)[2]. Where two festivals fell on the same day, *both* would not be found in calendars which were meant for the use, not of the pontifices themselves, but of the unlearned vulgar ; for the latter would not be able to distinguish, or to get one clear name for the day, and confusion would result. Now all Kalends and Ides were sacred to Juno and Jupiter respectively; all other rites falling on these days would stand a chance of being omitted, unless indeed they were noticed in later annotations such as we find cut in smaller letters in the Fasti Praenestini and others.

Luckily the entry in Philocalus' calendar is supplemented sufficiently from other sources. The earliest hint we get comes from the Greek historian Timaeus, and is preserved in a fragment of the twelfth book of Polybius[3]. Timaeus after the Greek fashion connects the horse-sacrifice with the legend of Troy and the wooden horse : but he also tells us the important detail that on a certain day *a war-horse was killed with a spear in the Campus Martius*[4]. The passage is no doubt characteristic of Timaeus, both in regard to the detail, and the

---

[1] Henzen, *Acta Fr. Arv.* 146. The deities to whom *piacula* are here to be sacrificed are deities of the grove of the Brethren : hence I should conclude that this Fons simply represented a particular spring there.

[2] *de Feriis*, &c., p. xi. To me this explanation does not seem quite satisfactory, though it seems to be sanctioned by Mommsen (*C. I. L.* i². 332, note on Id. Oct. sub fin.). It is however undoubtedly preferable to the view I had taken before reading Wissowa's tract, that the omission was due to an aristocratic neglect of usages which only survived among the common people and had ceased to concern the whole community.

[3] Polyb. xii. 4[b].

[4] Ἐν ἡμέρᾳ τινὶ κατακοντίζειν ἵππον πολεμιστὴν πρὸ τῆς πόλεως ἐν τῷ κάμπῳ καλουμένῳ. This is quoted from "τὰ περὶ Πύρρον."

R

mythology which Polybius despised. But though we do not know that Timaeus was ever at Rome, we may hope that he was correct in the one particular which we do not learn from other sources, viz. the slaughter of the horse with the sacred weapon of Mars.

Fuller information comes from Verrius Flaccus, as represented in the epitomes of Festus and Paulus Diaconus[1]. On this day there was a two-horse chariot race in the Campus Martius ; and the near horse of the winning pair was sacrificed to Mars—killed with a spear, if we may believe Timaeus. The place is indicated in Philocalus' calendar as ' ad nixas,' i. e. the *ciconiae nixae*, which seem to have been three storks carved in stone with bills crossing each other[2]: this however was non-existent under the Republic. The real scene of the sacrifice must have been an old ' ara Martis,' and that there was such an altar in the Campus we know for certain, though we cannot definitely fix its position[3]. The tail of the horse was cut off and carried with speed to the Regia so that the warm blood might drip upon the focus or sacred hearth there. The head also was cut off and decked with cakes ; and at one time there was a hard fight for its possession between the men of the two neighbouring quarters of the Via Sacra and the Subura. If the former carried off the prize, they fixed it on the wall of the Regia ; if the latter, on the turris Mamilia[4].

---

[1] Fest. 178 'October equus appellatur, qui in campo Martio mense Oct. immolatur quotannis Marti, bigarum victricum dexterior. De cuius capite non levis contentio solebat esse inter Suburanenses et Sacravienses, ut hi in regiae pariete, illi ad turrim Mamiliam id figerent ; eiusdemque coda tanta celeritate perfertur in regiam, ut ex ea sanguis distillet in focum participandae rei divinae gratia, quem hostiae loco quidam Marti bellico deo sacrari dicunt,' &c. Then follow three examples of horse-sacrifices. Paul. 179 adds no fresh information. Paul. 220 'Panibus redimibant caput equi immolati idibus Octobribus in campo Martio, quia id sacrificium fiebat ob frugum eventum, et equus potius quam bos immolabatur, quod hic bello, bos frugibus pariendis est aptus.' (The meaning of these last words will be considered presently.) Cp. Plutarch, *Qu. Rom.* 97 ; probably from Verrius, perhaps indirectly through Juba. Plut. by a mistake puts the rite on the Ides of December.

[2] See note in Preller's *Regionen der Stadt Rom*, p. 174. They are placed by Kiepert and Hülsen (map 2) close to the Tiber and near the Mausoleum of Augustus, and a long way from the old ara Martis. Perhaps the position of the latter had changed as the Campus came to be built over.

[3] Livy, 35. 10 ; 40. 45 (the censors after their election sat in Campo on their curule chairs ' ad aram Martis '). Roscher, *Lex.* s. v. Mars, 2389.

[4] What this was is not known : some think a kind of peel-tower.

It is probable[1], though not quite certain, that the congealed blood from the tail was used, together with the ashes of the unborn calves sacrificed on the Fordicidia, as 'medicine' to be distributed to the people at the Parilia on April 21.

The rite of the 'October-horse' had been adequately described and in some degree explained by Preller, Marquardt, Schwegler, and others[2], before the late Dr. Mannhardt took it in hand not long before his death[3]. Mannhardt studied it in the light of his far-reaching researches in folk-lore, and succeeded in treating it as all such survivals should be treated, i. e. in bringing it into relation with the practices of other peoples—not so much by way of explaining its original meaning precisely, as in order to make some progress by its help towards an understanding of the attitude of primitive man to the supernatural. His conclusions have been generally accepted, and, with very slight modifications, are to be found in Mr. Frazer's *Golden Bough* (ii. 64), and in Roscher's article 'Mars' in the *Mythological Lexicon* (2416). Recently, however, they have been called in question by no less a person than Prof. Wissowa[4] of Berlin, who seems to take a different view of the Mars-cult from that at which we thought we had at last safely arrived : it may be as well therefore to give yet another account of Mannhardt's treatment of the question, and to follow his track somewhat more elaborately than Mr. Frazer. It does not of course follow that he has said the last word ; but it is as well to begin by making clear what he *has* said.

1. This is *the last of the series of harvest festivals*, as we may call them generically. We have had the Ambarvalia and the plucking of the first ears by the Vestals in May : the Vestalia in June[5] ; the festivals of Consus and Ops Consiva in August ; and lastly we find this one coming after all the fruits of the land have been gathered in. In this respect it is parallel to the Pyanepsia and Oschophoria of the Greeks,

Possibly a tower in *quadriviis* : cf. definition of *compitum* in *Schol. Pers.* 4. 28.

[1] Ovid, *Fasti*, 4. 731 foll. ; Prop. 5. (4.) 1. 19. See on Parilia and Fordicidia.
[2] Preller, 1. 366 ; Marquardt, 334 ; Schwegler, *Röm. Gesch.* ii. 46 ; Roscher, *Apollo und Mars*, 64 foll.
[3] *Mythologische Forschungen*, 156–201.
[4] *de Feriis*, ix.
[5] I add this (see on Vestalia). Mannhardt had not handled it.

to the Jewish feast of Tabernacles[1], and to the true
Michaelmas harvest-festivals of modern Europe, which follow
at an interval the great variety of quaint harvest customs
which occur at the actual in-gathering. Even now in the
Roman Campagna there is a lively festival of this kind in
October.

It should be noticed that the harvest character of the rite
was suggested to Mannhardt by the passage from Paulus (220),
from which we learn that the head of the sacrificed horse was
decked with cakes, like those of the live draught-animals at the
Vestalia and Consualia and feriae Sementivae [q. v.]. This,
Paulus adds, was done 'quia id sacrum fiebat ob frugum
eventum,' which last words can hardly mean anything but
'on account of the *past* harvest[2].' There are, I may add, two
points open to doubt here, which Mannhardt does not point out:
(1) the reason here given may be only a guess of Verrius',
and not one generally understood at Rome[3]. (2) The concluding words of the gloss seem to make no sense, a fact which
throws some doubt on the whole passage. The rite is 'ob
frugum eventum,' yet 'a horse, and not an ox, is the victim,
because a horse is suited for war, and an ox is not[4].' However
this may be understood, we need not quarrel with the conclusion[5], that the real meaning of the adornment was to show
that the head was an object possessed of power to procure
fertility—an inference confirmed by the eagerness of the
rival city-quarters to get possession of it.

2. The *sacrificed horse represented a Corn-spirit.* The Corn-
spirit was Mannhardt's chief discovery, and its various forms
are now familiar to English readers of Frazer's *Golden Bough,*
and of Farnell's *Cults of the Greek States.* Almost every common
animal, wild or tame, may be found to represent the Corn-spirit
at harvest-time in one locality or another, where the nomadic

---

[1] Levit. 23 fin.

[2] Had they referred to the crops of the next season we might have
expected ' ob *bonum* frugum eventum.'

[3] So Wissowa, *de Feriis,* ix. He thinks that it was only an attempt to
explain the *panes*: but he is wrong in insisting that the Vestalia (where,
as we saw, the same decoration occurs) had *nothing* to do with 'frugum
eventus.'

[4] To me it looks as if some words had dropped out of the text, perhaps
after the word *eventum*; see the passage quoted above, p. 242, note 1.

[5] Given in Mannhardt's next section, p. 169.

age has given place to an agricultural one ; or a man, woman, boy or puppet represents the animal, and so indirectly the Corn-spirit [1]. Mannhardt produces from his stores of folk-lore many instances in which the horse thus figures, including the hobby-horse which in old England used to prance round the May-pole. Those examples, however, are not strong enough to convince us that the October horse was a Corn-spirit, though they prove well enough that the Corn-spirit often took this shape [2]. But we must remember that he is only suggesting an *origin* in the simple rites of the farm, indicating a class of ideas to which this survival may be traceable [3].

He does, however, produce an example which has one or two features in common with the Roman rite, only in this case the animal is a goat instead of a horse. In Dauphiné a goat is decked with ribbons and flowers and let loose in the harvest-field. The reapers run after it, and finally the farmer cuts off its head [4], while his wife holds it. Parts of its body (we are not told whether the head is among them) are kept as 'medicine' till the next harvest. So too the head, and also the tail and the blood, of the October horse were the seat of some great Power ; but whether this was a vegetation-spirit does not seem satisfactorily shown.

3. *The chariot-race was an elaborated and perhaps Graecized form or survival of the simple race of men and women so often met with in the harvest-field, often in pursuit of a representative of the Corn-spirit.*

Mannhardt gives examples from France and Germany of races in pursuit of cock, calf, kid, sheep, or whatever shape may be the one in vogue for the Corn-spirit ; often the animal is in some way decorated for the occasion. Two of a rather different kind may be mentioned here, though they occur, not on the harvest-field, but at Whitsuntide and Easter respectively ;

[1] See under May 15 (Argei).

[2] Mannhardt has not suggested what seems not impossible, that the horse represented Mars himself—in which case we might allow that Mars was, among other things, a vegetation deity.

[3] See his language at the top of p. 164.

[4] He ingeniously suggests that these cases of decapitation may be explained by the old custom of cutting off the corn-ears so as to leave almost the whole of the stalk. (See his *Korndämonen*, p. 35.) That this method existed in Latium seems proved by a passage in Livy, 22. 1 'Antii metentibus cruentas in corbem spicas cecidisse.'

but they show how horse-races may originate in the customs of the farm. In the Hartz the farm-horses, gaily decorated, are raced by the labourers for possession of a wreath, which is hung on the neck of the winning horse. In Silesia the finest near horse of the team, decorated by the girls, is ridden (raced?) round the boundary of the farm, and then round a neighbouring village, while Easter hymns are sung. We have already noticed the racing of horses and mules at the Consualia in August: according to Dionysius, these too were decked out with flowers [1]. Mannhardt makes also a somewhat lengthy digression to point out the possibility that in the original form of the Passover (on which was afterwards engrafted the Jahvistic worship and the history of the escape from Egypt) a race or something of the kind may be indicated by the custom of eating the victim with the loins girt.

There is undoubtedly a possible origin for the horse-racing of Greeks and Romans in the customs of the farm at different seasons of the year, and I accept Mannhardt's view so far, with a probability, not certainty, as to the Corn-spirit. We may perhaps be able to trace the development of the custom a little further in this case.

4. *The horse's head, fixed on the Regia or the turris Mamilia, is the effigy of the Corn-spirit, which is to bring fertility and to keep off evil influences for the year to come* [2].

Examples of this practice of fixing up some object after harvest in a prominent place in farm or village are so numerous as almost to defy selection, and are now familiar to all students of folk-lore [3]. Sometimes it is a bunch of corn or flowers, as in the Greek Eiresione [4], and to this day at Charlton-on-Otmoor, where it is placed over the beautiful rood-screen in the church. Such bunches are often called by the name of some animal; occasionally their place is taken by the effigy of an animal's head, e. g. that of a horse [5], which in course of time becomes a permanency.

5. *The cutting off the tail is explained by the idea that a remnant*

---

[1] Dion. Hal. i. 33, who compares an Arcadian Hippokrateia.
[2] Op. cit. p. 182.
[3] See *Golden Bough*, i. 68 foll., and Mannhardt, *A. W. F.* 214 foll.
[4] Mannhardt, *A. W. F.* l. c.
[5] Mannhardt, *Baumkultus*, 167.

of the body of the representative of the Corn-spirit is sufficient to produce this spirit afresh in the vegetation of the coming year.

The examples Mannhardt quotes are numerous, and only gain force when brought together : I must refer the reader to his work for them[1]. The word *tail* not only occurs frequently in harvest customs (e. g. the cutter of the last sheaf is called the wheat-tail or barley-tail[2]), but there is little doubt that virtue was believed to reside in a tail[3]. Who knows but that the preservation of the fox's brush by fox-hunters has some origin of this kind?

6. The use made of the blood, which was kept and mixed with the ashes of the unborn calves of the Fordicidia, and with sulphur and bean-straw as a medicine to be distributed to the people at the Parilia, tells its own story without need of illustration (see on April 15 and 21). The blood was the life[4]; the fire and sulphur-fumes were to purify and avert evil. Both men and beasts leapt over the fire into which this mixture was thrown at the Parilia, to gain new life and strength, and to avert the influences which might retard them.

Finally, Mannhardt has some remarks on the origin of the rite, which were suggested by Schwegler and Ambrosch[5]. The Campus Martius, the scene of the sacrifice, was originally *terra regis*, cultivated for him by the people[6]. When the king was the chief farmer, the horse's head was carried to his house (regia) and fixed thereon, and the tail allowed to drip on to his hearth. When the neighbouring community of the Subura was united with that of the Palatine, the seat of the oldest community, the remembrance of their duality survived in the contest for the head : if the men of the Subura won it, they fixed it on the turris Mamilia, which may have been the dwelling of their own chief. Such contests are even now well known, or have[7] but

---

[1] p. 185 foll. The tail in Roman ritual was ' offa penita.' Marq. 335, note 1.

[2] In Silesia, &c., the word is *Zâl, Zôl*, which I suppose = tail.

[3] *Golden Bough*, ii. 65. Jevons, Introduction to Plut. *Q. R.* p. lxix. He quotes an example from Africa.

[4] Robertson Smith, *Religion of the Semites*, Lect. ix. In this case, according to M., it was the life of the Corn-spirit—so of generation in general.

[5] Schwegler, *R. G.* i. 739 ; Ambrosch, *Studien*, 200 foll.

[6] Evidence for this in Liv. i 2 ; Serv. *Aen.* 9. 274.

[7] See e. g. Crooke's *Folklore of Northern India*, vol. ii. pp. 176 and 321. Crooke looks on these fights (he should have said, the possession of the

lately disappeared ; and some of them may owe their origin to
a fight for the Corn-spirit. Mannhardt gives some examples—
one very curious one from Granada, and one from Brittany.
At Derby, Hawick, Ludlow, and other places in this country,
they or the recollection of them may still be found.

On the whole we may agree with him that the rite was in
its origin one of the type to which he has referred it—a final
harvest festival of the Latin farm. There is yet, however,
a word to be said. He does not treat it from the point of view
of the Roman calendar, and thus fails to note the turn it took
when Latin farmers became Roman citizens. Wissowa, on the
other hand, takes the calendar as his sole basis for judging of
it, and with a strange perversity, as it seems to me, brushes
Mannhardt's conclusions aside, and would explain the rite simply
as a sacrifice to the god of war [1]. Now doubtless it had come to
be this in the organized city-calendar, as Mars himself began
to be brought into prominence in a new light, as the *iuvenes*
of the community came to be more and more employed in war
as well as agriculture, and as the Campus Martius came to be
used as an exercising-ground for the armed host. The Calendars
show us a curious correspondence between the beginning and
the end of the season of arms, i. e. the middle of March and the
middle of October, which leaves little doubt of the change which
had taken place in the accepted character of the rites of the two
periods by the time the Numan calendar was drawn up. This
correspondence has already been noted [2] ; it may be here briefly
referred to again.

On March 14 [3] there was a horse-race in the Campus Martius ;
on the 19th (Quinquatrus) was the *lustratio armorum* for the
coming war-season, as is seen from the fact that the *ancilia* of
the Salii at least—if not all arms—were *lustrata* on that day [4].

object which is the cause of the fight) as charms for rain or fertility.
So in the plains of N.-W. India, 'plenty is supposed to follow the side
which is victorious.'

[1] Veram huius sacri rationem inter veteres ii viderunt quorum senten-
tiam ita refert Festus 'equum hostiae loco Marti bellico deo sacrari'
(*de Feriis*, p. x`.   [2] See under March 14 and 19.

[3] Wissowa thinks it was originally the 15th (Ides) ; but Mommsen
dissents in his note on Oct. 15 (*C. I. L.* 332). It is the only feast-day in
the calendar which is an *even* number. Perhaps it was changed because of
the popularity of the revels, &c., on the Ides.

[4] Charisius, p. 81 ; Marq. 435.

So too on October 15 there was a horse-race, as we have seen, in the Campus Martius, and on the 19th we find the Armilustrium in the oldest calendars [1], a name which tells its own tale. The inference is that the horse-races on Oct. 15 and March 14 had much the same origin, and it is just this which induces Wissowa to slight Mannhardt's explanation of the former. He thinks that on each day the horses, like the arms, were lustrated (p. x.), i. e. before the war-season began, and after it was over. This is likely enough ; but might not the same have been the case with the horses of the farm ? The Roman farmer's year began with March, and the heavy work of carrying, &c., would be over in October. I am disposed to think that we must look on organized war-material as a development later than the primitive times to which Mannhardt would carry us back, a side of Roman life which only in course of time became highly specialized.

We must never forget that the oldest Roman calendar is the record of the life of an agricultural people. So much is clear on the face of it ; and in some instances, as in the Ambarvalia, Vestalia, Consualia, and in the October rite we have been discussing, something of the original intent can be made out from researches into modern folk-lore or savage custom. Yet this calendar is at the same time the table of feasts of a fully developed city-state, and in the process of its development the original meaning of the feasts was often lost, or they were explained by some mythical or historical event, or again they themselves may have changed character as the life of the people changed from an agricultural to a political one. In the rite of the October horse we may see an agricultural harvest custom taking a new shape and meaning as the State grew to be accustomed to war, just as Mars, originally perhaps the protector of man, herds, and crops alike, becomes — it may be even before Greek influence is brought to bear upon him — the deity of warriors and war-horses, of the yearly renewed strength of a struggling community [2]. It is looking with modern eyes at

---

[1] This point of the parallel was first noticed by Wissowa, who, as just noted, believes the day of Equirria to have been in each case the Ides.

[2] An apt illustration of this aspect of Mars, in combination with the older primitive form of ritual, is supplied by the strange sacrifice by Julius Caesar of two mutinous soldiers, recorded by Dio Cassius, 43. 24.

the institution of an old world if we try to separate the Roman warrior from the Roman husbandman, or the warlike aspect of his god from his universal care for his people.

XIV KAL. NOV. (OCTOBER 19).   N͞P.

ARM[ILUSTRIUM].   (ARV. SAB. MAFF. AMIT. ANT.)

The first three letters of this word, which alone appear in the calendars, are explained by Varro and Verrius : 'Armilustrium ab eo quod in armilustrio armati sacra faciunt . . . ab ludendo aut lustro, quod circumibant ludentes ancilibus armati [1].' This passage may be taken as referring both to March 19 and Oct. 19, and as showing that the Salii with the sacred shields were active on both days.   This can also be inferred from the fact that in 190 B. C. a Roman army, on its march into Asia, had to halt at the Hellespont, 'quia dies forte, quibus ancilia moventur, religiosi ad iter inciderant' [2]—its commander Scipio being one of the Salii.   It can be shown that this was in the autumn, as the army did not leave Italy till July 15 [3].   It may be taken as certain, then, that this was the last day on which the Salii appeared, and that *arma* and *ancilia* were now purified [4], and put away for the winter.

There are no festivals in any way connected with Mars from this day to the Roman new year, March 1.   As Roscher has remarked, his activity, like that of Apollo, is all in the warm season—the season of vegetation and of arms.   His priests, who seem in their dances, their song, and their equipment, to form a connecting link between his fertilizing powers and his warlike activity, are seen no more from this day till his power is felt again on the threshold of spring.

They were offered to Mars in the Campus Martius by the Flamen Martialis in the presence of the Pontifices, *and their heads were nailed up on the Regia.* (Hence Marq. infers that it was this flamen who sacrificed the October horse.)   Caesar was in Rome in *October* of the year to which D. C. attributes this deed, B.C. 46.

[1] *L. L.* 6. 62.   Cp. Festus, 19 'Armilustrium festum erat apud Romanos, quo res divinas armati faciebant ac dum sacrificarent tubis canebant.' See on March 19 and 23.

[2] Liv. 37. 33. 7.   Cp. Polyb. 21. 10. 12.

[3] Marq. 437, note 1.   The suggestion was Huschke's, *Röm. Jahr*, 363.

[4] Charisius, pp. 81. 20 (Keil), for *lustratio* in March.   The word Armi-lustrium, used for this day, speaks for itself.

We learn from Varro [1] that the place of *lustratio* on this day was the Aventine 'ad circum maximum.' I can find no explanation of this: we know of no Mars-altar in that part of Rome, which was the seat of the cults of Hercules and Consus. It was probably the last point in a procession of the Salii [2].

[1] *L. L.* 5. 153.
[2] We have a faint indication that they reached the *pons sublicius*, which was quite near to the Circus maximus. See Marq. 433, note 8.

MENSIS NOVEMBER.

Of all the months in the Roman year November is the least important from a religious point of view. It was the month of ploughing and sowing—not of holiday-time[1]; then, as now, it was a quiet month, and in the calendars, with the exception of the ludi plebeii, not a festival appears of any importance. Later on, the worship of Isis gained a hold upon the month[2], which remained open to intruders long after city-life had taken the place of November agricultural operations.

The ludi plebeii, as a public festival, date from 220 B.C.; they took place in the Circus Flaminius, which was built in that year[3]; they and the epulum Iovis (Nov. 13) are first mentioned by Livy four years later. The *epulum* has already been discussed in connexion with the ludi Romani. The plebeian games were probably at first on a single day (Nov. 13), and were gradually extended, like the ludi Romani; finally, they lasted from Nov. 4 to Nov. 17[4].

The 8th was one of the three days on which the *mundus* was open: see under Oct. 5.

ID. Nov. (Nov. 13). NP.

FERONIAE IN CAMPO[5]. (ARV., a later addition to the original.)
FORTUNAE PRIMIGENIAE IN COLLE. (ARV., a later addition to the original.)

This is the only mention we have of Feronia in Rome. She was a goddess of renown in Latium and central Italy, but

---

[1] Rustic calendars: 'Sementes triticariae et hordiar[iae].' Varro, *R. R.* i. 34.
[2] Mommsen in *C. I. L.* i.[2] 333.
[3] Friedländer in *Marq.* 499; Liv. 23. 30.
[4] See the table in *C. I. L.* i.[2] 335.
[5] Probably these notes belong to the Ides. In the Arval calendar the

never made her mark at Rome, as did others of her kind — Diana, Fortuna, Ceres; Flora—all of whom appear there with plebeian associations about them, as not belonging to the earliest patrician community [1]. It is curious to find this Feronia too in the calendar only in the middle of the ludi plebeii, and probably on the day which was the original nucleus of the games. We may either date the cult from the establishment of the *ludi* or guess that it was there before them, and was subsequently eclipsed by the cult of Jupiter.

The latter is perhaps the more probable conjecture; for the little that we know of the cult elsewhere points to a possible origin of the games which has not, so far as I know, been noticed. They took place, be it remembered, in the Circus Flaminius, which was in the Campus Martius; where also was this cult of Feronia. Now the most famous shrine of Feronia in Italy, that of Trebula Mutusca, was the centre of a great fair or market held on the feast-days of the goddess [2], and on the whole her attributes seem to be those of a deity of fertility and plenty [3]. Is it impossible that she had also some share in a fair in the Campus Martius long before the establishment of the *ludi*?

The connexion of Feronia with the plebs seems suggested not only by her position in the calendar, but by the devotion of *libertini* [4]. In the year 217 B.C. the Roman *freedwomen* collected a sum of money as a gift to Feronia [5]; though this offering need not be taken as destined for the Roman goddess, but rather for her of Soracte, to whom first-fruits and other gifts were frequently offered. The temple of Feronia at Terracina was specially devoted to the manumission of slaves, of which the process, as described by Servius, presents at least one feature of special interest [6]. Manumissions would take

---

entry is opposite the 14th, but from its position may be really meant as an additional note to the Ides. There is no other example of religious rites on a day *after* Ides. (Henzen, *Arv.* 240; *C. I. L.* i.[2] 296.) The same was the case with all 'dies postriduani.'

[1] See under Cerialia and Floralia.

[2] Liv. 1. 30. Roman merchants were seized by the Sabines in this market (Dion. Hal. 3. 32).

[3] Steuding in *Lex.* s. v. Feronia; Liv. 26 11. I cannot see any reason to connect her with November *sowing*, as Steuding does, p. 1480.

[4] Serv. *Aen.* 8. 564.   [5] Liv. 22. 1.

[6] The cutting of the hair, and putting on of the pileus. See Robertson Smith, *Religion of Semites*, p. 307.

place on public occasions, such as markets, when the necessary authorities and witnesses were to be easily found, and the temple of the market-goddess was at hand ; and this may be the original point of relation between this cult and the Roman plebs, which was beyond doubt by the third century B. C. largely composed of descendants of manumitted slaves.

The conjunction of Feronia on this day with Fortuna Primigenia (*in colle*) is curious, as both were goddesses of Praeneste, where Feronia in legend was the mother of Erulus, a daemon with threefold body and soul, who had to be killed three times by Evander [1]. The date of the introduction of this cult of Fortuna at Rome is 204 B. C. [2]

[1] Serv. *Aen.* l. c. The myth must be Graeco-Etruscan.
[2] Liv. 29. 36. The dedication was 194 B. C. (Liv. 34. 53).

MENSIS DECEMBER

In the middle of winter, until well on in January, the Roman husbandman had comparatively little to do. Varro [1] writes of sowing lilies, crocuses, &c., and of cleaning out ditches and pruning vines, and such light operations of the farm. Columella [2] tells us that the autumn sowing should be ended by the beginning of December, though some sow beans in this month; and in this he agrees with the rustic calendars which mention, besides this operation, only the manuring of vineyards and the gathering of olives.

It is not unnatural, then, that we should find in this 'slack time' [3] several festivals which are at once antique and obscure, and almost all of which seem to carry us back to husbandry and the primitive ideas of a country life. On the night of the 3rd or thereabouts was the women's sacrifice to the Bona Dea; on the 5th the rustic Faunalia in some parts of Italy, though probably not in Rome; on the 15th the winter Consualia; on the 17th the Saturnalia; and on the 19th the Opalia; and so on to the Compitalia and Paganalia. All this is in curious contrast with the absence of festivals in the busy month of November.

Women's Sacrifice to the Bona Dea.

This fell, in the year 63 B.C., on the night between Dec. 3 and 4, if we may trust Plutarch and Dio [4]; but the date does

---

[1] *R. R.* 1. 35. 2; Colum. 2. 8. 2.   [2] xi. 2.
[3] Cp. Hor. *Od.* 3. 18, 9-12. Ovid (*Fasti*, 3. 57) says of December—
   Vester (i.e. Faustuli et Larentiae) honos veniet, cum Larentalia dicam;
      Acceptus Geniis illa December habet.
Is this only an allusion to Larentia and Faustulus, or also to the general character of the month and its festivals?
[4] Plut. *Cic.* 19; Dio Cass. 37. 35.

not seem to have been a fixed one [1]. The rite does not appear in the calendars, and, though attended by the Vestals, did not take place in the temple of the goddess, but in the house of a consul or praetor, 'in ea domo quae est in imperio [2].' It seems to have been in some sense a State sacrifice, i. e. it was 'pro populo Romano' (according to Cicero) ; but it was not 'publico sumptu'[3], and it was never woven into the calendar by the pontifices, or it could hardly have occurred between the Kalends and the Nones. Its very nature would exclude the interference of the pontifical college, and there would be no need to give public notice of it.

The character of the goddess and her rites have already been discussed under May 1. All that need be said of the December sacrifice is that it was clearly a survival from the time when the wife of the chief of the community—himself its priest— together with her daughters (represented in later times by the Vestals), and the other matrons, made sacrifice of a young pig or pigs [4] to the deity of fertility, from all share in which men were rigorously excluded. It must have been originally a perfectly decorous rite, and so have continued to the famous sacrilege of Clodius ; it was only under the empire that it became the scene of such orgies as Juvenal describes in his second and sixth satires [5].

Non. Dec. (Dec. 5). F.

Here we have another festival unknown to the calendars, the Faunalia rustica, as it has been called. Our knowledge of it comes from the familiar ode of Horace (iii. 18), and from the comments of the scholiasts thereon :

> Faune, Nympharum fugientum amator,
> Per meos fines et aprica rura
> Lenis incedas abeasque parvis
>   Aequus alumnis,

[1] Cic. ad Att. 1. 12, and 15. 25.
[2] Cic. de Harusp. resp. 17. 37 'fit per Virgines Vestales, fit pro populo Romano, fit in ea domo quae est in imperio.' In 62 B C. it was in Caesar's house, and apparently in the Regia, if as pontifex maximus he resided there. See Marq. 346, note 1 ; 250, note 2.
[3] Fest. 245 publica sacra are 'quae publico sumptu pro populo fiunt.' See my article ' Sacra' in Dict. of Antiquities.
[4] Juvenal, 2. 86.   [5] 2. 83 foll. ; 6. 314 foll.

Si tener pleno cadit haedus anno,
Larga nec desunt Veneris sodali
Vina craterae, vetus ara multo
    Fumat odore.

Ludit herboso pecus omne campo
Cum tibi Nonae redeunt Decembres;
Festus in pratis vacat otioso
    Cum bove pagus;
Inter audaces lupus errat agnos;
Spargit agrestes tibi silva frondes;
Gaudet invisam pepulisse fossor
    Ter pede terram.

No picture could be choicer or neater than this; for once it is a treat to have our best evidence in the form of a perfect work of art. We are for a moment let into the heart and mind of ancient Italy, as they showed themselves on a winter holiday. There is an ancient altar—not a temple—to a supernatural being who is not yet fully god, who can play pranks like the 'Brownies' and do harm, but is capable of doing good if duly propitiated. On the Nones of December, possibly of other months too [1], he is coaxed with tender kid, libations of wine, and incense [2]; the little rural community of farmers (*pagus*), with their labourers, take part in the rite, and bring their cattle into the common pasture, plough-oxen and all. Then, after the sacrifice, they dance in triple measure, like the Salii in March.

Horace is of course describing a rite which was entirely rural, as the word *pagus* would indicate sufficiently, apart from other features. Unless he were the god of the Lupercalia, which is open to much doubt [3], Faunus was not introduced into the city of Rome till 196 B. C., when the aediles very appropriately built him a temple in the Tiber-island with money taken as fines from defaulting *pecuarii* [4], or holders of public land used for cattle-runs. We may assume that his settlement in the city was suggested by the pontifices, and that we have here a case of the transformation of a purely rustic cult into an urban one by priestly manipulation. It is not impossible that

[1] Probus on Virg. *Georg.* 1. 10 'In Italia quidam annuum sacrum, quidam menstruum celebrant.'

[2] The word is 'odore,' i.e. sweet herbs of the garden (Marq. 169 and note).

[3] See on Lupercalia, p. 312.

[4] Liv. 33. 42.

S

the idea that Faunus was the deity of the Lupercalia came in about the same time [1]. Both priests and annalists got hold of him, and did their best to rob him of his true character as an intelligible and useful god of woodland and pasture. He became a Rex Aboriginum [2], and the third on the list of mythical kings of Latium [3]. He became identified with the Greek Pan. But, in spite of all their efforts, Faunus would not tamely accept his new position. We hear no more of the *aedes* in the island : the Roman *vulgus* do not seem to have recognized him at the Lupercalia, and his insertion in the legends had no political effect. The fact that not a single inscription from Rome or its vicinity records his name shows plainly that he never took the popular fancy as a deity with city functions : and the absence of inscriptions in the country districts also, in most singular contrast to the ubiquitous stone records of Silvanus-worship, seems to show that he remained always much as wild as he was before the age of inscriptions began, while the kindred deity was adopted into the organized life and culture of the Italian and provincial farmer [4].

It may be as well, before leaving the subject of this singular being, to sum up under a very few heads what is really known about him. But so little is known about the cult of Faunus — and indeed it can hardly be said that any elaborate cult ever grew up around him — that it may be legitimate for once first to glance at the etymological explanations of his name which have been suggested by scholars.

(1) Faunus is connected with *favere*, and means 'the kind or propitious one,' like Faustus and Faustulus, and as some think, Favonius [5] and Fons. This derivation was known to Servius [6] : 'quidam Faunos putant dictos ab eo quod frugibus faveant.'

---

[1] The earliest hint of the connexion of Faunus with Evander and the Palatine legend is found in a fragment of Cincius Alimentus, who wrote at this time (H. Peter, *Fragm. Hist. Lat.* 41, from Servius, *Georg.* 1. 10).

[2] Dion. Hal. 1. 31 ; Suet. *Vitell.* 1. Cp. for a more truly Italian view, Virgil, *Aen.* 8. 314 foll.

[3] *Aen.* 7. 45 foll. The order was Saturnus, Picus, Faunus, Latinus.

[4] Wissowa in *Lex.* s. v. Faunus, 1458 : who, however, does not sufficiently explain the contrast. Silvanus became *tutor finium*, and *custos hortuli* (cp. *Gromatici Veteres.* p. 302). It was probably this turn given to his cult which saved him from the fate of Faunus. He takes over definite duties to the cultivator, while Faunus is still roaming the country in a wild state.

[5] Bouché-Leclercq, *Hist. de la Divination*, iv. 122.

[6] Ad *Georg.* 1. 10.

It is not in itself inconsistent with what we know of the rural Faunus, or with analogous supernatural beings, like the 'good people.' It was accepted by Preller and Schwegler, and has affected their conclusions about Faunus; e. g. Schwegler based on it the view, now generally held, that Evander is a Greek translation of Faunus[1].

(2) Faunus is from *fari*, i. e. the speaker, or foreteller. This too was known to Latin scholars: thus Isidorus (perhaps from Varro[2]), 'fauni a fando, ἀπὸ τῆς φωνῆς dicti, quod voce non signis ostendere viderentur futura.' It was revived not long ago by the late Prof. Nettleship: 'Once imagine Faunus as a "speaker," and all becomes clear. He is not only the composer and reciter of verses[3], but generally the seer or wise man, whose superior knowledge entitles him to the admiration and dread of the country folk who consult him. But as his real nature and functions are superseded, his character is mis-conceived: he becomes a divinity, the earliest king of Latium, the god of prophecy, the god of agriculture.' We may compare with this Scaliger's note on Varro, *L. L.* 7. 36: 'The Fauni were a class of men who exercised, at a very remote period, the same functions which belonged to the Magi in Persia, and to the Bards in Gaul.'

(3) Faunus may = Favonius, which itself may come from the same root as Pan (i. e. *pu* = purify). Thus Faunus, like Pan, might be taken as a mythological expression of the 'purifying breeze,' the god of the gentler winds[4]. The characteristics of Faunus are of course very like those of Pan; but as it is no easy matter to determine how far those of the Italian were taken over by the Roman litterati from the Greek deity, and as the etymology itself is confessedly a questionable one, this conjecture must be left to take its chance.

But the first two are worth attending to, and each finds some support in what we know of Faunus from other sources. Let us see in the next place what this amounts to.

(1) There is fairly strong evidence that Faunus was not

---

[1] Schwegler, *Röm. Gesch.* i. 351.

[2] Varro, *L. L.* 7. 36 'Faunos in silvestribus locis traditum est solitos fari futura.' Servius identifies Faunus and Fatuus; ad *Aen.* 6. 775.

[3] 'Versibus quos olim Fauni vatesque canebant.' Ennius in Varro, *L. L* 7. 36. See Nettleship, *Essays in Latin Literature*, p. 50 foll.

[4] Mannhardt, *A. W. F.* 113 foll.

originally conceived as a single deity, but as *multiplex*. Varro quotes the line of Ennius :

> Versibus quos olim Fauni vatesque canebant,

and comments thus[1] : 'Fauni dii Latinorum, ita ut Faunus et Fauna sit.' The evidence of Virgil, always valuable for rural antiquities, is equally clear :

> Et vos agrestum praesentia numina, Fauni,
> Ferte simul Faunique pedem Dryadesque puellae[2].

Servius has an interesting note on these lines : why, he asks, does the poet put Faunus in the plural, when there is but one ? We might be tempted to think Virgil wrong and his commentator right, the poet representing Greek ideas and the scholar Italian, but for a still more curious note of Probus on the same passage : ' Plures (Fauni) existimantur esse etiam praesentes: idcirco rusticis persuasum est incolentibus eam partem Italiae quae suburbana est, saepe eos in agris conspici.' My belief is that these words give us the genuine idea of Faunus in the rustic mind, surviving in central Italy long after he had been appropriated as a conventional Roman deity. We seem in the case of Faunus to be able to catch a deity in the process of manufacture—of elevation from a lower, multiplex, daemonistic form, to a higher and more uniform and more rigid one. Yet so excellent a scholar as Wissowa holds exactly the opposite view, that there was but one Faunus, and that his multiplication is simply the result of Roman acquaintance with Pan and the Satyrs[3]. It would have been more satisfactory if he had given us an explanation from his point of view of the passage of Probus just quoted, or had shown us how these Greek notions could have penetrated into the rural parts of Italy.

(2) Another point which comes out distinctly—unless our Roman authorities were wholly misled—is the *woodland* character of the Fauni. A passage of Varro, of which I quoted the first

---

[1] *L. L.* 7. 36.

[2] *Georg.* 1. 10. The introduction of the Greek Dryads may be thought to throw suspicion upon the Latinity of these Fauni of Virgil. But in *Aen.* 8. 314, the similar conjunction of Fauni and Nymphae is followed by words which seem to mark a true Italian conception.

[3] *Lex.* s. v. Faunus, 1454.

words just now, goes on thus: 'hos versibus quos vocant Saturnios *in silvestribus locis* traditum est solitos fari futura, a quo fando Faunos dictos.' This seems to be a genuine Italian tradition. Virgil was not talking Greek when he wrote [1]

> Haec nemora indigenae Fauni Nymphaeque tenebant
> Gensque virum truncis et duro robore nata,
> Queis neque mos neque cultus erat, &c.

The poet imagines an ancient race, sprung from the trees them-selves: a 'genus indocile et dispersum montibus altis,' living on the forest-clad hills [2], to whom foreign invaders brought the means of civilization. Why should not this tradition be a native one? It is singularly in accord with the most recent results of Italian excavation; for it is now absolutely certain that the oldest inhabitants of central Italy dwelt on the hill-tops, and that the first traces of foreign influence only occur in lower and later settlements [3]. The valleys were still undrained and malarious. These earliest inhabitants who have left their traces for the excavator, or a still older race scattered on the hills after their invasion, may have been the traditional repre-sentatives of what Preller has called 'the period of Faunus [4],' regarded by the later civilization, from their wild and woodland habits, as half demons and half men. The name of the kindred Silvanus tells its own tale; and his actual connexion with trees was even closer than that of Faunus [5].

(3) A third well-attested point is the attribution to Faunus or the Fauni of power for good or evil over the crops and herds, as we have seen it already implied in Horace's ode. Por-phyrion [6] in his commentary on this ode tells us that Faunus, on the Nones of December, wishes the cattle, which are under his protection, to be free from danger. Just before this passage he had spoken of him as 'deum inferum et pestilentem,' thus

---

[1] *Aen.* 8. 314.

[2] Cp. Ovid, *Fasti*, 3. 315 'Di sumus agrestes et qui dominemur in altis Montibus,' &c. Cp. Preller, i. 386.

[3] *Monumenti Antichi*, vol. v. (Barnabei). Von Duhn, translated in *Journal of Hellenic Studies*, 1896, p. 120 foll.

[4] *Röm. Myth.* i. 104 foll.

[5] Virg. *Aen.* 8. 601, and Serv.'s note: 'Prudentiores dicunt eum esse ὑλικὸν θεόν, hoc est deum ὕλης.' Silvanus may have been a true tree-spirit; Mannhardt, *A. W. F.* 118 foll.; Preller, i. 392.

[6] Vol. i. 335, ed. Hauthal.

giving us the dark and hurtful side of his power as well as the bright and gracious. The same combination of the powers of doing and averting harm is seen in Mars, as we have already learnt from the hymn of the Arval Brethren and the formula of prayers preserved by Cato [1].

Under this head may be mentioned the belief that both Faunus and Silvanus were dangerous for women, an idea which finds expression in the significant word *incubus*, so often applied to them [2]. We may perhaps find a reason for the identification of Faunus as god of the Lupercalia in the most striking feature of the festival—the pursuit of the women by the *creppi*, who struck them with thongs in order to render them productive [3].

(4) The last characteristic of the Fauni to be noticed is that they had the power of foretelling the future. The verse of Ennius already quoted is the earliest literary evidence we have of this; but the quaint story of the capture of Picus and Faunus by Numa [4], who caught them by making them drunk with wine at the fountain where they came to drink, and compelled them as the price of their liberty to reveal the art of staying a disaster, has an unmistakeable old-Italian ring. The idea seems to have been, not that Faunus was a 'god of prophecy,' as Preller seems to fancy, but that there was an ancient race of Fauni, who might be coaxed or compelled to reveal secrets. Sometimes indeed they 'spoke' of their own accord; when a Roman army needed to be warned or encouraged on its march, their voice was heard by all as it issued from thicket or forest. Cicero and Livy [5] write of these voices with a distinctness which (as it seems to me) admits of no suspicion that they are inserting Greek ideas into Roman annals.

There are also traces to be found of a belief in the existence of local woodland oracles of Faunus and his kind. It was in a grove sacred to Faunus that Numa, in Ovid's vivid description [6],

---

[1] See above, p. 126. It may be noticed that the Bona Dea, whose solemn rite occurs also at the beginning of this month, was identified with Fauna, the female form of Faunus (R. Peter, in *Lex.* s.v. Fauna); i.e. their powers for good and evil were thought to be much alike.

[2] Preller, i. 381 and reff.   [3] See under Lupercalia, p. 320.

[4] Ovid, *Fasti*, 3. 291 foll. I am glad to see that Wissowa accepts this story as genuine Italian (*Lex.* s.v. 1456).

[5] Cic. *de Div.* 1. 101 ; Livy, 2. 7 (Silvanus), and Dion. Hal. 5. 16 (Faunus) of the battle by the wood of Arsia.

[6] *Fasti*, 4. 649 foll.

slew two sheep, the one to Faunus, the other to Sleep, and after twice sprinkling water on his head, and twice wreathing it with beech-leaves, stretched himself on the fleeces to receive the prophetic inspiration as he slumbered. Almost every touch in this story seems to me to be genuine; and especially the conditions necessary to success—the continence of the devotee, and the removal of the metal ring from the finger. Virgil, with something more of foreign adornment, tells in exquisite verse what is really the same story as Ovid's [1]. And a later poet writes of a sacred beech-grove, where under like conditions of temperance, &c., the shepherds might find the oracles of Faunus inscribed on the bark of a beech-tree [2]. All this reminds us of Dodona and the oldest Greek oracles: we have here the quaint methods of primitive shepherds, appealing to prophetic powers localized in particular woodland spots. Roman exigencies of state drew by degrees the whole of the secrets of fore-knowledge into the hands of a priestly aristocracy, with its fixed doctrine and methods of divination; but the country folk long retained their faith in the existence of an ancient race, possessed of prophetic power, which haunted forest and mountain.

These four points, taken together, i. e. the multiplicity of the Fauni, their woodland character, and their supposed powers of productivity and prophecy, seem by no means to exclude the possibility of the human origin suggested long ago by Scaliger, and recently by Prof. Nettleship, though I would shape the explanation somewhat differently. Wild men from the hills and woods, for example, might well be supposed to be possessed of supernatural powers, like the gipsies of modern times [3]. And the striking absence of any epigraphical survivals of a definite cult may possibly be explained by a persistence of the belief in the Italian mind that Faunus was never really and truly a god, but one of a race with some superhuman attributes—a link in the chain that always in antiquity connected together the human and the divine. Horace's ode shows the divine element predominating; some local Faunus has, so to speak, been caught and half deified; and yet, even then, the process is hardly complete.

---

[1] *Aen.* 7. 81 foll.   [2] Calpurnius, *Ecl.* 1. 8 foll.
[3] Cp. Tylor, *Primitive Culture*, i. 341 foll.; Sir A. Lyall, *Asiatic Studies*, ch. 2.

There is, however, another explanation of conceptions of this kind to which I must briefly allude, which was based by Dr. Mannhardt on an exhaustive examination of the attributes of creatures like the Fauni, as they occur in various parts of Europe and elsewhere [1]. The general result of his investigation may be stated thus. Spirits which seem to have their origin in woods and mountains find outward expression for their being in the *wind*; so also do those which seem to have their origin in corn and vegetation generally. We thus find three ingredients· in their composition : (1) trees, (2) corn, (3) wind. We have only to think how the invisible wind moves the branches of the trees, or bows the corn before it, to see how closely, in the eyes of men used to attribute life to inanimate things, the idea of the wind might run together with that of objects to which it seems to give motion and life. The result of its mysterious agency is the growth of a variety of creatures of the imagination, often half bestial, like Pan and the Russian Ljeschi, sometimes entirely animal, like the Rye-wolf and many another animal corn-spirit now familiar to readers of Frazer's *Golden Bough*; sometimes entirely human, like Silvanus, perhaps Faunus himself [2], or the Teutonic 'wild man of the woods.' Mannhardt endeavours, not wholly without success, to bring the attributes of Faunus into harmony with this theory. His prophetic *vox* comes from the forest in which the wind raises strange noises ; his relation to crops and flocks is parallel to that of many other spirits who can be traced to a woodland origin ; and the word Favonius, used for the western moist and fertilizing breeze, is kindred, if not identical, with Faunus ; and so on.

This theory, resting as it does on a very wide induction from unquestionable facts, beyond doubt explains many of the conceptions of primitive agricultural man ; whether it can be applied satisfactorily to the Italian Faunus is perhaps less evident. At present I rather prefer to think of the Fauni as arising from the contact of the first clearers and cultivators of

---

[1] *Antike Wald- und Feldkulte*, p. 152.

[2] See the cuts of two bronze statuettes which Wissowa, following Reifferscheid, believed to represent the un-Graecized Italian Faunus, at the end of the article 'Faunus' in *Lex*. 1460. But it is at least very doubtful whether Reifferscheid was right in his opinion.

Italian soil with a wild aboriginal race of the hills and woods.
But on such questions certainty is impossible, and dogmatism
entirely out of place.

III Id. Dec. (Dec. 11). N̄P.

AG. IN. . . . (AMIT.).   AG[ONIA] (MAFF. PRAEN. ANT.)
SEPTIMONTIA (PHILOC.).   SEPTIMONTIUM, GUID. SILV.[1]

For Agonia see on Jan. 9. This (Dec. 11) is the third day
on which this mysterious word appears in the calendars. The
AG. IN. of the Amiternian calendar was conjectured by Mommsen
in the first edition of *C. I. L.*, vol. i, to indicate 'Agonium
Inui'[2]; but in the new edition he withdraws this; 'ab incertis
coniecturis abstinebimus.' This is done in deference to Wissowa,
who has pointed out that there is no other case in the calendars
of a festival-name inscribed in large letters being followed
immediately by the name of a deity[3]. We must fall back on
the supposition that AG. IN. . . . is simply a cutter's error for
the AGON. of three other calendars.

It is impossible to determine what was the relation between
this agonium, or solemn sacrifice, and the Septimontium or
Septimontiale sacrum, which appears only in very late calendars,
or whether indeed there was any relation at all. It is not
absolutely certain that the so-called Septimontium took place
on this day. It was only a conjecture of Scaliger's (though
a clever one) that completed the gloss in Festus on the word
'Septimontium'[4] [*Septimontium dies ap*]*pellatur mense* [*Decembri
qui dicitur in f*]*astis agonalia.* The word Septimontium suggested
itself, as the gloss occurred under letter S. Other support for
the conjecture is found in the two late calendars, and in
a fragment of Lydus[5], who connects the two ceremonies.

But even if Scaliger's conjecture be right, it does not follow
that the Agonium was identical with or was part of the Septimontiale sacrum. The latter does not appear in the old calendars,

---

[1] By an error Silvius has entered it on the 12th.

[2] For Inuus see on Lupercalia, and Livy, i. 5.

[3] *de Feriis*, xii. His other argument, that Inuus is not a nomen, but
a cognomen, is less satisfactory. Can we always be sure which is which?
(e. g. Saturnus, Janus).

[4] Festus, p. 340.

[5] *de Mensibus*, p. 118, ed. Bekk. ; quoted by Mommsen, *C. I. L.* i[1]. 336.

as it was not 'pro populo,' but only 'pro montibus' (see below) ;
and if it was there represented by the word Agonium, it is not
easy to see how the latter should have found its way into the
calendar. It seems better to conclude that the two were distinct.

About the Septimontium itself we have just enough information to divine its nature, but without details. The word is
used by Varro both in a topographical and a religious sense :
'Ubi nunc est Roma, erat olim Septimontium ; nominatum ab
tot montibus, quos postea urbs muris comprehendit[1].' Here
he implies that the old name for Rome was Septimontium ; but
this is only a guess based on the name of the festival: 'Dies
Septimontium nominatur ab his septem montibus, in quis sita
urbs est ; feriae *non populi sed montanorum* modo, ut Paganalia,
quae sunt aliquoius pagi[2].'

The *montes* here meant are the three divisions of the Palatine,
viz. Palatium, Cermalus, Velia ; the three of the Esquiline, viz.
Mons Oppius, Mons Cispius, and the Fagutal, together with the
lower ground of the Subura[3]. I believe that Mommsen is
right in thinking that these were never political divisions—in
other words, that they were not originally distinct communities[4],
but probably religious divisions of a city which began on the
Palatine, and gradually took in new ground on the Esquiline.
The same process can be traced at Falerii, and at Narce a few
miles above it ; what we seem to see is not the accretion of
villages—not συνοικισμός—but the extension of a city from one
strong position to another[5]. This is especially clear at Narce,
where it is distinctly proved by the pottery found in the
excavations, that the hill (Monte li Santi) subsequently added
to the original city was not co-eval with the latter as a settle-

---

[1] *L. L.* v. 41.   [2] Ibid. vi. 24.

[3] Antistius Labeo, ap. Festum, 348: 'Septimontio, ut ait Antistius Labeo,
hisce montibus feriae. Palatio, cui sacrificium quod fit Palatuar dicitur.
Veliae, cui item sacrificium, Fagutali, Suburae, Cermalo, Oppio, Cispio
monti.' Before 'Cispio' the MS. has 'Caelio monti,' which must be
a copyist's blunder. The Subura is by courtesy a *mons* ; also a *pagus*
(Festus, 309), a *regio* (ib.), and a *tribus* (ib.).

[4] *Staatsrecht*, iii. 112. O. Gilbert has made a great to-do about the development of these communities ; *Gesch. u. Topogr.* i. 39 foll. But where else
will he find three distinct settlements in a space as small as that of the
Palatine ? The discoveries at Falerii and Narce would have saved him the
labour of much web-spinning. Plutarch, *Q. R.* 69, has (accidentally
perhaps) expressed the matter rightly.

[5] *Monumenti Antichi*, vol. v. p. 15 foll.

ment; i. e. that it was the absorption by an older settlement of a probably uninhabited position which here took place, and not the synoecizing of distinct political communities [1]. In the later Rome the *montani* of the seven districts, together with the *pagani*, or inhabitants of what had originally been the farm-country around Rome, formed the united city [2]. It is most interesting to find that the earliest divisions, i. e. of the *montes*, were imitated in the foundation of some colonies — we should find them probably in many if we had the necessary information [3].

All we know of the cult of the *montani* on this day is as follows: (1) There was a sacrifice on the Palatium (which seems to have been the first in dignity of the *montes*) by the Flamen Palatualis [4]; but we do not know to what deity, and can only guess that it was Pales, or Palatua [5]. (2) On this day no carts or other vehicles drawn by beasts of burden were allowed in the city, as we learn from Plutarch, who asks the reason of this, and gives some quaint answers [6]. But the explanations are useless to us, and we cannot even guess whence Plutarch drew his knowledge of the fact, unless it was from personal observation. Let us remember, however, that this was a feast of *montani*: is it not likely that this was a survival from a time when the farm-waggons of the *pagani* really never ascended to the 'hills'?

PRID. ID. DEC. (DEC. 12). EN.

CONSO IN AVENTIN[O]. (AMIT.)

XVIII (ANTE CAES. XVI [7]) KAL. IAN. (DEC. 15). NP.

CONS[UALIA]. (MAFF. PRAEN. AMIT. ANT.) FERIAE CONSO (PRAEN. AMIT.)

For these see on Aug. 21. If the conclusions there arrived at are sound we might guess that these winter rites of Consus

---

[1] *Mon. Ant.* p. 110 foll. (Barnabei).   [2] Cic. *de Domo*, 28. 74.

[3] At Ariminum, and Antioch in Pisidia (Mommsen, *Staatsrecht*, iii. 113, note).

[4] Festus, 348, cp. 245.   [5] Preller, i. 414.

[6] *Q. R.* 69. Plutarch does not say in what parts of the city the vehicles were forbidden. The feast existed in his day, and indeed long afterwards (Tertull. *Idololatr.* 10). It seems to have become a general feast of the whole people.   [7] Macrob. i. 10. 2.

arose from the habit of inspecting the condition of the corn-
stores in mid-winter [1]. It is this day that has the note attached
to it in the Fasti Praenestini, 'Equi et [muli floribus coronantur]
quod in eius tu[tela] . . . itaque rex equo [vectus ?],' which was
commented on under Aug. 21. See also under Aug. 25
(Opeconsivia); Wissowa, s. v. Consus, in *Lex. Myth.*; and *de
Feriis*, vi foll.

XVI (Ante Caes. xiv [2]) Kal. Ian. (Dec. 17). NP.

SATURNALIA. (maff. amit. guid. rust. philoc.)
FERIAE SATURNO. (maff. amit)
SATURN[O] AD FO[RUM]. (amit.)
FERIAE SERVORUM. (silv.)

This was the original day of the Saturnalia [3], and, in a strictly
religious sense, it was the only day. The festival, in the sense
of a popular holiday, was extended by common usage to as
much as seven days [4]: Augustus limited it to three in respect
of legal business, and the three were later increased to five [5].

Probably no Roman festival is so well known to the general
reader as this, which has left its traces and found its parallels
in great numbers of mediaeval and modern customs [6], occurring about the time of the winter solstice. Unfortunately,
it is here once more a matter of difficulty to determine what
features in the festival were really of old Latin origin, in spite
of information as to detail, which is unusually full; for both
Saturnus himself and his cult came to be very heavily overlaid
with Greek ideas and practice.

---

[1] See below on Saturnalia, p. 271.

[2] Macrob. 1. 10. 2. Macr. tells us that after the change some people in
error held the festival on the 19th, i. e. on the day which was now xiv
K. Ian.

[3] Hartmann, *Der Röm. Kalender*, p. 203 foll., thinks it was originally one
of the *feriae conceptivae*, like the Compitalia, Paganalia, &c., and only
became fixed (*stativae*) when it was reorganized in 217 B. C. But if so,
why is it marked in the calendars in large letters? And Hartmann
himself points out (p. 208) that Dec. 17 is the first day of Capricornus, i.e.
the coldest season, which in the oldest natural reckoning would be likely
to fix the day (Colum. 11. 2. 94).

[4] Macr. l.c.; Cic. *Att.* 13. 52. 　　　　[5] Mommsen, *C. I. L.* i. 337.

[6] Frazer, *Golden Bough*, ii. 172; Brand, *Popular Antiquities*, ch. 13; Usener,
Religionsgeschichtliche Untersuchungen, 1. 214 foll. See for Italy, *Academy*, Jan.
20, 1888.

That Saturnus was an old agricultural god admits, however, of no doubt; the old form of the word was probably Säëturnus, which is found on an inscription on an ancient vase [1], and this leads us to connect him with *serere* and *satio*; and popular tradition attributed to him the discovery of agricultural processes [2]. But the Roman of the historical age knew very little about him, and cared only for his Graecized festival; like Faunus, he is the object of no votive inscriptions in Rome and its neighbourhood [3]; and this conclusively proves that he was never what may be called popular as a deity. As the first king of Latium there were plenty of legends about him, or as the first civilizer of his people, the representative of a Golden Age [4]; but no one has as yet thoroughly investigated these [5], with a view to distinguish any Italian precipitate in the mixture of elements of which they certainly consist. We are still without the invaluable aid of the contributors to Roscher's *Lexicon*.

More promising at first sight is the tradition which connects him in Rome itself with the Capitoline hill. Varro tells us positively that this hill was originally called Mons Saturnius; and that there was once an *oppidum* there called Saturnia, of which certain vestiges survived to his own time, including a 'fanum Saturni in faucibus,' i. e. apparently the ara Saturni of which Dionysius records that it was at the 'root of the hill,' by the road leading to the summit [6], in fact on the same spot where stood later the temple of which eight columns are still standing. Close to this, it may be noted, was a sacellum of Dis Pater [7], the Latinized form of Plutus; in the temple was the aerarium of later Rome [8], and built into the rock behind, the chambers of records (tabularia). But it would be idle to found upon these facts or traditions any serious hypothesis as to the original nature of the Roman cult of Saturn; all attempts

---

[1] *C. I. L.* i. 48. But Prof. Gardner tells me that the reading Saet. is not certain.

[2] Macrob. i. 10. 19 foll.; i. 7. 24 and 25; Marq. p. 11 note 3. The conjunction of Ops with him in this function is rejected (rightly, I think) by Wissowa, *de Feriis*, iv. But see below on Opalia.

[3] Jordan's note on Preller, ii. 10.   [4] e.g. Virg. *Aen.* 8. 321.

[5] See, however, Schwegler, *R. G.* i. 223 foll.

[6] Varro, *L. L.* 5. 42; Dion. Hal. i. 34 (cp. 6. 1); Fest. 322; Solinus, i. 13; Servius, *Aen.* 2. 115; Middleton, *Rome in 1885*, p. 166.

[7] R. Peter, s. v. Dis in *Lex.* 1181; Macr. i. 11. 48.

[8] Lucan, 3. 153; Middleton, op. cit. 167.

must fail in the bewildering fog of ancient fancy and ancient learning. Saturnus belongs, like Janus, with whom he was closely connected in legend [1], to an age into whose religious ideas we cannot penetrate, and survived into Roman worship only through Greek resuscitation [2], and in the feast of the Saturnalia. All we seem to see is that he is somehow connected with things that are put in the earth [3]—seed, treasure, perhaps stores of produce; to which may just be added that the one spot in Rome at all times associated with him is close to the *market*, and that market-days (nundinae) were said to be sacred to him [4]. The temple of Janus is also close by, and it is not impossible that both these ancient gods had some closer relation to the Forum and the business done there than we can at present understand with our limited knowledge. Neither of them, it may be noted, had a flamen attached to his cult; from which we may infer that they did not descend from the primitive household or the earliest form of community, but rather represented some place or process common to several communities, such as a forum and the business transacted there [5]. It is precisely such gods who figure in tradition as kings, not of a single city, but of Latium.

But to turn to the festival; if the god was obscure and uninteresting, this was not the case with his feast. It seems steadily to have gained in popularity down to the time of the empire, and still maintained it when Macrobius wrote the dialogue supposed to have taken place on the three days of the Saturnalia, and called by that name. Seneca tells us that in his day all Rome seemed to go mad on this holiday [6]. Probably its vogue was largely due merely to the accident of fashion,

---

[1] Preller, ii. 13 ; i. 182.

[2] The temple was traditionally dated B.C. 497 (Livy, 2. 21) ; cp. Aust, *de Aedibus sacris*, p. 4 : so too the festival, though both had an older origin (Ambrosch. *Stud.* 149). The latter was reorganized in Greek fashion in obedience to a Sibylline oracle in B.C. 217 (Livy, 22. 1).

[3] Plut. *Q. R.* 34 notes the cult of such gods when all fruits have been gathered.

[4] Macr. 1. 8. 3 and 1. 16. 30 (also, but probably in error, attributed to Jupiter). Plut. *Q. R.* 42, and *Poplic.* 12, states it distinctly ; but there is no indication of the source from which he drew.

[5] Cp. the legendary connexion of both with ship-building and the coining of money ; though it is of course possible that this was simply suggested by the Janus-head and the ship of early Roman coins.

[6] Seneca, *Ep.* 18. 1. Martial is full of Saturnalian allusions ; e. g. 12. 62.

partly perhaps to misty ideas about the Golden Age and the reign of Saturn[1]; but it seems to be almost a general human instinct to rest and enjoy oneself about the time of the winter solstice, and to show one's good-will towards all one's neighbours[2]. In Latium, as elsewhere, this was the time when the autumn sowing had come to an end, and when all farm-labourers could enjoy a rest[3]. Macrobius alludes also to the completion of all in-gathering by this date: 'Itaque omni iam fetu agrorum coacto ab hominibus hos deos (Saturnus and Ops) coli quasi vitae cultioris auctores[4].' The close concurrence of Consualia, Opalia, and Saturnalia at this time seems to show that some final inspection of the harvest work of the autumn may in reality have been coincident with, or have immediately preceded, the rejoicings of the winter solstice.

There are several well-attested features of the Saturnalia as it was in historical times[5]. On Dec. 17 there was a public sacrifice at the temple (formerly the *ara*) of Saturn by the Forum[6], followed by a public feast, in breaking up from which the feasters shouted 'Io Saturnalia'[7]. During the sacrifice Senators and Equites wore the toga, but laid it aside for the convivium, which reminds us of the ritual of the Fratres Arvales, except that the toga was in the latter case the praetexta[8]. These proceedings of the first and original day of the festival might seem pretty clearly to descend from the religion of the farm, yet the convivium is said by Livy to have been introduced as late as 217 B.C.[9]

[1] Popularized, of course, by the poets: Virg. *Georg.* ii. 538; Tibull. i. 3. 35, &c.

[2] Was this one of the reasons why Christmas was fixed at the winter solstice? Cp. John Chrysostom, tom. iii. 497 e: quoted by Usener, op. cit. p. 217.

[3] Varro, *R. R.* 1. 35. 2 'Dum in xv diebus ante et post brumam ut pleraque ne facias.' Columella, 2. 8. 2, seems to follow Varro. Virg. *Georg.* 1. 211 extends the time 'usque sub extremum brumae intractabilis imbrem' (cp. Serv. ad loc.).

[4] *Sat.* i. 10. 19 and 22, and Dion. Hal. 3. 32; Plut. *Q. R.* 34.

[5] See Marquardt's excellent summary in *Staatsverwaltung*, iii. 357, and Preller, ii. 15 foll.

[6] Dion. Hal. 6. 1. Fasti Amit. Dec. 17. We do not know who was the sacrificing priest; perhaps the Rex Sacrorum, or a magistrate.

[7] Macrob. 1. 10. 18.

[8] Martial, 14. 1; at least this seems to be the inference from 'Synthesibus dum gaudet eques dominusque senator.' Cp 6. 24.

[9] Livy, 22. 1. 19 'lectisternium imperatum et convivium publicum.'

On the 18th and 19th, which were general holidays, the day began with an early bath [1]; then followed the family sacrifice of a sucking pig, to which Horace alludes in familiar lines:

> Cras genium mero
> Curabis et porco bimenstri
> Cum famulis operum solutis [2].

Then came calls on friends, congratulations, games, and the presentation of gifts [3]. All manner of presents were made, as they are still at Christmas : among them the wax candles (*cerei*) deserve notice, as they are thought to have some reference, like the yule log, to the returning power of the sun's light after the solstice. They descended from the Saturnalia into the Christmas ritual of the Latin Church [4]. The sigillaria, or little paste or earthenware images which were sold all over Rome in the days before the festival [5], and used as presents, also survived into Christian times ; thus, in the ancient Romish Calendar, we find that all kinds of little images were on sale at the confectioners' shops, and even in England the bakers made little images of paste at this season [6]. What was the original meaning of the custom we do not know ; but it reminds us of the oscilla of the Latin festival and the Compitalia [7].

But the best known feature of the Saturnalia is the part played in it by the slaves, who, as we all know, were waited on by their masters, and treated as being in a position of entire equality. The earliest reference to this is in a fragment of Accius, quoted by Macrobius [8]:

> Iamque diem celebrant, per agros urbesque fere omnes
> Exercent epulas laeti, famulosque procurant
> Quisque suos: nostrique itidem, et mos traditus illinc
> Iste, ut cum dominis famuli epulentur ibidem.

But even this custom, as Marquardt points out, may not have been of genuine Latin origin : ' Though the Romans looked

---

[1] Tertull. *Apol.* 42.

[2] *Odes*, 3. 17. Cp. Martial, 14. 70. The pig-offering indicates an earth-deity : Henzen, *Acta Fratr. Arv.* p. 22 ; Marq. 173.

[3] Martial, bk. 14, is the *locus classicus* for all this.

[4] Brand, *Pop. Ant.* 183.

[5] Macr. i. 10. 24 ; 11. 49. In the latter passage he says 'quae homines pro se atque suis piaculum pro Dite Saturno facerent.'

[6] Brand, 180.

[7] Marq. 192, and the passages there quoted.

[8] *Sat.* 1. 7. 37. For later evidence see Marq. 588.

on it as a reminiscence of the Golden Age when all men were equal, it may have begun with the lectisternium of 217 B.C., for such entertainments were a characteristic of lectisternia.' When we turn, however, to the same author's account [1] of the Greek forms of religion introduced through the Sibylline oracles, of which the lectisternium was one, we do not find slaves included in the ritual of any of them. There was no general exclusion of outsiders or women, but nothing is said of slaves. And on the whole we may still perhaps consider the other explanation possible, that the slaves here represent the farm-servants of olden time, whatever social position they may have held, who at the end of their year's work were allowed to enjoy themselves 'exaequato omnium iure.'

XIV (ANTE CAES. XII) KAL. DEC. (DEC. 19). NP.

OPAL[IA]. (MAFF. AMIT.)
FERIAE OPI: OPI AD FORUM. (AMIT.)

For Ops see on Aug. 25, when the sacrifice was in the Regia, the significance of which I endeavoured to explain. Here it is 'ad forum,' which has lately aroused a little unfruitful dispute. Is the temple of Saturn meant, which was also described as 'ad forum' in the same calendar? This is still the view of Mommsen [2], who seems to hold the old opinion that there was a sacellum Opis attached to the aedes Saturni, or that this aedes was dedicated to both deities [3]. H. Jordan made up his mind that 'ad forum' meant the Regia [4]; but this is not supported by any similar entry in the *Fasti*. Aust and Wissowa believe that Ops had a separate temple 'ad forum,' of which all traces are lost, as has happened with many others [5]; and the latter, as we have already seen, disbelieves in any connexion between Saturnus and Ops, attributing it entirely to Greek influence.

However this may be, the one interesting fact about the

---

[1] p. 50, and note 13. [2] *C. I. L.* i[2]. 337.
[3] O. Gilbert (i. 247 note) holds this latter view.
[4] *Ephem. Epigr.* i. 37. Wissowa (*de Feriis*, v) points out that all such entries, in which the god's name in the dative is followed by the place of sacrifice, apply to consecrated temples only—and the Regia was not one.
[5] Aust, *de Aedibus sacris Populi Romani*, p. 40. Wissowa, l.c., who should not, I think, write of an aedes *in foro*.

temple—or whatever it was—is that it was 'ad forum.' The conjunction of Saturnus and Ops at this place and time must surely indicate some connexion of function between the two. But what it was is not discoverable; under Saturnalia I have merely suggested the direction in which we may look for it.

XII (Ante Caes. x). Kal. Ian. (Dec. 21). NP.
DIVA[LIA]. (MAFF. PRAEN.)

Praen. adds a terribly mutilated note, which Mommsen thus fills up from stray hints in Varro, Pliny (following Verrius), and Macrobius [1]:

FERIAE DIVA[E ANGERONAE, QUAE AB ANGINAE MORBO] APPELL-
[ATUR, QUOD REMEDIA EIUS QUONDAM] PRAE[CEPIT. STATUE-
RUNT EAM ORE OBLIGATO] IN AR[A VOLUPIAE, UT QUI NO]SSET
N[OMEN] OCCUL[TUM URBIS, TACERET. S]UNT TAMEN, [QUI FIERI
ID SACRU]M AIUNT OB AN[NUM NOVUM; MANI]FESTUM ESSE
[ENIM PRINCIPIU]M [A]NNI NOV[I].

The date given by Pliny and Macrobius proves that Angerona was the deity of the Divalia; but the etymology of the latter is useless, and the statement of Pliny as to the statue with the mouth gagged and sealed fails to give us any clue to the nature or function of the goddess [2]. Angerona is, in fact, the North Pole of our exploration: no one has ever reached her, and probably no one ever will. The mention of Volupia by Macrobius gives no help; she is only elsewhere mentioned as one of the numina of the Indigitamenta by Augustine [3]. The only possible clue is that of which Mommsen has taken advantage in the very clever completion of Verrius' last words, viz. the fact that this day (21st) is the centre one of the winter solstice.

---

[1] Varro, *L. L.* 6. 23 'Angeronalia ab Angerona, cui sacrificium fit in curia Acculeia et cuius feriae publicae is dies.' Pliny, *N. H.* 3. 5. 65 'Nomen alterum dicere [nisi] arcanis caerimoniarum nefas habetur;... non alienum videtur hoc loco exemplum religionis antiquae ob hoc maxime silentium institutae; namque diva Angerona, cui sacrificatur a.d. xii Kal. Ian., ore obligato obsignatoque simulacrum habet.' Macr. *Sat.* i. 10 'xii (Kal. Ian.) feriae sunt divae Angeroniae, cui pontifices in sacello Volupiae sacrum faciunt; quam Verrius Flaccus Angeroniam dici ait, quod angores ac sollicitudines animorum propitiata depellat.'

[2] See Wissowa, s. v. Angerona, *Lex.* 350.

[3] *Civ. Dei*, 4. 8.

He here even allows himself an etymology, and derives Angeronalia 'ab angerendo, id est ἀπὸ τοῦ ἀναφέρεσθαι τὸν ἥλιον' : quoting
Plutarch (*de Iside*, ch. 52) for similar Egyptian ideas of the
sun's birth at this time. Though the etymology may be doubtful, the inference from the date of the festival is certainly
acceptable, in the absence of anything more definite : and the
'Praenestine fragments' clearly suggest the word 'annus.'

x (Ante Caes. viii) Kal. Ian. (Dec. 23). NP.
LAR[ENTALIA]. (maff. praen.)

Here again Praen. has a valuable note, which, in this case, is
fairly well preserved : FERIAE IOVI. ACCAE LARENTIAE.
. . . HANC ALII REMI ET ROM[ULI NUTRICEM ALII] MERETRI-
CEM, HERCULIS SCORTUM [FUISSE DIC]UNT : PARENTARI EI
PUBLICE, QUOD P[OPULUM] R[OMANUM] HE[REDEM FECE]RIT
MAGNAE PECUNIAE, QUAM ACCEPE[RAT TESTAME]NTO TARUTILI
AMATORIS SUI [1].

As regards the feriae Iovi we are utterly in the dark.
Macrobius explains it thus : 'Iovique feriae consecratae, quod
aestimaverunt antiqui animas a Iove dari et rursus post mortem
eidem reddi,' which is obviously a late invention. I can see
no possible connexion of Jupiter with the Larentalia, and believe
the conjunction to be accidental.

Mommsen writes : 'De origine Larentalium ipsiusque Laren-
tinae indole ac natura parum constat.' He himself has investigated the myth of Acca Larentia in a memorable essay [2], and
we may take his opinion on the Larentalia as at present conclusive. It is to be noted, however, that the view he formerly
held as to the impossibility of connecting Lārentia and Lăres [3]
is not re-asserted in the new edition of the *Corpus* (vol i) ; the
connexion, he says, may be right, but does not help us to
explain the 'feriae Iovi' or the parentatio (performance of
funeral rites) at the grave of Larentina (or Larentia).

This parentatio seems to me the one thing known to us about

---

[1] Macrob. *Sat.* i. 10. 11 ; Fest. 119 ; and Lact. *Inst.* i. 20. 4 mention the
Larentalia.
[2] *Röm. Forschungen*, vol. ii. p. 1 foll. See also Roscher, s.v. in *Lex.* 5.
[3] Cp. Ovid, *Fasti*, 3. 55.

the Larentalia which can possibly aid us. We are told by Varro that it took place in the Velabrum, 'qua in Novam viam exitur, ut aiunt quidam, ad sepulcrum Accae [1].' The Flamen Quirinalis took part in it, and the Pontifices [2]. Now the Parentalia took place in February. Is it possible that this is a survival from a time when it was in December—a survival, because it was at the tomb of a semi-deity, and was a public function [3]? It is very curious that we have a record of a private parentatio wilfully transferred from February to December, and probably to this day. Cicero, in a mutilated passage from which Plutarch has apparently drawn one of his 'Roman Questions,' seems to have stated that Dec. Brutus (consul 138 B.C.) used to do his parentatio in December [4]. Whether Cicero was here alluding to the Larentalia we do not know ; but Plutarch notes the fact of the parentatio of Larentia in December, and is led thereby to write the quaestio next in order on the story of Larentia [5]. Was the learned Brutus simply a pedant, changing his parentatio to a date which he believed to be the real original one, or had he some special reason for connecting his family with December and Larentia ?

However we may answer this question, there is, perhaps, a bare possibility that the Larentalia was originally a feast of the dead of the old Rome on the Palatine, preserved in the calendar of the completed city only through the reputed survival of the tomb of Larentia in the Velabrum at the foot of the rock.

[1] L. L. 6. 23. The passage is in part hopelessly corrupt.
[2] Gellius, N. A. 7. 7 ; for the Flamen Quir. cf. Gilbert, 1. 88. Cic. Ep. ad Brut. 1. 15. 8. Varro, l.c. says vaguely 'sacerdotes nostri.' Plut. Romulus, 4, gives ὁ τοῦ Ἄρεος ἱερεύς, wrongly.
[3] 'Sacerdotes nostri publice parentant' (Varro, l.c.).
[4] Cic. de Legibus, 2. 21. 54 ; Plut. Q. R. 34.
[5] Plutarch is often led on in this work from one question to another by something he finds in the book he is consulting for the first.

MENSIS IANUARIUS.

THE period of winter leisure which began for the agriculturist in December continued into January. From the solstice to Favonius (i. e. Feb. 7) is Varro's eighth and last division of the agricultural year, in which there is no hard work to be done out of doors (*R. R.* i. 36 : cf. Virg. *Georg.* 1. 312 ; Colum. xi. 2). So too the rustic calendars; 'palus aquitur, salix harundo caedetur.' Columella tells us, however, that if the weather be favourable, it may be possible from the Ides of January 'auspicari culturarum officia.' We have seen that in December this easy time was occupied with a series of religious rites of such extreme antiquity that their meaning was almost entirely lost for the Roman of later ages. After the solstice this series cannot be said to continue : the calendars have only three festivals in January marked with large letters, the Agonia on the 9th, and the two Carmentalia on the 11th and 15th. On the other hand, there were two *feriae conceptivae* in this month which do not appear in the calendars ; the Compitalia (which might, however, fall before the beginning of the month), and the Paganalia towards the end of it. Both these were originally festive meetings in which rural folk took part together, and seem to indicate that agricultural labours had not yet really begun.

KAL. IAN. (JAN. 1). F.

[AESCU]LAPIO, VEDIOVI IN INSULA. (PRAEN.)

This temple of Vediovis was vowed by the praetor L. Furius Purpureo in 200 B. C., and dedicated six years later[1]. For this

---

[1] Livy, 31. 21 ; 34. 53. The MSS have 'deo Iovi' in the former passage, and 'Iovis' in the second ; but it is almost certain that Vediovis is the

obscure deity see on May 21. The connexion between him and Aesculapius (if there were any) is unexplained. The latter was a much older inhabitant of the Tiber island (291 B.C.), and became in time the special deity of that spot [1], which is called by Dionys. (5. 13) νῆσος εὐμεγέθης 'Ασκληπιοῦ ἱερά. Is it possible that an identification of Vediovis with Apollo [2]—so often a god of pestilence—brought the former to the island seat of the healing deity? The connexion between Apollo and Aesculapius is well known.

Another invasion of the island took place almost at the same time. In 194 B.C. a temple of Faunus was dedicated there which had been vowed two years earlier [3]; and it may be worth noting that Faunus also had power to avert pestilence and unfruitfulness, as is seen in the story of Numa and the Faunus-oracle. (Ovid, *Fasti*, 4. 641 foll.)

On Jan. 1, under the later Republic, i. e. after the year 153 B.C., in and after which the consuls began their year of office on this day, it was the custom to give New Year presents by way of good omen, called *strenae* [4]; a word which survives in the French *étrennes*. It is likely enough that the custom was much older than 153 B.C. : the word was said to be derived from a Sabine goddess Strenia, whose sacellum at the head of the Via Sacra is mentioned by Varro (*L. L.* v. 47 [5]), and from whose grove certain sacred twigs were carried to the arx (in procession along the Sacred Way?) at the beginning of each year [6]. But we are not told whether this latter rite always took place on Jan. 1, or was transferred to that day from some other in 153 B.C.

---

deity referred to. See Mommsen in *C. I. L.* i². 305 for the confusion in these passages, and in Livy, 35. 41. (Cp. Ovid, *Fasti*, i. 291-3.)

[1] Livy, *Epit.* 11, and 10. 47; Preller, ii. 241; Plut. *Q. R.* 94; Jordan, in *Comm. in hon. Momms.* p. 349 foll.

[2] See under May 21. Deecke, *Falisker*, 96.

[3] Livy, 33. 42, 34. 53; Jordan, l. c.

[4] These and their later history are the subject of a most exhaustive treatise by Martin Lipenius, in Graevius' *Thesaurus*, vol. xii, p. 405. See also Marq. *Privatleben*, I², 245. For the sentiment implied in the *strenae* see Ovid, *Fasti*, 1. 71 foll. and 175.

[5] Cp. Fest. 290.

[6] Symmachus, ep. 10. 35 'Ab exortu paene urbis Martiae strenarum usus adolevit, auctoritate Tatii regis, qui verbenas felicis arboris ex luco Strenuae anni novi auspices primus accepit.'

III Non. Ian.–Non. Ian. (Jan. 3–5). C.

3	LUDI		LUDI	
4	LUDI	(PHILOC.)	LUDI COMPITALES	(SILV.)
5	LUDI		(COMITALIS, MS.)	

The Compitalia were not *feriae stativae* until late in the
Empire, and then perhaps only so by tradition[1]. They took
place at some date between the Saturnalia (Dec. 17) and Jan. 5;
and we may infer from Philocalus and Silvius as quoted above
that the tendency was to put them late in that period. Not
being a great state-festival, they could be put between Kalends
and Nones.

The original meaning of *compitum* is explained by the
Scholiast on Persius, 4. 28[2] 'Compita sunt loca in quadriviis,
quasi turres, ubi sacrificia, finita agricultura, rustici celebra-
bant. . . . Compita sunt non solum in urbe loca, sed etiam
viae publicae ac diverticulae aliquorum confinium, ubi aediculae
consecrantur patentes. In his fracta iuga ab agricolis ponuntur,
velut emeriti et elaborati operis indicium[3].' From this we
gather that where country cross-roads met, or where in the
parcelling out of agricultural allotments one *semita* crossed
another[4], some kind of altar was erected and the spot held
sacred. This is quite in keeping with the usage of other
peoples: the 'holiness' of cross-roads is a well-known fact in
folk-lore[5]. It may be doubted, however, whether the Scholiast
is right in his explanation of the 'fracta iuga,' which may rather
have been used as a spell of some kind, than as 'emeriti operis
indicium.' Thus Crooke[6] mentions an Indian practice of fixing

[1] Varro, *L. L.* 6. 25 'quotannis is dies concipitur' (for the right reading
of the rest of the passage see Mommsen, *C. I. L.* 305). Macrobius (1. 16.
6) reckons them as conceptivae, in the fourth century; Philoc. and Silv.
may be representing a *traditional* date for a feast which was *iure conceptivus*.
So Momms. Cp. Gell. 10. 24. 3. where the formula for fixing the date is
given; and Cic. *in Pis.* 4. 8. It was the praetor (urbanus ?) who in this
case made the announcement.

[2] Cp. Philargyrius, *Georg.* 2. 382 '[compita] ubi pagani agrestes buccina
convocati solent certa inire consilia'; no doubt discussion about agricultural matters.

[3] Cp. Ovid, *Fasti*, 1. 665, of the Paganalia: 'Rusticus emeritum palo
suspendat aratrum.' (Cp. Tibull. ii. 1. 5.) Such features were perhaps
common to all these rustic winter rejoicings.

[4] *Grom. Vet.* 302. 20 foll.

[5] For Greece see Farnell, *Cults*, ii. 561 and 598.

[6] *Folklore in Northern India*, i. 77.

up a harrow perpendicularly where four roads met, apparently with the object of appeasing the rain-god.

In the city of Rome the *compita* were the meeting-places of *vici* (streets with houses), where sacella were erected to the Lares compitales [1]—two in each case. For the inhabitants of the vici which thus crossed each other, the compitum was the religious centre; and thus arose a quasi-religious organization, which, as including the lowest of the population and even slaves [2], became of much importance in the revolutionary period in connexion with the machinery of electioneering. The 'collegia compitalicia' were abolished by the Senate in B. c. 64, and reconstituted in B. c. 58 by a bill of Clodius *de collegiis.* Caesar again prohibited them, and the ludi compitalicii with them; but the latter were once more revived by Augustus and made part of his general reorganization of the city and its worship [3].

The Compitalia, which the Romans ascribed to Servius Tullius or Tarquinius Superbus [4], was probably first organized as part of the religious system of the united city in the Etruscan period, though it doubtless had its origin in the rustic ideas and practice of which we get a glimpse in the passage quoted from the Scholiast on Persius. Two features of it seem to fit in conveniently with this conjecture: (1) that already mentioned, that even the slaves had a part in it, as well as the plebs; (2) the fact that the *magistri vicorum*, who were responsible for the festival, wore the *toga praetexta* on the day of its celebration [4]—which looks like a Tarquinian innovation in an anti-aristocratic sense.

v Id. Ian. (Jan. 9). ℞?

AGON. (MAFF. PRAEN.) A mutilated note in Praen. gives the word Agonium.

It may be doubted whether the Roman scholars themselves

---

[1] Marq. 203; Dion. Hal. 4. 14; Ovid, *Fasti*, 2. 615 and 5. 140. Wissowa (*Myth. Lex.* s.v. Lares, p. 1874) would limit them in origin to the pagi outside the septem montes, as the latter had their own sacra.

[2] Dion. Hal. 4. 14 οὐ τοὺς ἐλευθέρους ἀλλὰ τοὺς δούλους ἔταξε (i.e. Serv. Tull.) παρεῖναί τε καὶ συνιερουργεῖν, ὡς κεχαρισμένης τοῖς ἥρωσι τῆς τῶν θεραπόντων ὑπηρεσίας (Cic. pro Sestio, 15. 34).

[3] Marq. 204; Rushforth, *Latin Historical Inscriptions*, p. 59 foll.

[4] Pliny, *N. H.* 36. 204; Macrob. 1. 7. 34; Dion. l.c.

[5] Asconius, p. 6, K. Sch. Livy, 34. 7. 2.

knew for certain what was meant by AGON, and whether the explanations they give are anything better than guesses based on analogy[1]. Ovid calls the day 'dies agonalis':

> Ianus agonali luce piandus erit (*Fasti*, I. 318).
> Nomen agonalem credit habere diem (Ibid. I. 324).

and gives a number of amusing derivations which prove his entire ignorance. Festus[2] gives Agonium as the name of the day (which agrees with Verrius in Fast. Praen.), and says that *agonia* was an old word for hostia. Varro calls the day 'agonalis'[3]; Ovid in another place Agonalia[4]. A god Agonius mentioned by St. Augustine[5] is probably only an invention of the pontifices. The fact is that the Romans knew neither what the real form of the word was, nor what it meant. The attempt to explain it by the apparitor's word at a sacrifice, *agone*? (shall I slay?) is still approved by some, but is quite uncertain[6].

The original meaning of the word, if it ever were in common use, must have vanished long before Latin was a written language. The only traces of it, besides its appearance in the calendars, are in the traditional name for the Quirinal hill, Collis Agonus, in its gate, 'porta agonensis,' and its college of Salii agonenses[7]. It would seem thus to have had some special connexion with the Colline city.

The same word appears in the calendars for three other days, March 17 (Liberalia), May 21 (Agon. Vediovi), Dec. 11 (Septimontium); but it is impossible to make out any connexion between these and Jan. 9. Nor can we be sure that the sacrifice (if such it was), indicated by Agon, had any relation to the other ceremonies of the days thus marked[8]. On Jan. 9

---

[1] So Wissowa, *de Feriis*, xii note. Cp. his article 'Agonium' in the new edition of Pauly's *Real-Encycl.*

[2] p. 10. Cp. Ovid, *Fasti*, I. 331 'Et pecus antiquus dicebat agonia sermo.'

[3] He uses the plural: 'Agonales (dies) per quos rex in regia arietem immolat' (*L. L.* 6. 12). But only Jan. 9 seems to be alluded to.

[4] *Fasti*, I. 325: cf. Macrob. I. 16. 5.

[5] *Civ. Dei*, 4. 11. 16. Ambrosch (*Studien*, 149) thinks it possible that Agonius may have been a god of the Colline city.

[6] Bücheler, *Umbrica*, p. 30. B. apparently sees in the Umbrian 'sakreu perakneu' an equivalent to 'hostias agonales.' The Iguvian ritual is certainly the most likely document to be useful; it at least shows how large was the store of sacrificial vocabulary.

[7] Fest. p. 10. For the Salii, Varro, *L. L.* 6. 14.

[8] Wissowa, *de Feriis*, xii.

Ovid does indeed say that Janus was 'agonali luce piandus,' and
on May 21 the Fasti Venusini add a note 'Vediovi' to the letters
AGON; but there is no distinct proof that the agonium was
a sacrifice to Janus or to Vediovis. We are utterly in the
dark [1].

On this day the Rex sacrorum offered a ram (to Janus?)
in the Regia. Ovid says [2] that though the meaning of Agon
is doubtful,

> ita rex placare sacrorum
> Numina lanigerae coniuge debet ovis.

It is provokingly uncertain whether this ram was actually
sacrificed to Janus : Varro does not say so, and Ovid only
implies it [3]. But we may perhaps assume it on the ground that
once at least in the ritual of the Fratres Arvales [4] the ram is
mentioned as Janus' victim.

If this be so, we are carried back by this sacrifice to the very
beginnings of Rome, and get a useful clue to the nature of the
god Janus. The Rex sacrorum was the special representative in
later times of the king ; the king, living in the Regia, was the
equivalent in the State of the head of the household. The two
most important and sacred parts of the house are the door
(ianua, ianus), and the hearth (vesta) [5], and the numina inhabiting and guarding these are Janus and Vesta, who, as is well
known, were respectively the first and the last deities to be
invoked at all times in Roman religious custom. The whole
house certainly had a religious importance, like everything else
in intimate relation to man; and Macrobius is not romancing
when he says (quoting *mythici*) 'Regnante Iano omnium domos

[1] When Varro writes (*L. L.* 6. 12) that the dies agonales are those in which
the Rex sacrorum sacrifices a ram in the Regia, he may be including all the
four days, and not only Jan. 9. I think this is likely ; but we only know
it of Jan. 9.

[2] *Fasti*, i. 333. Varro *L. L.* 6. 12 'Agonales (dies) per quos rex in regia
arietem immolat.'

[3] Cp. lines 318 and 333.

[4] Henzen, 144. An 'agna' is the only other animal sacrifice we know
of to Janus (Roscher, in *Lex.* 42).

[5] Roscher, in *Lex.* s. v. Ianus, 29 foll. (cp. for much interesting kindred
matter, De-Marchi, *Il Culto privato*, p. 20 foll.). Roscher's attempt to find
an analogy between the Forum and the house is interesting, but unluckily
the positions 'ad Forum' of the 'Ianus geminus' and the 'aedes Vestae' do
not exactly answer to those of the door and hearth of a Roman house.

religione et sanctitate fuisse munitas [1].' But the door and the hearth were of special importance, as the folk-lore of every people fully attests ; and it is hardly possible to avoid the conclusion that we must look for the origin of Janus in the ideas connected with the house-door, just as we have always found Vesta in the fire on the hearth. Whatever be the true etymology of Janus, and however wild the interpretations of his nature and cult both in ancient and modern times, we shall always have firm ground to stand on if we view him in relation to the primitive worship of the house [2]. There is hardly an attribute or a cult-title of Janus that cannot be deduced with reason from this root-idea.

The old Roman scholars, who knew as little about Janus as we do, started several explanations of a cosmical kind, which must have been quite strange to the average Roman worshipper. He was a sun-god [3], and his name is the masculine form of Diana (= moon) ; he was the *mundus*, i. e. the heaven, or the atmosphere [4]. These were, of course, mere guesses characteristic of a pedantic age which knew nothing of the old Roman religious mind. If Janus ever had been a nature-deity, his attributes as such were completely worn away in historical times, or had lost their essential character in the process of constant application to practical matters by a prosaic people. How far the Roman of the Augustan age understood his great *deorum deus* may be gathered from Ovid's treatment of the subject, itself no doubt a poetical version of the learned speculation of Varro and others. The poet 'interviews' the deity with the object of finding out the lost and hidden meaning of his most obvious peculiarities, and the old god condescends to answer with a promptness and good temper that would do credit to the victims of the modern journalist. The curious thing is that the real origin, humble, simple, and truly Latin,

---

[1] *Sat.* i. 9. 2 ; Procopius, *B. G.* i. 25, who says that 'Janus belonged to the gods whom the Romans in their tongue called Penates,' seems to be alluding to the same connexion of this god and the house.

[2] We owe this explanation of Janus chiefly to Roscher's article, and Roscher himself owed it to the fact that his study of Janus for the article was a second and not a first attempt. In *Hermes der Windgott* (Leipzig, 1878) he had arrived at a very different and a far less rational conclusion. The influence of Mannhardt and the folk-lorists set him on the right track.

[3] Nigidius Figulus in Macrob. i. 9. 8.

[4] See Roscher, *Lex.* 44.

escaped the observation both of the interviewer and the deity.

Before I state more definitely the grounds on which this simple explanation of Janus is based, it will be as well to deal shortly with the more ambitious ones.

1. The theory that Janus was a sun-god has the support of Roman antiquarians [1], and was probably suggested by them to the moderns. Nigidius Figulus, the Pythagorean mystic, seems to have been the first to broach the idea: we have no evidence that Varro gave his sanction to it. It was Nigidius who first suggested the idea of the relation of Janus to Diana (Dianus, Diana = Janus, Jana), which found much favour with Preller and Schwegler [2] at a time when neither comparative philology nor comparative mythology were as well understood as now. But the common argument, both in ancient and modern times, has been that which Macrobius quotes from certain speculators whom he does not name: ' Ianum quidam solem demonstrari volunt, et ideo geminum quasi utriusque ianuae coelestis poten- tem, qui exoriens aperiat diem, occidens claudat,' &c. It is obvious that this is pure speculation by a Roman of the cosmo- politan age: it is an attempt to explain the Janus geminus as the representation of one of the great forces of nature. But it has nothing to do with the ideas of the early Italian farmer.

2. The theory that Janus was a god of the ' vault of heaven ' was also started by the ancients, as may be seen from the chapter of Macrobius quoted above. Recently it has been adopted by Professor Deecke in his Etruscan researches [3]. He seems to hold that Janus in Etruria, as a god of the arch of

[1] Macrob. 1. 9. 9 ; Lydus, de Mensibus, 4. 6 (who quotes Lutatius).

[2] Schwegler, R. G. i. 218 foll.; Preller, 1. 168 foll. The etymology is weak ; the god and goddess have nothing common in cult or myth ; it is not certain that Diana was originally the moon ; and the great Italian deities are not coupled together in this way.

[3] ii. 125 foll. Cf. Müller's Etrusker (ed. Deecke), ii. 58 foll. Müller, with his usual good sense, concluded from the evidence that the Latin Janus was a god of gates ; but he thought that an Etruscan deity of the vault or arch of heaven had been amalgamated with him. This is not impossible, if there was really such an Etruscan god ; and Deecke finds him in Ani, who in Etruscan theology seems to have had his seat in the northern part of the heaven (Mart. Capell. 1. 45) where Janus was also represented in the templum of Piacenza (Lex. s. v. Janus, p. 28). But this must remain a doubtful point, even though Lydus (4. 2) tells us that Varro said that the god παρὰ Θούσκοις οὐρανὸν λέγεσθαι.

heaven, was represented on arches and gates in that country, and came to Rome when the Romans learnt the secret of the arch from the Etruscans. That the Romans were the pupils of the Etruscans in this particular seems to be true ; but if Janus only came to Rome with the arch (Deecke says in Numa's time) it is hard to see how he could have so quickly gained his peculiar place in Roman worship and legend. I cannot think that Deecke has here improved on the conclusions of his predecessor.

Speculations about Janus as a heaven-god have been pushed still further. Here is a passage from a book which is almost a work of genius[1], yet embodies many theories of which its author may by this time have repented : 'He who prayed (in ancient Italy) began his prayer looking to the East, but ended it looking to the West. Herein we find expressed the conception of the unity and indivisibility of Nature ; whose symbol is the most characteristic figure of the Italian religion, the double-headed Janus, the highest god, and the god of all things, all times, and all gods. He unites the dualistic opposites which complete the world—beginning and end, morning and evening, outgoing and ingoing. He is the god of the year, which finds its completion in its own orbit, and as he is the god of time, so he is the god of the Kosmos, which like a circle displays both beginning and end at once.' He then quotes a passage from Messalla, which Macrobius has preserved, in support of this astonishing product of the rude mind of the primitive Roman[2]. Of this Messalla we only know that he was consul in 53 B.C., and that (as Macrobius tells us) he was augur for fifty-five years, in the course of which period, after the fashion of his day, he wrote works of which the object was to find a philosophic basis for the quaint phenomena of the Roman religion. His speculations on the double head of Janus cannot help us to discover the primitive nature of our deity ; Janus may have been the ancient heaven-god of the Latins, but these guesses are the product of a spurious and eclectic Greek philosophy.

3. There is another possible explanation of Janus, which is not mentioned in Roscher's article, but is perhaps worth as much consideration as the two last. Professor Rhys, in

---

[1] Nissen, *Templum*, p. 228. [2] Macrob. 1. 9. 16.

his *Hibbert Lectures on Celtic Mythology*[1], somewhat casually identified Janus with the Celtic god Cernunnos, whom he considers to be the Gallic deity called by Caesar *Dis Pater*. The one striking fact in favour of this equation is that Cernunnos was represented as having three faces, and like Janus, as a head without a body—the lower portion of the block being utilized for other purposes[2]. He seems to have been a chthonic deity, and is compared to and even identified by Rhys with Heimdal of the Norsemen and Teutons, who was the warder or porter of the gods, and of the underworld[3], who sits as the 'wind-listening' god, whose ears are of miraculous sharpness, who is the father of man, and the sire of kings. Both Cernunnos and Heimdal are thought further to have been, like Janus, the *fons et origo* of all things. According to Caesar the Gauls believed themselves to be descended from their deity; and both the Celtic and Scandinavian gods seem to have had, like the Roman, some connexion with the divisions of time.

It must be allowed that these two gods taken together supply parallels to Janus' most salient characteristics; and even to one or two of the less prominent and more puzzling ones, such as the connexion with springs[4]. It is not impossible that all three may have grown out of a common root; but in the cases of Cernunnos and Heimdal it does not seem any longer possible to trace this, owing to heavy incrustations of poetical mythology. In the case of the Roman, the chance is a better one, in spite of philosophical speculation, ancient and modern.

We return from philosophers and mythologists to early Rome. The one fact on which we must fix our attention is that on the north-east of the forum Romanum was the famous Janus geminus, which from representations on coins[5] we can see was not a temple, but a gateway, with entrance and exit connected by walls, within which was, we may suppose, the double-headed figure of Janus which is familiar on Roman coins. The same word janus is applied to the gate and to the

---

[1] p. 93 foll.; Caes. *B. G.* 6. 18.
[2] M. Mowat thought that this was Janus naturalized in Gaul; but with Prof. Rhys (p. 81 note) I cannot but think this unlikely.
[3] See *Corpus Poeticum Boreale*, ii. 465.
[4] Roscher, in *Lex.* 18; Rhys, l. c. 88.
[5] Roscher, *Lex.* 17; Jordan, *Topogr.* 1. 2. 351.

numen who guarded it, lived in it, and was as inseparable from it as Vesta from the fire on the hearth[1]. The word does not seem to have been used for the gate of a city, but for the point of passage into a space within a city, such as a market, or a street. At Rome there were several such jani[2]; probably two or more leading into the forum, as well as the more famous one, which alone appears to have had a strictly religious signification[3]. The connexion of the god with entrances is thus a certainty, though we are puzzled by his apparent absence from the gates of the city[4]. The double head would signify nothing transcendental, but simply that the numen of the entrance to house or market was concerned both with entrance and exit. It is not peculiar to Italy, or to Janus, but is found on coins in every part of the Mediterranean (Roscher, *Lex.* 53 foll.): in no case, it is worth noting, does the double head represent any of the great gods of heaven, such as Zeus, Apollo, &c., but Dionysus, Boreas, Argos, unknown female heads[5], &c. Its history does not seem to have been worked out; but we can be almost sure that it does not represent the sun, and has no relation to the arch of heaven.

Now keeping in mind the fact that Janus is the guardian spirit of entrances, let us recall again the fact that he was the first deity in all invocations both public and private[6], and that Vesta was the last[7]. Vesta in the house was, as Cicero expresses it, 'rerum custos intimarum'; she presided over the penetralia—the *last* part of the house to which any stranger could be admitted; exactly the opposite position to that of Janus

[1] Cic. *De Nat. Deorum*, 2. 27. 67 'Transitiones perviae iani, foresque in liminibus profanarum aedium ianuae nominantur.' Cp. Macrob. 1. 9. 7.

[2] On the whole question see Jordan, *Topogr.* 1. 2. 215 foll. Ovid (*Fasti*, 1. 257) asks the god 'Cum tot sint iani, cur stas sacratus in uno?'

[3] From Falerii came another janus, with a four-headed simulacrum, which was set up in the Forum transitorium (Macr. 1. 9. 13; Jordan, *Top.* 1. 2. 348).

[4] Preller made an attempt, which Roscher approves, to identify Portunus with Janus, Portunus being, according to Varro, 'Deus portuum portarumque praeses' (Interpr. Veron. *Aen.* v. 241). But see on Aug. 17.

[5] The nearest approach to Janus is the Hermes θυραῖος or στροφαῖος (single head only?) and Hermes with two, three, or four heads at the meeting-points of streets. These are points which suggested to Roscher in his older work an elaborate comparison of Hermes and Janus (p. 119 foll.).

[6] See Marq 25, 26 and notes.

[7] Cic. *N. D.* 2. 27; Preller, ii. 172.

at the entrance [1]. Both deities retained at all times the essential mark of primitive ideas of the supernatural : they resided in, and in a sense were, the doorway and the hearth respectively. What we know of the priests who served them tells the same tale of an origin in the house, and the family—the foundation of all Italian civilization. Vesta was served by her sacred virgins, and these, we can no longer doubt, were the later representatives of the daughters of the head of the family, or the headman of the community [2]; the innermost part of the house was theirs, the care of the fire, the stores (penus), and the cooking. To the father, the defender of the family, belonged naturally the care of the entrance, the dangerous point, where both evil men and evil spirits might find a way in. And surely this must be the explanation of the fact that no priest is to be found for Janus in the Roman system but the Rex sacrorum [3], the lineal representative of the ancient religious duties of the king, and therefore, we may infer with certainty, of those of the primitive chief, and of the head of the household [4]. In the most ancient order of the priesthoods, the Rex sacrorum came first, just as Janus was the first of all the gods [5]: then came the three great Flamines, and then the Pontifex maximus, in whose care and power were the Vestals. Translating the order into terms of the primitive family, we have first the head of the house, next the sons, and lastly (as women do not appear in these lists), the daughters represented by the later priesthood, to which they were legally subordinated. The order of the gods, the order of the priests, and the natural position of the entrance to the house, all seem to lead us to the same conclusion, that the beginning of Janus and his cult are

[1] For the evidence of this position of Janus in the cults of the house see Roscher, *Lex.* 32 ; it is indirect, but sufficiently convincing.

[2] See my article 'Vestales' in *Dict. of Antiquities*, ed. 2.

[3] Marq. 321 foll. Besides the sacrifice in the Regia on Jan. 9, the Rex and his wife, the Regina sacrorum, sacrificed to Juno in the Regia on the Kalends of every month, and apparently also to Janus (Junonius) to whom there were twelve altars (in the Regia ?) one for each month. Macr. 1. 9. 16 and 1. 15. 19.

[4] For the father as the natural defender of the family, see Westermarck, *Hist. of Human Marriage*, ch. 3.

[5] Festus, 185 'Maximus videtur Rex, dein Dialis, post hunc Martialis, quarto loco Quirinalis, quinto pontifex maximus.' For the corresponding place of Janus, Liv. 8. 9. 6; Cato, *R. R.* 134 ; Marq. 26.

to be sought, and may be found, in the early Italian family dwelling.

We may agree with Roscher, who has worked out this part of the subject with skill, that this position of Janus in the worship of the family and the state is the origin of all the practices in which he appears as a god of beginnings. For these the reader must be referred to Roscher's article[1], or to Preller, or to Mommsen, who sees in this aspect of the god, and rightly no doubt, that which chiefly reflects the notion of him held by the ordinary Roman. He was himself the oldest god, the beginner of all things, and of all acts[2]; to him in legend is ascribed the introduction of the arts, of agriculture, ship-building, &c.[3]. He is an object of worship at the beginning of the year, the month, and the day[4]. All this sprang, not from an abstract idea of beginning—an idea which has no Roman parallel in being sanctified by a presiding deity, but from the concrete fact that the entrance of the house was the *initium*, or beginning of the house, and at the same time the point from which you started on all undertakings.

Such developments of the original Janus were no doubt as old as the State itself. In the Salian hymn he is already 'deorum deus'[5], and 'duonus cerus'[6], which Festus tells us meant creator bonus. But even in the State there are, as we have seen, sufficiently clear traces of his original nature to forbid us to attribute these titles to any lofty and abstract philosophical ideas of religion.

The known cult-titles of Janus are for the most part explicable in the same way. Geminus, Patulcius, Clusius, and Matutinus, speak for themselves. Junonius probably arose from the con-currence of the cults of Janus and Juno on the Kalends of each month, as Macrobius tells us[7]. Consivius[8] is explained by Roscher as connected with *serere*, and used of Janus as creator (beginner of life: cf. *duonus cerus*). Curiatius, Patricius, and

---

[1] *Lex.* 37 foll.; Preller, 1. 166 foll.; Mommsen, *R. H.* i. 173.

[2] Ἔφορος πάσης πράξεως, says Lydus, 4. 2, quoting Varro; cp. Ovid, *Fasti*, 1. 165 foll.

[3] Plut. *Q. R.* 22.

[4] Macrob. 1. 9. 16; Horace, *Sat.* ii. 6. 20 foll.

[5] Macrob. 1. 9. 14.

[6] Varro, *L. L.* 7. 26; Fest. 122.   [7] Macr. 1. 9. 16.

[8] Macr. l. c. Wissowa (*de Feriis*, vi) says the true form is consevius; but the etymology holds.

Quirinus[1] are titles arising from the worship of the god in gentes, curiae, and the completed state, and have no significance in regard to his nature.

III Id. Ian. (Jan. 11). ℞.
KARM[ENTALIA]. (praen. maff.)

XVIII Kal. Feb. (Jan. 15). ℞.
KAR[MENTALIA]. (praen. maff. phil. caer.)

The full name of the festival is supplied by Philoc. and Silv. There is a much mutilated note in Praen. on Jan. 11 which is completed by Mommsen thus[2]: '[Feriae Carmenti ... quae partus curat omniaque] futura ; ob quam ca[usam in aede eius cavetur ab scorteis tanquam] omine morticino.'

The first point to be noticed here is that the same deity has two festival days, with an interval of three days between them. There is no exact parallel to this in the calendar, though there are several instances of something analogous[3]. The Lemuria are on May 9, 11, 13 ; but here are three days, and no special deity. Kindred deities have their festivals separated by three days, as Consus and Ops (Aug. 21, 25) ; and we may compare the Fordicidia and Cerealia on April 15 and 19, and the Quinquatrus and Tubilustrium, both apparently sacred to Mars, on March 19 and 23. All festivals occur on days of uneven number ; and if there was an extension to two or more days, the even numbers were passed over[4]. But the Romans did not apparently consider the two Carmentalia to be two parts of the same festival, but two different festivals, or they would not have tried to account as they did for the origin of the second day. It was said to have been added by a victorious general who left Rome by the Porta Carmentalis to attack Fidenae[5], or by the matrons who had refused to perform the function of women, in anger at being deprived by the Senate of the right of

[1] Roscher, *Lex.* 21, 26, 40.

[2] *C. I. L.* I. 307, on the evidence of Ovid, *Fast.* I. 629 and Varro, *L. L.* 7. 84.

[3] Wissowa, *de Feriis,* viii.   [4] Mommsen, *C. I. L.* I. 288.

[5] Fast. Praen. on Jan. 15 (mutilate l). Cp. Ovid, *Fast.* I. 619 and Plut. *Q. R.* 56. Festus, 245.

riding in *carpenta*; and who, when the decree was withdrawn, testified their satisfaction in this curious way.

It does not seem possible to discover the real meaning of the double festival. It has been suggested[1] that the two days represent the so-called Roman and Sabine cities, like the two bodies of Salii and Luperci. This guess is hardly an impossible one, but it is only a guess, and has nothing to support it but a casual statement by Plutarch that the Carmentalia were instituted at the time of the *synoikismos* of Latin and Sabine cities[2].

There is fortunately little doubt about the nature of Carmenta and the general meaning of the cult. In all the legends into which she was woven[3] her most prominent characteristic is the gift of prophecy; she is the 'vates fatidica,' &c.,

> Cecinit quae prima futuros
> Aeneadas magnos et nobile Pallanteum.

So Ovid, at the end of his account of her:

> At felix *vates*, ut dis gratissima vixit,
> Possidet hunc Iani sic dea mense diem.

The power is expressed in her very name, for *carmen* signifies a spell, a charm, a prophecy, as well as a poem. Now there is clear evidence that either women alone had access to the temple at the Porta Carmentalis, or that they were the chief frequenters of it; and they are even said to have built a temple themselves[4]. Where we find women worshipping a deity of prophecy we may be fairly sure that that deity also has some influence on childbirth. 'The reason,' writes the late Prof. Nettleship[5], 'why the Carmentes are worshipped by matrons is because they tell the fortunes of the children'—and also,

---

[1] By Huschke, *Röm. Jahr*, 199. There was probably more than one Carmenta (Gell. 16. 16. 4), if we consider Porrima and Postverta as two forms of the goddess; and the two days may have some relation to this duality. Perhaps there were two altars in the temple. Ovid, *Fasti*, 1. 627.

[2] Plut. *Romulus*, 21.

[3] See Wissowa in *Lex. Myth.* i. 851; Ovid. *Fasti*, 1. 461 foll.; Virg. *Aen.* 8. 336. The eighth Aeneid, it may be remarked, should be learnt by heart by all investigators into Roman antiquity.

[4] Plut. *Q. R.* 56: cp. Dion. Hal. 1. 31. 1-9, from whom Plutarch may have drawn his information, directly or perhaps through Juba. For the temple they built cp. Gell. 18. 7. 2. If this temple be a different one from that under the Capitol, it may suggest an explanation of the double festival.

[5] *Studies in Latin Literature*, p. 48 foll.; *Journal of Philology*, xi. 178.

surely, because they tell the fortunes of the women in child-birth[1].

I am inclined to agree with my old tutor that the Carmentes may originally have been wise women whose skill and spells assisted the operation of birth. I do not think we can look for an explanation of the titles Porrima and Postverta elsewhere than in the two positions in which the child may issue from the womb, over each of which a Carmentis watched[2]; and there is in fact no doubt that Carmenta was a birth-goddess[3]. The argument then would be that the spiritual origin attributed to superior knowledge transforms the owner of the knowledge into a divine person. As Sir A. Lyall says[4] (of the genesis of local deities in Berar), 'The immediate motive (of deifica-tion) is nothing but a vague inference from great natural gifts or from strange fortunes to supernatural visitation, or from power during life to power prolonged beyond it.'

Of the cult of Carmenta we know hardly anything. She had a flamen of her own[5], like other ancient goddesses, Palatua, Furrina, Flora. His sacrificial duties must have been confined to the preparing of cereal offerings, for there was a taboo in this cult excluding all skins of animals—all leather—from the temple.

> Scortea non illi fas est inferre sacello[6],
> Ne violent puros exanimata focos.

Varro writes 'In aliquot sacris et sacellis scriptum habemus: Ne quid scorteum adhibeatur ideo ne morticinum quid adsit.' We could wish that he had told us what these sacra and sacella were[7]; as it is we must be content to suppose that a goddess

---

[1] See on Fortuna, above, p. 167.

[2] Ovid, *Fast.* I. 633; Varro in Gell. 16. 6. 4. Nettleship takes a different view of these words. But see Wissowa in *Lex.* I. 853; Preller, i. 406.

[3] St. Augustine, *C. D.* 4. 11 'In illis deabus quae fata nascentibus canunt et vocantur Carmentes.'

[4] *Asiatic Studies*, p. 20.

[5] Cic. *Brut.* 14. 56; *C I. L.* vi. 3720; and *Eph. Ep.* iv. 759. The rite of Jan. 11 is called 'sacrum pontificale' by Ovid (*Fast.* I. 462), whence we infer that the pontifices had a part in it as well as the flamen.

[6] Ovid, *Fast.* I. 629. Cp. Varro, *L. L.* 7. 84. This passage of Varro may possibly raise a doubt whether the taboo did not arise from a mistaken interpretation of the words *scortum* and *pellicula*, as Carmenta was especially worshipped by matrons.

[7] The more so as we have no inscriptions relating to Carmenta. Though her flaminium continued to exist under the Empire, she herself

of birth could have nothing to do with the slaughter of animals.

The position of the temple was at the foot of the southern end of the Capitol, near the Porta Carmentalis [1], where, according to Servius, she was said to have been buried (cp. Acca Larentia, Dec. 23). It is noticeable that the festivals of this winter period are connected with sites near the Capitol and Forum ; we have already had Saturnus, Ops, and Janus.

If the reader should ask why a goddess of birth should be specially worshipped in the depth of winter, he may perhaps find a reason for it after reading the third chapter of Westermarck's *History of Human Marriage*. As far as we can judge from the calendar, April was the month at Rome when marriages and less legal unions were especially frequent [2]; during May and the first days of June marriages were not desirable [3]. In January therefore births might naturally be expected.

Ovid tells us (1. 463) that *Juturna* was also worshipped on Jan. 11 [4]; but whether in any close connexion with Carmenta we do not know. They are both called Nymphs; but from this we can hardly make any inference. Juturna was certainly a fountain-deity : I can find no good evidence that this was one of Carmenta's attributes. The fount of Juturna was near the Vesta-temple [5], and therefore close to the Forum : its water was used, says Servius, for all kinds of sacrifices, and itself was the object of sacrifice in a drought. All took part in the festival who used water in their daily work ('qui artificium aqua exercent'). But the Juturnalia appears in no calendar, and Aust is no doubt right in explaining it only as the dedication-festival of the temple built by Augustus in B.C. 2 [6].

---

practically disappeared. I am inclined to guess that her attributes were to some extent usurped by the more popular and plebeian Fortuna.

[1] Solinus, 1. 13 ; Serv. *Aen.* 8. 336 and 337.

[2] See especially under April 1 and 28, the days of Fortuna virilis and Flora.

[3] Ovid, *Fasti*, 6. 223 foll.

[4] Juturnalia, Serv. *Aen.* 12. 139.

[5] Jordan, *Topogr.* 1. 2. 370 ; Wissowa in *Lex.* s. v. Iuturna.

[6] Aust, *de Aedibus sacris*, p. 45.

FERIAE SEMENTIVAE [1]. PAGANALIA.

Under date of Jan. 24–26, Ovid [2] writes in charming verse of the *feriae conceptivae* called Sementivae (or -tinae), which from his account would seem to be identical with the so-called Paganalia [3]. Just as the Compitalia of the city probably had its origin in the country (see on Jan. 3–5), though the rustic *compita* were almost unknown to the later Romans, so the festival of sowing was kept up in the city ('a pontificibus dictus,' Varro, *L. L.* 6. 26) as Sementinae, long after the Roman population had ceased to sow. In the country it was known— so we may guess—by the less technical name of Paganalia [4], as being celebrated by the rural group of homesteads known as the *pagus*.

As to the object and nature of the festival, let Ovid speak for himself:

> State coronati plenum ad praesaepe iuvenci:
>   Cum tepido vestrum vere redibit opus.
> Rusticus emeritum palo suspendat aratrum [5]:
>   Omne reformidat frigida volnus humus.
> Vilice, da requiem terrae, semente peracta:
>   Da requiem terram qui coluere viris.
> Pagus agat festum: pagum lustrate, coloni,
>   Et date paganis annua liba focis.
> Placentur frugum matres, Tellusque Ceresque,
>   Farre suo, gravidae visceribusque suis.
> Officium commune Ceres et Terra tuentur:
>   Haec praebet causam frugibus, illa locum.

Ceres and Tellus, 'consortes operis,' are to be invoked to bring to maturity the seed sown in the autumn, by preserving it from all pests and hurtful things; and also to assist the sower in his

---

[1] Sementinae, according to Jordan in Prell. 2. 5, note 2.

[2] *Fasti*, 1. 658 foll.

[3] Paganicae (feriae), Varro, *L. L.* 6. 26. Varro seems to separate the two: after mentioning the Sementinae, which he says was 'sationis causa susceptae,' he goes on 'Paganicae eiusdem agriculturae susceptae, ut haberent in agris omnes pagi,' &c. But the distinction is perhaps only of place; or if of time also, yet not of object and meaning.

[4] So Marq. 199, and Hartmann, *Röm. Kal.* 203. Preller thinks the Sementinae were in September, before the autumn sowing; and it is possible that there were two feasts of the name, one before the autumn, another before the spring, sowing. Lydus (*de Mens.* 3. 3) speaks of two days separated by seven others; on the former they sacrificed to Tellus (Demeter), on the latter to Ceres (Κόρη); two successive nundinae (market-days) are here meant.

[5] Cp. Scholiast on Persius, 4. 28; and see under Compitalia, Jan. 3–5.

work in the spring that is at hand. This at least is how
I understand the lines (681, 682):

> Cum serimus, caelum ventis aperite serenis;
> Cum latet, aetheria spargite semen aqua.

Or if it be argued that both these lines may very well refer
to the spring, it is at least certain that the poet understood the
festival to cover the past autumn sowing:

> Utque dies incerta sacro, sic tempora certa,
> Seminibus iactis est ubi fetus ager[1].

Varro tells us[2] that the time of the autumn sowing extended
from the equinox to the winter solstice; after which, as we
have seen, the husbandmen rested from their labours in the
fields, and enjoyed the festivals we have been discussing since
Dec. 17 (Consualia). The last of these is the Paganalia, i. e. the
one nearest in date, if we may go by Ovid, to the time for
setting to work at the spring sowing, which began on or
about Feb. 7 (Favonius)[3]. It would thus be quite natural that
this festival should have reference not only to the seed already
in the ground, but also to that which was still to be sown.
If Ovid lays stress on the former, Varro and Lydus seem to be
thinking chiefly of the latter[4].

Ovid has told us what was the nature of the rites. According
to him, Ceres and Tellus were the deities concerned, and with
this Lydus agrees. We need not be too certain about the
names[5], considering the 'fluidity' and impersonality of early
Roman *numina* of this type; but the type itself is obvious.
There were offerings of cake, and a sacrifice of a pregnant sow;
the oxen which had served in the ploughing were decorated
with garlands; prayers were offered for the protection of the
seed from bird and beast and disease. If we may believe

---

[1] Ovid, 1. 661.   [2] *R. R.* 1. 34; Plin. *N. H.* 18. 204.

[3] Cp. Varro, *R. R.* 1. 29, 36. Cp. the Rustic Calendars for February.

[4] Varro, *L. L.* 6. 26 'sationis causa'; and Lydus says that the feast could
not be 'stativae,' because the ἀρχὴ σπόρου cannot be fixed to a day. Lydus'
reason is not a good one, if the sowing did not begin till Feb. 7; but it is
plain that he understands the rites as *prophylactic*. I may note that
Columella seems to know little about spring sowing (11. 2: cp. 2. 8).
Mommsen, *R. H.* ii. 364, says that spring sowing was exceptional.

[5] See under Cerialia, April 19.

a note of Probus'[1], *oscilla* were hung from the trees, as at the Latin festival, &c., doubtless as a charm against evil influences.

VI KAL. FEB. (Jan. 27). C.

AEDIS [CASTORIS ET PO]LLUCIS DEDICA[TA EST . . .]. (PRAEN.)

Mommsen's restoration of this note in the Fasti of Praeneste is based on Ov. *Fast.* I. 705-8:

> At quae venturas praecedet sexta Kalendas,
>   Hac sunt Ledaeis templa dicata deis.
> Fratribus illa deis fratres de gente deorum
>   Circa Iuturnae composuere lacus.

But Livy[2] gives the Ides of July as the day of dedication, and a difference of learned opinion has arisen[3]. July 15, B.C. 496, is the traditional date of the battle of Lake Regillus, and the temple was dedicated B.C. 484—the result of the Consul's vow in that battle[4]. Mommsen infers that Livy confused the date of the dedication with that of the battle, and that Jan. 27 is right. Aust and others differ, and refer the latter date to a restoration by Tiberius, probably in A.D. 6[5]. The mistake in Livy is easy to explain, and Mommsen's explanation seems sufficient[6]. Three beautiful columns of Tiberius' temple are still to be seen at the south-eastern end of the Forum, near the temple of Vesta, and close to the lacus Juturnae, where the Twins watered their steeds after the battle[7].

The very early introduction of the Dioscuri into the Roman worship is interesting as being capable of unusually distinct proof. They must have been known long before the battle

---

[1] Ad Virg. *Georg.* 2. 385 ; Marq. 200 and 192, where the old explanation (Macr. I. 7. 34) seems to be adopted, that these were substitutes for human or other victims (cp. Bötticher, *Baumkultus*, 80 foll.). We have no clear evidence for this, and I am not disposed to accept it.

[2] 2. 42. So Plut. *Coriol.* 3.

[3] Momms. *C. I. L.* I. 308 ; Jordan, *Eph. Ep.* I. 236 ; Aust, *de Aedibus sacris*, 43.

[4] Dion. Hal. 6. 13 ; Liv. 2. 20.

[5] Suetonius, *Tib.* 20 ; Aust, op. cit. p. 6.

[6] Weight must, however, be given to the fact that the transvectio equitum took place on July 15. Aust, 43, and Furtwängler in *Lex.* s. v. Dioscuri.

[7] Middleton, *Ancient Rome*, p. 174 ; Lanciani, *Ruins and Excavations of Ancient Rome*, p. 271 foll.

of the Regillus; and they took a peculiarly firm hold on the Roman mind, as we see from the common oaths Edepol, Mecastor, from their representation on the earliest denarii [1], from their connexion with the equites throughout Roman history, and from the great popularity of their legend, which was reproduced in connexion with later battles [2]. The spread of the cult through Southern Italy to Latium and Etruria (where it was also a favourite) is the subject of a French monograph [3].

[1] Mommsen, *Münzwesen*, 301, 559.

[2] Pydna, Cic. *N. D.* 3. 5. 11 ; Verona (101 B.C.), Plut. *Mar.* 26. The most famous application of the story is in the accounts of the great fight between Locri and Kroton at the river Sagra : this was probably the origin of the Italian legends. See Preller, ii. 301.

[3] Albert, *le Culte de Castor et Pollux en Italie*, 1883. Cp. Furtwängler, l. c.

MENSIS FEBRUARIUS

THE name of the last month of the old Roman year is derived from the word *februum*, usually understood as an instrument of purification [1]. This word, and its derivatives were, as we shall see, best known in connexion with the Lupercalia, the most prominent of the festivals of the month. Now the ritual of the Lupercalia seems to suggest that our word 'purification' does not cover all the ground occupied by the 'religio' of that festival; nor does it precisely suit some of the other rites of February. We are indeed here on difficult and dangerous ground. Certainly we must not assume that there was any general lustration of the whole people, or any period corresponding in religious intent to the Christian Lent, which in time only is descended from the Roman February. Assuredly there were no such ideas as penitence or forgiveness of sins involved in the ritual of the month. Let so much be said for the benefit of those who are only acquainted with Jewish or Christian history.

What at least is certain is that at this time the character of the festivals changes. Since the middle of December we have had a series of joyful gatherings of an agricultural people in homestead, market-place, cross-roads; now we find them fulfilling their duties to their dead ancestors at the common

---

[1] Paulus, 85 'Quaecumque purgamenti causa in quibusque sacrificiis adhibentur, februa appellantur. Id vero quod purgatur, dicitur *februatum.*' The verb februare also occurs. Varro (*L. L.* 6. 13) says that *februum* was the Sabine equivalent for *purgamentum*: 'Nam et Lupercalia februatio, ut in Antiquitatum libris demonstravi' (cp. 6. 34). Ovid renders the word by 'piamen' (*Fasti*, 2. 19). Februus, a divinity, is mentioned in Macr. 1. 13. 3; he is almost certainly a later invention (see *Lex. Myth.* s. v.). The etymology of the word is uncertain.

necropolis, or engaged in a mysterious piacular rite under the walls of the oldest Rome. The Parentalia and the Lupercalia are the characteristic rites of February; we shall see later on whether any of the others can be brought into the same category. If pleasure is the object of the mid-winter festivals, the fulfilment of duties towards the gods and the *manes* would seem to be that of the succeeding period.

From an agricultural point of view February was a somewhat busy month ; but in the time of Varro the work was chiefly the preparatory operations in the culture of olives, vines and fruit-trees [1]. The one great operation in the oldest and simplest agricultural system was the spring sowing. Spring was understood to begin on Feb. 7 (Favonius) [2], and it is precisely at this point that the rites change their character. We are in fact close upon the new year, when the powers of vegetation awake and put on strength ; but the Romans approached it as it were with hesitation, preparing for it carefully by steady devotion to work and duty, the whole community endeavouring to place itself in a proper position toward the *numina* of the land's fertility, and the dead reposing in the land's embrace.

Before taking the rites one by one, it will perhaps be as well to say a word in general about the nature of Roman expiatory rites, in order to determine in what sense we are to understand those of February.

The first point to notice is that these rites were applicable only to *involuntary* acts of commission or omission—an offence against the gods (nefas) if wittingly committed, was inexpiable. In this case the offender was *impius*, i. e. had wilfully failed in his duty ; and him no rites could absolve [3]. But by ordinary offences against the gods we are not to understand *sin*, in the Christian sense of the word ; they were rather mistakes in

---

[1] Varro, *R. R.* I. 29. Cp. Colum. xi. 2 ; and the rustic calendars.

[2] Varro, *R. R.* I. 28. See above, p. 295.

[3] This is very distinctly stated by Cicero (*de Legibus*, I. 14. 40 ' In deos impietatum nulla expiatio est': cp. 2. 9. 22 'Sacrum commissum quod neque expiari poterit, impie commissum est'). Even the sailor in Horace's ode (I. 28), whose duty does not seem exactly binding, is told, if he omits it, ' teque piacula nulla resolvent.' On the general question, cp. De-Marchi, *La Religione nella vita domestica*, 246 ; and Marq. 257. The pontifex Scaevola ' asseverabat prudentem expiari non posse ' (Macrob. I. 16. 10). Ovid's account (*Fasti*, 2. 35 foll.) is that of a layman and a modern, but not less interesting for that reason.

ritual, or involuntary omissions—in fact any real or supposed or possible errors in any of a man's relations to the *numina* around him. He might always be putting himself in the wrong in regard to these relations, and he must as sedulously endeavour to right himself. In the life of the ' privatus ' these trespasses in sacred law would chiefly be in matters of marriages and funerals and the regular sacrifices of the household ; in the life of the magistrate they would be mistakes or omissions in his duties on behalf of the State[1]. Whether in private or public life, they must be duly expiated. It is needless to point out how powerful a factor this belief must have been in the growth of a conscience and of the sense of duty ; or how stringent a ' religio ' was that which, assuming that a man could hardly commit an offence except unwittingly, made the possible exceptional case fatal to his position as a member of a community which depended for its wholesome existence on the good will of the gods.

Remembering that among the divine beings to whom it was most essential for each family to fulfil its duties, were the *di manes*, or dead ancestors and members of the family, we see at once that February with its Parentalia was an important month in the matter of expiatory rites. Ovid, though suggesting a fancy derivation for the name of the month, expresses this idea clearly enough :

> Aut quia *placatis* sunt tempora pura sepulcris
> Tum cum ferales praeteriere dies[2].

But the other etymology given by the poet is, as we have seen, the right one, and may bring us to another class of *piacula*, of which we find an example this month in the Lupercalia.

> Mensis ab his dictus, secta quia pelle Luperci
> Omne solum lustrant, idque piamen habent[3].

Not only was the Roman most careful to expiate involuntary offences, and also to appease the wrath of the gods, if shown in any special active way, e. g. by lightning and many other prodigia[4], but he also sought to avert evil influences *before-*

---

[1] Varro, *L. L.* 6. 30 ' Praetor qui tum (i. e. die nefasto) fatus est, si imprudens fecit, piaculari hostia facta piatur ; si prudens dixit, Q. Mucius ambigebat eum expiari ut impium non posse.'

[2] *Fasti*, 2. 33.   [3] Ib. 31.

[4] See Marq. 259 ; Bouché-Leclercq, *Les Pontifes*, 101 foll.

hand, which might possibly emanate from hostile or offended *numina*. This religious object is well illustrated in the sacrifice of the *hostia praecidanea*, which was offered beforehand to make up for any involuntary errors in the ritual that followed[1]. But it is also seen in numerous other rites of which we have had many examples; all those, for instance, which included a *lustratio*. We generally translate this word by 'purification'; but it also involves the ideas of intercession, and of the removal of unseen hostile influences which may be likely to interfere with the health and prosperity of man, beast, or crop. At such rites special victims were sometimes offered, or the victim was treated in a peculiar manner; we find, perhaps, some part of it used as a charm or potent spell, as the strips of skin at the Lupercalia, or the ashes of the unborn calves at the Fordicidia, or the tail and blood of the October horse[2]. To the first of these, at least, if not to the other two, the word *februum* was applied, and we may assume it of the others: also to many other objects which had some magical power, and carry us back to a very remote religious antiquity. Ovid gives a catalogue of them[3]:

> Februa Romani dixere piamina patres,
>   Nunc quoque dant verbo plurima signa fidem.
> Pontifices ab rege petunt et flamine *lanas*,
>   Quis veterum lingua februa nomen erat.
> Quaeque capit lictor domibus purgamina †ternis†[4]
>   Torrida cum mica farra, vocantur idem.
> Nomen idem *ramo*, qui caesus ab arbore pura
>   Casta sacerdotum tempora fronde tegit.
> Ipse ego flaminicam poscentem februa vidi:
>   Februa poscenti *pinea virga* data est.
> Denique quodcunque est, quo corpora nostra piantur,
>   Hoc apud intonsos nomen habebat avos.

Objects such as these, called by a name which is explained by *piamen*, or *purgamentum*, must have been understood as charms potent to keep off evil influences, and so to enable nature to take its ordinary course unhindered. Only in this sense can we call them instruments of *purification*.

---

[1] Marq. 180, Bouché-Leclercq, 178.
[2] See Robertson Smith, *Religion of the Semites*, p. 406.
[3] *Fasti*, 2. 19 foll.
[4] This difficult line has occasioned much conjecture, and seems still inexplicable. See Merkel, *Fasti*, clxvi foll.; and De-Marchi, op. cit. p. 246.

The use of the *februa* in the Lupercalia was, as we shall see, to procure fertility in the women of the community. Here then, as well as in the rites of the Fornacalia and Parentalia, is some reason for calling the month a period of purification ; but only if we bear in mind that at the Parentalia the process consisted simply in the performance of duties towards the dead, which freed or purified a man from their possible hostility ; while at the Lupercalia the women were freed or purified from influences which might hinder them in the fulfilment of their natural duties to their families and the State. Beyond this it is not safe to go in thinking of February as a month of expiation.

KAL. FEB. IUNONI SOSPITAE. N.

This was the dedication-day of a temple of the great Lanuvian goddess, Juno Sospita, in the Forum olitorium [1]. It was vowed in the year 197 B. C. by the consul Cornelius Cethegus, but had fallen into decay in Ovid's time [2]. For the famous cult of this deity at Lanuvium, see Roscher, in *Lex.* s. v. Iuno, 595.

ID. FEB. FAUNO [I]N INSUL[A]. *C. I. L.* vi. 2302. NP.

This temple was vowed almost at the same time as the last, 296 B. C., by plebeian aediles ; it was built by fines exacted from holders of ager publicus who had not paid their rents [3]. See under Dec. 5, p. 257.

FORNACALIA : FERIAE CONCEPTIVAE, ending Feb. 17.

I have drawn attention to the change in the character of the festivals at this season. But before we go on to the Parentalia and Lupercalia, which chiefly mark this change, we have to consider one festival which seems to belong rather to the class which we found in December and January. This was the

---

[1] Aust, *De Aedibus sacris*, pp. 21, 45. 48. On this last page are some useful remarks on the danger of drawing conclusions as to the indigenous or foreign origin of deities from the position of their temples inside or outside the pomoerium.

[2] *Fasti*, 2. 55 foll.

[3] Livy, 33. 42 ; 34. 53. Jordan, in *Commentationes in hon. Momms.* 359 foll. ; Aust, op. cit. p. 20.

Fornacalia, or feast of ovens; one which does not appear in the calendars, as it was a moveable feast (conceptivae) ; and one which was a *sacrum publicum* only in the sense of being pro curiis, as the Paganalia were pro pagis, the Septimontium pro montibus, and the Argean rite pro sacellis [1]. Each curia conducted its own rites, under the supervision of its curio and (for the last day) of the Curio Maximus [2]: the great priests of the State had no official part in it. In this it differs in some degree from the Fordicidia (April 15), the other feast of the curiae, which appears in three of our calendars, and in which the Pontifices and Vestals took some part [3].

This is not the place to investigate the difficult question of what the *curiae* really were. So much at least is clear, that while, like the montes, pagi, and sacella (argea), they were divisions of the people and the land, they were more important than the others, in that they formed the basis of the earliest political and military organization [4]. It need hardly be said that each curia had also itself a religious organization : their places of assembly, though not temples, were quasi-religious buildings [5], used for sacred purposes, but furnished with hearth and eating-room like an ordinary house [6]. We hear also of tables (mensae, τράπεζαι) 'in quibus immolabatur Iunoni quae Curis appellata est [7].' There is no need to assume any etymological connexion between Cŭris and Cūria [8] ; but the cult of the goddess of the spear is interesting here, as seeming at once to illustrate the military importance of the curiae, the power of the paterfamilias [9], and the necessity of continuing the family through

[1] See *Dict. of Antiq.* s. v. sacra. Fest. 245 a 'Publica sacra, quae publico sumptu pro populo fiunt : quaeque pro montibus, pagis, curiis, sacellis.'

[2] Ovid, *Fasti*, 2. 527. See under Quirinalia.

[3] See on April 15. There must have been at one time a tendency to amalgamate the two kinds of *sacra publica*. The *argei* were also attended by Pontifices and Vestals. I should conjecture that the Pontifices claimed supervision over rites in which they had originally no official *locus standi*, and brought the Vestals with them.

[4] Mommsen, *Staatsrecht*, iii. 1. 89 foll.

[5] Ἱεραὶ οἰκίαι, Dion. Hal. 2. 23 ; Fest. 174 b ; Marq. 195.

[6] Dion. Hal. 2. 23.

[7] Ib. 2. 50. The Latin words are from Paul. 64.

[8] Jordan, on Preller, i. 278 note. Roscher, in *Lex.* s. v. Iuno, 596. Curis = hasta in Sabine ; Fest. 49 ; Roscher, l. c. ; Ovid, *Fasti*, 2. 477.

[9] Cp. the parting of the bride's hair with a spear, Marq. vii. 44 and note 5 ; Plut. *Q. R.* 87 ; Bötticher, *Baumkultus*, 485 ; Schwegler, *R. G.* i. 469.

the fertility of woman, an idea which we shall come upon again
at the Lupercalia [1]. Lastly, each curia had its own curio, or
religious superintendent, and its own flamen, and at the head
of all the curiae was the Curio Maximus ; officers who coincide
with the general character of the curiae in being (like the heads
of families) not strictly priests, but capable of religious duties,
for the performance of which they are said to have been
instituted [2].

The ritual of the Fornacalia has been evolved with difficulty,
and without much certainty, from a few passages in Ovid,
Dionysius, Varro, Festus, and Pliny [3]. We seem to see—1. An
offering in each private house in each curia : it consisted of *far*,
i. e. meal of the oldest kind of Italian wheat, roasted in antique
fashion in the oven which was to be found in the *pistrina* of
each house, and made into cakes by crushing in the manner
still common in India and elsewhere [4]. 2. A rite in which
each curia took part as a whole. This is deduced from the fact
that on the 17th (Quirinalia) any one who by forgetfulness or
ignorance had omitted to perform his sacra on the day fixed by
the curio for the meeting of his own curia, might do so then
at a general assembly of all the thirty curiae [5]. This was the
reason why the Quirinalia was called ' stultorum feriae.' It has
also been conjectured that the bounds of each curia were beaten
on this day, on which its members thus met : for Pliny says
' Numa et Fornacalia instituit farris torrendi ferias *et aeque*

---

[1] The same connexion between *curiae* and the armed deity of the
female principle is found at Tibur (Serv. *Aen.* 1. 17), ' in sacris Tibur-
tibus sic precantur : Iuno curritis (sic) tuo curru clipeoque tuere meos
curiae vernulas,' Jordan, in *Hermes*, 8. 217 foll. Possibly also at Lanuvium
(*Lex.* s.v. Iuno, 595).

[2] Varro, *L. L.* 5. 83 and 155 ; Marq. 195.

[3] This has been done by O. Gilbert (*Gesch. und Topogr.* 2. 129 foll.), an
author who is not often so helpful. He is followed by Steuding, in *Lex.
Myth.* s. v. Fornax.

[4] Paul. 93 (cp. 83), ' Fornacalia feriae institutae sunt farris torrendi
gratia quod ad fornacem quae in pistrinis erat sacrificium fieri solebat.'
Dionysius was probably referring to this when he wrote (2. 23) that he
had himself seen ancient wooden tables spread with rude cakes of primitive
fashion in baskets and dishes of primitive make. He also mentions
καρπῶν τινων ἐπαρχάς (cp. Ovid, l. c. 520), which might indeed suggest
a feast of curiae at a different time of year. For the *far*, see Marq. vii.
399 foll. The cakes were *februa*, according to Ovid ; see above, p. 301.

[5] Comp. Ovid, l. c. with Fest. 254 ; Paul. 316 ; Varro, *L. L.* 6. 13 ; Plut.
Q. R. 89.

religiosas terminis agrorum[1].' 3. What happened on the Quirinalia Ovid shall tell us himself[2]:

> Curio legitimis nunc Fornacalia verbis
>   Maximus indicit, nec stata sacra facit ;
> Inque foro, multa circum pendente tabella,
>   Signatur certa curia quaeque nota :
> Stultaque pars populi, quae sit sua curia, nescit,
>   Sed facit extrema sacra relata die.

It should be noted that no certain connexion can be made out
between Quirinus and curia, and I imagine it was only accident
or convenience that made this day the last of the Fornacalia[3].
Ovid's words ' nec stata sacra facit' seem to me to imply that
the Curio Maximus carefully abstained from using a formula
of announcement likely to confuse the 'stultorum feriae' with
the Quirinalia, which was always on the same day. But it may
well have been the case that by usage the two coincidd.

Ovid's lines make it clear that on the 17th (as a rule) the
Forum was the scene of a general meeting of curiae, each of
which had a certain space assigned it, indicated by a placard.
Is it possible that this was merely a survival of the assembly of
the armed host in comitia curiata, now used only for religious
purposes? If so, the tendency to fix it on the festival of
Quirinus might find a natural explanation.

The meaning and object of the Fornacalia are very far from
being clear. Preller[4] fancied it was the occasion of the first
eating of the fruits of the last harvest: but it is hardly possible
to imagine this postponed as late as February. On the other
hand Dionysius' description[5], already quoted, of what he saw
in the curiae, would suit this well enough if it could be set down
to a suitable time of year: it suggests a common meal, in which
the first-fruits are offered to the god, while the worshippers eat
of the new grain. But this cannot have been in February.
Steuding (in the *Lex.*) suggests that the object was to thank
the gods for preserving the corn through the winter, and to

---

[1] *H. N.* 18. 8 ; Lange, *Röm. Alt.* 1². 245. [2] *Fasti*, 2. 527 foll.
[3] That it was so is proved by Fest. 254, and Varro, *L. L.* 6. 13. It must
have been a custom fairly well fixed.
[4] ii. 9.
[5] 2. 23, Ἐγὼ γοῦν ἐθεασάμην ἐν ἱεραῖς οἰκίαις δεῖπνα προκείμενα θεοῖς ἐπὶ
τραπέζαις ξυλίναις ἀρχαϊκαῖς, ἐν κάνῃσι καὶ πινακίσκοις κεραμέοις ἀλφίτων μάζας
καὶ πόπανα καὶ ζέας καὶ καρπῶν τινων ἐπαρχάς &c.

pray for the welfare of the seed still in the ground (i. e. in a lustratio). Ovid says (though Steuding does not quote him)

> Facta dea est Fornax: laeti Fornace coloni
> Orant, ut fruges temperet illa suas [1].

But neither Steuding's conjecture, nor the German parallels he appeals to, seem convincing. I am rather inclined to think that the making of cakes in each household was simply a pre-liminary to the *sacra* that followed in the curia, i. e. each family brought its contribution to a common religious meal. The roasting was naturally accompanied by an offering to the spirit of the oven [2] (fornax); hence the name Fornacalia. The object of the sacra in the curia is doubtful; but they probably had some relation to the land and its fertility, in view of the new year about to begin. Of the final meeting of all the curiae in the forum I have already suggested an explanation: the phrase 'stultorum feriae' was, in my opinion, of late origin, and illus-trates the diminishing importance of the curiate organization after the admission of plebeians [3].

Id. Feb. (Feb. 13). NP.

VIRGO VESTALIS PARENTAT. (PHIL.)

PARENTATIO TUMULORUM INCIPIT. (SILV.)

The *dies parentales*, or days of worshipping the dead (placandis Manibus), began at the sixth hour on this day, and continued either to the 21st (Feralia), or the 22nd (cara cognatio) [4]. The parentatio of the Vestal was at the tomb of Tarpeia, herself a Vestal [5]. Undoubtedly, the Feralia (21st) was the oldest and the best known of these days, and the only one which was a public festival: it appears in three calendars (Caer. Maff. Farn.) in large letters. Yet there is reason for believing that even the Feralia was not the oldest day for worshipping the

---

[1] *Fasti*, 2. 525. What does Ovid mean by *fruges*?

[2] Paul. 93, quoted above; Ovid, l.c. 525. Fornax as a spirit may be at least as old as those of other parts of the house, Janus, Vesta, Limentinus, &c.

[3] Mommsen, *Röm. Forschungen*, i. 149 foll.

[4] Lydus, *de Mens.* 4. 24. Lydus gives the 22nd as the final day; Ovid, *Fasti*, 2. 569, gives the 21st (Feralia).

[5] Dion. Hal. 2. 40.

manes : it was in part at least a dies fastus, and none of the dies parentales are marked N in the calendars ; and this, according to Mommsen [1], shows that the rites of those days were of later origin than those of the Lemuria (May 9–13), which are all marked N. This seems also to have been the opinion of Latin scholars [2].

Whatever the Lemuria may have been, it is certain that the Parentalia were not days of terror or ill-omen ; but rather days on which the performance of duty was the leading idea in men's minds. Nor was the duty an unpleasant one. There was a general holiday : the dead to be propitiated had been duly buried in the family tomb in the great necropolis, had been well cared for since their departure, and were still members of the family. There was nothing to fear from them, so long as the living members performed their duties towards them under the supervision of the State and its Pontifices [3]. They had their *iura*, and the relations between them and their living relations were all regulated by a *ius sacrum* : they lived on in their city outside the walls of the city of the living [4], each family in their own dwelling : they did not interfere with the comfort of the living, or in any way show themselves hostile or spiteful. Such ideas as these are of course the result of

---

[1] *C. I. L.* I[2]. 309 : cf. 297 (Introduction. p. 9). The Lupercalia (15th) is an exception ; but for reasons connected with that festival. The 21st (Feralia) is F P (Caer.) F (Maff.). See Introduction, p. 10. F P, according to Mommsen, = fastus principio.

[2] If Ovid reflects it rightly in *Fasti*, 5. 419 foll. Cp. Porph. on Hor. *Ep.* 2. 2. 209. See on Lemuria, above, p. 107.

[3] On the vast subject of the jus Manium and the worship of the dead, the following are some of the works that may be consulted : Marq. 307 foll., and vii. 350 foll. ; De-Marchi, *Il Cu'to Privato*, p. 180 foll. ; Roscher, *Lex.* articles Manes and Inferi ; Bouché-Leclercq, *Pontifes*, 147 foll. ; Rohde, *Psyche*, p. 630 foll. Two old treatises still form the basis of our knowledge : Gutherius, *de iure Manium*, in Graevius' *Thesaurus*, vol. xii. ; and Kirchmann, *de Funeribus* (1605). Valuable matter has still to be collected (for later times) from the *Corpus Inscriptionum*.

[4] This was the universal practice in Italy from the earliest times, so far as we have as yet learnt from excavations. For the question whether burial in or close to the house, or within the city walls, preceded burial in necropoleis, see *Classical Review*, for February, 1897, p. 32 foll. Servius (Ad *Aen.* 5. 64 ; 6. 152 ; cp. Isidorus, 15. 11. 1) tells us that they once buried in the house, and there were facts that might suggest this in the cult of the Lares, and in the private ghost-driving of the Lemuria ; but we cannot prove it, and it is not true of the Romans at any period. Not even the well-known law of the XII Tables can prove that burial ever regularly took place within the *existing* walls of a city.

a well developed city life; experience has taught the citizen how his conduct towards the Di Manes can best be regulated and organized for the benefit of both parties. The Parentalia belong to a later stage of development than the Lemuria, though both have the same original basis of thought. The Parentalia was practically a yearly renewal of the rite of burial. As *sacra privata* they took place on the anniversary of the death of a deceased member of the family, and it was a special charge on the heir that he should keep up their observance[1]. On that day the family would go in procession to the grave, not only to see that all was well with him who abode there, but to present him with offerings of water, wine, milk, honey, oil, and the blood of black victims[2]: to deck the tomb with flowers[3], to utter once more the solemn greeting and farewell (Salve, sancte parens), to partake of a meal with the dead, and to petition them for good fortune and all things needful. This last point comes out clearly in Virgil's picture:

> Poscamus ventos, atque haec me sacra quotannis
> Urbe velit posita templis sibi ferre dicatis.

The true meaning of these lines is, as Henry quaintly puts it[4], 'Let us try if we cannot kill two birds with one stone, and not only pay my sire the honours due to him, but at the same time help ourselves forward on our journey by getting him to give us fair winds for our voyage.'

As we have seen, the dies parentales began on the 13th; from that day till the 21st all temples were closed, marriages were forbidden, and magistrates appeared without their insignia[5]. On the 22nd was the family festival of the *Caristia*, or *cara cognatio*: the date of its origin is unknown, but Ovid[6]

---

[1] Cic. *De Legg.* 2. 48. Cp. Virg. *Aen.* 5. 49:
   Iamque dies, ni fallor, adest, quem semper acerbum,
   Semper honoratum—sic di voluistis—habebo.

[2] Marq. 311 foll.

[3] Purpureosque iacit flores, Virg. *Aen.* 5. 79. Cp. Cic. *pro Flacco*, 38. 95.

[4] *Aeneidea*, 3. 15. He well compares Lucan, 9. 990. Tylor, *Prim. Cult.* ii. 332. Aeneas is here, as always, the true type of the practical Roman.

[5] Marq. 311 and reff.

[6] *Fasti*, 2. 617 foll. Among the calendars it is only mentioned in those of Philocalus and Silvius, and in the rustic calendars. Valerius Maximus is the next writer after Ovid who mentions it: 2. 1. 8. Cp. *C. I. L.* vi. 10234. Martial calls it 'lux propinquorum' (9. 55, cp. 54). For an inter-

writes of it as well established in his time, and it may be very
much older.   He describes it as a reunion of the living
members of the family after they have paid their duties to
the dead :

> Scilicet a tumulis et qui periere, propinquis
> Protinus ad vivos ora referre iuvat ;
> Postque tot amissos quicquid de sanguine restat,
> Aspicere, et generis dinumerare gradus.

It was a kind of love-feast of the family, and gives a momen-
tary glimpse of the gentler side of Roman family life.   All
quarrels were to be forgotten [1] in a general harmony : no guilty
or cruel member may be present [2].   The centre of the worship
was the Lares of the family, who were 'incincti,' and shared
in the sacred meal [3].

We might naturally expect that, especially in Italy—so
tenacious of old ideas and superstitions—we should find
some survival of primitive folk-lore, even in the midst of this
highly organized civic cult of the dead.   Ovid supplies us with
a curious contrast to the ethical beauty of the Caristia, in
describing the spells which an old woman works, apparently on
the day of the Feralia [4].   'An old hag sitting among the girls
performs rites to Tacita : with three fingers she places three
bits of incense at the entrance of a mouse-hole.   Muttering
a spell, she weaves woollen threads on a web of dark colour,
and mumbles seven black beans in her mouth.   Then she
takes a fish, the *maena*, smears its head with pitch, sews its
mouth up, drops wine upon it, and roasts it before the fire : the
rest of the wine she drinks with the girls.   Now, quoth she,
we have bound the mouth of the enemy :

> Hostiles linguas inimicaque vinximus ora,
> Dicit discedens, ebriaque exit anus.'

In spite of the names of deities we find here, Tacita and Dea

esting conjecture as to the special meaning of *carus*, see Lattes quoted in
De-Marchi, op. cit. 214, note 2.

[1] Val. Max. l.c. and Silvius' *Calendar*.

[2] Ovid, *Fasti*, 2. 623,
> Innocui veniant : procul hinc, procul impius esto
> Frater, et in partus mater acerba suos.

[3] Ovid, *Fasti*, 2. 633-634. On such occasions the Lares were clothed
in tunics girt at the loins ; see a figure of a Lar on an altar from Caere in
Baumeister, *Denkmäler*, vol. i. p. 77.

[4] *Fasti*, 2. 571 foll.

Muta[1], and of the pretty story of the mother of the Lares
which the poet's fancy has added to it, it is plain that this is no
more than one of a thousand savage spells for counteracting
hostile spirits[2]. The picture is interesting, as showing the
survival of witchcraft in the civilized Rome of Ovid's time, and
reminds us of the horrible hags in Horace's fifth epode; but it
may be doubted whether it has any real connexion with the
Feralia. Doubtless its parallel could be found even in the
Italy of to-day[3].

XV. KAL. MART. (FEB. 15). NP.

LUPER(CALIA). (CAER. MAFF. FARN. PHILOC. SILV. AND
RUSTIC CALENDARS.)

There is hardly another festival in the calendar so interesting
and so well known as this. Owing to the singular interest
attaching to its celebration in B.C. 44, only a month before
Caesar's death, we are unusually well informed as to its details;
but these present great difficulties in interpretation, which the
latest research has not altogether overcome[4]. I shall content
myself with describing it, and pointing out such explanations of
ritual as seem to be fairly well established.

On Feb. 15 the celebrants of this ancient rite met at the cave
called the Lupercal, at the foot of the steep south-western
corner of the Palatine Hill—the spot where, according to the
tradition, the flooded Tiber had deposited the twin children
at the foot of the sacred fig-tree[5], and where they were
nourished by the she-wolf. The name of the cave is almost

[1] Line 583. See Wissowa in Lex. s.v. Dea Muta.
[2] See e.g. Crooke, Folklore of Northern India, ch. 5 (the Black Art), and especially pp. 264 foll.
[3] See e.g. Leland, Etruscan Roman remains in popular legend, pp. 3 and 195 foll.
[4] The chief attempts are those of Unger, in Rhein. Mus., 1881, p. 50, and Mannhardt in his Mythologische Forschungen, pp. 72–155. The former is ingenious, but unsatisfactory in many ways; the latter conscientious, and valuable as a study in folk-lore, whether its immediate conclusions be right or wrong. See also Schwegler, R. G. i. 356 foll.; Preller, i. 387 foll.; and article s.v. in Dict. of Antiquities (2nd edition); Marq. 442 foll. The ancient authorities are Dion. Hal. 1. 32. 5, 79, 80; Ovid, Fasti, 2. 267 foll.; Plutarch, Caes. 61, Rom. 21; Val. Max. 2. 2. 9; Propert. 5. (4.) 1. 26; and many other passages which will be referred to when necessary.
[5] Dion. Hal. 1. 32. 5.

without doubt built up from *lupus*, 'a wolf' [1]; but we cannot be equally sure whether the name of the festival is derived directly from Lupercal, or on the analogy of Quirinalia, Volcanalia, and others, from Lupercus, the alleged name of the deity concerned in the rites, and also of the celebrants themselves [2]. In any case we are fairly justified in calling this the wolf-festival ; the more so as the wolf was the sacred animal of Mars, who was in a special sense the god of the earliest settlers on the Palatine [3].

The first act of the festival seems to have been the sacrifice of goats (we are not told how many), and of a dog [4]; and at the same time were offered sacred cakes made by the Vestals, from the first ears of last year's harvest. This was the last batch of the *mola salsa*, some of which had been used at the Vestalia in June, and some on the Ides of September [5].

Next, two youths of high rank, belonging, we may suppose, one to each of the two collegia of Luperci (of which more directly), were brought forward : these had their foreheads smeared with the knife bloody from the slaughter of the victims, and then wiped with wool dipped in milk. As soon as this was done they were obliged to laugh. Then they girt themselves with the skins of the slaughtered goats, and feasted luxuriously [6]; after which they ran round the base of the Palatine Hill, or at least a large part of its circuit, apparently in two companies, one led by each of the two youths. As they ran they struck at all the women who came near them or offered themselves to their blows, with strips of skin cut from the hides of the same victims ; which strips, as we have seen, were among the objects which were called by the priests *februa*.

---

[1] Jordan, *Kritische Beiträge*, 164 foll. Unger's attempt, after Serv. *Aen.* 8. 343, to derive the word from *luo* ('to purify') is generally rejected.

[2] Wissowa, *Lex.* (s. v. Lupercus) takes the latter view, but rightly, as I think, rejects the deity.

[3] Virg. *Aen.* 8. 630 'Mavortis in antro.' Roscher, in *Lex.* s. v. Mars, 2388 ; Preller, i. 334.

[4] Plut. *Rom.* 21. After mentioning the goats, he says, ἴδιον δὲ τῆς ἑορτῆς τὸ καὶ κύνα θύειν τοὺς Λουπέρκους (cp. *Q. R.* 111).

[5] Marq. 165. See above, p. 110.

[6] So Val. Max. l.c. From Ovid's version of the aetiological story of Romulus and Remus (*Fasti*, 2. 371 foll.) we might infer that the feasting took place after the running.

Here, in what at first sight looks like a grotesque jumble, there are two clearly distinguishable elements; (1) an extremely primitive ritual, probably descended from the pastoral stage of society; (2) a certain co-ordination of this with definite local settlements. The sacrifices, the smearing and wiping, the wearing of the skins, and the striking with the *februa*, all seem to be survivals from a very early stage of religious conceptions; but the two companies of runners, and their course round the Palatine, which apparently followed the most ancient line of the pomoerium, bring us into touch with the beginning and with the development of urban life. Surviving through the whole Republican period, with a tenacity which the Roman talent for organization alone could give it, the Lupercalia was still further developed for his own purposes by the dictator Caesar, and thenceforward lived on for centuries under his successors into the age of imperial Christianity.

Let us now examine the several acts of the festival, to see how far they admit of explanation under the light of modern research into primitive ideas and ritual.

It began, as we saw, with the sacrifice of goats and a dog. Unluckily we cannot be sure of the god to whom they were offered, nor of the sacrificing priest. According to Ovid[1] the deity was Faunus; according to Livy it was a certain mysterious Inuus, of whom hardly anything else is known[2], though much has been written. There was no Lupercus, as some have vainly imagined; much less any such combination as Faunus Lupercus, which has been needlessly created out of a passage of Justin[3]. Liber is suggested by Servius[4]; who adds that others fancied it was a 'bellicosus deus.' Recently Juno has been suggested, because the strips which the runners carried were called 'Iunonis amiculum'[5]. Thus it is quite plain that the Roman of the literary age did not know who the god was. The

---

[1] 'Cornipedi Fauno caesa de more capella' (*Fasti*, 2. 361). Cp. 5. 101. So Plut. *Rom.* l. c.

[2] Livy, 1. 5. Unger (p. 71 foll.) has much to say about Inuus in the worst style of German pseudo-research. See *Lex.* s. v. (Steuding).

[3] Schwegler, i. 351 foll.; Justin, 43. 1. I had long ago arrived at this conclusion, and was glad to see it sanctioned by Wissowa in *Lex.* s. v. Lupercus.

[4] *Aen.* 8. 343 : the only reason given is that the goat was Liber's victim.

[5] Arnobius, 2. 23. See Mannhardt, 85; Huschke, *Röm. Jahr*, 12.

common idea that he was Faunus is discredited by Livy's
account and his mention of Inuus, and also by the fact that
Faunus is not associated with urban settlements: and may
easily be accounted for by the myth of Evander and the
Arcadians, whose Pan Lycaeus was of course identified with
Faunus[1], or by the girding of the Luperci with skins, which
made them resemble the popular conception of the Fauni[2].
Possibly the name was a secret; for there was a tendency to
avoid fixing a god's name in ritual, in order to escape making
mistakes, and so offending him. 'Iure pontificum cautum est
ne suis nominibus dii Romani appellarentur, ne exaugurari
possint[3].' We must also remember that the Lupercalia undoubtedly descends from the very earliest period of the Roman
religion, when the individuality of deities was not clearly
conceived, and when their names were unknown, doubtful, or
adjectival only. In fact, we need not greatly trouble ourselves
about the name of the god: his nature is deducible to some
extent from the ritual. The connexion with the Palatine, with
the wolf, and with fructification, seems to me to point very
clearly in the direction of Mars and his characteristics.

It would be almost more profitable if we could be sure of the
sacrificing priest; but here again we are in the dark. Ovid
says, 'Flamen ad haec prisco more Dialis erat[4]'; but it is impossible that this priest could have been the sacrificer (though
Marquardt committed himself to this), for he was expressly
forbidden to touch either goat or dog[5], which seem to have
been excluded from the cult of Jupiter. Even in the case
of such exceptional *piacula* as this no doubt was, we can hardly
venture without further evidence to ascribe the slaughter of the
sacred animal to the great priest of the heavenly deity in whose
cult it was tabooed. Plutarch says that the Luperci themselves sacrificed[6]; and this is more probable, and is borne out

---

[1] Schwegler, i. 354 foll. : the general result is given in *Lex.* s.v. Evander,
vol. i. 1395. Evander himself = Faunus. It is possible that there may be
some basis of truth in the Arcadian legend : we await further archaeological inquiry.

[2] See on Dec. 5 ; and *Lex.* s.v. Faunus, p. 1458.

[3] Serv. *Aen.* 2. 351. The whole passage is very interesting. See on
Dec. 21 ; and Bouché-Leclercq, *Pontifes*, 28 and 49.

[4] *Fasti*, 2. 282 ; Marq. 443.

[5] Plut. *Q. R.* 111 ; Gell. 10. 15 ; Arnob. 7. 21.

[6] *Rom.* 21 : quoted above, p. 311. Val. Max. l. c. seems also to imply it :

by comparison with other cases in which the priest clothes himself, as the Luperci did, in the skin of the victim. It does not indeed seem certain that the two youths who thus girt themselves had also performed the sacrifice ; but they represent the two collegia of Luperci, and lead the race [1], as Romulus and Remus did in the explanatory legend.

As regards the victims, there is here at least no doubt that both goat and dog were exceptional animals in sacrifice [2], and that their use here betokens a piacular rite of unusual 'holiness.' Thus their offering is a mystic sacrifice, and belongs to that ' small class of exceptional rites in which the victim was drawn from some species of animals that retained even in modern times their ancient repute of natural holiness [3].' It is exactly in this kind of sacrifice that we find such peculiar points of ritual as meet us in the Lupercalia. 'The victim is sacrosanct, and the peculiar value of the ceremony lies in the operation performed on its life, whether that life is merely conveyed to the god on the altar (i. e. as in burnt-sacrifices) or is also applied to the worshippers by the sprinkling of the blood, or some other lustral ceremony [4].' The writer might very well have been thinking of the Lupercalia when he wrote these lines. The meaning of these rites was originally, as he states it, that the holiness of the victim means kinship to the worshippers and their god, 'that all sacred relations and all moral obligations depend on physical unity of life, and that physical unity of life can be created or reinforced by common participation in living flesh and blood.' We may postpone consideration of this view as applied to the Lupercalia till we have examined the remaining features of the ceremony.

After the sacrifice was completed, Plutarch [5] tells us that the

---

'Facto sacrificio caesisque capris, epularum hilaritate ac vino largiore provecti, divisa pastorali turba, cincti pellibus immolatarum hostiarum, iocantes obvios petiverunt.'

[1] Even this point is not quite certain ; but see Hartung, *Rel. der Römer*, ii. 178, and Mannhardt, 78.

[2] Ox, sheep and pig were the usual victims ; the dog was only offered to Robigus (see on April 25), to the Lares Praestites and to Mana Geneta ; the goat only to Bacchus and Aesculapius, foreign deities (Marq. 172). The goat-skin of Juno Sospita is certainly Greek : *Lex.* s. v. Iuno, 595. The goat was a special Hebrew *piaculum* (Robertson Smith, 448 ; cf. 453).

[3] Robertson Smith, 379.   [4] Ib. 381.

[5] *Rom.* 21 οἱ μὲν ᾑμαγμένῃ μαχαίρᾳ τοῦ μετώπου θιγγάνουσιν, ἕτεροι δ'

foreheads of the two youths were touched with the bloody
knife that had slain the victims, and the stain was then wiped
off with wool dipped in milk, after which the youths had to
laugh. This has often been supposed to indicate an original
human sacrifice[1], the he-goats being substituted for human
victims, and the death of the latter symbolized by the smearing
with their blood. This explanation might be admissible if
this were the only feature of the ceremony; but it is so entirely
out of keeping with those that follow—the wearing of the
skins and the running—that it is preferable to look for another
before adopting it. At the same time it may be observed that
no reasonable hypothesis can be ruled out of court where our
knowledge of the rite is so meagre and so hard to bring
satisfactorily into harmony with others occurring among other
peoples[2].

There is a curious passage in Apollonius Rhodius[3], where
purification from a murder is effected by smearing the hands
of the murderer with the blood of a young pig, and then
wiping it off ἄλλοις χύτλοισι; and the Scholiast on the lines
describes a somewhat similar method of purification which was
practised in Greece. This would raise a presumption that the
youths were not originally the victims at the Lupercalia, but
rather the slayers; and that they had to be purified from the
guilt of the blood of the sacrosanct victim[4]. When this was
done they became one with the victim and the god by the
girding on of the skins, and were able to communicate the new
life thus acquired in the course of their lustratio of the city by
means of the strips of skin to the women who met them. This
explanation is open to one or two objections; for example, it
hardly accounts for the laughter of the youths, unless we are

---

ἀπομάττουσιν εὐθὺς ἔριον βεβρεγμένον γάλακτι προσφέροντες. Γελᾶν δὲ δεῖ τὰ
μειράκια μετὰ τὴν ἀπόμαξιν.

[1] So Schwegler. l.c. and reff. in Marq. 443 notes 11–13. Dion. Hal. (1.
32) compared the human sacrifice in the cult of Zeus Lycaeus in Arcadia.
See Farnell, *Cults*, i. 40 foll.

[2] We ought to have the whole *history* of the Lupercalia if we are to
explain it rightly; it is impossible to guess through what stages and
changes it may have passed.

[3] 4. 478 (quoted in a valuable section (23) of Hermann's *Gottesdienstliche
Alterthümer der Griechen*).

[4] For examples of this idea see under Feb. 24 (Regifugium); Robertson
Smith, 286; Mannhardt, *Myth. Forsch.* 58 foll.

to suppose that it was an expression of joy at their release from blood-guiltiness [1]. And we have indeed no direct evidence that the youths were ever themselves the sacrificers, though the collateral evidence on this point, as I have already said, seems to be fairly strong [2]. Yet I cannot but think that the true significance of the essential features of the ceremony is to be looked for somewhere in the direction thus indicated.

There is, however, another explanation of the application of the bloody knife, the wiping, and the laughing, which Mannhardt proposed, not without some modest hesitation, in his posthumous work [3]. In his view these were symbolic or quasi-dramatic acts, signifying death and renewed life. The youths were never actually killed, but they were the figures in a kind of acted parable. The smearing with blood denoted that they partook of the death of the victim [4]; the wiping with milky wool signified the revival to a new life, for milk is the source of life. The laughing is the outward sign of such revival : the dead are silent, cannot laugh [5]. And the meaning of all this was the death and the revival of the Vegetation-spirit. I have already more than once profited by Mannhardt's researches into this type of European custom, and they are now familiar to Englishmen in the works of Mr. Frazer, Mr. Farnell, and others. Undoubtedly there are many bits of grotesque custom which can best be explained if we suppose them to mean the death of the Power of growth at harvest-time, or its resuscitation in the spring, perhaps after the death of the powers of winter and darkness. But whether the Lupercalia is one of these I cannot be so sure. These rites do not seem to have any obvious reference to *crops*, but rather to have come down from the

---

[1] It may indeed be misrepresented by Plutarch (who is the only writer who mentions it), and may have been originally an ὀλολυγή. For the confusion of mournful and joyful cries at a sacrifice see Robertson Smith, 411.

[2] Robertson Smith notes (p. 396) that young men, or rather lads, occur as sacrificers in Exodus xxiv. 5.

[3] p. 91 foll.

[4] Mannhardt is not lucid on this point ; he was evidently in difficulties (pp. 97-99). He seems clear that the application of the blood produces an *identity* between victim and youths ; but in similar cases it is not through death that victim, god, and priest become identical, but through the life-giving virtue of the blood. The blood-application must surely mean the acquisition of new life ; but he makes it symbolic of death.

[5] Frazer, *G. B.* ii. 242.

pastoral stage of society : and it is not in this case the *fields* which are lustrated by the runners, but the *urbs* and its women [1]. And the earlier parts of the ritual bear the marks of a *piaculum* so distinctly that it seems unnecessary and confusing to introduce into it a different set of ideas.

There is a similar divergence of opinion in explaining the next feature, the wearing of the skins of the victims [2]. Dr. Mannhardt believed that this was one of the innumerable instances in which, at certain times of the year, animals are personated by human beings, e. g. at Christmas, at the beginning of Lent (Carnival), and at harvest. These he explained as representations of the Vegetation-spirit, which was conceived to be dead in winter, to come to life in spring, and at harvest to die again, and which was believed to assume all kinds of animal forms. This has been generally accepted as explaining several curious rites both in Greece and Italy, e. g. that of the Hirpi Sorani at Soracte not far from Rome [3]. But it is a question whether it will equally well explain the Luperci and their goat-skins. In this case Mannhardt is driven to somewhat far-fetched hypotheses ; he derives Lupercus from *lupus-hircus* [4] (p. 90), and suggests that the two collegia represented respectively wolves and goats, according to the view of the Vegetation-spirit taken by the two communities of Palatine and Quirinal [5]. But this solution, the result of a bias in favour of his favourite Vegetation-spirit, does not strike us as happy, and Dr. Mannhardt himself does not seem well pleased with it [6].

It would seem safer to take this as one of the many well-

[1] Mannhardt seems to have felt this difficulty (p. 86), and to have tried to overcome it, but without success.

[2] I here omit the feasting, as it is by no means certain at what point of time it took place. If the victims themselves were eaten, it would be part of the sacrificial act and would precede the running ; but this is not common in the case of such *piacula*. and one victim, we must remember, was a dog. It is more likely that Val. Max. is here wrong (see above, p. 311, note 6).

[3] See Mannhardt, *Antike Wald- und Feldkulte*, 318 foll., and for other examples, Frazer, *G. B.* ii. 1 foll. ; Preller-Robert, *Griech. Myth.* i. 144 (Zeus-festival on Pelion).

[4] After Schwegler, i. 361 ; rejected by Marq. (439, note 4).

[5] p. 101. The 'wolves' represent of course the Palatine city.

[6] See his eminently modest and sensible remarks at the end of his 5th section, p. 113.

known *piacula* in which the worshipper wears the skin of
a very holy victim, thereby entering sacramentally into the
very nature of the god to whom the victim is sacrificed[1].
Whether or no we are to look for the origin of these practices
in a totemistic age, is a question that cannot be discussed
here; and there is no sign of totemism in the Lupercalia
save this one[2].

But if this be the right explanation, what, we may ask, was
meant by the name Luperci? If it meant wolves, are we not
rather thrown back on Mannhardt's theory? To this it may
be answered; (1) that no classical author suggests that the
runners were looked upon as representing wolves; by the
common people we are told that they were called *creppi*[3],
the meaning of which is quite uncertain, though it has been
explained as = *capri*, and as simply arising from the fact that
the runners were clad in goat-skins[4]. There is in fact no
necessary connexion at all between the skins and the name
Luperci. If that name originally meant wolf-priests, its
explanation is to be found rather in .connexion with the wolf
of Mars, and the cave of the she-wolf, than in the skins of the
sacrificed goats, which were worn by only two members of
the two collegia bearing the name.

We must now turn our attention to the last features of the
festival; the course taken by the runners round the Palatine
Hill, and the whipping of women with the strips of sacred
skin. The two youths, having girded on the skins (though
otherwise naked) and also cut strips from them, proceeded to
run a course which seems almost certainly to have followed
that of the pomoerium at the foot of the Palatine. The starting-
point was the Lupercal, or a point near it, and Tacitus[5] has

[1] Robertson Smith, *Religion of the Semites*, 416 foll.; *Encycl. Brit.* art.
'Sacrifice'; and for the Lupercalia, *Academy*, Feb. 11, 1888, where a totemistic origin is suggested.

[2] See also Lobeck, *Aglaoph.* pp. 183 6; Lang, *Myth, Ritual and Religion*,
vol. ii. 177 (cp. 106) and reff., 213; *Dict. of Antiquities*, art. 'Sacrificium,'
p. 584.

[3] Festus, p. 57 'Creppos, id est lupercos, dicebant a crepitu pellicu-
larum,' &c.

[4] Preller, i. 389. On this Jordan has added no comment.

[5] *Ann.* 12. 24; Jordan, *Topogr.* i. 163 foll., has examined Tacitus's account
with great care. Tacitus starts the pomoerium from the Forum boarium,
while Dionysius and Plutarch start the runners from the Lupercal; but
the two are close together.

described the course of the pomoerium as far as the 'sacellum Larum forumque Romanum': in his day it was marked out by stones ('cippi'). We are concerned with it here only so far as it affects the question whether the running was a *lustratio* of the Palatine city. The last points mentioned by Tacitus, the 'sacellum Larum, forumque Romanum [1],' show plainly that the course was round the Palatine from south-west to north-east, but they do not bring the runners back to the point from which they started, and complete the circle [2]. Varro is, however, quite clear that the running was a *lustratio*: 'Lupercis nudis lustratur antiquum oppidum Palatinum gregibus humanis cinctum.' The passage is obscure, and attempts have been made to amend it; but there can be no doubt that it points to a religious ceremony [3].

This lustratio, then, as we may safely call it, was at the same time a beating of the bounds and a rite of purification and fertilization. Just as the peeled wands of our Oxford bound-beaters on Ascension Day [4] may perhaps have originally had a use parallel to that of the *februa*, so the parish boundaries correspond to the Roman pomoerium. We have already had examples of processional bound-beating in the rites of the Argei and the Ambarvalia; in all there is the same double object—the combination of a religious with a juristic act; but the Lupercalia stands alone in the quaintness of its ritual, and may probably be the oldest of all.

Before we go on to the *februa* and their use, mention must be made of a difficulty in regard to the duality of the collegia of Luperci and the runners. These have been supposed to have originated from two gentile priesthoods of the Fabii and

[1] The reading is not quite certain; the MSS. have 'Larum de forumque.'

[2] The Sacellum Larum has generally been supposed to be that in summa sacra via (Jordan, op. cit. ii. 269). Kiepert and Huelsen make it the sacellum or ara Larum praestitum at the head of the Vicus Tuscus.

[3] *L. L.* 6. 34. Mommsen proposed 'a regibus Romanis moenibus cinctum.' But it is safer to keep to the MS. reading and make the best of it. Jordan sees in the words a 'scurrilous' allusion to the *luperci*.

[4] For modern practices of the kind in England see Brand, *Popular Antiquities*, ch. 36; and for Oxford, p. 209. As Brand puts it, the beaters (i.e. ministers, churchwardens, &c.), '*beg a blessing on the fruits of the earth, and preserve the rights and boundaries of their parish.*' The analogy with the old Italian processions is very close.

Quinctii[1]; and as we know that the gens Fabia had a cult on the Quirinal[2], it is conjectured that the Luperci Fabiani represented the Sabine city, and the Quinctiales the Romans of the Palatine, just as we also find two collegia of Salii, viz. Palatini and Collini[3]. If, however, the running of the Luperci was really a lustratio of the Palatine, we must suppose that the lustratio of the Quirinal city by its own Luperci was given up and merged in that of the older settlement[4]; and such an abandonment of a local rite would be most surprising in Roman antiquity. It is true that there is no other explanation of the existence of the two guilds; but we may hesitate to accept this one, if we have to pay for it by so bold a hypothesis[5].

The last point to be noticed, the whipping with the strips of skin[6], might have attracted little notice as a relic of antiquity in the late Republic but for the famous incident in the life of Caesar, when Antonius was one of the runners. We have it on excellent evidence, not only that the runners struck women who met them with the strips, but that they did so in order to produce fertility[7]. Such an explanation of the object would hardly have been invented, and it tallies closely with some at least of a great number of practices of the kind, which have been investigated by Mannhardt[8]. His parallels

---

[1] So *C. I. L.* 6. 1933 'lupercus Quinctialis vetus.' See Mommsen, *Forsch.* i. 117. Unger, however (p. 56 foll.), argues for the form Quintilianus, as it appears in Fest. 87, and Ovid, *Fasti*, 2. 378; and also denies that the names indicate gentile priesthoods. But his arguments depend on a doubtful etymology. See Marq. 440, note.

[2] Liv. 5. 46. Mommsen connects the name *Kaeso*, which is found in both gentes, with the cutting of the strips at the Lupercalia. The Fabii in Ovid's story (361 foll.) are led by Remus, and the Quintilii by Romulus.

[3] See under March 1, p. 41.

[4] So Mannhardt, 101, who tries to explain it as we have seen.

[5] Gilbert, *Gesch. und Topogr.* i. 86, note, tries to make out that the Fabii belonged to the Palatine proper; and the other guild, not to the Quirinal, but to the Cermalus, and thus also to account for the fact that in Ovid's story the Fabii come first to the feast; but all this is pure guesswork.

[6] Plut. *Rom.* 21 and *Caes.* 61; Ovid, *Fasti*, 2. 425 foll.; Paul. 57; Liv. fragm. 12 (Madvig); Serv. *Aen.* 8. 343. All these passages make it clear that the object was to procure fertility in women. Nic. Damasc., *Vita Caesaris* 21, does not specify women (cp. Dion. Hal. 1. 80).

[7] Liv. l. c. and Serv. l. c. are explicit on this point.

[8] Op. cit. 113 foll. and his *Baumkultus*, p. 251 foll. (see also Frazer, *G. B.* ii. 214 and 232 foll.). An example of the same kind of practice in India is in

are not indeed all either complete or convincing; but the collection is valuable for many purposes, and the general result is to show that whipping certain parts of the body with some instrument supposed to possess magic power is efficacious in driving away the powers of evil that interfere with fertilization. Whether the thing beaten be man, woman, image, or human or animal representative of the Vegetation-spirit, the object is always more or less directly to quicken or restore the natural powers of reproduction; the notion being that the hostile or hindering spirit was thus driven out, or that the beating actually woke up and energized the power. The latter is perhaps a later idea, rationalized from the earlier. In any case the thongs, as part of the sacrosanct victim, were supposed to possess a special magical power [1]; and the word applied to them, *februa*, though not meaning strictly instruments of purification in our sense of the word, may be translated *cathartic* objects, since they had power to free from hostile influences and quicken natural forces. And those who wielded them were regarded in some at least as priests or magicians; they were naked but for the goat-skins, and probably had wreaths on their heads [2]. Their wild and lascivious behaviour as they ran is paralleled in many ceremonies of the kind [3].

It is singular that a festival of a character so rude and rustic should have lived on in the great city for centuries after it had become cosmopolitan and even Christian. This is one of the many results due to the religious enterprise of Augustus, who rebuilt the decayed Lupercal, and set the feast on a new footing [4]. It continued to exist down to the year 494 A.D. when the Pope, Gelasius I, changed the day (Feb. 15) to that of the Purification of the Virgin Mary [5].

Crooke, *Religion and Folklore*, vol. i. p. 100. See under May 1 (Bona Dea), p. 104.

[1] They were also called 'amiculum Iunonis' (Fest. 85 : cp. Ovid, *Fasti*, 2. 427 foll.); Juno here, as so often, representing the female principle. Farnell (*Cults*, i. 100) aptly compares with this the Athenian custom of carrying Athena's *aegis* round Athens, and taking it into the houses of married women.

[2] Lactantius, *Inst.* 1. 21. 45, describes them as 'nudi, uncti, coronati, personati, aut luto obliti currunt'; but we have no certain confirmation from earlier sources except as to the nakedness (Ovid, *Fasti*, 2. 267).

[3] '*Iocantes* obvios petiverunt' (Val. Max.). Mannhardt, *My.h. Forsch.* 140 foll.

[4] Mon. Ancyr. iv. 2; Marq. 446. [5] Baronius, *Annal. Eccles.* viii. 60 foll.

XIII Kal. Mart. (Feb. 17). NP.

QUIR[INALIA]. (CAER. MAFF. FARN. PHILOC.)
QUIRINO IN COLLE. (FARN. CAER.)

How the festival of Quirinus came to be placed at this time
I cannot explain : we know nothing of it, and cannot assume
that it was of an expiatory character, like the Lupercalia
preceding it, and the Feralia following. Of the temple 'in
colle' we also know nothing[1] that can help us. We have
already learnt that this day was called 'stultorum feriae,' and
why ; but the conjunction of the last day of the sacra of the
curiae with those of Quirinus is probably accidental ; we
cannot safely assume any connexion through the word 'curia.'
The name Quirinalia was familiar enough[2] ; but it may be that
it only survived through the *stultorum feriae.*

The Roman of the later Republic identified Quirinus with
Romulus ; Virgil, e. g. in the first *Aeneid* (292) speaks of 'Remo
cum fratre Quirinus[3].' We have no clue to the origin of this
identification. It may have been suggested by the use of the
name Quirites ; but neither do we know when or why that
name came to signify the Roman people in their civil capacity,
and the etymology of these words and their relation to each
other still entirely baffles research[4].

There is, however, a general agreement that Quirinus was
another form of Mars, having his abode on the hill which still
goes by his name. That Mars and Quirinus were ever the
same deities was indeed denied by so acute an inquirer as
Ambrosch[5] ; but he denied it partly on the ground that
no trace of the worship of Mars had been found on the
Quirinal ; and since his time two inscriptions have been
found there on the same spot, one at least of great antiquity,

[1] Aust, *de Aedibus sacris*, p. 11 ; Jordan, *Eph. Epigr.* iii. 238.
[2] e. g. Cic. *ad Quint. Fratr.* 2. 3. 2.
[3] See other references in Preller, i. 374, note. Ambrosch (*Studien*, 169,
note 50) observes that Cicero (*de Off*. 3. 10) writes with a trace of scepticism :
'Romulus fratre interempto sine controversia peccavit, pace vel Quirini
vel Romuli dixerim.'
[4] See Jordan on Preller, i. 369. The article 'Quirinus' in *Myth. Lex.*
has not yet appeared as I write.
[5] *Studien*, 169.

which indicate votive offerings to Mars and Quirinus respectively[1]. From these Mommsen concludes that Quirinus was at one time worshipped there under the name of Mars; which involves also the converse, that Mars was once worshipped under the adjectival cult-title Quirinus. Unluckily Mars Quirinus is a combination as yet undiscovered; and as the existence of a patrician Flamen Quirinalis distinct from the Flamen Martialis points at least to a very early differentiation of the two, it may be safer to think of the two, not as identical deities, but rather as equivalent cult-expressions of the same religious conception in two closely allied communities[2].

That the Quirinal was the seat of the cult of Quirinus admits of no doubt; and the name of the hill, which we are told was originally Agonus or Agonalis[3], arose no doubt from the cult[4]. Here were probably two temples of the god, the one dating from B.C. 293, and having June 29 as its day of dedication; the other of unknown date, which celebrated its birthday on the Quirinalia[5]. A 'sacellum Quirini in colle' is also mentioned at the time of the Gallic invasion[6] (this was perhaps the predecessor of the temple of June 29), and also the house of the Flamen Quirinalis which adjoined it. To the Quirinal also belong the Salii Agonenses, Collini, or Quirinales, who correspond to the Salii of the Palatine and of Mars[7]. And here,

---

[1] *C. I. L.* i. 41 = vi. 475 and i. 630 = vi. 565. The older one is attributed by Mommsen to the consul P. Cornelius of B.C. 236: 'P. Corn[elios] L. f. coso[l] prob[avit] Mar[te sacrom].' The other, 'Quirino L. Aimilius L. f. praitor,' must be set down to an Aemilius praetor in 204, 191, or 190. The inference is that Mars became known as Quirinus in that spot at the end of the third century B C. It is worth noting that the legendary smith, Mamurius, had a statue on the Quirinal (Jord. *Top.* ii. 125).

[2] This is much what Dion. Hal. 2. 48 says was one view held in his time: οὐκ ἔχοντας εἰπεῖν τὸ ἀκριβὲς εἴτε Ἄρης ἐστὶν εἴτε ἕτερός τις ὁμοίας Ἄρει τιμὰς ἔχων.

[3] See on Jan. 9. Fest. 254.

[4] Gilbert, i. 283, points out that in the Argean itinerary (Jord. *Top.* ii. 237 foll.) one of the *divisions* of the Quirinal bears the name, and infers the gradual spread of the cult of Quirinus over the whole hill; but he insists that it was introduced from the Palatine. The general result of his wild but ingenious combinations is to infer a religious conquest of the Quirinal from the Palatine.

[5] Aust, op. cit. pp. 11 and 33. Mommsen, *C. I. L.* i. 310, takes the one of unknown date as the older.

[6] Aust, op. cit. 51, where for Liv. 4. 21 read Liv. 5. 40.

[7] Preller, i. 356.

lastly, seems to belong the mysterious Flora or Horta Quirini, whose temple, according to Plutarch[1], was 'formerly' always open. About the cult of Quirinus on his hill we know, however, nothing, except that there were two myrtles growing in front of his temple, one called the patrician and the other the plebeian[2], and to which a curious story is attached. Preller[3] noted that these correspond to the two laurels in the *sacrarium Martis* in the Regia, and conjectured that each pair symbolized the union of the state in the cults of the two communities.

Of the duties of the Flamen Quirinalis we have already seen something[4]: unluckily they throw little or no new light on the cult of Quirinus. He was concerned in the worship of Robigus, of Consus, and of Acca Larentia, all of them ancient cults of agricultural Rome ; and he seems to have been in close con- nexion with the Vestal Virgins[5]. These are just such duties as we might have expected would fall to the Flamen of Mars ; and probably the two cults were much alike in character.

VII KAL. MART. (FEB. 23.) NP.

TER[MINALIA].   (CAER. MAFF. RUST. PHILOC. SILV.)

Was there any connexion between the Terminalia and the end of the year ? The Roman scholars thought so; Varro[6] writes, 'Terminalia quod is dies anni extremus constitutus ; duodecimus enim fuit Februarius, et quum intercalatur, in- feriores quinque dies duodecimo demuntur mense.' So Ovid,

> Tu quoque sacrorum, Termine, finis eras.

But Terminus is the god of the boundaries of land, and has nothing to do with time ; and the Terminalia is not the last festival of the year in the oldest calendars. The Romans must have been misled by the coincidence of the day of Terminus with the last day before intercalation. The position in the

---

[1] *Q. R.* 46; Ennius ap. Nonium 120; Gell. 13. 23.
[2] Plin. *H. N.* 15. 120.   [3] i. 373.
[4] See under April 25, Aug. 21, Dec. 23. Marq. 335 ; Schwegler, i. 334.
[5] Liv. 5. 40, 7 and 8.
[6] *L. L.* 6. 13. According to Macrob. (1. 13. 15) the five last days of February were added after the intercalation, in order that March might follow on Feb., and not on the intercalated days.

year of the rites to be described seems parallel to that of
the Compitalia and Paganalia, which were concerned with
matters of common interest to a society of farmers: and we
may remember that Pliny[1] said of the Fornacalia that it
was 'farris torrendi feriae et *aeque religiosae terminis agrorum.*'

The ritual of the Terminalia in the country districts is
described by Ovid[2]. The two landowners garlanded each his
side of the boundary-stone, and all offerings were double[3]. An
altar is made; and fire is carried from the hearth by the
farmer's wife, while the old man cuts up sticks and builds
them in a framework of stout stakes. Then with dry bark the
fire is kindled; from a basket, held ready by a boy[4], the little
daughter of the family thrice shakes the fruits of the earth into
the fire, and offers cakes of honey. Others stand by with
wine; and the neighbours (or dependants) look on in silence
and clothed in white. A lamb is slain, and a sucking-pig,
and the boundary-stone sprinkled with their blood; and the
ceremony ends with a feast and songs in praise of holy
Terminus.

This rite was, no doubt, practically a yearly renewal of that
by which the stone was originally fixed in its place. The latter
is described by the gromatic writer Siculus Flaccus[5]. Fruits
of the earth, and the bones, ashes, and blood of a victim which
had been offered were put into a hole by the two (or three)
owners whose land converged at the point, and the stone was
rammed down on the top and carefully fixed. The reason
given for this was of course that the stone might be identified
in the future, e. g. by an arbiter, if one should be called in[6];
but it also reminds us of the practice of burying the remains

---

[1] *H. N.* 18. 8. See above, p. 304. [2] *Fasti,* 2. 643 foll.
[3] Te duo diversa domini pro parte coronant,
      Binaque serta tibi binaque liba ferunt.
[4] This must be a son of the family. We have, therefore, in this
charming picture the predecessors of the Rex, the Regina sacrorum, the
flamines, and the Vestal Virgins.

      Stat puer et manibus lata canistra tenet.
      Inde ubi ter fruges medios immisit in ignes,
      Porrigit incisos filia parva favos.

De-Marchi, p. 231, gives a cut of a painting at Herculaneum which may
represent a scene of this kind.
[5] *Gromatici veteres,* i. 141. See Rudorff in vol. ii. 236 for an interesting
discussion of the religio terminorum and its ethical and legal results.
[6] Rudorff, l. c. 237.

of a victim[1], and the use of the blood shows the extreme
sanctity of the operation.

That the stone was regarded as the dwelling-place of a *numen*
is proved by the fact that it was sprinkled with blood and garlanded[2] ; and the development of a god Terminus is perfectly
in keeping with Roman religious ideas. It is more difficult to
determine what was the relation of this Terminus to the great
Jupiter who was so intimately associated, as we have seen[3],
with the idea of keeping faith with your neighbours. Was he
the *numen* originally thought to occupy the stone, and is the
name Terminus, as marking a distinct deity, a later growth?
I am disposed to think that this was so ; for we saw that there
is some reason to believe that Jupiter did not disdain to
dwell in objects such as trees and stones, and there is no need
to look to Greece for the origin of his connexion with boundaries[4].
But Jupiter and Terminus remained on the whole distinct ; and
a Jupiter Terminus or Terminalis is first found on the coins of
Varro the great scholar, probably in B. C. 76[5].

The close connexion of the two is seen in the legend that
when Jupiter was to be introduced into the great Capitoline
temple, from the Capitolium vetus on the Quirinal, all the gods
made way for him but Terminus[6]:

> Quid nova cum fierent Capitolia? nempe deorum
> Cuncta Iovi cessit turba, locumque dedit.
> Terminus, ut veteres memorant, inventus in aede
> Restitit, et magno cum Iove templa tenet.

This, as Preller truly observes, is only a poetical way of
expressing his stubbornness, and his close relation to Jupiter,
with whom he continued to share the great temple. It seems
certain that there was in that temple a stone supposed to be

---

[1] Jevons, *Introduction to the History of Religion*, 149.

[2] Robertson Smith, *Religion of the Semites*, 187 foll.

[3] See under September, p. 229 foll. I may here notice the very curious
'oraculum' in *Grom. Vet.* p. 350 (ex libris Vegoiae) which connects Jupiter
with the introduction of termini in Etruria.

[4] Ζεὺς ὅριος he is called by Dion. Hal. (2. 74), where the cult is ascribed
to Numa. Farnell, *Cults of the Greek States*, i. 159.

[5] Aust, in *Myth. Lex.* s. v. Iuppiter, 668.

[6] *Fasti*, 2. 667 ; Liv. 1. 55 ; Serv. *Aen.* 9. 448. Augustine, *C. D.* 4. 23, adds
Mars, and Dion. Hal. 3. 69 Iuventus to Terminus, who could not be
'exauguratus.'

that of Terminus, over which there was a hole in the roof[1] :
for all sacrifice to Terminus must be made in the open air.

> Nunc quoque, se supra ne quid nisi sidera cernat,
> Exiguum templi tecta foramen habent[2].

Precisely the same feature is found in the cult of Semo
Sancus or Dius Fidius[3], who was concerned with oaths and
treaties ; and of Hercules we are told that the oath taken
in his name must be taken out of doors[4].

Of the stone itself we know nothing. It is open to us to
guess that it was originally a boundary-stone, perhaps between
the ager of the Palatine city and that of the Quirinal. The
mons Capitolinus seems to have been neutral ground, as we
may guess by the tradition of the asylum there ; it was
outside the pomoerium, and in the early Republic was the
property of the priestly collegia[5]. It was, therefore, a very
appropriate place for a terminus between two communities[6].

From Ovid (679 foll.) we gather that there was a terminus-
stone at the sixth milestone on the via Laurentina, at which
public sacrifices were made, perhaps on the day of the Terminalia: this was probably at one time the limit of the ager
Romanus in that direction.

vi Kal. Mart. (Feb. 24). N.

'REGIF[UGIUM]. (caer. maff. philoc.) regifugium, cum
tarquinius superbus fertur ab urbe expulsus. (silv.)

This note of Silvius is based on a very old and natural
misapprehension. Ovid[7], and probably most Romans, believed

---

[1] Serv. *Aen.* 9. 448 'Unde in Capitolio prona pars tecti patet, quae
lapidem ipsum Termini spectat.' This is the 'Capitoli immobile saxum'
of Virgil ; see above, p. 230.

[2] Ovid, l. c. 671. [3] See above, p. 140. Varro, *L. L.* 5. 66.
[4] Plut. *Q. R.* 28. [5] Ambrosch, *Studien*, 199 foll.
[6] It would exactly correspond to the spot of sacred ground on which
the terminus-stone stood between two properties (Rudorff, l. c.). In the
latter case, it is worth noting, the sacrifices and sacrificers are doubles,
as with the Salii, Luperci, &c., of the two Roman settlements. Mr. Granger
(*Worship of the Romans*, 163) suggests that this stone was 'a relic from the
original dwellers by the Tiber,' i.e. pre-Roman. But the question is, How
did the Romans come to associate it with Terminus ?

[7] *Fasti*, 2. 685 foll. He is probably following Varro and common opinion,
which latter Verrius refers to (Paul. 279) 'Regifugium sacrum dicebant,

that the expulsion of Tarquin was commemorated on this day.
There is, however, strong indirect evidence to show that the
'flight of the king' on Feb. 24 was something very different.

1. We have already had a 'flight of the people' (Poplifugia)
on July 5; and we saw that this was probably a purificatory
rite of which the meaning had been lost—the sacrifice perhaps
of a sacred animal followed by the flight of the crowd as
from a murder. It seems impossible, at any rate unwise, to
separate Poplifugia and Regifugium in general meaning, for
there is no other parallel to them in the calendar. Both
were explained historically by the Romans, because in both the
obscure (and perhaps obsolete) religious rite was inexplicable
otherwise; and we must also endeavour to treat both on the
same principle.

2. It seems pretty clear that Verrius Flaccus did not believe
in the historical explanation of the Regifugium. In Festus,
page 278, we find a mutilated gloss which evidently refers
to this day, and is thus completed by Mommsen [1] :—

[*Regifugium notatur in fastis dies a. d.*] vi kal. [*Mart. qui
creditur sic dict*]us quia [*eo die Tarquinius rex fugerit ex urbe*].
Quod fal[*sum est; nam e castris in exilium abisse eum r*]*ettul*[*e-
runt annales. Rectius explicabit qui regem e*]*t Salios* [2] [*hoc die . . .
facere sacri*]*ficium in* [*comitio eoque perfecto illum inde fugere
n*]*overit. . .*

It may be said that this is all guesswork, and no evidence;
but it is borne out by the following passage in Plutarch's sixty-
third Roman question:

Ἔστι γοῦν τις ἐν ἀγορᾷ θυσία πρὸς τῷ λεγομένῳ Κομητίῳ πάτριος, ἣν
θύσας ὁ βασιλεὺς κατὰ τάχος ἄπεισι φεύγων ἐξ ἀγορᾶς.

Whence Plutarch drew this statement we cannot tell. He
does not give the day on which the sacrifice and flight took

quo die rex Tarquinius fugerit e Roma.' The word *dicebant* seems to show
that this was not Verrius' own opinion.

[1] *C. I. L.* i. 289. This gloss is no doubt the equivalent in Festus to that
of Paulus just quoted; but the leading word Regifugium is lost. I have
only quoted so much as is needed for our purpose. For other completions
of the gloss see Müller, *Festus*, l. c., and Huschke, *Röm. Jahr*, p. 166.

[2] If this gloss really refers to Feb. 24, the presence of the Salii is difficult to account for, as their period of activity begins in March. Frazer in
an interesting note (*G. B.* ii. 210) suggests that the use of the Salii was to
drive away evil demons; if the Regifugium was a solemn piaculum, and
the victim a scapegoat, this explanation might serve for Feb. 24.

place; and Huschke[1] has denied that he refers to the Regifugium at all. He believes that Plutarch is thinking of the days marked Q. R. C. F. (March 24 and May 24), on which Varro says, or seems to say, that the Rex sacrorum sacrificed in the Comitium[2]; and this may have been so, for the note in the Fasti Praenestini on March 24 shows that there was a popular misinterpretation of Q. R. C. F, which took the letters to mean, 'quod eo die ex comitio fugerit rex.' In this confusion we can but appeal to the word Regifugium, which is attached to Feb. 24 only. Taking this together with Plutarch's statement, and remembering the great improbability of the historical explanation being the true one, we are justified in accepting Mommsen's completion of the passage in Festus, and in concluding that there was really on Feb. 24 a flight of the Rex after a sacrifice.

And this view is strengthened by the frequent occurrence of sacerdotal flights in ancient and primitive religions. These were first collected by Lobeck[3], and have of late been treated of and variously explained by Mannhardt, Frazer, and Robertson Smith[4]. The best known examples are those of the Bouphonia ('ox murder') at Athens, in which every feature shows that the slain ox was regarded, 'not merely as a victim offered to a god, but in itself a sacred creature, the slaughter of which was sacrilege or murder'[5]; and the sacrifice of a bull-calf to Dionysus at Tenedos, where the priest was attacked with stones, and had to flee for his life[6]. We do not yet know for certain whether the origin of these ideas is to be found in totemism, or in the sanctity of cattle in the pastoral age, or in the representation of the spirit of vegetation in animal form. The second of these explanations, as elucidated by Robertson Smith, would seem most applicable to the Athenian rite; but in the case of the Roman one, we do not know what the victim

---

[1] *Röm. Jahr*, 166 foll.

[2] *L. L.* 6. 31, where Hirschfeld has conjectured 'litat ad comitium' for the MS. 'dicat.'

[3] *Aglaophamus*, 676.

[4] Mannhardt, *Myth. Forsch.* 58 foll.; Frazer, *Golden Bough*, ii. 35 foll.; Robertson Smith, *Religion of the Semites*, 286 foll. Cp. Lang, *Myth, Ritual and Religion*, ii. 233 foll. See also Farnell, *Cults of the Greek States*, i. 88 foll., who agrees in the main with Robertson Smith.

[5] Frazer, l. c.   [6] Aelian, *N. A.* 12. 34.

was. It is also just possible, as Hartung long ago suggested [1], that the victim was a scapegoat carrying away pollution, and therefore to be avoided ; but I do not find any example of flight from a scapegoat, among the many instances collected by Mr. Frazer (*Golden Bough*, ii. 182 foll.).

III KAL. MART. (FEB. 27). N̄P.
EQ[UIRRIA]. (MAFF. CAER. : cp. Varro, *L. L.* 6. 13).

We have no data whatever for guessing why a horse-race should take place on the last day of February, or why there should be two days of racing, the second being March 14. This has not, however, prevented Huschke [2] from making some marvellous conjectures, in which ingenuity and learning have been utterly thrown away.

We saw [3] that the oldest races of this kind were connected with harvest rejoicings ; and Mannhardt [4] suggested that they originated in the desire to catch the spirit of vegetation in the last·sheaf or in some animal form. Races also occur in various parts of Europe in the spring—e.g. at the Carnival, at Easter, and at Whitsuntide ; and of these he says that they correspond with the others, and that the idea at the bottom of them is ' die Vorstellung des wetteifernden Frühlingsein-zuges der Vegetationsdämonen.' However this may be, we cannot but be puzzled by the doubling of the Equirria, and are tempted to refer it to the same cause as that of the Salii and Luperci [5].

That both were connected with the cult of Mars is almost beyond question. They were held in the Campus Martius, and were supposed to have been established by Romulus in honour of Mars [6] ; and we have already had an example of the occurrence of horses in the Mars-cult. It would seem, then,

---

[1] *Relig. der Römer*, ii. 35. Cp. Gilbert, i. 343, note. The presence of the Salii (see above, p. 328), if a fact, would be in favour of this explanation.

[2] *Röm. Jahr*, 199.   [3] See on Aug. 21 (Consualia).

[4] *Myth. Forsch.* 170 foll. ; *Baumkultus*, 382 foll.

[5] This, though with impossible combinations, is what Huschke does (199, note 53). Feb. 27 is the Roman, March 14 the Quirinal Equirria, in his view. That the Quirinalia falls in February may perhaps give some support to the view.

[6] Varro, *L. L.* 6. 13 ; Fest. 81. See under Oct. 15.

that the peculiar features of the worship of Mars began even *before* March 1. Preller noticed this long ago [1], and suggested that even the Lupercalia and the Quirinalia have some relation to the Mars-cult, and that these fall at the time when the first beginnings of spring are felt—e.g. when the first swallows arrive [2]. We may perhaps add the appearance of the Salii at the Regifugium to these foreshadowings of the March rites. Ovid seems to bear out Preller in his lines on this day [3]:

> Iamque duae restant noctes de mense secundo,
> Marsque citos iunctis curribus urget equos:
> Ex vero positum permansit Equirria nomen,
> Quae deus in Campo prospicit ipse suo.
> Iure venis, Gradive. Locum tua tempora poscunt,
> Signatusque tuo nomine mensis adest.

I may aptly add Ovid's next couplet, now that we have at last reached the end of the Roman year:—

> Venimus in portum, libro cum mense peracto.
> Naviget hinc alia iam mihi linter aqua.

[1] i. 361.
[2] So Ovid, on Feb. 26, writes (2. 853):
> Fallimur, an veris praenuntia venit hirundo,
> Et metuit ne qua versa recurrat hiems?
This would be early now for central Italy; but Columella, 11. 2, gives Feb. 23 as the date.
[3] *Fasti*, 2. 857 foll.

CONCLUSION

At the end of the introductory chapter a promise was made that when we had completed the round of the year, we would sum up our results, sketch in outline the history of Roman religious ideas, and estimate the influence of all this elaborate ceremonial on the life and character of the Roman people. This undertaking I must now endeavour to fulfil, though with doubt and diffidence; for even after the most careful examination of the Calendar, both the character and the history of the Roman religious system must still in great degree remain a mystery. With such knowledge however as may have been gleaned in the preceding pages, the reader may be able to appreciate or criticize a few conclusions of a more general character.

The Roman religion has been ably discussed in general terms by several writers of note in the century just closing. Mommsen's chapters in the early books of his Roman History are familiar to every one. The introduction to Marquardt's volume on our subject is indispensable; and Preller, less exact perhaps, but more sympathetic and inspiring, still holds the field with the opening chapters of his work on Roman Mythology. To these classical works may be added the section on the Roman religion in the second volume of the *Religionsgeschichte* of Chantepie de la Saussaye, and the first chapter of Boissier's work on the Roman religion from Augustus onwards. Professor Granger's *Worship of the Romans* also contains here and there some suggestive remarks, though as a rule these are not based upon any elaborate investigation of the cult. Lastly I may mention a small but valuable treatise, published as long ago as 1837 by Leopold Krahner, on the history of the decay of the Roman religion down to the time of Augustus, which fell into my hands many years ago, and is in almost every sentence of value to the student of Roman history.

In all these works the one point insisted on at the outset is this: that the Romans were more interested in the cult of their deities, that is, in the ritual and routine by which they could be rightly and successfully propitiated, than in the character and personality of the deities themselves. This is indeed a truth which has been abundantly borne out in our examination of the Calendar, and might be further illustrated in almost every public act of procedure in the Roman State. Cicero himself expresses it well in the second book of his *De Natura Deorum* (2. 3. 8) 'Si conferre volumus nostra cum externis, ceteris rebus aut pares aut etiam inferiores reperiemur, religione, id est cultu deorum, multo superiores.' The second book of his work *De Legibus* is also an invaluable witness to the conviction, lasting on even in an age of scepticism and indifference among the educated, that the due performance of sacred rites was a necessary function of the State, on which its very existence depended. The Christian Fathers, some of whom, like St. Augustine and Tertullian, were men of learning who had studied the voluminous works of Varro, were well aware of this character; and Tertullian in a curious passage went so far as to suggest that the Devil had here perpetrated an imitation or parody of the minute ritual of Leviticus [1]. So far as externals go, the comparison he suggested is a useful one; but there is an essential difference in the religious spirit which lay at the root of the two ceremonial systems—a difference that makes it impossible that any work should be written on the Roman religion as inspiring for the student of religious history as *The Religion of the Semites* so often quoted in these pages.

This elaborate Roman ceremonial consisted in the main of sacrifices of different kinds, conducted with an endless but ordered variety of detail, of prayers, processions, and festivities, the object of which was either to obtain certain practical results, to discover the will of the gods, or to rejoice with the

---

[1] Tertullian, *de Praescriptionibus Haereticorum*, 40.

divine inhabitants of the city over the prosperous event of some undertaking. When we survey it in the Calendar as a whole, it seems to fall naturally into three divisions, which correspond with and illustrate the development of the State from its constituent materials. The Calendar contains in fact in a fossilized condition the remains of three different strata of religious or social development.

(1) Here and there we find survivals of what we can only regard as the most primitive condition of human life in ancient Latium : that of men dwelling on forest-clad hill-tops, surrounded by a world of spirits, some of which have taken habitation in, or are in some sort represented by, objects such as trees, animals, or stones. Examples of such objects are the oak of Jupiter Feretrius, the sacred fig-tree of Rumina, the stone of Terminus with its buried sacrifice, and the wolf, the wood-pecker, and spear of Mars. To this earliest stratum may also belong in their ultimate origin those quaint sacrificial or semi-dramatic rites of which we have had examples in the Lupercalia, the Fordicidia, and the Parilia. The casting of the Argei into the Tiber may perhaps also be reckoned here, though connected later on with certain divisions of the developed city of which the meaning and origin are lost to us. This primitive popula-tion knew also of charms and spells and omens, not reduced indeed as yet to a definite system, of which the Calendar naturally supplies hardly any indications, while in Ovid and Cato not a few survivals meet us. But the investigation of the oldest culture of central Italy is more especially the province of archaeology, and to the archaeologists, who are now in Italy doing excellent and elaborate work, I must be content to leave it.

(2) We next come conjecturally to clearly-defined evidence of a period in which the ordered processes of agriculture, and the settled life of the farm-house, are the distinctive features. We have the beginnings of a calendar in the observation of the quarters of the moon and their connexion with the deities of light. We have the discipline of the house, represented in the cult of Vesta the hearth-spirit, under the care of the daughters of the family, while the sons as *flamines* have their special sacrificial duties, the head of the house presiding over all, and having as his own special department the worship of

the spirit of the door-way (Janus). The occupations of the
family are reflected in the series of festivals which represent
the processes and perils of pastoral and agricultural industry:
e. g. the Robigalia, Ambarvalia, Vestalia, Consualia, Opiconsivia, Vinalia, Saturnalia, and Terminalia: this last indicating
also the idea of property, whether of the community or the
individual. We have also clear traces of the union of farms
in a group (*pagus*); for the Paganalia still survived in the
full-grown city, and both at the Saturnalia and Compitalia
the households met together at the winter period of ease and
rejoicing.

(3) The further development of social life is also reflected
in the annual rites we have been investigating. We see the
aggregation of small communities in the Septimontium, in
the Fornacalia or feast of the Curiae, possibly also in the
ritual of the twenty-four or twenty-seven Sacella Argeorum,
round which a procession seems to have gone in March and
May. The Parentalia again is the systematized cult of the
dead in their own city, outside the walls of the city of
the living. The Lares Praestites, worshipped on May 1, are
the guardian spirits of the whole community. The Regia, the
dwelling of the king, is its political and religious centre, with
its sacrarium of Mars, the peculiar deity of the stock, and with
the house and hearth of Vesta close by, now grown to be the
symbol of the State's vitality. The Vestals and Flamines have
become priests of special worships in an organized state, and
at the head of all is the Rex, still specially concerned with the
cult of Janus, but representing in his priestly capacity the
whole community. The steadily increasing tendency to organize,
a tendency rooted in the very fibre of this people, is producing
colleges of pontifices and augurs, to assist by associated effort
in making sure of the laws of intercourse with the unseen
world, and of the best methods of divining its will and
intention. And lastly, not only have we found in the festivals
traces of the growth and systematization of the life of the city,
but in the great Latin festival we have also religious evidence
of the early tendency of the cities of Latin blood to combine in
some sort with each other.

We have thus reached what has been called by Preller the
period of Numa, the king with whose name and personality

the Romans always associated the redaction of the Fasti and
the state-organization of their religion: a personality so clearly
conceived by them as to bear witness at once to its own
historical reality, and to their conviction of the vital importance
of his work. Before we go further, let us pause here to
interrogate the Calendar as to the nature of the divine beings
who in these same stages of development were the objects of
popular worship. The simplest way to do this will be to
present a table showing the list of the most ancient festivals,
with the deities concerned in them, so far as they can be
identified, in a parallel column:—

Festivals.	*Deities.*
KALENDS	JUNO.
IDES	JUPITER.
EQUIRRIA	MARS.
LIBERALIA	LIBER.
FORDICIDIA	TELLUS ?
CERIALIA	CERES.
PARILIA	PALES ?
ROBIGALIA	ROBIGUS.
LEMURIA	Ghosts (unburied).
ARGEORUM SACRA	Unknown.
AGONIA	VEDIOVIS ?
VESTALIA	VESTA.
MATRALIA	MATER MATUTA.
POPLIFUGIA	Unknown.
LUCARIA	,,
NEPTUNALIA	NEPTUNUS.
FURRINALIA	FURRINA ?
PORTUNALIA	PORTUNUS.
VINALIA	JUPITER.
CONSUALIA	CONSUS.
VOLCANALIA	VOLCANUS.
OPICONSIVIA	OPS CONSIVA
MEDITRINALIA	Unknown.
FONTINALIA	FONS ?
AGONIA	Unknown.
CONSUALIA	CONSUS.
SATURNALIA	SATURNUS.
OPALIA	OPS.
DIVALIA	ANGERONA ?
LARENTALIA	LARENTIA ?
AGONIA	JANUS ?
CARMENTALIA	CARMENTA.
LUPERCALIA	Unknown.
QUIRINALIA	QUIRINUS.
FERALIA	BURIED ANCESTORS.
TERMINALIA	TERMINUS.
REGIFUGIUM	Unknown.

Here it will be noticed that in those festivals which seem to be survivals from the oldest stratum of civilization (the period of Faunus, as Preller has named it), viz. the Lupercalia, Parilia, Fordicidia, Argeorum Sacra, the deities concerned are either altogether doubtful, or so wanting in clearness and prominence as to be altogether subordinate in interest to the details of the ceremony. The Parilia and Fordicidia were believed in later times to have belonged to Pales and Tellus; but our authority for the grounds of such belief is not strong, and as a matter of fact these two, together with the sacrifice of the October horse, were interconnected by details of antique ceremonial, rather than separately defined by their relation to particular *numina*. In other festivals which may have possibly come down from the oldest period, the deity is almost entirely lost. Here is good evidence of the indistinctness of the Roman conception of the divine; the cult appealed to this people as the practical method of obtaining their desires, but the unseen powers with whom they dealt in this cult were beyond their ken, often unnamed, and only visible in the sense of being seated in, or in some sort symbolized by, tree or stone or animal. They are often multiplex, like the Fauni, Silvani, Lares, Penates, Semones, Carmentes; or they run into each other, like Bona Dea, Maia, Tellus, Ceres, Dea Dia, and others. Only the great deity of the stock stands out at all clearly; Father Mars of the Romans; Father Diovis of the whole Latin race; to these we may perhaps add the Hercules or Genius, and Juno, representing respectively the male and female principles of human life.

In the second and third of the strata which the Calendar offers to the excavator, representing the ordered life of the household and afterwards of the city, we still find much of the same indistinctness. Vesta indeed, the spirit of the hearth-fire, becomes clearly though not personally delineated; so too, but in a less degree, does Janus the spirit of the doorway. Two other groups of spirits also occupy the house; the Lares, who may have been the spirits of dead ancestors duly buried, and the Penates or spirits of the store-chamber; both of them becoming sufficiently clear in the popular conception to be represented by images at a very early period. But in the round of ancient festivals, some at least of the so-called gods,

z

so far as we can guess at their original nature, hardly deserve that name. Liber and Ceres seem to have been originally general names for an ill-defined class of spirits ; Robigus is the spirit of the mildew ; Consus and Ops are not personalities, but *numina* protecting the gathered harvest, as Saturnus probably protected the sown seed. The Compitalia was concerned only with the Lares Compitales, spirits of the crossways ; in the Paganalia we have but very indistinct information as to the object of worship. The Vinalia, marking a later and more skilled agricultural process, seems on the other hand always to have been clearly connected with Jupiter himself.

Thus in the so-called period of Numa, the period of the earlier monarchy and the first organization of the city-state, the religious life of the community had become highly systematized in respect of the cult, of the priest in charge of it, and the *ius* which governed all the citizens in their relation to the world of divinities. Of any real change however in the character of these divinities, of any approach to polytheism in the way of an increased individuality of conception, of iconic representation, or definite temple-worship, the Calendar then drawn up supplies no certain evidence. There may indeed have been a tendency towards a clearer definition of *numina*, arising from the very fact of the definite organization of prayer and sacrifice, and of the allotment of cults to particular priesthoods or families. There may, even at that early stage in Roman history, have been an influence at work on the Roman mind, coming from Etruria and Greece, where polytheism found its nourishment in works of art and mythological fancy. These are possibilities of which we must take account, but the Calendar has nothing positive to tell us of them.

It is when we advance to the later monarchy, which we may speak of without hesitation as an Etruscan dynasty, that we find a change beginning, both in the forms and objects of the cult, which marks an epoch in Roman religious history. The oldest Calendar, that of the large letters in the Fasti, tells us of course nothing of this. But in the *additamenta ex fastis*, and in later literary allusions, we have a considerable body of material to help us in following out the character and consequences of this change. It is at this point, or rather at the end of the monarchy, that we begin to hear of the building

of real temples, as distinct from luci, sacella, arae, or fana ; of
the introduction into these of statues of the gods, of the *Graecus
ritus* in sacrifice, and of the appearance of new deities, some of
them apparently connected with new elements of population.

This epoch is most clearly marked by the building of the
great temple on the Capitol of Jupiter, Juno, and Minerva,
an Etruscan Trias, perhaps ultimately of Greek origin, whose
statues, as we have seen, were invited in true polytheistic
fashion to partake of a feast every year on the Ides of
September, the *dies natalis* of the temple. This temple was
dedicated in B.C. 509, directly after the expulsion of Tarquinius
Superbus. The next of which we hear is that of the old
Roman Saturnus (B.C. 497), now strangely represented by a
fettered statue, and worshipped henceforward *Graeco ritu*, with
the head uncovered. Next comes Mercurius (B.C. 495), a god
unknown to the most ancient Fasti; then Ceres, the Greek
Demeter under a familiar Italian name (B.C. 493); next Fortuna with a statue (B.C. 486), an imported goddess, to whom
Servius Tullius, if tradition can be trusted, had already erected
temples. To this same age belongs probably the temple of
Diana on the Aventine, with a Greek ξόανον; and the introduction of Apollo-worship as a popular cult. If we follow the
catalogue of dedications during the two centuries following the
abolition of the monarchy [1], we find that out of fourteen of
which the dates are known to us, six are Greek or Graeco-
Etruscan, three more admit before long a non-Roman ritual
under the influence of the *duoviri sacris faciundis*, and five are
known to have contained statues from an early period. Only
three, those of Dius Fidius, of Juno Lucina, and of Mater Matuta,
can be said to have been genuine Roman foundations. Without
doubt a great change is here indicated which has come over
the Roman religion, both in cult and theology. New elements
of population, new relations with conquerors or conquered,
new commercial enterprise, new experiences of war, famine,
and pestilence, bring in new deities, suggest recourse to new
divine aids. The old Rome is almost a thing of the past; the
cults and deities of the Numan period no longer suffice, and
are perhaps already beginning to be forgotten; the oldest

---

[1] Collected by Aust in his work *de Aedibus sacris*, pp. 4 foll.

priesthoods begin to give place in all except empty externals
to the semi-political colleges of pontifices and augurs, and to
the important new foundation of *duoviri sacris faciundis*; the
old Italian ritual of simple apparatus and detailed ceremony
is becoming overshadowed by the showy ceremonial of lectisternia and supplicationes.

Was there no reaction, we may well ask, against a tendency
so expansive and denationalizing? I answer this question with
hesitation, for so far as I am aware it has never yet been fully
investigated. But I am strongly disposed to believe that there
was such a reaction in the third century B. C., in the period, that
is, between the Samnite wars and Hannibal's invasion of Italy.
This, unlike the preceding century, was a period of almost
uniform success of the Roman arms, and one in which the
State was at no time in serious peril; and the temptation to
have recourse to strange divinities, as a patient betakes himself
to new physicians, would not present itself to the minds of the
senate or the priesthoods. If we pursue the history of the
temple-foundations of this period, under Aust's invaluable
guidance, the result is very remarkable. Between 304 and
217 B.C. we know the dates of twenty-five foundations; and
of these no less than twenty are in honour of indigenous, or
at least what I may perhaps call, home-made deities. No
doubt there is a growing tendency to identify Roman gods
with Greek; but this does not show itself plainly till the end
of the century, and the only genuine Greek foundation is that
of Aesculapius, the consequence of a severe pestilence in 293 B.C.
Three or four, e.g. those of Fors Fortuna, Minerva Capta, and
Feronia, were probably of non-Roman origin; but they were
transplanted from the near neighbourhood of Rome and may
almost count as indigenous.

In contemplating the Roman foundations of this period we
are struck by certain indications of the activity of the *pontifices*,
as distinguished from the *duoviri sacris faciundis*; i. e. the
activity of that college of priests whose special charge was
the Roman religion proper, and who were only indirectly concerned with foreign introductions. For example, we may note
with interest a group of four agricultural deities, to whom
temples were dedicated in the eight years between 272 and
264 B. C., the years, that is, of the pacification and settlement

of Italy after the invasion of Pyrrhus [1]. These deities were Consus, Tellus, Pales, and Vortumnus. Owing to the loss of Livy's second decade we cannot be very certain of the immediate object of these foundations; but we may guess that they had a definite meaning in connexion with the events of the time, and that they were chiefly the work of the pontifical college. Less distinct perhaps, but still worth noticing, is a group of foundations in honour of deities connected with water [2], i.e. to Tempestates, Juturna and Fons, which seem to have had some reference to the naval operations of the First Punic War. The temple of Juturna was vowed by Lutatius Catulus in the battle at the Aegates Insulae in 241 B.C.; that to the Tempestates by Cornelius Scipio, when the fleet was almost destroyed near Corsica in 259 B.C.; and that of Fons in the Corsican war in 231 B.C. It was characteristic of the Roman mind, and of the pontifical methods, thus to connect the spirits of the springs in Rome with those of the sea and its tempests.

It is at this time also that we notice the appearance of abstractions resolved into deities, such as Salus, Spes, Fides, Honos et Virtus, Concordia, and Mens. These, as I have said elsewhere [3], are not genuine old Roman cults, but pontifical creations in the spirit of the old Roman impersonal and daemonic ideas of divine agency. In connexion with these I may mention the conviction which has grown upon me in the course of these investigations, that it was in this reactionary period, as we may call it, that the pontifices drew up that extraordinary list of deities, classified according to their functions in relation to man and his activity and suffering, which we know as the *Indigitamenta*. This seems to me characteristic of the period, inasmuch as it was probably based on the old Roman ideas of divine agency, now systematized by something like scientific terminology and ordered classification. It is the old national belief in the ubiquity of the world of spirits, now edited and organized by skilled legal theologians. But it would be beyond the province of this work to venture further into this tangled question.

From the Hannibalic war to the end of the Republic is the

---

[1] Aust, op. cit., p. 14, note 1. [3] Aust, op. cit., p. 15, note 1.
[2] Above, p. 190.

period of the decay and downfall of the old Roman religion.
This period need not detain us long; it has been no part of
my plan to exhibit this religion on its death-bed, for the Fasti
do not admit us to that scene. They show us a living and
genuine, not a spurious and enfeebled religious life. A few
salient facts shall suffice as illustrations of the slow process of
this dissolution.

At the very outset of the period we mark the solemn
introduction into Rome of Cybele, the Magna Mater Idaea,
and the stone which was supposed to represent her; and we
are thus warned that even the Greek cults, with all their
adjuncts of art and mythology, are no longer sufficient for
Roman needs. The State is once more in peril, and the far-
reaching struggle with Hannibal has brought her into touch
with new peoples and cults. The Greeks do indeed continue
to be the chief invaders of the Roman religious territory, but
the religion they bring with them is a debased one. The
extraordinary rapidity with which the orgiastic rites of
Dionysus spread over Italy in 186 B. C. proves at once that
the Italian religious forms were wearing out, and that the
Greek substitute was no longer a wholesome one [1]. From
this time forward the lower strata of population show a
tendency to run after exciting Oriental forms of worship,
which neither the attempted restoration of the old religion
by Augustus, nor the subsequent rapid growth of Christianity,
could entirely and permanently check. Among the educated
classes the old beliefs were being eaten away by the acids of
a second-hand philosophy. The Greeks had long begun to
inquire into the nature of the gods, and they passed on their
disintegrating criticism to their conquerors. Euhemerus, the
arch-destroyer of ancient faiths, became known to the Romans
through a translation by Ennius at the beginning of the second
century B. C. ; and it took only another century and a half to
produce the sceptical and eclectic treatise of Cicero, *De Natura
Deorum*.

Again, nothing is more characteristic of this period than the
contempt and neglect into which the old priesthoods gradually
fell; Rome now swarmed with a mongrel population that
knew little of them and cared less. In the year 209 B. C. even

[1] See especially the speech of the consul Postumius in Livy 39. 15.

the priesthood of Jupiter was filled by the youthful black sheep of an old patrician family, apparently for no other reason than the hope that so objectionable a character might be reformed by the many quaint restrictions imposed upon the office [1]. Of the flamines in general, of the Fratres Arvales, Salii, Sodales Titii, and others of the ancient priesthoods we henceforward hear little or nothing until the revival of learning and religion in the Augustan age. Old forms continued to be used, but mainly for political purposes, like the *obnuntiatio* or observation of lightning; and only those religious offices which had considerable political power continued to be sought after by men of light and leading.

Temples continued to be vowed and built, especially in the earlier part of this period; but their cults are, with few exceptions, of Greek origin, or are new and fanciful forms of old worships, such as the Lares Permarini, Venus Verticordia, Fortuna Equestris, Ops Opifera, Fortuna Huiusce Diei. Before the fall of the Republic a great number of the old temples had fallen almost irretrievably into decay; Augustus tells us in his record of his own reign that he restored no less than eighty-two of them. This too is the period when the identification of Roman gods with Greek became a general fashion; a process which had begun long before, but originally with a genuine meaning and object, not as the sport of a sceptical society educated in Greek speculation. Salus takes the attributes of Hygieia, Mater Matuta becomes Leucothea, Faunus Pan, Sancus Hercules, Carmenta Nicostrate, Neptunus Poseidon, the god of Soracte, Apollo Soranus; and even the greater gods like Mars, Diana, and others assume more and more the likeness and mythical adornment of their supposed Greek equivalents.

The civil troubles of the age of revolution completed the work of disintegration. Men became careless, reckless, self-regarding; the δεισιδαιμονία of which Polybius could say only just before the revolution began, that more than anything else it served to knit the Roman state together, was lost to view in the tumult of political passion and personal greed. Not indeed that it was altogether extinct; that could never be, and never has been the case in Italy. Augustus, who

[1] See a paper by the author in *Classical Review*, vol. vii. p. 193 foll.

came by degrees to know the people he governed better than any statesman in Italian history, was well aware that to inspire the Roman world once more with confidence, he must bring the religious instinct into play again. The task he thus set himself he accomplished with extraordinary skill and tact; the old religion seemed to live again, the old priesthoods were revived, the old minutiae of worship were restored. He did what he could to bring to life again even the spirit and the principles of the old *religio*; and in the *Carmen Saeculare* of Horace, written to his order at a moment when he wished to make these things obvious to the eyes of all Romans, we probably have the best succinct exposition of them to be found in Roman literature[1]. But of the Augustan revival, and of the reasons why it could not be permanent, I must forbear here to speak further.

I have yet to say a few words in answer to the interesting question whether the religious system we have been examining had any appreciable influence on the character of the Roman people: whether it contributed to build up that *virtus* of the State and the individual which enabled them to subdue and govern the world, as the *pietas* of Aeneas in the poem armed him for the subjugation and civilization of the wild Italian tribes. The question may at first sight seem a superfluous one, since the religion of a people is rather the expression of its own genius for dealing with the perplexities of human life, than a *vera causa* in determining its character; yet it is worth asking, for it is unquestionable that the peculiar turn taken by a nation's religious beliefs and practices does in course of time come to react upon its character and morals.

It has often been said of the Roman religion that it had nothing to do with righteousness, and was without ethical value. The admirable criticism of it given by Mommsen in the first volume of his History may originally have suggested this view; but if so, the copyists have exaggerated the opinion of the master in one particular point, failing to give due weight to the general tenor of his exposition. However this may be,

---

[1] Note for example the way in which Horace has contrived to introduce in combination the ideas of the fertility of crops and herbs, of marriage and the increase of population, of public morality and prosperity.

we certainly are now always invited to conclude that this great people, which in its dealings with human beings discovered an extraordinary genius for expansion and adaptation, in its attitude to the supernatural remained cooped up within curiously narrow mental limits, drawing no real sustenance either from its primitive beliefs or its quaint and detailed practice. The current views of this kind have just lately been so well summed up in an admirable English work on the latest age of Roman society and thought, that I cannot do better than borrow a few sentences from it [1] :—

'The old Roman theology was a hard, narrow, unexpansive system of abstraction and personification, which strove to represent in its Pantheon the phenomena of nature, the relations of man in the State or in the clan, every act and feeling and incident in the life of the individual. Unlike the mythologies of Hellas and the East, it had no native principle of growth, or adaptation to altered needs of society and the individual imagination. It was also singularly wanting in awe and mystery. The religious spirit which it cultivated was formal, timid, and scrupulous. . . . The old Roman worship was businesslike and utilitarian. The gods were partners in a contract with their worshippers, and the ritual was characterized by the hard and literal formalism of the legal system of Rome. The worshipper performed his part to the letter with the scrupulous exactness required in pleadings before the praetor. To allow devotional feeling to transgress the bounds prescribed by immemorial custom was "superstitio."'

It is impossible to deny that there is much truth in all this ; yet I may venture to express a doubt whether it contains the whole truth. The fact is that the subject needs a more historical treatment, and perhaps also something of the historical imagination, to do it full justice.

In the earliest periods of Roman civilization, those of the family and the beginnings of the State, the Roman attitude towards the supernatural was, if I am not mistaken, a real contributing cause towards the formation of *virtus*. It was not merely an attitude of business and bargaining. So far

---

[1] It gives me pleasure to quote this passage from *Roman Society in the last century of the Western Empire* (p. 63) by my old friend Professor Dill.

as we know it, the common form of address to the gods was not 'send me what I want—sun, rain, victory, &c., and you shall then have these gifts'; but 'I give you these sacrifices and expect you to do your part; in taking all this trouble to act correctly by you, I establish a right as against you.' It is true that in one particular form of dealing with the gods, the vow, or solemn undertaking (*votum*), the transaction wears more the character of a definite bargain ; if the god will do certain things, he shall then have his reward.   So Cloanthus in Virgil addresses the gods of the sea [1]—

> Di, quibus imperium est pelagi, quorum aequora curro,
> Vobis laetus ego hoc candentem in litore taurum
> Constituam ante aras, *voti reus*, extaque salsos
> Proiciam in fluctus et vina liquentia fundam.

But the *votum* was the exception, not the rule ; it was a promise made by an individual at some critical moment, not the ordered and recurring ritual of the family or the State.   It takes its peculiar form simply because the maker of the vow is not at the particular moment in a position to fulfil it.   The normal attitude of the Roman in prayer and sacrifice was not this ; it is much more exactly expressed in the formula of the farmer's prayer already quoted in these pages : 'Father Mars, I pray and beseech thee be willing and propitious to me, my household, and my slaves ; for the which object I have caused this threefold sacrifice to be driven round my farm and land.' This is the usual and natural attitude of all peoples in sacrificing to their gods, and is far from being peculiar to Rome ; but it was the nature of the Roman to express it in a more formal and definite way than others, and this led to an outward religion of formulae which has done much to obscure for us, as indeed for the Romans themselves, the real thought underlying them.

These exact formulae of invocation and sacrifice were really the outward expression of a fear of the unknown, and its power to hinder and injure man ; for the old Roman did not know his gods intimately, inasmuch as they took no human shape, and did not dwell in buildings made by hands.   We have illustrated this ignorance of his again and again, and the

[1] *Aen.* 5. 235.

vagueness and fluidity of the religious conceptions of the
Roman mind. The remedy for this weakness was found, as
with the Jews, in a remarkable formularity of ritual, both
as regards time, place, and method of worship : in a series
of elaborate prescriptions drawn up by experts, going even so
far as to anticipate the consequence of an unintentional
omission or error by piacular acts. This in time, and under
State organization, became a science, and finds its parallel in
the science of legal formulae. But there was a difference
between the two sciences, even for the Roman. In religious
acts, the human mind is dealing with the unseen and unknown, not with human beings who can be calculated with
or outwitted. His fear of the unknown was thus for the
primitive Roman a wholesome discipline ; and his attitude
towards it he aptly and characteristically called *religio*, because
it *bound* him to the performance of certain regulated duties,
calculated to keep his footsteps straight as he walked daily
in this unseen world : duties which even in the family and
clan must have been to some extent systematized, and which
when the city-state was reached took the definite form of
a calendar of public prayers, sacrifices, and festivities.

Now surely in this motive of fear, thus remedied by exact
ritual, we may trace a true civilizing element—the idea of
Duty, Pietas, which as Cicero defined it, was 'iustitia erga
deos': righteous dealing towards the gods, in expectation of
righteous treatment on their part. And he would be a bold
man who should assert that 'iustitia erga deos' had no effect
in inducing the habit of 'iustitia erga homines': in other
words that it could not react upon conduct. In the *pietas* of
the one typical Roman in literature both these elements are
equally present. The *pietas* of Aeneas is a sense of duty
towards god and man alike ; to his father, his son, and his
people, as well as to the will of the gods, and to that solemn
mission which is at once the religion of his life and the key
to the great Roman poem [1]. This is indeed that same sense
of duty and responsibility which governed every Roman in
authority in the best days of the State, whether paterfamilias,
patronus, priest, or magistrate, and which was the motive
power in the working of a constitution which lasted for cen-

[1] See Nettleship, *Essays in Latin Literature*, pp. 103, 104.

turies, though only resting on a basis of trust. In this *pietas*, it is true, we find no sense of contrition for sin, no humbling of the individual self before an almighty Governor of the world; but we do find a very sensitive conscientiousness, arising from the dread of neglect or trespass in the discharge of religious observance, in the trust committed by family or State to its constituted representative. And this trust included also the discharge of duties to other men, the neglect of which might bring down the anger of the Unknown, and even compel the surrender of a criminal as *sacer* to an offended deity. We find abundant evidence of this aspect of the *religio* in the language of solemn oaths and treaties, and especially in connexion with the cult of the great Jupiter.

I maintain then that in this Roman religion, in spite of its dryness and formality, there was a distinct ethical and civilizing element. And in conclusion I may perhaps raise the question whether it was really, as has been so often asserted, such a conception of the unseen as could never admit of elevation and expansion. A religion, which in its best and simplest forms, could bind men together in the orderly dutiful life of family, gens, state, and federation, could hardly, if left to itself, have speedily become an inanity, even though based on the motive of fear rather than that of brotherly love. But this religion, as the State became more fully matured, came under the influence of two retarding causes. First, its ritual, always obnoxious to formularism, was gradually deprived of its meaning by great priesthoods which from causes which need not be here discussed became powerful political agencies. Secondly, the contact with a mature system of polytheism, adorned and in some sort materialized by art and literature, drew away the mind of the simple and wondering Roman from the task of developing his religious ideas in his own way. When a new world of thought broke on the conquering Roman of the Republic, his own religious motives were already drying up under the influence of a powerful State-organization. His *pietas* lived on after a fashion for centuries, but more and more it lost that hold on the conscience, that appeal to trust and responsibility, which had once promised it a vigorous life and growth. While foreign gods and cults attracted his attention and admiration, or appealed to his sense that there was no quarter from which supernatural aid might not be called in for the advancement of his State, they failed to bind his conscience with the wholesome motives which lay at the root of his old native *religio*. And neither in the reaction of the fourth century B.C., nor in the protests of an austere Cato in the second, nor in the elaborate revival of Augustus, much less in any later effort of philosopher or autocrat to return to the old ways, was any permanent resuscitation of discipline or conduct possible. The problem of giving a real religion to the world-state into which the Roman dominion had then grown, was not to be solved either by Roman *pietas* or Hellenic polytheism.

NOTES ON TWO COINS.

A. DENARIUS OF P. LICINIUS STOLO (p. 42).

Obv. **AVGVSTVS TR POT** Augustus, laureate, on horseback to r.

Rev. **P. STOLO** Helmet (apex) between two shields.
IIIVIR

The forms of the helmet and shields are very archaic and interesting, appearing to point to a very early period. The helmet bears a marked likeness to that worn on Egyptian monuments by the Shardana, one of the races that invaded Egypt about the thirteenth century B.C. The shield seems to consist of two small round bosses connected by an oval boss. It is strikingly like the Mycenaean shield as shown on a number of monuments, and far earlier than the so-called Boeotian shield which was common in Greece from the sixth century onwards. The Roman writers themselves seem to have been puzzled by this shape (Marindin, article 'Salii' in Smith's *Dict. Antiq.*), and there can be little doubt that it came down from a time when the 'Mycenaean' civilization was common to Greece and Italy.

The figure on the coins of M. Sanquinius (Babelon, *Mon. de la Répub. Rom.* ii. 417), who wears a horned helmet and long tunic and carries a herald's staff and round shield, has been identified by several authorities as one of the Salii. This, however, is certainly wrong. Both on this coin, and later coins of Domitian, the personage is closely connected with the Ludi Saeculares. Dr. Dressel, in the *Ephem. Epigr.* viii. 314, maintains him to be a herald proclaiming the festival. This would admirably suit the caduceus ; but the decorations of the helmet seem to me to be not plumes, as Dr. Dressel thinks, but horns, like those on the headpiece of Juno Lanuvina. In any case the person is no Salius.

B. DENARIUS OF L. CAESIUS (p. 101).

Obv. Youthful bust l., hair disordered, striking with thunderbolt. Behind, a monogram.

Rev. **L. CAESI** Two young male figures seated to r. Each has drapery wrapped round waist, and grasps a spear. Between them, a dog, which one of them caresses. In field, in monograms, **LARE** Above, head of Vulcan and pinchers (moneyer's

mark). The monogram of the obverse was read by Mommsen **AP** for Apollo ; but the closed **P** was not at that time in use : the interpretation of Montagu (*Numismatic Chronicle*, 1895, p. 162) as Roma is therefore to be preferred. The head appears to be that of Vedius or Vejovis, whose statue at Rome carried in the hand a sheaf of arrows, which would naturally be confused with the Greek thunderbolt. Other heads of Vejovis on Roman coins, as those of the Gens Fonteia, are more Apolline in type, with long curls and laurel-wreath.

The two seated figures of the reverse are identified by the inscription as Lares. They are clearly assimilated to the Greek Dioscuri, early adopted at Rome. The dog, however, which sits between them is an attribute properly belonging to them. Dr. Wissowa in Roscher's *Lexicon* (p. 1872) says that they are clad in dogs' skins ; this, however, is certainly not the case, an ordinary cloak or chlamys falls over their knees.

This representation of the Lares stands by itself, the deities are frequently represented in later art, especially wall-paintings and bronze statuettes, but their type is that of boys who hold cornucopiae or drinking vessel, and are fully clad.

P. G.

INDEX OF SUBJECTS

INDEX OF LATIN WORDS

INDEX OF LATIN AUTHORS QUOTED

---

[1] Both excerptors being contained in the same volume, they are here combined for convenience.

INDEX OF GREEK AUTHORS QUOTED

THE END